W9-ACL-716

KNITTING
A STEP-BY-STEP GUIDE

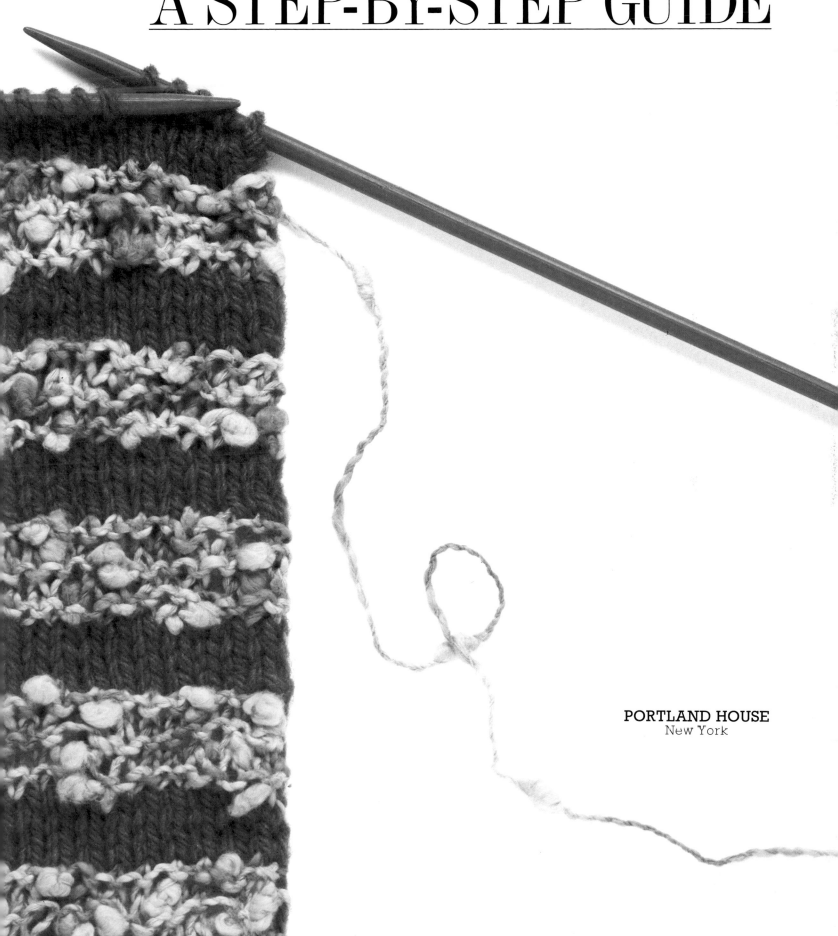

KNITTING
A STEP-BY-STEP GUIDE

PORTLAND HOUSE
New York

Copyright © 1985, 1990 by Marshall Editions Limited

First published under the title *The Knit Kit* in the United States by Villard Books, a division of Random House, Inc., New York, and simultaneously in Canada by Random House of Canada Limited, Toronto. First published in Great Britain by William Collins Sons & Co. Ltd.

Conceived, edited and designed by Marshall Editions Ltd., 170 Piccadilly, London W1V 9DD

This 1990 edition published by Portland House, a division of dilithium Press, Ltd. Distributed by Crown Publishers, Inc., 225 Park Avenue South, New York, New York 10003.

Authors
Design Your Own
Sandy Carr
Knitting Basics
Josie May, Eleanor Van Zandt

Managing editor   **Ruth Binney**
Editor   **Eleanor Van Zandt**

Art editor   **Daphne Mattingly**

Picture coordinator   **Zilda Tandy**
Picture assistant   **Sarah Wergan**

Assistant editor   **Louise Tucker**

Pattern subeditor   **Suzi Read**
Pattern checker   **Marilyn Wilson**
Proof reading and index   **Fred and Kathie Gill**

Production   **Barry Baker**

Typeset by Servis Filmsetting Ltd., Manchester, U.K.
Reproduction by Adroit Photo Litho Ltd., Birmingham, U.K.
Printed in Singapore

ISBN 0-517-02888-3

h g f e d c b a

CONTENTS

INTRODUCTION

Flexibility is the keynote of this book. It has been designed to meet the needs of knitters with widely varying degrees of skill—from the absolute beginner to the most accomplished. Above all, however, it is intended for anyone, irrespective of experience, who wants to explore the craft of knitting in a creative, imaginative way. How you use this book will depend on your present level of skill and on your goals as a knitter; but we hope that as you continue to use it both your skill and your goals will continue to develop and expand.

Three distinct but interrelated parts make up the book: the Pattern Portfolio and the two preceding sections, "Design Your Own" and "Knitting Basics." The Portfolio contains 46 original patterns, each giving complete instructions for making a garment or household item. The designs have been chosen to include a wide range of styles to suit men, women, and children and to cater for different degrees of knitting proficiency.

A moderately experienced knitter can use any of these patterns without referring to other pages. For the less experienced, or for the person who wants to adapt the pattern in some way, the book will provide invaluable guidance.

"Knitting Basics" (pp. 99–140) includes detailed, illustrated instructions for all the essential knitting skills, from casting on to joining the seams. Any unfamiliar terms or techniques in any pattern can be readily clarified by referring to this section. For the complete beginner in this craft "Knitting Basics" will, of course, be the best starting point.

For the knitter seeking help in adapting a pattern—adjusting the size, for example, or following one of the "Options" provided with many of the patterns—"Design Your Own" offers a wealth of information and ideas. But this section of the book is more than a work of reference: it is a comprehensive exploration of design as the "heart" of knitting and, therefore, as a subject of interest to all knitters, whatever their level of skill.

Beginning with an introduction to yarns, in all their amazing variety, "Design Your Own" goes on to explain clearly the "building blocks" of knitting design—gauge and measurements—and to demonstrate how these can be applied to altering the size or style of an existing pattern. Sections on surface decoration and color-patterned knitting, plus a library of stitch patterns, offer countless possibilities for creating interesting fabrics and embellishing plain ones. Even a comparative beginner can employ these suggestions creatively within the confines of a printed knitting pattern.

From this point it is but a short step to designing simple garments using only rectangular shapes. Here the book takes you step by step through the design process, using three hypothetical garments and showing how to combine vital data, such as body measurements and gauge, with aesthetic and practical considerations to create a garment that is your own "designer's original."

Essentially the same process (although rather more complex) is used to show you how to design three classic garments—that is, garments in which some or all of the pieces are shaped.

You can use these example garments in various ways. By substituting your own body measurements, but using the same type of yarn and the specified stitch pattern, you could make a garment closely resembling the model. Or you could follow the basic idea and the same steps to make a quite different garment, using another stitch pattern and/or a different type of yarn (as well as, naturally, your own measurements). You could also make structural changes to the design by incorporating one or more of the features described on pp. 92–97.

Whether or not you feel inclined to use any of these examples in a practical way, simply reading and studying them will help you to understand the process of knitting design and will remove any mystery from it. When you do begin to design your own knitwear, they will serve again and again as guides to solving particular design problems.

Throughout the book—in both "Design Your Own" and "Knitting Basics"—you will find useful tips and special features that will enable you to perform a certain technique in the most efficient way, to prevent mistakes or accidents, or to achieve a professional-looking finish.

We believe that knitting should be as enjoyable and satisfying as possible. The combined experience of several knitting experts (and that of a few enthusiasts, also) has gone into the making of this beautiful book, and we hope that this experience will enhance your enjoyment of this endlessly stimulating craft.

The Editors

PATTERN PORTFOLIO

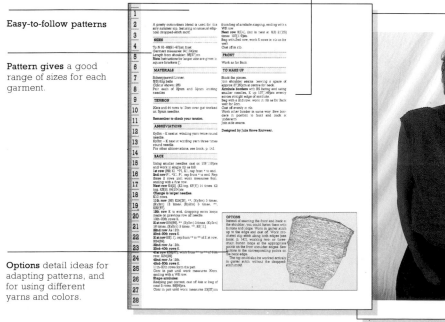

Pattern includes clear instructions for finishing.

Easy-to-follow patterns

Pattern gives a good range of sizes for each garment.

Options detail ideas for adapting patterns, and for using different yarns and colors.

Full-color photograph of the finished garment shows its major design features.

Life-size close-up of the yarn enables you to substitute another yarn of your choice.

DESIGN YOUR OWN

Text explains the design process in easy stages.

Illustrations show the vital elements of knitwear design, including making a sketch, choosing yarn and stitch pattern, and calculating the dimensions of each garment piece.

Detailed examples make it simple to work out your own designs.

KNITTING BASICS

Expert tips suggest alternatives, short cuts, and fail-safe knitting methods.

Charts illustrate multicolor knitting and other techniques.

Clear line drawings show knitting techniques step by step.

Photographs of knitted samples show finished effects.

Special features explain finer points of knitting technique.

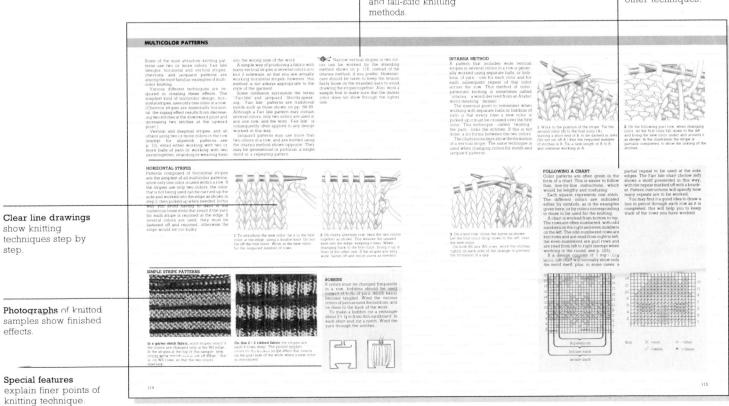

In the last few years there has been a revolution in knitting design. This ancient craft has been "discovered" by some of the world's top fashion designers and in the process has shed much of its homespun image. In striking contrast to the situation that prevailed in the past, when most knitting patterns were dull and depressingly utilitarian, today knitters can choose from hundreds of designs that are exciting and, above all, fashionable.

One result of all this interest is that many people have not only taken up knitting but also developed an urge to translate their own ideas into knitwear. However satisfying it is to make up someone else's designs, it is potentially even more satisfying to create something original and unique.

Apart from the pleasure of expressing your own ideas, there are some practical reasons for learning to design. In spite of the countless knitting patterns published in leaflets, magazines, and books, it is often difficult to find the exact shape and style you want in the yarn you want and in an appropriate size. Most patterns are inevitably restricted in the number of sizes that are offered, and if you happen to be an unorthodox shape, it can be almost impossible to find something that will fit. Sometimes it is possible to make adjustments to an existing pattern, but often it proves no more difficult to begin at the beginning and design a completely new

garment. There is, however, a persistent mystique about knitting design that deters many people. Unlike a dressmaking pattern, which consists of readily identifiable shapes presented full-size for instant duplication, a knitting pattern looks rather like a scientific—or even magical—formula. As every knitter knows, it takes only a little experience to be able to follow the formula; but to create such a formula oneself seems a rash enterprise: remember what happened to the sorcerer's apprentice! Even the most expert knitters who can follow highly complex patterns to perfection are reluctant to deviate in the slightest way from the formula they have been given, as if to do so would invite disaster.

In fact, knitting design—like any other craft—is based on perfectly intelligible principles. To begin with, it is geared to the familiar proportions of the human body (and specifically, if you are doing the design, to those of your own body). It also depends on an understanding of knitted fabric and the way it behaves—an understanding that can be acquired by experimenting with different yarns and stitch patterns. Inevitably, combining these factors to create a knitted garment entails some calculations. However these are simple ones: addition, subtraction, division, multiplication; and since the advent of the pocket calculator even the most innumerate have no excuse for not trying.

THE SCOPE OF DESIGN

Doing your own design can be as simple as knitting stripes into a pattern for a plain jacket or as complex as working out a pattern for a raglan-sleeved Aran cardigan using five different stitches. Basically it means creating something that is distinctively yours, putting the stamp of your own individuality and taste on to an object or garment.

Naturally, when you begin designing for yourself, you will have some stunning creation in mind; but, as in all things, it is essential to learn to walk before you can run. Start with something simple, such as a garment based on squares and rectangles (see pp. 44–55). In this way you can easily gain some experience in creating an original fabric, relating yarn to stitch pattern, taking measurements, and making simple calculations. Do not attempt anything too large (or too expensive) to begin with. You need quick results without having too much at stake. Later you will be able to try more complex designs.

GETTING IDEAS

Ideas for knitting designs can come from all kinds of sources—some obvious and some unlikely. There are three basic elements you will need to consider: shape, texture, and color. An awareness of all these can be cultivated by looking closely at the world around you—in both its

natural and its man-made aspects.

Fashion is, clearly, a primary source of inspiration. Study the work of professional designers—not only of knitwear but of other clothing as well. Isolate the features that appeal to you and that might be adapted and interpreted in your own designs.

Other visual arts and crafts, and books devoted to them, will yield interesting color schemes, patterns, and motifs. Visit museums and art galleries—not purposefully to "get an idea," but in a relaxed manner, to develop the habit of seeing; ideas will take shape in your mind without your striving for them. Many designers use beautiful old textiles as source material: embroideries, lace, quilts, tapestries, printed fabric. But you can also find inspiration in quite different crafts—ceramics, stained glass, printing, and marquetry, for example.

The natural world, also, can heighten your visual sensitivity. Examine the shapes, colors, and textures to be found in fruit and flowers, rocks and shells, water and clouds. Once you start looking you will find that there is no end to the possibilities.

Of course the idea for a design might come from within the craft of knitting itself—from one of the hundreds of stitch patterns that have been created over the centuries by resourceful, imaginative knitters. The time you spend trying out these patterns in different yarns is never wasted.

PLANNING AHEAD

Knitting design is a craft in which planning ahead really does pay dividends. If you have some marvelous yarn and a good idea for a garment, it is tempting just to pick up some needles and get on with it. However, if you want to avoid disappointment or hours of wasted work and unraveling, it is best to take a deep breath and accept the fact that a good many hours of preparatory work are needed before you can start knitting. Taking the correct measurements, finding a suitable gauge, and working out your pattern—or at least the broad outlines of it—in advance will save you a great deal of trouble and frustration later.

Of course this does not mean that you cannot change your mind as you go along. It may become apparent that a color scheme or pattern is just not working, or you may decide to make the cardigan a coat or the pullover a dress. Even so, you will be less likely to come unstuck if you have worked out a good basic pattern at the outset.

WHAT YOU NEED

Apart from the usual knitting equipment (see p. 18), there are several other items that will come in useful when designing. A pocket calculator is essential unless your arithmetic is infallible. Keep track of your calculations by writing them down in a notebook. You can also use this notebook, or another one, to keep a kind of designer's diary, in which you record your various experiments with yarns, gauge, and stitch patterns.

Tags or small cards are useful for labeling swatches with pertinent information. You will also need a sketch pad for roughing out ideas, tracing paper for tracing motifs from books and magazines, and graph paper for plotting shaping lines and color patterns. It is also possible to buy a special kind of graph paper known as a gauge grid, which is based on the proportions of knitted stitches and is useful for charting pictorial motifs, among other things; however, if this is not available in your area you can easily construct your own gauge grid (see p. 42).

For color patterns you will need pencils or pens in a wide range of colors. An eraser and some correction fluid will be necessary for correcting errors in charts. For charting curves it may be helpful to use a flexible curve or stencils or a compass.

Above all, collect yarns in as wide a variety as possible. If you have been knitting for a few years you should already have acquired an assortment of left-over yarns that can be used for stitch pattern experiments. Add to this stock frequently, keeping your eye open for new and unusual textures. Yarn is the very essence of knitting and an inexhaustible source of inspiration.

ALL ABOUT YARNS

At one time wool was virtually the only yarn available for hand knitting. Fine silk and cotton yarns had been popular in the late eighteenth and early nineteenth centuries, when they were used for delicate, lacy garments; but when these garments went out of fashion toward the end of the 1800s, wool resumed its traditional place as the standard knitting yarn.

Since the early 1970s, however, in reaction to a new wave of interest in knitting, there has been a welcome flood of wonderful new yarns on to the market. Not only are there new yarns in natural fibers other than wool—cotton, silk, linen, angora, alpaca, cashmere—but there are also many more synthetic yarns, and their quality has improved enormously. Also, these less-common fibers are often mixed with each other and/or with wool to widen the choice and produce yarns that usefully combine the best of the individual fibers.

Besides the greater variety of fibers available, there has also been a great increase in the range of yarn types in terms of weight and finish. There are far more thicknesses, from the finest threadlike yarns to huge bulky ones, and many more unusual or novelty yarns with unconventional, even bizarre finishes. (Sometimes, however, these fascinating-looking yarns do not fulfill their promise when they are knitted up.) Slubbed, nubbly, bouclé, tweedy, flecked, metallic, ribbon, and brushed yarns of every kind are available in profusion.

This marvelous richness and diversity can in itself be a source of great inspiration to the would-be designer. Often an exceptionally beautiful yarn can spark off an idea for a design. But it also presents another kind of problem: with such a bewildering array to choose from, how do you select the right yarn for a design? Is it just a matter of taste, or are other factors important?

The "wrong" yarn can, in fact, totally wreck a potentially good design. Before choosing yarn it is important to know something about the various properties of the different fibers and yarn types, how they will react in different circumstances—both in making and wearing—and whether they are suitable for the purposes you have in mind.

FIBER CONTENT

All yarns are made either from natural fibers or from synthetic, or man-made, fibers. Natural fibers include those of animal origin—wool, mohair, silk, and so on—and those of plant origin such as cotton and linen. Synthetics include fibers, such as acrylic, which are products of the chemical industry and originate in nonorganic substances—oil, for example—and those, such as rayon, which are regenerated from some fibrous organic substance—wood pulp, for example, or cotton

waste. Wool remains the archetypal knitting yarn, and for many people nothing can match its superb qualities as a knitting material, which include elasticity, warmth, durability, wearability, and excellent receptivity to dye in an immense range of colors, from the most brilliant primaries to the subtlest pastels. The range of thicknesses available is also large, with fine Shetland laceweight at one end of the spectrum and extra-bulky and thick rug yarns at the other.

Pure wool yarns require special care if the garments made from them are to retain their shape and softness. Hand washing or dry cleaning is essential in most cases, although some wool yarns are now labeled "superwash," which means that they are machine washable.

Wool is spun from the coat, or fleece, of sheep. It is gathered by shearing the coat at regular intervals; or, in some cases (Shetland laceweight, for example), it is plucked or combed from the animal. The quality of the wool depends on the age of the sheep and also on the particular breed. Lambswool, for example, comes from the first shearing of the animal and is renowned for its warmth and softness. Botany wool is named after Botany Bay, in Australia, and is spun from the fleece of merino sheep. It is exceptionally fine and soft.

The wool from breeds other than merino is collectively known as crossbred. It includes most of the standard knitting wools as well as unusual types such as Jacob's wool, Herdwick, and Swaledale—coarse, rather hairy yarns, which are hard to find and are available only in their natural colors (from creamy white to dark brownish black).

There are also various special wool yarns, spun for specific types of knitting and often associated with a strong folk knitting tradition. Fisherman wool, for example, is a medium-weight plain yarn used for Aran sweaters; it shows up the textures of Aran cables and lattice stitches particularly well. The traditional undyed creamy white yarn is known as "bainin." Guernsey wool is a tightly twisted, five-ply yarn used for knitting Guernsey sweaters. It is always worked to a tight gauge, producing a firm weather-proof fabric. Shetland wool is a loosely twisted, two-ply yarn available in a wide range of colors and is especially suitable for the multicolored patterns of Fair Isle and traditional Shetland knitting. Shetland laceweight is an extremely fine yarn used for knitting delicate lacy shawls—sometimes called "ring" shawls because they will pass through a wedding ring. The color range is usually limited to white and soft pastels.

Mohair is the second most commonly used animal fiber after wool. It is a beautiful yarn with long, fluffy fibers and a slight

sheen. It is strong and hard wearing, despite its delicate appearance, but less elastic than wool and more expensive. Because of this, mohair is rarely available in its pure form and is often mixed with wool or acrylic. Mohair takes dye well and can be obtained in a good range of strong colors. However, many people find the long fibers scratchy if worn next to the skin. Kid mohair (from the young animal's coat) is softer but more expensive.

Angora is an exceptionally fluffy yarn with long, soft, silky fibers. It looks and feels extremely luxurious and is, in fact, very expensive—more so than mohair. It comes from the fur of the Angora rabbit, which in its natural state is pure white and shiny (the coat is combed at three- or four-monthly intervals to obtain the fibers). Angora dyes well and is sometimes (depending on fashion) available in a good variety of colors. The yarn is so slippery that it can be difficult to work. Avoid using angora for baby clothes, since it tends to shed its fibers, which can cause sneezing and even choking in young children.

Cashmere is another yarn made from goat hair. Only rarely available as a knitting yarn, and in a limited range of colors, it is fine, soft, light, warm, but also expensive. The main disadvantages of cashmere, apart from the cost, are that it is not hard wearing, felts easily, and has to be washed with great care to prevent shrinking.

Alpaca is a soft, silky yarn spun from the coat of a relative of the South American llama. You can sometimes find llama wool itself, and also vicuña, which is similar. Alpaca is used in its pure form in some knitting yarns and also mixed with wool. The natural cream, fawn, and brown shades are popular, but it is also possible to find alpaca dyed in a good range of medium to dark colors.

1 Pure wool fisherman yarn
2 Fine wool bouclé
3 Cotton, wool, mohair and synthetic tweed
4 Smooth wool tweed
5 Pure wool Guernsey
6 Pure wool tweed

7 Bulky pure Cheviot wool
8 Bulky wool and mohair blend
9 Angora and wool mix
10 Mohair and silk

11 Fine mohair, wool and nylon mixture
12, 13 Pure alpaca

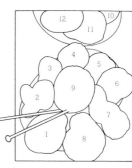

Silk is harvested from silkworm cocoons. The silkworm spins many hundreds of yards of silk fibers in a single cocoon, and this is then processed in various ways. Reeled silk is the shiny variety and is made by unwinding the cocoon into a single long thread. Yarns made by twisting together strands of reeled silk are usually extremely expensive. Spun silk—made from short fibers—is slightly coarser and cheaper. Tussah, or raw silk, is coarser still and has a slubbed texture. Silk is often mixed with other fibers, especially wool. It is very strong and durable.

Cotton comes from the plant of that name and is the third most important natural-fiber knitting yarn after wool and mohair. The range of cotton yarns has widened considerably in recent years, and it is now available in many different thicknesses and finishes. Traditionally used for household items, cotton is also ideally suited to summer garments, being cool to wear; and it dyes well to strong, bright colors.

Some cotton is "mercerized"; that is, it has undergone a process that gives it extra strength and luster. The disadvantages of cotton are that it lacks the resilience of wool (so that ribbing, for example, does not spring back into shape) and that it takes a long time to dry. Many people also find cotton hard to knit with—again because of its lack of elasticity. However, it is remarkably strong and is moth resistant.

Linen comes from the fibers in the stem of the flax plant. Because it tends to be heavy, linen is normally available for knitting only in fine strands. The finish is slubbed, and it is often mixed with cotton for both economy and texture.

Synthetic yarns are made from a number of different substances—nylon, acrylic, and polyester, among others. They are almost always less expensive than yarns made from natural fibers. They also have several practical advantages. Most synthetics are resistant to moths and mildew; they are easily washed (often machine washable) and quickly dried; they can be shrinkproof in water and they do not felt, as does wool; they are also usually strong and hard wearing. Synthetics are also light, which makes them economical—one ball of acrylic, for example, will go a lot farther than the same weight of wool or cotton.

The disadvantages of synthetics are mainly aesthetic ones. Although they have improved a great deal, they do not have the wonderful tactile qualities of natural yarns; nor are they, on the whole, as beautiful. Also, although strong, they often do not wear well. Garments made from 100 per cent synthetic yarn frequently become shapeless after they have been washed a few times. They are also sometimes subject to static electricity and can be uncomfortable to wear. Synthetics can be clammy in warm weather and insufficiently warm when it is cold. However, they do provide an alternative for people who are allergic to wool or mohair, and they include some interesting novelty yarns which cannot be duplicated with natural fibers. As a rule, synthetics are most successful when mixed with natural fibers.

1, 2 Linen and
   cotton slub
3, 4 Pure silk
5 Mohair, cotton,
   and nylon slub
6 Acrylic, cotton,
   and linen
   multicolor
7 Pure cotton
   ribbon
8 Synthetic twisted
   thread and tape
9 Pure pearl cotton

10 Shiny viscose
11 Cotton, viscose
   and linen slub
12 Cotton and
   acrylic
13 Wool and
   synthetic medium-
   weight yarn
14 Cotton and
   synthetic mixture

15 Pure pearl cotton
16 Cotton and nylon
   bouclé
17 Pure cotton
18 Wool and silk
19 Cotton, linen,
   and acrylic
   mixture

YARN SIZE

Yarns are available in a range of thicknesses. They are usually formed of several single strands, or plies, twisted together. The thickness of the strands may vary considerably from one yarn type to another and therefore the number of strands cannot be used to determine the thickness of the yarn.

Certain twisted yarns are designated on the label as "fingering," "sport yarn," "knitting worsted," and so on, and these commonly used terms give an approximate indication of the relative thickness of the yarn. Fingering yarns include various fine yarns such as those used for lace knitting and baby garments. "Sport" weight is a term applied to a lightweight yarn that is widely available. It is a standard, all-purpose yarn found in a full range of fibers. "Knitting worsted" is the generic name given to a type of medium-weight yarn. It is thicker than sport weight and produces a medium-to-heavy fabric.

One whole category of yarns is described as "fisherman's." These are a little thicker than knitting worsted but not as thick as bulky yarn. Both fisherman and bulky yarns are best used for outdoor garments. Finally there is extra-bulky yarn, suited to heavy coats and jackets.

A 4-ply yarn expanded

A 4-ply yarn

A 2-ply yarn

A 2-ply yarn expanded

A yarn's ply is not an absolute guide to its thickness, as these examples show.

Recommended needle sizes

Some yarn labels give a recommended size of needle to be used with the yarn. Where this is not given, you can use the table below as a guide when starting to make gauge samples.

yarn	needle size
fingering	3
sport	5
knitting worsted	8
fisherman	9
bulky	10
extra-bulky	13

American-British yarn equivalents

American and British yarns are classified under different names. This table shows the approximate equivalents in the two systems—but note that these are *approximate*. American yarns are very slightly thicker, category for category, than British and Continental yarns. Substituting one for the other yarn can thus be difficult. It is essential to test a substitute yarn carefully by making a 6-inch square gauge swatch. If the gauge is correct but the knitted fabric is too flimsy or too stiff, you will have to try a thicker or thinner yarn respectively. Remember that the yarn names on the chart are not technical terms. They are a handy guide for specifying the relative thickness of a yarn, but the thickness in each category can vary.

American	British
fingering	2-ply
fingering	3-ply
sport	4-ply
knitting worsted	double knitting
fisherman	Aran
bulky	chunky
extra-bulky	extra-chunky

Raffia

Rags

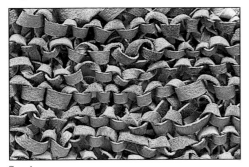

Suede

1 Latex, wool, and
  synthetic mixture
2 Acrylic chenille
3 Synthetic "tinsel"
4 Shiny synthetic
  "interrupted"
  chenille
5 Slubbed bouclé;
  wool and
  synthetic
6 Fine glitter
7 Shoe laces

8 Ribbon
9 Suede
10 Plastic
11 Feathers

YARN FINISHES

The finish of a yarn—the way in which it has been spun and processed—has a dramatic effect on the knitted fabric. It is this, along with the fiber content and stitch pattern, which determines the texture of the garment. The largest category among the various finishes includes the standard smooth, plain knitting yarns—sometimes called "classic" yarns. These can be loosely twisted, like Shetland wool; medium twisted, like most ordinary sport and knitting worsted yarns; or tightly twisted, like Guernsey yarns.

Generally, the more tightly twisted the strands of the yarn, the more hard wearing it will be. Some of the most loosely spun of all yarns are the thick homespun yarns made of a single thick strand (Lopi Icelandic yarn, for example). The exceptional softness of these yarns means that they break easily, especially during the knitting process. Most tightly twisted of all are the crêpe yarns. Tightly twisted yarns will show up a stitch pattern most clearly.

There are many other special finishes: bouclé and loop yarns are curly and produce a crunchy-textured fabric which is unsuitable for anything but the plainest of stitch patterns. Cotton bouclé can look like terry cloth when knitted up. Brushed yarns are fluffy; chenille (from the French word for caterpillar) is usually velvety in appearance and is either synthetic or, increasingly, made from cotton. Slubbed yarns and flake yarns are uneven in thickness and knit up to more or less lumpy textures unsuitable for fancy stitches.

Yarns containing plies (or strands) of different texture and/or fiber content often contain some variation in color to give them additional interest. This variation may be slight, producing only an effect of richness and depth; or somewhat more pronounced, as in flecked, tweedy yarns; or dramatic, as in some novelty yarns. Knitting with such yarns can be especially interesting—and designing even more so—for the effect when the yarn is knitted up can seldom be predicted from its appearance in the ball.

Other multicolored effects can be achieved by random dyeing or space dyeing the yarn. These techniques involve dyeing the yarn different colors along its length, either haphazardly or according to a set pattern. These yarns, too, can be fun to knit with, although they require additional experimentation and planning by the designer. The true effect of a space-dyed yarn cannot be judged from a 4-in square sample; when knitted over a width of 15 in or more, the colors will change in a quite different pattern. For this reason, such yarns are best used for simple garments, without pockets or other trimmings that might introduce an unwelcome contrast, and for simple stitch patterns.

NOVELTY YARNS

Many fascinating new materials are being manufactured into knitting yarn, and these can be exploited to great effect in producing unusual fabrics, textures, and finishes for knitted garments and other items. The most long-standing of these novelty yarns are the metallic glitter yarns. These are available in fine threads as well as mixed with thick wools and cottons. They are perfect for adding a little sparkle and glamour to evening wear and accessories. Strips of fur or feathers, knitted or threaded into the fabric, give a luxurious touch.

Ribbon yarns are also more common. They are manufactured either as narrow, flat ribbon strips or as knitted flattened tubes and are usually made of cotton or a synthetic fiber. These yarns are best knitted loosely and in plain stitches. Another "fabric" yarn is rag yarn—flat bias strips of woven cotton fabric with raw cut edges. The same yarn can be made at home, using left-over fabric; but this is not so economical as it sounds—an astonishing amount of fabric is needed to make the yarn for a small T-shirt. Raffia is also available as knitting yarn and is specially treated to make it soft enough to wear next to the skin. Another newcomer is simulated leather or suede.

Apart from manufactured novelties, there are many other materials that can be used for knitting—anything, in fact, which is in the form of, or can be made in the form of, a long, thin, pliable strand. Materials from other crafts (macramé, for example) can be appropriated, if desired. All the hemps, jutes, and twines can be knitted and often provide exactly the right material for household items such as rugs and shopping bags. Fine wire can be knitted into pieces of jewelry. Plastic and polyethylene strips, embroidery threads, lace, ribbons, and braids may all, at some time, be exactly what you need.

MIXING YARNS

Despite the vast range of yarns available, it may be impossible to find exactly the right color in the thickness or fiber you want. In such cases the solution may be to mix two or more yarns. You can mix colors together, using two or three sharp contrasts for a tweedy or flecked effect, or harmonizing colors to give exactly the desired nuance or shade. You can also mix fine yarns to make up the thickness necessary for a particular purpose, or to achieve some special effect of color or texture: mix a curly bouclé with a smooth yarn or mohair, for example, or run a glitter yarn along with a fine silk or cotton. There are many such creative possibilities.

The main point to remember when mixing yarns in this way is that the yarns you choose must be compatible, especially in regard to after-care.

CHOOSING YARN

Selecting the correct yarn for a design is one of the most important factors in its success. Of course there is no one "correct" yarn; there may be hundreds that will suit a particular idea—but there are also hundreds that will spoil it. All sorts of factors enter into the choice, including the individual preference of the person who will wear or use the item. There are general commonsense considerations to do with the purpose of the garment or object; for example, if it is a garment, will it be worn in summer or winter? during the day or evening? on casual or dressy occasions?

There are also certain more technical points to bear in mind: for one thing, it is most important that the yarn and the stitch pattern be compatible. As a general rule, do not use textured yarns for textured stitch patterns, especially if the texture of the stitch pattern is a rather subtle one (see p. 60, for example). Some fluffy or very fine bouclé yarns can be successfully used for strong stitch patterns such as cables. On the whole, however, textured stitches look best in plain, smooth yarns.

Lacy stitches require even more careful treatment. The yarn used should not be too heavily textured (brushed, mohair, and angora can work well, but not bouclés) nor should it be too thick.

Color patterns can be worked in a variety of yarns, depending on the desired effect. If a crisp, sharp-edged pattern is required, choose a smooth yarn. Anything fluffy, such as mohair, will make the effect fuzzier, but this can be appealing. Sometimes touches of a textured yarn in an otherwise smooth scheme will add much-needed interest. Traditional designs, such as Fair Isle, are best worked in traditional materials.

BUYING YARN

Yarns come in balls, skeins, spools, hanks, and cones and are sold in amounts varying from 1 oz upward. The most common ball and hank sizes are 1 oz, 2 oz, and 4 oz or 25 g, 50 g, and 100 g. Spools are usually smaller, and cones (intended mainly for machine knitting) are much larger. If you buy in bulk and from a mail order supplier, you can often make considerable savings. Mail order suppliers will usually send shade cards or fringes to enable you to choose colors. If there is a charge for these, it will be specified. Department stores and specialist yarn stores are the other main suppliers of knitting yarns.

If you intend to design your own garments, it is a good idea to begin building up a stock of many different kinds of yarn, apart from the yarn you buy for specific projects. These odds and ends of yarn are useful in many ways. You can experiment

Bluebell lace pattern in a fisherman yarn (top), mohair blend, and (most successfully) smooth, light-weight cotton.

Trinity stitch works well in fine mohair (top) and sport yarn; it is obscured in multicolored bouclé.

Reverse stockinette stitch works well in knitting worsted (top), a mohair blend, and a tweed.

A check pattern looks good in two smooth yarns; it is completely lost in hairy, flecked yarn.

weight
color
dye lot

fiber content
for machine knitting
gauge
needle/hook size

ESTIMATING YARN QUANTITIES

One problem in designing your own knitting is that you have to estimate the total amount of yarn required as soon as possible after you begin, in order to ensure that you can obtain all of the yarn from the same dye lot. This is a problem because there is no sure way of knowing exactly how much you need short of actually knitting up your design. The best you can do is estimate, and it is always better to overestimate. A few balls left over are not a problem for the dedicated designer. Rather, they serve as a source of inspiration for future projects.

There are two ways of making a reasonable guess about yarn needs. One method is to knit up a section of the garment (the back, for example) weigh it, and work out from that how much more you will need, bearing in mind the relative sizes of other parts of the garment. This method is feasible if you can knit the first section fairly quickly and know that ample yarn in the same dye lot is available. (Some stores will reserve yarn for a short period or allow you to return excess yarn within a reasonable time.)

Another method is to knit up at least one ball and see how far you have gotten, then divide the area knitted with one ball into your estimate of the total area of the completed garment (see below). The result will be the approximate number of balls needed.

A word of caution: you must estimate with your chosen yarn, even if you are using the second method. Another, similar yarn (another knitting worsted, for example, or another sport yarn) will not give you a sufficiently accurate result. In some cases the amount of yarn needed can differ even between two colors of the same yarn (dark colors contain more dye than light ones, and so the length of yarn will be less in a given weight); so to be as accurate as possible, use your intended color, as well as the intended yarn, when making an estimate.

with colors, textures, and mixtures, or try out new stitch patterns in various types of yarn to see which works best. Make sure, however, to keep all yarn samples linked to their labels for future reference.

The labels and ball bands on yarns often contain a great deal of useful information. Any information about fiber content is obviously crucial. In some cases it will correct any false impression conveyed by the brand name or the name given to the yarn quality; the words "mohair type," for example, may be applied to a yarn that is mainly, or entirely, synthetic.

There may also be a recommended needle size printed on the label. This will give you some idea of the thickness of the yarn and provide a starting point for making gauge samples (although you may well end up using a different-size needle). There may even be a recommended gauge measurement, stating the number of stitches and rows (usually of stockinette stitch) obtained over a given number of inches using the suggested needles. Many labels also contain after-care and washing instructions (see p. 134).

Whatever other information the label may include, it will always give the color code and dye lot. When buying yarn for a particular project it is almost always desirable to obtain all the balls you need from the same dye lot. This is particularly true of a garment made in one color. The variation in color from one dye lot to another can be considerable and would be easily visible on the garment.

ESTIMATING YARN REQUIREMENTS FROM ONE BALL

This example illustrates the procedure used if you wish to estimate your yarn requirements after knitting up one ball of your chosen yarn.

Suppose that one 2 oz ball knits the first 6 in of the back, which measures 17¾ in across. Multiply 6 in by 17¾ in to get 106½ sq in—the area of knitting produced by one ball.

Now multiply the length and width of each piece of the garment: back, front, each sleeve, and any extra pieces such as collar or edging bands. (If the pieces have shaping, include the "cut out" areas in your calculations; you can later round down *slightly* the figure for the total area.) This will give you the area, in square inches, of each piece.

Add all the areas together to obtain the total area of the knitting. In this hypothetical example the result is 1,285 sq in.

Finally, divide the total area, 1,285 sq in, by 106½ sq in (the amount produced by one ball) to get the number of balls required: 13 (approximately 12, plus an extra ball for safety).

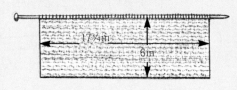

Area 6 × 17¾ in = 106½ sq in

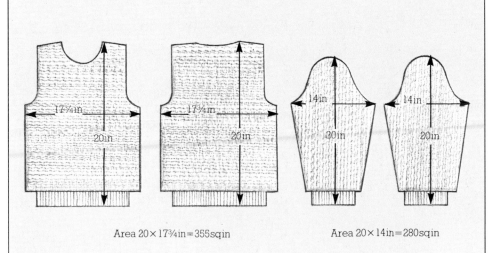

Area 20 × 17¾ in = 355 sq in

Area 20 × 14 in = 280 sq in

EQUIPMENT

Compared with other crafts, hand knitting requires little in the way of equipment. The only essential tools are the needles. Knitting needles have changed very little in hundreds of years, although they are probably manufactured with much greater precision nowadays than they were in the past. Wood, bone and metal were the most common materials used for needles in earlier times; today, metal and wood are still used, but plastic has replaced bone.

The most basic requirements of needles are that they be strong (that is, not bend with use), light, smooth and durable. The points should be rounded rather than sharp, in order to avoid splitting the yarn. Metal needles come closest to fulfilling all these requirements, although the smaller sizes will bend if they are not carefully handled and stored. Metal needles are also the most widely available in a wide range of sizes and types.

Some people, especially those troubled with arthritis or rheumatism in their hands, may prefer plastic needles, which tend to feel warmer and are lighter than metal ones. The main disadvantage of plastic needles is that they can become rather sticky in use. Wooden needles are widely available in some of the larger sizes, and it is occasionally possible to find fine bamboo needles; however, bamboo needles bend easily and are consequently uncomfortable to use.

TYPES OF NEEDLES

Straight, single-pointed needles come in a range of sizes, from 0 to 15 (it is also sometimes possible to find size 50 needles), and lengths of 10 to 16 in. Usually they are of uniform thickness throughout the length, but in Europe, in particular, one can find "quick-knit" needles, which are the thickness for their size only at the points; the rest of the needle is narrower. This makes it possible to use bulky yarns and the large needle size required, without the weight of large metal needles or the "sticky" quality of plastic.

Another new type of needle has metal points on a plastic rod, giving the strength of metal with the comfort and lightness—for those who need it—of plastic. All single-pointed needles are used for ordinary flat knitting. They come in pairs.

Circular needles—sometimes called "twinpins"—consist of a length of flexible, plastic-coated wire with a short, pointed rod at each end. They are available in sizes from 0 to 10½ and in lengths between 16 in and 40 in. Circular needles are used for knitting large items in the round and for flat knitting where the number of stitches is too great for single-pointed needles. Because a circular needle distributes the weight of the knitting evenly between the two hands, it is also useful if the work is exceptionally heavy. In fact, some people prefer to use circular needles, rather than single-

pointed ones, for most flat knitting.

When used for tubular knitting, a circular needle must be chosen carefully according to size: it must not be so long that the stitches are stretched around it. The rule of thumb is that the needle should measure, from point to point, at least 2 in less than the circumference of the knitting. In some cases, however—for example, on a curved yoke—this is difficult to estimate. The chart on p. 142 is a guide to selecting the correct circular needle for a given number of stitches.

Double-pointed needles are also used for tubular knitting, especially for knitting items such as gloves, socks, and turtle neck collars, which are too small to be knitted on a circular needle. They are also used for knitting flat medallion shapes—circles and squares knitted either from the center out or from the outside into the center. The needles are packaged in sets of four or five. They are available in a narrower range of sizes (usually 0–10½) than single-pointed needles, and in lengths between 7 in and 16 in. The longer ones can be used for knitting a garment in the round—this is the traditional way of knitting a Guernsey sweater, for example. In such cases, however, more than one pack of needles may be required in order to accommodate the large number of stitches.

Cable needles are used—as their name suggests—for cable patterns, which in-

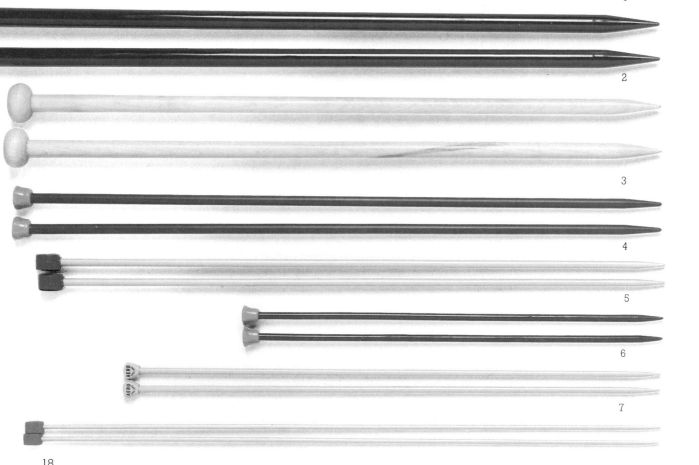

volve moving stitches from their usual position in a row. The cable needle holds the stitches safely while this maneuver is being carried out. Some cable needles are simply short double-pointed needles; others are bent, so as to hold the stitches more securely.

ACCESSORIES

There are several other pieces of knitting equipment which, although not essential, are certainly useful from time to time. A needle gauge measures the needle size. The needle size is usually marked on the knob of single-pointed needles, but sometimes this is lost or worn away. When this happens the needle gauge is useful. The gauge is also useful for measuring double-pointed and circular needles, which are not marked.

Stitch holders are used for holding stitches in waiting while another section of a garment is being completed—for example, neckband stitches. A length of yarn can do the same job for a large number of stitches, and a safety pin is adequate where there are only a few.

A row counter can be slipped on to a single-pointed needle close to the knob. This will help you to keep track of the rows in a complicated pattern.

Ring markers are small plastic rings that are used for marking a particular stitch in a row—for example, in tubular knitting,

where it is important to keep track of the beginning of each round. A loop of yarn in a contrasting color will serve the purpose.

Stitch stoppers, also known as "needle guards," are rubber or plastic knobs that can be placed on the ends of needles to prevent the stitches from slipping off when the work is temporarily laid aside.

Bobbins are small, usually plastic, yarn holders which can be used in color-patterned knitting (see pp. 38 and 114), when several different colors are being handled simultaneously. They help prevent the various strands from becoming tangled. Acceptable substitutes can be made from pieces of thin cardboard.

Apart from these, the only other things you will need are a tape measure for taking body measurements, a ruler for measuring gauge samples, some glass-headed pins—also for measuring gauge samples and for blocking—a pair of scissors, and some tapestry needles for finishing.

1, 3, 5 Plastic needles	13 Safety pins
2 Wooden needles	14 Row counter
4, 6, 7 Metal needles	15 Stitch stopper or "needle guard"
8 Double-pointed needles	16 Scissors
9 Needle gauge	17 Glass-headed pins
10 Cable needles	18 Stitch holders
11 Circular needle	19 Bobbin
12 Ring markers	20 Tape measure

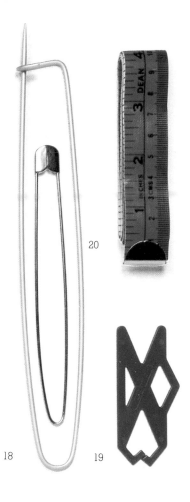

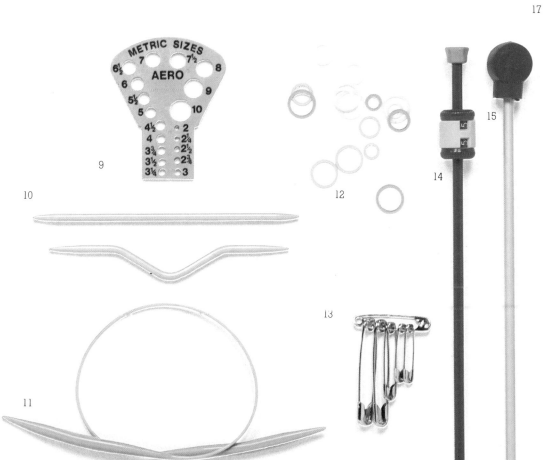

GAUGE—KEY TO SUCCESS

Knitters frequently ignore the gauge measurement given in knitting patterns, and the results, in terms of ill-fitting, misshapen garments are all too evident. It is impossible, however, for the would-be designer to ignore gauge, since it is the basis of all knitting design.

The approach of a knitter following an existing pattern is quite different from that of a designer creating a garment from scratch. The knitter has to match her gauge to that given in the pattern if the garment is to be the correct size and shape; she does this by making gauge samples, measuring the gauge, and adjusting it, if necessary, by changing the needle size.

The designer has to create her own gauge, but this does not mean that *any* gauge will do. A great deal depends on the type and thickness of yarn, the stitch pattern, the type of garment or object, and its purpose. Gauge, for the designer, means matching needle size to yarn, in order to find the gauge that produces the desired feel or "handle" in the fabric and that best displays or enhances the stitch pattern. This is done by making samples until these requirements are met. The final sample is then measured, and the results form the figures on which the calculations for the garment are based. So both knitter and designer must know how to make gauge samples and how to measure and adjust tension. But, first of all, it helps to understand what gauge means and how it is affected by stitch pattern and yarn.

WHAT IS GAUGE?

Gauge is simply a measurement of the tightness or looseness of the knitted fabric. It is expressed in terms of the number of stitches and rows there are to a given measurement (usually 4 in).

The thickness of the yarn is obviously a major influence on the gauge measurement. There will be far fewer stitches to 4 in if the yarn is bulky than if it is fingering-weight. Apart from that, the nature of the yarn is also important, irrespective of thickness. Some yarns are better knitted quite firmly; others produce a more pleasing fabric if the gauge is looser. Any brushed or fluffy yarn, such as mohair or angora, is best knitted rather more loosely than is a plain yarn of a similar thickness. Heavily textured yarns—bouclés, chenilles and so on—can also take a looser gauge. On the other hand, if the gauge is too loose the stitches will be uneven, and the garment will hang badly and wash badly. If it is too tight the fabric will be stiff and uncomfortable, and it will be difficult to work the stitches. Tightly twisted yarns such as Guernsey five-ply can usually be knitted more tightly.

Like the yarn thickness, needle size has a direct and obvious effect on gauge. The same yarn knitted on different needle sizes will vary widely in its gauge measurement. It is precisely this which enables one to adjust the gauge measurement in a particular pattern or design to produce the desired result.

The effect of different stitch patterns on the gauge measurement is less widely appreciated. In fact, the same yarn, knitted on the same needles, can show striking variations in gauge when worked in different stitch patterns. The greatest differences are between in-pulling stitches such as ribs and cables, and openwork patterns such as lace and eyelets; but even in apparently similar stitches such as garter stitch and stockinette stitch there is considerable variation in both row and stitch gauge.

MAKING GAUGE SAMPLES

When matching your own tension to that given in a pattern, use the needle size specified in the gauge measurement and the yarn you intend to use for the garment (and in the same colour—there can even be gauge differences between two colours of the same yarn). Knit up a sample in the stitch pattern specified in the gauge measurement. Ideally you should knit up a sample a little larger than the 4 in usually given. Where the measurement is specified as "over pattern" the stitch pattern given for the garment must be used. Work enough whole repeats of the pattern to make at least 4 in (or whatever gauge measurement is given). Work a few more rows than are specified in the gauge measurement. Bind off the stitches, then block or press the sample.

For the designer the procedure is a little different, since one does not have a given gauge to match. However, on ball bands and yarn labels there is often a recommended needle size and sometimes also a recommended gauge measurement over stockinette stitch; these can provide useful starting points. If no needle size is recommended, use your experience of similar yarns to guide you, or consult the chart given on page 14. In any case, these are only guidelines for making your samples; the size you select eventually will depend on the results you obtain from the sample.

Knit the sample in the yarn and stitch pattern you intend to use. If there will be several stitch patterns, make a sample in each one, including ribbings and edgings. You will then have to use your judgment as to whether the fabric has the correct feel. One test is to squeeze it gently and then stretch it both ways. If it springs back into shape quite readily after these manipulations then it will hold its shape well in wear. Also, look to see whether the stitches are reasonably even and neither distorted nor squashed together. Does the stitch pattern show up well—the holes in eyelet patterns, the bobbles and cables in textured stitches? It may well be necessary to make several samples on different needle sizes before these conditions are satisfied. Once the desired effect has been achieved, block or press the sample.

size 7

size 5

size 3

The effect of needle size on gauge is shown by these samples, each with 22 cast-on stitches and worked in the same yarn.

A fuzzy yarn should be knitted to a relatively loose gauge. The mohair blend, *above right*, is approximately the same thickness as the smooth 4-ply, *above left*, but if knitted on a needle size appropriate for the 4-ply (size 3), it produces a stiff, unattractive fabric. Larger needles (size 8) reveal its soft texture, *center*.

MEASURING GAUGE

Lay a rigid ruler horizontally across the sample, aligning the top of the ruler with the edge of one row of stitches. Place a pin at the 0 in point and another at the 4 in point. Count the stitches between the pins. The result is the stitch gauge of that sample. If you are matching the gauge specified in a pattern, check your results against the pattern gauge. If you have more stitches your sample is too tight; make another one using larger needles. If you have fewer stitches it is too loose; make another one using smaller needles.

You will also need to measure your row gauge. Place the ruler vertically on the sample, aligning the right-hand edge with the edge of a column of stitches. Place a pin at the 0 in mark and another at the 4 in mark and count the stitches between the pins. This figure is the row gauge of your sample. To match your gauge, check it against the gauge measurement given in the pattern and adjust it as for stitch gauge if necessary. If it proves impossible to match both row and stitch gauge simultaneously, adjust the needles to gain the correct stitch gauge and adjust the number of rows as explained on p. 26.

COMPLICATED STITCH PATTERNS

Counting stitches and rows is relatively easy with simple patterns such as stockinette stitch and garter stitch. However, if the stitch pattern is a lacy stitch or involves complicated crossover motifs and cables it can be a little more difficult. In such cases, if you are matching a given gauge, place a marker (a small tag of yarn in another color will do) just before the third or fourth stitch when working the first row and another after the number of stitches specified by the pattern. Do the same on the row given as the figure for the row gauge (for example, the 22nd row if it is "22 rows to 4 in"). When the sample is completed, measure between these points. If the measurement either way is more than 4 in the sample is too loose; if less it is too tight. Adjust the needle size.

The designer should proceed a little differently. Make sure that your sample includes at least two pattern repeats and note the number of cast-on stitches. When the sample is completed, measure the width and divide the number of stitches by the answer to find the number of stitches per inch. For example 60 stitches ÷ 5 in = 12 stitches per inch.

When making gauge samples, label each one with the yarn and needle size. The samples can then be compiled into a useful archive which can be consulted at a later date, so eliminating much needless duplication.

Measure gauge by pinning out the sample as shown. Mark the specified number of stitches with pins and measure the distance between them. It should be 4 in.

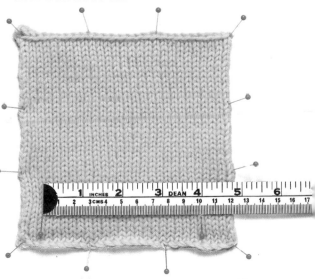

MEASURING UP

One of the advantages of designing your own garments is that you can achieve a perfect fit. Patterns are always written to standard measurements, but few people actually conform to these model dimensions in every respect. Smaller sizes are normally based on the assumption that people are shorter as well as thinner; larger sizes assume that they are taller as well as fatter. In real life, of course, this is not necessarily so. It is also surprisingly common for a person to have arms or legs that are not quite the same length. Growing children rarely conform to commercial stereotypes, and ill-fitting clothes can be distressing for them, as well as impractical.

A well-fitting garment is one in which the wearer feels utterly comfortable and which hangs well in relation to the chosen style. There should be no friction or pulling on any part of the garment, even if it is tight-fitting. Necklines and wrists must allow for comfortable putting on and off or they will become worn and eventually tear. A good fit is thus not only visually pleasing but also of practical importance.

TAKING MEASUREMENTS
The first step to a perfect fit is to take accurate and appropriate body measurements. The number and nature of such measurements depend on the type of garment (skirt, dress, or sweater, for example) and on how you intend to design it. If your design is to be a simple shape based on squares and rectangles (see pp. 44–55) you will need fewer measurements than if it is to be a fully-tailored classic. In the first case you may need only four: bust/chest width, length from shoulder, armhole depth, and neck width. For a raglan sweater dress, on the other hand, there could be nine or ten (see pp. 84–85). The diagrams given here show all the body measurements you are likely to need for most garments and where on the body they should be taken.

When taking measurements use a good quality dressmaker's tape measure: accurate body measurements cannot be taken with a rigid rule. It is impossible to measure your own body successfully, so if you are designing a garment for yourself, get someone to help. Always take *all* measurements on the person for whom the garment is intended. Make sure that he or she is standing perfectly upright but in a relaxed, natural position (not "to attention"). When taking upper arm and chest measurements, hold the tape smoothly over the body, neither pulling it tightly nor allowing any slack. When taking length measurements (sweater back or skirt length, for example) the best method is simply to let the tape hang, in order to ensure that it is truly vertical.

ALLOWANCE FOR EASE
Body measurements are not the same as garment measurements. To each body measurement you must usually add an allowance for ease or tolerance. This allowance is dependent on the styling of a garment—whether it is to be loose or tight-fitting—and also to some extent on the thickness of the yarn; it is usually necessary to increase the ease allowance for garments made in thick yarns. If the garment is to be tight-fitting (a "boob tube" or skinny rib, for example) the allowance can be negative; that is, it is subtracted from the body measurement, rather than added.

The range of these allowances is enormous—from, say, 2 in for a body-clinging sweater to twice or three times the body measurements for a huge, ballooning coat or cloak. The amount of ease is fundamental to the basic style or character of a garment and thus closely related to fashion trends. The table opposite is only a guide to the kinds of ease allowance that are necessary to achieve certain classic fittings. The type of garment—as well as its style—will also affect the ease allowance. For example, a garment that is worn next to the skin will need less ease to look baggy than will a coat or jacket, which is intended to be worn over other garments. Garments for children may have extra ease added to certain sections to allow for growth.

The ease allowance should not be uniformly applied all over a garment. Certain sections of a garment must fit the body measurements exactly. Following the table at right, add ease only to the bust/chest (A), hip (C), armhole (O), upper arm (P), wrist (Q), thigh (U), and ankle (W).

For convenience when designing, make a complete list of measurements for yourself and any other adult for whom you may design often, using the diagram here as a guide. Keep the measurements among your designing equipment and revise them as necessary after any gain or loss of weight or growth in height.

Key to measurement diagrams

A bust/chest—measure around the fullest part
B waist—measure loosely around the natural waistline
C hips—measure around the fullest part
D shoulder to shoulder—measure straight across to just inside the edge for set-in sleeves
E neck to underarm—measure from top of spine to required top of side seam (this is dependent on style)
F waist to underarm (or desired top of side seam)
G length from shoulder to desired lower edge of garment
H length from back neck to lower edge
I length from back neck to waist
J around neck—measure around the base of the neck
K front neck depth—measure from top of shoulder slope to desired neckline depth
L neck width—measure straight across back for desired width of neckline
M shoulder depth—measure from top of spine to shoulder width line (D)
N neck to sleeve edge—measure from top of spine with arm hanging down
O around armhole—measure from top of shoulder, under arm, and back
P upper arm—measure around fullest part
Q wrist
R around face
S inside leg
T outside leg
U thigh—measure around fullest part
V skirt length
W ankle
X crotch—measure from the waistline, between the legs, and back to the waistline

EASE

Approximate allowances (in inches) using medium-weight yarn (e.g. knitting worsted).

BODY MEASUREMENTS	FIT				
bust/chest (A) hips (C)	tight	close-fitting	standard	loose	baggy
26in	−1¼	− ¾	+1½	+3	+5 up
28in	−1¼	− ¾	+1½	+3½	+5½ up
30in	−1½	− ¾	+2	+3½	+6 up
32in	−1½	−1	+2	+4	+6½ up
34in	−1¾	−1	+2	+4	+7 up
36in	−1¾	−1¼	+2½	+4½	+7 up
38in	−2	−1¼	+2½	+4½	+7½ up
40in	−2	−1¼	+2½	+5	+8 up
42cm	−2¼	−1¼	+2½	+5	+8½ up
44cm	−2¼	−1½	+3	+5½	+8½ up
46cm	−2½	−1½	+3	+5½	+9 up
armhole (O) upper arm (P) wrist (Q) thigh (U) ankle (W)	−5%	0%	+10%	+25%	+40% up

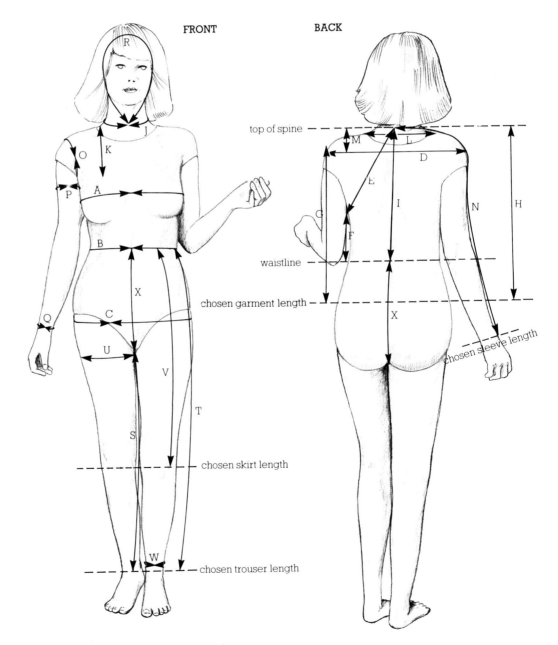

FRONT BACK

top of spine

waistline

chosen garment length

chosen sleeve length

chosen skirt length

chosen trouser length

ADAPTING EXISTING PATTERNS

Thousands of knitting patterns are published every year, but it is often difficult to find precisely the right one. This is, of course, one of the main incentives for learning to design your own garments. Sometimes, however, you can find an existing pattern which is exactly what you are looking for, except for one or two details. Perhaps the neckline is too deep or too shallow, or the sleeves are straight and you prefer them tapered. Perhaps you cannot find the recommended yarn, or do not like it, or you might prefer a plainer or more elaborate stitch pattern.

It could be that the sizing is not right for you. The sleeves may be too long or too short. The body may be too baggy or too tight. There is a limit to the number of sizes that can be given in a knitting pattern, so if you can find one that fits you exactly you are fortunate. Even if the pattern appears to fit—that is, the chest or bust measurement coincides with your own—it is still worthwhile checking the other measurements against your own measurements. The pattern may include a measurement diagram or a list of measurements. If not, or if these are not sufficiently detailed, it is a relatively easy matter to construct your own.

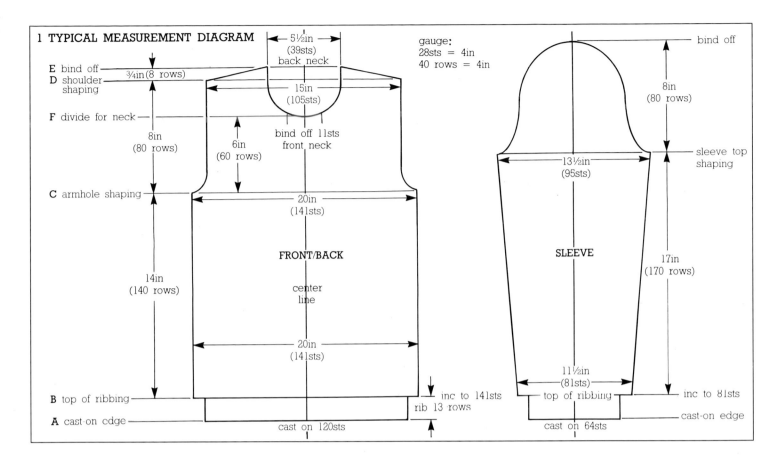

1 TYPICAL MEASUREMENT DIAGRAM

E bind off
D shoulder shaping
¾in (8 rows)

5½in (39sts) back neck

gauge:
28sts = 4in
40 rows = 4in

bind off

8in (80 rows)

15in (105sts)

F divide for neck

8in (80 rows)

6in (60 rows)

bind off 11sts front neck

sleeve top shaping

13½in (95sts)

C armhole shaping

20in (141sts)

FRONT/BACK

SLEEVE

center line

14in (140 rows)

17in (170 rows)

20in (141sts)

11½in (81sts)

B top of ribbing

inc to 141sts
rib 13 rows

top of ribbing

inc to 81sts

A cast-on edge

cast on 120sts

cast on 64sts

cast-on edge

CONSTRUCTING A MEASUREMENT DIAGRAM

It is usually obvious from the way a pattern is laid out how many separate pieces there are to be worked. For a classic crew-neck pullover it is a back, front, and two sleeves. The back and front are usually the same as far as the neck shaping, and the sleeves should be identical, so your diagram need show only a combined back and front and one sleeve.

A typical measurement diagram is shown in illustration 1. When drawing your own, you could use graph paper to facilitate symmetry and correct proportions. (The horizontal lines on the back/front are marked "A," "B," and so on, simply for ease in identifying them here, this is unnecessary when drawing your own diagram.)

Start with the number of cast-on stitches for the back and draw a horizontal line ("A") to represent the lower edge of the sweater. If this is worked in ribbing, you will not be able to work out the width of this line unless—which is very unusual—you are given a gauge measurement for the ribbing. The pattern may then give you a measurement or number of rows to be worked in ribbing. Draw another horizontal line ("B") to represent the end of the ribbing. The last rib row will probably be an increase row. Using the stitch gauge calculate the width after the increase row.

Sometimes the length up to the armhole

is given in the pattern. If it is not, work out the number of rows to the armhole shaping and, using the row gauge, calculate the length of that section. Draw a horizontal line ("C") to mark the beginning of the armhole shaping. Use the stitch gauge to calculate the width of the garment at this point. (If the pattern does not give the number of stitches just before the shaping, you will need to add the number of increases—if any—worked after line B to the number of stitches at B.) Mark off the measurement on line C, centering it above the ribbing. Join lines B and C to form the side edges, cross-checking with the pattern for shaping.

Next, draw a line ("D") at the point just before the shoulder shaping begins, using the measurement given in the pattern, or the row gauge, to find the armhole depth. Using the pattern for the back and the stitch gauge, work out the shoulder width and mark off this measurement on line D, centering it above the ribbing. Draw two vertical lines from line D down to line C.

Work out the depth of the shoulder up to the back neck, and draw a horizontal line ("E") at this point. Mark the width of the back neck at this point and draw diagonal lines to join the sides of the neck to the shoulder points. Mark the front neck shaping (line "F" and the vertical shaping lines) on the same diagram.

Construct a similar diagram for the

sleeve, drawing horizontal lines at the bottom edge, top of the ribbing, underarm point (that is, before the beginning of the sleeve cap shaping), and the top of the sleeve.

Mark the calculated measurements and number of stitches or rows at all the appropriate points as shown.

Compare the diagram with your body measurements, taking into account the allowances that will have been made for ease (see p. 23), and calculate the necessary adjustments.

25

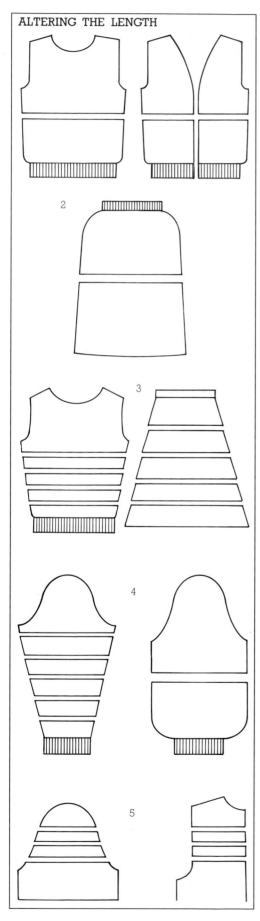

ALTERING THE LENGTH

LENGTH ALTERATIONS

Altering the length of a garment is usually much easier than altering the width, since it is largely just a matter of working more or fewer rows. Altering the width is much more complicated, so if you are choosing which size to knit from a given range, always select a pattern that will give you suitable width, rather than length, measurements. Also, where possible, always make alterations in straight, rather than shaped, sections of a garment.

Over-all length In straight-sided garments (illustration **2**), lengthen or shorten in the part above the ribbing or edging, and below the armhole shaping (or waist, if it is a skirt). Work more rows for a longer garment and fewer for a shorter one. If there is a pattern to be matched across the sleeve cap and you do not intend to adjust the sleeve length, make the alteration immediately above the ribbing, so that you end on the same pattern row at the armhole as in the original pattern. (This may entail beginning the stitch pattern part-way through the repeat.)

If the sides of the garment are shaped, the adjustment must be evenly distributed along the length (illustration **3**). For example, if the number of rows between the ribbing and the armhole shaping is 120, and the stitches are increased every 10th row, and you need to add 24 rows to lengthen the garment, work an extra 2 rows between each increase: 120 (rows) ÷ 10 (increase rows) = 12 (number of segments), and 24 (rows to be added) ÷ 12 = 2 (number of rows added per segment).

Sleeve length Make the alteration between the top of the ribbing and the sleeve cap shaping (illustration **4**). If the pattern needs to be matched at the armhole, work additional or fewer pattern rows just above the ribbing if you do not intend to adjust the body length also. If the sleeve is tapered, distribute the adjustment evenly between the increases.

Armhole depth If the armhole depth is to be adjusted, matching alterations must be made on the sleeve and the body (illustration **5**). On shaped set-in sleeves the same number of rows must be added or subtracted after the initial bind-off rows for armhole shaping and before the last few bind-off rows at the top. If the sleeve top is straight and is joined to a straight edge (see p. 89), the number of stitches in the bind-off row on the sleeve must be adjusted to fit the new armhole depth.

WIDTH ALTERATIONS

In garments knitted from the bottom up, the chest or bust width can be adjusted only by altering the number of stitches on the needle. Calculate the number of stitches you will need to achieve the new width at the underarm. Half of the increase or decrease must be worked on the back and half on the front. If the garment is not shaped at the sides these stitches can be added to or subtracted from the cast-on stitches (make sure that the number is compatible with the stitch pattern multiple—see p. 56).

If the garment is bloused at the top of the ribbing but straight thereafter, the new width must be achieved partly by altering the number of increases at that point. Some of the adjustment must be made in the cast-on stitches; for example, if you need to add 15 stitches to the width, you can add 10 to the cast-on stitches and the remaining 5 by extra increases above the ribbing. Distribute the increases above the ribbing evenly across the width (see p. 91).

Where the sides of a garment are shaped, make the adjustment to the number of cast-on stitches and maintain the arrangement of increases in the side seams (every sixth or tenth row, for example); although the number of stitches on the needle will, of course, be different from that specified (or understood) in the pattern, the number of stitches increased will remain the same throughout.

The adjustment to the width will also affect the armhole, shoulder, and neck shaping. Be especially careful to allow for the difference when you are dividing the garment to work the neck—the stitches worked before turning and completing one side of the section should include half the adjustment.

Any alterations to the width must take account of stitch or color patterns. In the latter case, if you cannot add or subtract one complete repeat, make sure that the pattern is correctly centered and that there is still a good match at the side seams (see p. 40). In garments with complex stitch or color patterns it is usually essential to add or subtract at least one whole pattern repeat.

Where panel patterns are used (see p. 56) the increase or decrease can often be accommodated in the background stitches or by adding, for example, a vertical rib or narrow cable divider, or, in the case of Aran patterns, by making the alteration in the all-over stitches at the sides or in the center of the Aran panels. Again, you should make sure that the panels are correctly centered and that the arrangement is symmetrical (unless you are deliberately aiming for an unorthodox effect).

The width of the sleeves can be altered in the same way as for the back and front.

RESTYLING GARMENTS

Apart from altering the size of a garment it is also possible to make some simple changes in the styling without too much difficulty. If large-scale changes are required it is probably just as easy to design from scratch exactly the garment you want. However, if the rest of a garment is ideal and you only want to change the neckline, perhaps, or the sleeve shape, or the collar, then restyling becomes a practical alternative to a full-scale new design.

Collars and necklines The shape of a collar or the cut of a neckline is a major feature of the over-all look or feeling of a design. It is also something about which most people have strong individual preferences. Some people, for example, feel that they cannot wear V-necks, or turtleneck collars, or square necklines.

In some cases the change is very easy to effect. You can alter a crew-neck sweater into a turtleneck simply by continuing the ribbed neckband to the required depth. To substitute a collar for a round neckband, cast on the number of stitches given for picking up around the neck edge and work a rectangle. Sew the collar on to the neck edge with the short edges meeting at the center front.

The shape of the neckline itself can also be altered (illustration **6**). A round neck can be squared off by binding off the same number of stitches for the front as are bound off for the back neck, then working each side of the neck straight up.

To work a classic V-neck, divide for the neck a couple of rows after the beginning of the armhole shaping. If there is an even number of stitches, divide them exactly in half; if an odd number, leave the center stitch on a safety pin to be picked up as part of the neckband. The number of stitches that must be decreased on each side is equal to half the number of stitches left for the back neck (minus one if the front section contains an odd number). Divide the number of decreases into the number of rows between the beginning of the neck shaping and the bound-off edge to find the intervals between the decreases. For example, 100 rows ÷ 20 decreases = 5; so you would decrease one stitch at the neck edge on every 5th row.

Sleeves To make a full straight sleeve into a tapered sleeve, take the number of stitches that are increased in the mass increase row at the top of the ribbed cuff and divide them into the number of rows between the top of the cuff and the sleeve cap shaping; multiply the result by 2 to get the intervals between increases. For example, if the number of stitches increased is 20 and the number of rows is 120, the interval between increases should be 12: 120 ÷ 20 = 6; 6 × 2 = 12; so you should increase one stitch at each end of every 12th row. (See also p. 91.)

To make a tapered sleeve into a full, straight sleeve, subtract the number of cast-on stitches from the number of stitches in the last row before the sleeve cap shaping and increase that number evenly across the last row of the ribbing. Then work straight to the beginning of the sleeve cap shaping.

Making a pullover into a cardigan This is most easily done with a round- or square-necked pullover. Allow for overlapping front button and buttonhole bands about 1 in wide. Using the stitch gauge, calculate the number of stitches in 1 in and subtract half that number from the cast-on stitches for each front of the cardigan (half the number cast on for the back). Work straight to the armhole shaping. If stitches are increased just above the ribbing, work half the number of increases in each section. Shape the armhole on the right-hand side of the left front and on the left-hand side of the right front. Shape each side of the neck as instructed in the original pattern. Button and buttonhole bands, each 1 in wide, should be worked separately and sewn on. (See illustration **7**.)

It is also possible, of course, to convert a cardigan into a pullover. Simply work the front as for the back up to the neck shaping (see p. 81).

SUBSTITUTING YARNS

One of the most radical alterations you can make to a pattern is to substitute a different yarn for the one specified. By changing the yarn you can make a winter garment into a summer one, a slipover into a sleeveless top, a sporty outdoor cardigan into a glitzy cover-up for evening wear.

You may also wish to change the yarn for other, more practical reasons: the yarn specified may not be available in the color you want; its fiber content may be unsuitable for you or for the person for whom you are making it; you may even have found

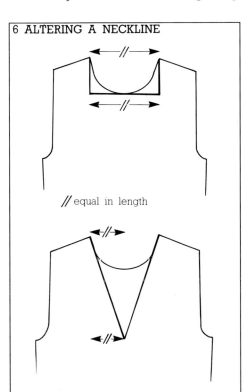

6 ALTERING A NECKLINE

// equal in length

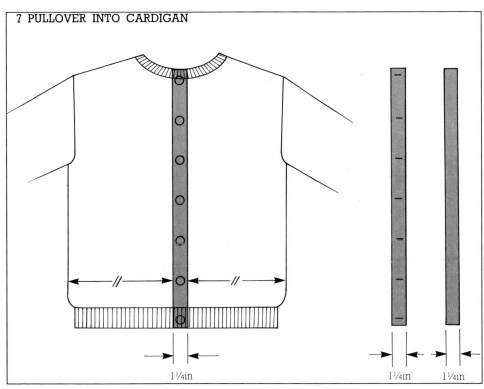

7 PULLOVER INTO CARDIGAN

1¼in

1¼in   1¼in

some wonderful yarn at a bargain price in a sale or on a market stall and be looking for an appropriate use for it. Whatever the reason, how can you be sure that the substitute will work as well as the original yarn?

First check that the substitute falls into the same general weight category (sport, knitting worsted, extra bulky, and so on). Even if it does not belong technically to one of these categories, it may be described on the yarn label in terms of its thickness (''knits as sport yarn,'' for example). If there is no indication of the thickness, compare the gauge and recommended needle size of the original yarn specified by the pattern with any such information given on the label of the proposed substitute. (This comparison of the gauge measurements is only relevant if it is given over the same stitch pattern in both cases.) If these are significantly different (size 5 needles compared with size 12 needles, for example, or 15 stitches to 4 in compared with 25 to 4 in) the proposed substitute is unlikely to be suitable. If they are within a couple of needle sizes or a few stitches, you are probably on the right track.

Buy one ball of the proposed substitute and make a gauge swatch. If you can match the gauge with the new yarn, then provided it meets all the other criteria of suitability for its purpose and compatibility with the stitch pattern (see p. 16), it will almost certainly be a successful substitute.

Quantities You cannot assume that you will need the same quantity of the new yarn as was given for the original one. The determining factor in the amount of yarn needed for a project is the length of the yarn, not the weight. However, most yarns are sold by weight rather than length, and differences in fiber content will have a considerable effect on the weight of a yarn.

Some yarns are intrinsically heavier than others, regardless of the thickness of the thread. Synthetics tend to be lighter (unless they have a metallic component) than wools; cottons and silks tend to be heavier. The heavier yarns will have less length of thread for a given weight than the lighter ones, so you would need, for example, fewer ounces of an acrylic sport yarn than you would of a wool sport yarn for the same garment or object.

When buying a substitute yarn you can either use your knowledge of the fiber content of the new yarn and that of the original to make an educated guess, or estimate the quantity as for an entirely new design, following the guidelines on p. 17.

SUBSTITUTING STITCH PATTERNS

Another device for dramatically altering a design is substituting stitch patterns. A simple garment shape, such as a round-necked pullover, will look strikingly different in an all-over lace pattern from the way it looks in stockinette stitch, or in a series of cabled panels, or a bobble pattern, or a series of Fair Isle bands. However, the variation in gauge between different stitch patterns (see p. 20) means that you cannot knit, for example, a stockinette stitch cardigan in a lacy or color pattern and assume that it will end up the same size and/or proportions as the original. Unless you are to make drastic alterations to the numbers of stitches and rows (in which case, you might as well design a completely new garment) the gauge of the substitute pattern has to be the same as the original. It is essential to knit gauge swatches in the new stitch pattern before embarking on the whole project.

You are most likely to find a successful match if you choose a substitute within the same general group of patterns (in other words, a different lacy pattern, or a different Fair Isle pattern, and so on). In some cases it is possible to work simple color patterns into a plain garment without affecting the gauge (see p. 41); stripes and motifs worked by the intarsia method can easily be incorporated. Even so, it is always best to make a gauge check to be on the safe side.

RENOVATING EXISTING GARMENTS

Even the most perfectly-made garments are subject to a degree of wear and tear and occasionally to unfortunate accidents—snags, burns, permanent stains, and such. Some garments are quickly outgrown; others become outmoded. There can be any number of reasons why a garment that is otherwise perfectly sound is no longer worn. Rather than consigning such casualties to the ragbag, why not see if there is some way in which they can be rescued or renovated?

WEAR AND TEAR

Certain sections of garments are particularly prone to wear and tear. The cast-on and bound-off edges of ribbing, for example, are subject to great stress when an article is put on or taken off, and they frequently break. You can help to prevent this on cast-on edges by casting on with a double length of yarn, and on bound-off edges by binding off in ribbing. If the edge does break, however, it is possible to re-knit the entire ribbed section. If the ribbed edging has been knitted on to a previously-worked section (for example, around a neck edge or an armhole), it can easily be unraveled back to the edge where the stitches were picked up, and the whole band can be re-knitted following the original instructions. (If you do not want to rip out shoulder seams, re-knit neckbands in the round on double-pointed needles.)

If the ribbing is above the cast-on edge, the procedure is rather different. First rip out any side seams up to an inch or so above the damaged area. With the point of a tapestry or yarn needle pull a thread at the side seam just above the affected part and cut it, then gently pull out that thread right across the row, slowly easing the top and bottom sections of the knitting apart. If the yarn is slippery you can secure the stitches in the top part of the split on a knitting needle as you go. Finally, re-knit the ribbing in reverse.

Elbows, sock heels, and any other parts of a garment that have worn thin can be reinforced with Swiss darning in a matching yarn (this was the original purpose of Swiss darning, hence its name). Alternatively, make a virtue out of necessity and patch holes or damaged parts with brightly-colored knitted shapes, edged with bold embroidery (blanket stitch—see p. 34—is ideal for this).

OUTGROWN GARMENTS

Children always seem to shoot up astonishingly quickly, and however much allowance you make for this, they inevitably outgrow their clothes long before they wear them out. Sleeves are a constant problem, but with a little forethought you can avert the problem. Always knit cuffs on children's garments at least twice as long as they need to be. To begin with, they can be turned back; later on, the extra will be needed to cover lengthening arms.

An effective way to lengthen a garment is to insert contrasting stripes. This way, you do not have to worry about matching yarns. Simply rip out a row at the chosen point (as described for re-knitting ribbing above), pick up the lower section of the garment on a needle and knit the stripe for the required depth. Finally, graft the last row of the stripe to the top section of the garment (see p. 137). This method can be used to lengthen fronts and backs, sleeves, and legs, and also to increase armhole depth (in this case, the same adjustment must be made to the sleeve cap and armhole).

OUTMODED GARMENTS

There are lots of things you can do to existing garments to give them a new look. Try surface decoration in the form of embroidery, beading, Swiss darning, or fringe (see pp. 30–37). Re-knit borders in a new stitch or color. Insert a band of lace or Fair Isle knitting. Take out the sleeve and knit on armbands to make a pullover into a slipover or a cardigan into a vest. Make a pullover into a cardigan: machine-stitch four vertical rows of stitching up the center front, then cut between the second and third rows of stitching with sharp scissors and knit on a button band and buttonhole band. Add some patch pockets.

SURFACE DECORATION

The use of trimmings and embroidery is a relatively easy way to add style and individuality to a knitted garment or household item, whether it is something you have designed yourself or something you have made from a pattern. Cords have a practical function as ties and drawstrings, but they can also be appliquéd on to the knitted fabric in a decorative manner. Pompoms and tassels can be used to trim ties and to create unusual fringes for shawls, blankets, pillows, and clothes; but they, too, can be incorporated into appliqué designs. Ready-made trimmings, obtainable in notions departments, also come in handy from time to time. Lace, ribbons of all kinds, fringe, beads, sequins, and, of course, buttons can all play a part in surface decoration.

Embroidery has traditionally been used in Norwegian knitting and even more prominently in Tyrolean knitting, which is characterized by pretty floral motifs; but it can also be used for bold, strikingly modern effects. Swiss darning, also called "duplicate stitch," is a kind of embroidery that imitates knitted stitches and makes it possible to introduce color patterning after the knitting is completed. Smocking provides both textural and linear interest and can be used to shape a knitted fabric.

CORDS

Ready-made cords in various materials are obtainable, but it is often preferable to make a cord from the same yarn as the knitted item, or in one that harmonizes with it. There are many different ways of making cords—some derived from other crafts, such as crochet and macramé, which produce variously ornate results. Among the simplest and best suited to knitted garments are twisted cords, braided cords, and knitted cords.

Making a twisted cord Twisted, rope-like cords can be made in any thickness, depending on the number and thickness of the strands used. A smooth and elegant effect can be achieved by making the cord from a plain fingering or a fine glitter yarn; a coarse, rustic effect, by using a bulky tweed yarn. A particular advantage of this type of cord is that several different types of yarn can be combined, enabling you to mix textures and colors to achieve unusual, original trimmings.

To estimate the number of strands you will need, twist a few together and then double them. Then cut the required number of strands, making them three times the finished length of cord. Knot them together at each end. Hook one of the knots around a door handle or some other con-

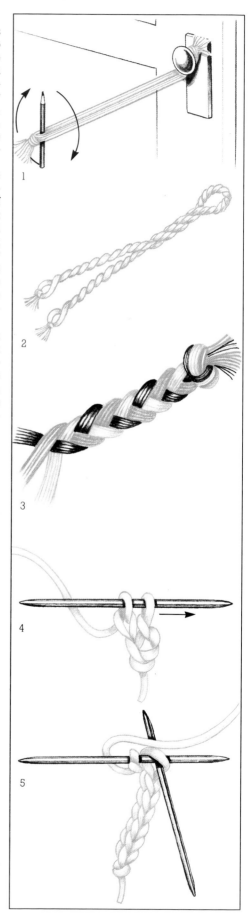

Twisted cord in glitter yarn

Twisted cord in multicolor mohair blend

Knitted cord in mohair blend

Knitted cord in medium-weight yarn

Twisted cord in three colors of medium-weight yarn

Braided cord in solid-color and tweed yarn

30

venient anchor and slip a pencil or a cable needle through the other end (illustration **1**). Pull the strands taut and rotate the pencil until they are twisted tightly together. The strands must be so well twisted that they kink up if the tension is relaxed.

Carefully fold the twisted strands in half and hold both knotted ends firmly together. The twisted strands will twist once more around each other **(2)**. Shake the cord to smooth out the twist. Secure the folded and knotted ends with two more knots, and trim them to form small tassels.

Making a braided cord Although braided cords have a rather more primitive look than twisted cords, they are useful for children's clothes and some accessories. Use enough strands to achieve the necessary thickness and cut them slightly longer than the desired finished length. Knot them at one end and anchor the knot securely. Divide the strands into three equal groups and braid them in the usual way **(3)**. Knot the other end.

Making a knitted cord This cord takes a little more time to make than a twisted or braided cord, but it is attractive and ideally suited to knitted fabrics. Only one strand of yarn is used, so the thickness of the cord depends on the weight of the yarn. It is not possible to make a multicolored cord in this way unless you use space-dyed yarn. To work beads into the cord, thread them on to the yarn first (see p. 122) and work them in as you go.

Using two double-pointed needles, cast on two stitches and knit them as usual. Without turning the work, slide the stitches across to the working end of the needle **(4)**. Pull the yarn firmly across the back from left to right and knit the two stitches again. Without turning, slide the stitches to the working end and knit them again. Continue in this way **(5)** until the cord is long enough. Knit the two stitches together, and bind off.

Using cords Appliqué contrasting cords on to plain knitted fabrics, using fine thread and slipstitch. Try bright geometric patterns on pillow covers or swirling spirals and whorls on a child's jacket.

To use a cord as a drawstring you will need to work a casing for it. The normal method is to work a row of eyelets (see p. 113) a few rows in from the edge of the sleeve, neckline, or lower edge. Remember to allow for a hem (p. 128) if one is to be included. Often a casing is placed immediately above a ribbed waistband; if the stitches need to be increased for the main fabric, work the increases on the last (wrong-side) row of the ribbing, then work the eyelets in the first (right side) row of the main fabric.

Cords can also be used for bag handles, for "cording" the edges of pillows, and also on their own, twisted and coiled together to make belts and soft jewelry.

TASSELS AND POMPOMS

Decorations such as tassels and pompoms can be made separately and included in fringe or attached to cords and ties. They can also be sewn directly on the garment. Both trimmings require a fair amount of yarn (depending on the desired size). The yarn can be the same yarn as the main fabric, a contrasting one, or a combination of several different yarns. Pompoms are best made with fine yarns.

Making a tassel Cut a rectangle the length of the tassel out of stiff cardboard. Wind the yarn around the card lengthwise (the number of times you wind determines the thickness of the tassel). Tie all the strands together at one end of the card and cut through the folds at the other end **(6)**. Bind the tassel about an inch from the tied end and trim the ends neatly.

Making a pompom Cut two circles the desired diameter of the pompoms out of stiff cardboard. Cut a circle out of the middle of each one. Place the disks together and bind yarn tightly and evenly around the disk **(7)** until the hole in the center is filled. Take a pair of scissors and, slipping the blades between the disks, cut through the yarn at the edges **(8)**. Part the disks slightly to allow you to tie a length of yarn securely around the middle of the pompom **(9)**. Cut away the cardboard and fluff out the yarn ends. Speckled and spotted effects can be achieved by binding the disks with yarns of different colors.

Using tassels and pompoms Tassels and pompoms are often used to trim the ends of cords and ties at necklines, cuffs, and waists. Alternatively, you can sew them directly on to a garment. Pompoms made in brilliant primary colors will create an amusing clownlike effect; made in dark, sultry chenille yarn they give a luxurious touch to sophisticated evening wear. Small pompoms could make jolly buttons for a child's outfit; larger ones could serve as earmuffs on a cap. A pompom is often used as a topknot for a hat or beret. Use tassels to finish the corners of a square pillow or the ends of a bolster.

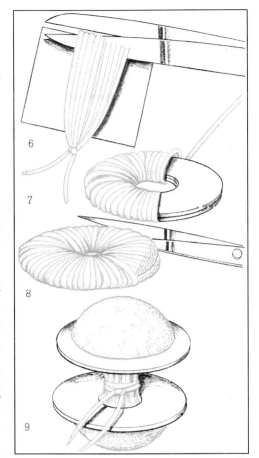

31

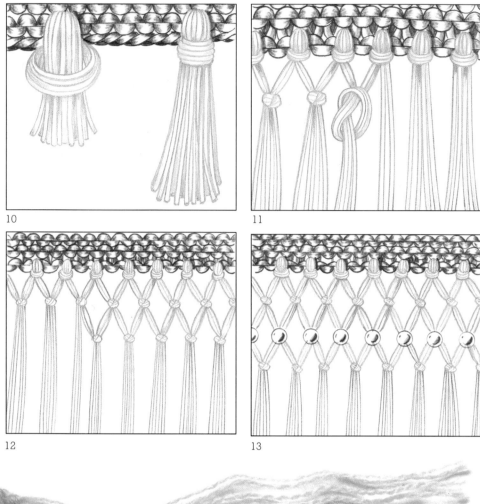

10

11

12

13

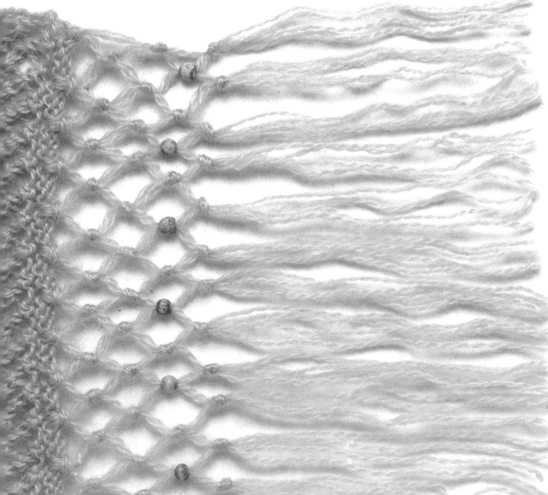

FRINGE

A fringe can be bought ready-made and sewn on, or you can make one yourself using yarn to match or harmonize with the fabric. A knotted fringe, worked directly on the edge or the main body of the fabric, is a versatile trimming which can be as simple or elaborate as you wish. Basically it consists of a series of tassels, but by making the tassels longer and knotting them together—perhaps adding beads— you can produce elegant, lacy effects.

Making a simple fringe The fringe will be a little less than half the length of the strands used to make it. Make one tassel before cutting the lengths needed for the whole fringe so that you can see the finished effect. Unless the yarn is very thick, cut several strands for each tassel.

First fold the strands in half. Using a crochet hook if necessary, thread the folded end from front to back through the edge (or through a stitch in the main fabric). Bring the fold back to the front and pass the ends through it, tightening the knot firmly (illustration **10**). Repeat this across the edge at regular intervals.

Making a knotted fringe For this fringe each tassel should be fairly long (4 in or more) and rather thinner than is needed for a simple fringe. Knot the tassel into the edge as for a simple fringe, but at slightly wider intervals; you will need to experiment with the thickness of tassel and the spacing to find appropriate proportions. Leaving a space, knot half of each tassel with half of the adjacent one **(11)**, using a simple overhand knot as follows: loop the threads into a circle in a counter-clockwise direction and pass the ends behind the circle and through the loop, tightening the knot firmly.

Successive rows of knots are staggered to produce a lattice effect **(12)**. You can also substitute beads for some of the knots to add glitter and color **(13)**. Trim the ends when the fringe is completed.

Using fringe A long, generous fringe adds a wonderful sweeping feeling to shawls and stoles. Straight, unhemmed, unribbed edges of jackets, coats, and skirts can also be finished with fringe—an excellent way, too, of adding immediate color to something plain and dull. For a cowboy flavor, try fringing the yoke area and upper armhole seams of a cardigan or jacket.

READY-MADE TRIMMINGS

Beads can be knitted in (see p. 122) or sewn on when the garment is finished. Make sure that the weight of the beads is not too great for the fabric. On the other hand, if the beads are too small they will be lost in the stitches. Always experiment with small swatches before making a final decision.

Beads can be used in countless different ways. For an all-over beaded effect, work them in regularly throughout the fabric. Or use them to emphasize the texture of an interesting stitch pattern. Beads and eyelet patterns are especially compatible. Beads can also be used to create abstract patterns of color and pictorial motifs.

Since the beads have to be threaded on to the yarn before you begin knitting, any multicolor scheme must be carefully worked out in advance. Calculate the number of beads you will need in each color for each ball of yarn to be used. This may be difficult to achieve with total accuracy—thread more beads rather than fewer, if in doubt. Thread them in reverse order from the order in which they will be knitted.

Beads also combine well with some kinds of embroidery—particularly with French knots. When used in this way, they should be sewn on to the completed fabric. One advantage of this method is that relatively small beads can be used, since they are strung on to ordinary sewing thread. When sewing on the beads, anchor each one with a small backstitch and work the thread through the wrong side of the fabric, taking care to keep it fairly loose.

Sequins can also be knitted into a fabric, since they are usually lighter than beads, you can use them much more densely with no risk of distorting the fabric. Ready-made sequin strings and motifs can be sewn on for instant glamour.

Lace edgings of all kinds can be bought by the yard and used to trim necklines, armholes, and other edges. Apply lace flat or gather the straight edge, using small running stitches, before sewing it to the knitted fabric. (For knitted lace edgings see pp. 74–75.)

Ribbons are available in many different colors, types, and widths. Thread them through eyelet patterns or tie them in bows and sew them on. Use them as ties on baby clothes and on delicate lacy garments.

Buttons are thought of primarily as fastenings, but they are obviously decorative as well. The right button can provide the perfect finishing touch for a garment, complementing the color and texture of the knitting and sometimes adding a note of whimsy or glamour. Brass buttons give a smart, military look to a classic cardigan; a horn toggle enhances the rugged look of a bulky jacket; buttons in the form of animals or flowers are a charming touch on young children's clothes.

EMBROIDERY

It is possible to work embroidery on knitting just as if it were a woven fabric. However, some of the most interesting and attractive uses of embroidery take the texture of knitting—and, sometimes also the specific stitch pattern—into account. Lines of chain stitch, for example, can follow the twists and turns of a cable pattern. French knots can nestle in the hollows of a lattice or honeycomb stitch. In Tyrolean knitting the "lazy daisy" leaves and flowers that are typical of the style are always set off or framed by some feature of the knitting. Even a plain knitted background has its own character, which can be complemented by the stitchery. The grid-like surface of stockinette stitch, for example, lends itself to cross stitch motifs.

Always work embroidery fairly loosely on knitting to allow for the elasticity of the fabric. As a general rule, choose materials that are sympathetic to the underlying yarns—wool embroidery thread on a wool fabric, cotton on cotton, silk on silk. Interesting effects can be created, however, by using contrasting materials—a silk embroidery thread, for example, on a mohair-blend knitted fabric. If you are choosing a contrasting thread, make sure the materials are compatible in terms of the after-care they require.

While bearing such practical considerations in mind, experiment with the wealth of materials that can be used for embroidery—not only traditional embroidery threads but also fine ribbons and braids, buttons and beads, and knitting yarns themselves. Smooth yarns can be used for simple motifs, Swiss darning, and smocking. Slubbed and fuzzy yarns that may be difficult to use in the needle can be applied to the surface of the fabric using the couching technique described below. There are a great many suitable embroidery stitches; the following are some of the easiest and most effective.

Cross stitch (illustration 1) used for abstract patterning or motifs, or for lines and borders. Use the lines formed by the rows and stitches of the knitting as a guide for working the embroidery. All of the cross stitches should slant the same way; to ensure this, work the stitch in two stages as shown.

Blanket stitch (2) can be used to finish an edge and also as a purely decorative stitch on the main part of a garment. The stitches can be worked evenly or irregularly, for an interesting modern effect; spaced widely or close together. For stylized flowers, work the stitches radiating from a central point as shown (3).

Couching (4) is used to catch down other threads, cords or ribbons laid loosely on the surface of the fabric. On knitting it is normally used for outlining rather than for filling a shape; although it can also be

1

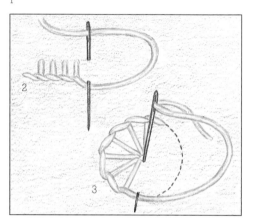

2

3

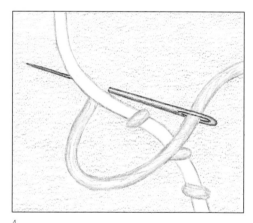

4

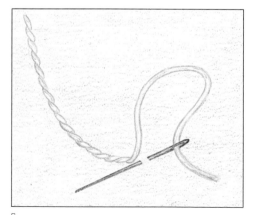

5

Cross stitch

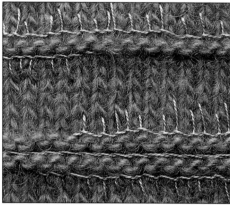

Blanket stitch

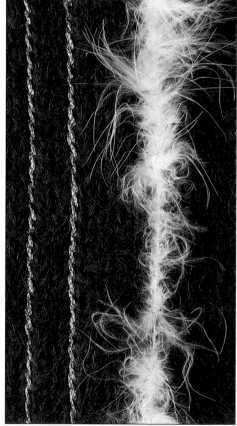

Stem stitch and couched feather yarn

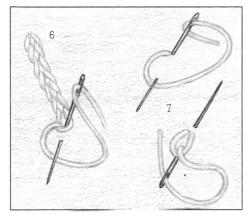

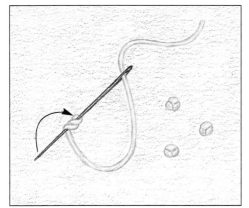

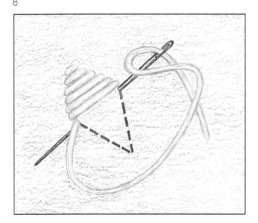

8

Tyrolean-style embroidery—chain stitch and French knot

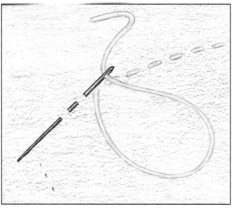

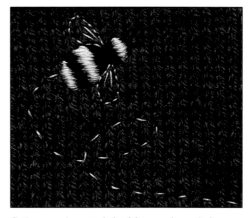

9

10

Satin, running, and double running stitch

effectively used to "draw" a motif in a free and easy fashion.

Lay the thread to be couched on the surface, leaving a short extra length at each end. The thread used for the stitching can be a fine matching thread or a thicker, contrasting one. When the couching is completed, thread the ends into a large-eyed needle. Take them to the wrong side, and fasten them with a few stitches using ordinary thread.

Stem stitch (5) can be used for fine continuous lines. The working thread must be kept on the same side of the needle throughout.

Chain stitch (6) worked vertically over a single column of stitches can look just like a knitted stitch, but it can also be worked against the grain in straight lines or curves. Use the knitted stitches to help keep the "links" even. Worked singly **(7)**, chain stitches can be used for leaves and flowers. This is often called "lazy daisy stitch."

French knots (8) create small raised dots of color and are generally used along with other stitches. The size of the knot can be varied by using two or more strands of thread.

Satin stitch (9) is a filling stitch used for solid shapes and motifs. The shape to be filled should be outlined with small running stitches before being filled in. For a padded effect, work two layers, slanting the stitches in different directions.

Running stitch (10) is very simple, but with imaginative use of color and different yarns or thread textures you can create a variety of attractive effects. All sorts of woven and checkered patterns can be worked. Two superimposed lines—called "double running stitch"—make a more solid line.

Some embroidery stitches are easier to work if the knitting is first basted to a piece of organdy, which is then mounted in an embroidery frame (*not* including the knitting). Later, the cloth can be trimmed away around the stitching.

SMOCKING

A form of embroidery, smocking is not only decorative but also functional: it is used to gather in fullness in a fabric. Its use in knitting is somewhat limited, for most knitted fabrics are too thick to be gathered up as required for conventional smocking. However, there is a simple technique that gives the appearance of one type of smocking—honeycomb stitch.

The smocking must be planned in advance. The area to be smocked must be at least a third again as wide as is required in the finished garment, and it must be worked in a rib pattern; the three-by-one rib given here lends itself well to this technique.

Choose a light- to medium-weight yarn for the knitting; on heavier fabrics the results can appear ugly and cumbersome. The yarn used to work the smocking can be the same as that used for the knitting, perhaps in a contrasting color. Or you could use an embroidery thread, such as pearl cotton.

Working smocking Work the background fabric in twisted three-by-one rib on a multiple of four stitches, plus three extra, as follows:

1st row (RS) K1, (K1 tb1, P3) to last 2 sts, K1 tb1, K1.
2nd row (WS) K1, (P1 tb1, K3) to last 2 sts, P1 tb1, K1.

Repeat these two rows until the area to be smocked is the required depth. Thread a tapestry needle with the yarn to be used for the smocking and secure it on the wrong side at the lower right-hand corner of the ribbed area. Bring the needle out just to the left of the second rib from the right. Take it down just to the right of the first rib and up beside the second rib as before. Pull tightly to draw the two ribs together (illustration 1). Take the yarn back over the ribs twice more. After the third stitch, take the needle under the fabric and bring it up to the left of the fourth rib. Join the fourth and third ribs in the same way. Continue across the width of the fabric, joining adjacent pairs of ribs, carrying the yarn loosely across the wrong side.

Work the next row of smocking a short distance above the first, this time joining the second and third ribs, the fourth and fifth, and so on **(2)**. Alternate these rows to create the honeycomb effect **(3)**.

Using smocking Smocking is often used in knitting—as in dressmaking—to control fullness in certain areas of a garment, such as the yoke of a dress or the cuffs of a full-sleeved sweater. This application of the technique is particularly appropriate to clothes for children and babies. Smocking can also be used in a purely decorative way: a fabric smocked over its entire surface could be used for an interesting vest or jacket. A panel of smocked knitting might be set into a pillow cover or a sweater worked mainly in a plain stitch. The simple honeycomb pattern can be embellished with the use of interesting threads and beads; small pearls worked into the smocking stitches create a pretty effect, as shown below.

To make sure that the rows of smocking are evenly spaced, count the number of stitches in the ribs each time you begin a new row.

1

2

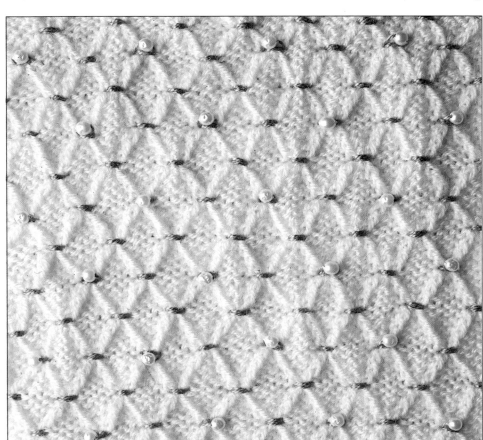

Smocking worked in pearl cotton and decorated with pearl beads

3

SWISS DARNING (DUPLICATE STITCH)

This is a type of embroidery specifically designed for fabrics knitted in stockinette stitch. It originated as a means of renovating worn patches (hence the name), but nowadays it is used to cover knitted stitches with duplicate embroidery stitches in a contrasting color. In this way you can create color patterns of all kinds that look as though they have been knitted in. The effects of intricate multicolored motifs can be achieved without the considerable problems involved in handling several different yarns at once. You can plan this into your design from the start or use the technique to revitalize a tired-looking or uninteresting garment.

Swiss darning is also useful for concealing mistakes, and for working fine diagonal or vertical lines or outlining a motif—all rather difficult to achieve by knitting.

Much of the success of Swiss darning depends on a thoughtful choice of yarn or thread with which to work it. If the desired effect is an exact imitation of the knitted stitches—a genuinely knitted-in look—then choose a yarn that matches the original as closely as possible in thickness, texture, and fiber content. If an exact match is not important you can use another yarn to create a special effect: Lurex or silk, for example, would add a rich effect on an evening sweater. Fluffy and bouclé yarns are not easy to work with, for the fibers tend to get caught between the background stitches. If the yarn is too thin, it will not cover the stitches properly. If it is too thick, it will not lie flat.

The type of background yarn is also important. Swiss darning is most successfully worked on a smooth, plain background. Dark colors can be a problem, since it is difficult to distinguish the individual stitches clearly. If the background yarn is too fine, the work could become very laborious.

Swiss darning is generally worked in rows, beginning at the bottom right-hand corner of a pattern or motif, working from right to left for one row then from left to right for the next row and so on. Only one color is used at a time. Work all the stitches required in one color before going on to the next one. Use a tapestry needle to avoid splitting the stitches. Secure the yarn on the wrong side. Work fairly loosely and keep an even tension.

Horizontal lines Bring the needle to the front through the base of the stitch to be covered. Insert it from right to left behind the stitch immediately above (illustration **1**), then take it to the back of the work through the base of the first stitch, pulling the yarn through gently. Bring the needle back to the front through the base of the next stitch to the left (**2**). Repeat the process for the required number of stitches. Work the next row in the same way,

but from left to right and inserting the needle from left to right through the base of the stitch in the row above (**3**). If you are working a pattern the row will not necessarily be solid. If you have to skip a few stitches, carry the yarn loosely and evenly across the back. Do not pull too tightly or the work will be distorted. If a large number of stitches must be skipped, break the yarn, finish the end and begin again in the appropriate place.

Vertical lines Begin at the bottom of the line by bringing the needle through the base of the first stitch. Insert the needle behind the base of the stitch above, then back through the base of the first stitch. Now bring the needle out through the base of the stitch above. Repeat the process (**4**) for the required number of stitches. When working solid areas of color, always work in horizontal lines: the finished effect is much smoother and neater.

Motifs for Swiss darning are usually worked from charts similar to those used for color-pattern knitting and cross-stitch embroidery. Each square on a grid represents one stitch of embroidery and the different colors or symbols on the chart represent the colors to be used.

It is quite feasible to use or adapt charts designed for other crafts (embroidery or rug-making, for example), so long as you remember that the shape of a knitted stitch,

unlike that of the square on graph paper, is rarely exactly square. More often it resembles a rectangle which is shorter than it is wide. This means that the finished effect will be slightly distorted unless you re-chart the pattern on a gauge grid (see p. 42). However, unless the design is a pictorial motif, the distortion may not significantly affect the results. In charts designed for knitting patterns this effect is already taken into consideration. If you are using a motif designed for another garment, however, there may be a slight distortion due to gauge differences between the original pattern and the one you are working.

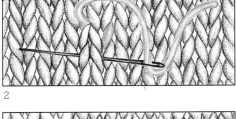

1

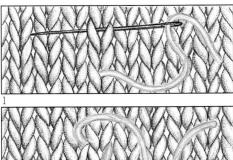

2

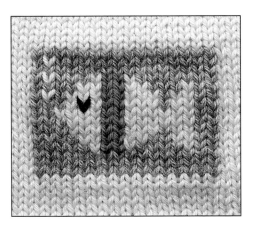

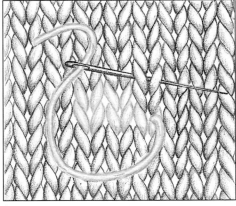

3

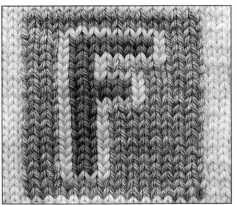

Swiss-darned motifs

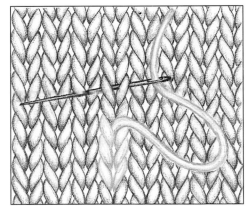

4

37

THE PRINCIPLES OF PATTERN

The introduction of contrasting color into a knitted fabric can be as simple as a sequence of horizontal or vertical stripes or as complex as an all-over pictorial design using dozens of different hues. Color can be used to enhance the effect of a textured stitch pattern, or it can form a pattern in its own right.

Generally, where the focus of interest is to be the color pattern itself, the fabric is worked in stockinette stitch, which presents the smoothest possible "canvas" for colorwork. Even a single stitch in a different color is sharply defined on this fabric, making it possible to work quite intricate patterns successfully. All the most celebrated traditions of color-patterned knitting—Fair Isle, Shetland, Scandinavian, Icelandic—are worked in stockinette stitch.

Almost all colorwork involves using two or more colors in a single row. There are, however, a few exceptions to this rule, and these may be good starting points for those who would like to add color to their designs but are put off by the problems of handling the yarns (see p. 114). In slipstitch patterns (see p. 72) only a single color is handled in any one row, but the simple technique of slipping some of the stitches, rather than knitting them in the new color, makes it possible to create some interesting patterns—including variations on stripes, checks, and striking geometric designs. Most of these patterns are by nature rather small scale and subtle, but with a clever use of strong, contrasting colors, bolder effects can be produced.

Another simple way of adding color interest to knitting is by the use of embroidery, especially Swiss darning, or duplicate stitch (see p. 37); but the simplest method of all—apart from using multicolored yarn—is by knitting horizontal stripes, which is no more difficult than joining in a new ball of yarn.

HORIZONTAL STRIPES

Although they may be the easiest color pattern to achieve in knitting, horizontal stripes can be worked in literally innumerable ways. You can use two colors or 20, repeating them in a regular sequence or at random. And if you knit the garment sideways, the horizontal stripes become vertical.

Working a garment in stripes of varying depth and color is an excellent way to use up bits of yarn. Alternatively, work the stripes in an orderly sequence of two, three, four, or more colors. They can be worked to any depth simply by varying the number of rows in each color. It is advisable, however, to keep the stripes to even numbers of rows (two, four, six, and so on) if you want to carry colors up the side of the work; this way, the yarn will always be in the right place for beginning a new stripe. Reverse stockinette stitch produces subtle broken-stripe effects.

If you wish the stripes to continue around the back of a garment, make sure to knit them in exactly the same sequence on the back as on the front, or fronts, so that they match at the side seams. To match stripes at an armhole seam, work the same sequence from the beginning of the sleeve cap shaping as from the armhole shaping on the body. If necessary, use the row gauge to calculate the number of rows in each piece so that you can plan the stripes accurately. Alternatively, you could stop the stripes below the armholes. If you cannot match the stripes properly it is usually better to work the sleeves in an entirely different sequence altogether or leave them in one color.

Working horizontal stripes should not affect the over-all gauge of the fabric, so long as the same yarn is used throughout. For this reason it is usually safe to knit horizontal stripes into an existing pattern for a solid-color garment.

SCALING UP A DESIGN

A design can be enlarged or reduced photographically, if you live near a photocopier that offers this service. Alternatively, you can adjust the size yourself. In the example shown, a motif is enlarged; the same method, in reverse, is used for reducing a design.

Trace the motif. Using a ruler and pencil, draw a grid of horizontal and vertical lines over the motif, making sure that the lines are equally spaced (about ½ in, or less, apart) and at right angles to each other. Draw a rectangle around the motif, as shown (**1**).

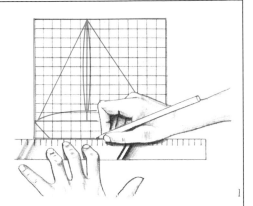

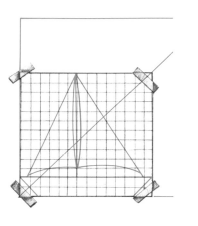

Pin or tape the tracing to a larger sheet of paper, at the lower left-hand corner. Decide on the finished width or height of the motif (depending on which dimension is more important), and extend the bottom or left-hand line to this distance. Draw a diagonal line through the tracing from the lower left-to upper right-hand corner, extending it over the increased width or height. Draw a line perpendicular to the base line to intersect the diagonal (**2**).

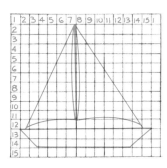

Remove the tracing. Using the lines already ruled on the paper as a guide, draw the remaining sides of the enlarged rectangle. Divide the rectangle into the same number of squares as are contained within the original rectangle, spacing the lines evenly. Number the squares vertically and horizontally on both rectangles (**3, 4**).

Copy the design on to the larger rectangle (**4**), positioning each part of the drawing in the square corresponding to the one it occupies in the original tracing.

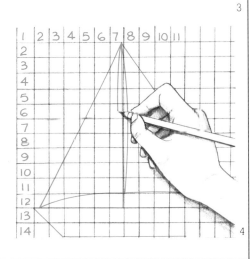

REPEATING PATTERNS

Most color-patterned knitting involves repeating patterns. These may be abstract geometric shapes—for example squares, triangles, or diamonds—or pictorial motifs, such as hearts, flowers, animals, birds, or butterflies. In a printed knitting pattern the instructions for such designs are either written out row by row or displayed in the form of a chart, in which each square represents one stitch and is colored or coded with a symbol to denote the appropriate yarn used to knit that stitch (see p. 115). The chart will usually show the pattern repeat and edge stitches, if any. The edge stitches may be needed to accommodate extra sizes, to balance the pattern, or to achieve a neat match at seams.

The rules for using repeating color patterns are similar to those for any other stitch pattern. The gauge swatch must be knitted in the pattern that is being used for the garment itself, and the number of cast-on stitches must be compatible with the pattern repeat plus any edge stitch or stitches needed to balance the pattern. If necessary, the number of stitches across the width must be adjusted to fit. For example, if the number of stitches across the width has been calculated at 120, and the pattern repeats over 12 plus 1, the number of stitches can be adjusted to 121.

It is usually possible to achieve an accommodation between the number of stitches in the width and the number required for the pattern repeat, so long as the pattern repeat is not too large (and/or the yarn used is not too thick). If the pattern repeat is large, it may be difficult to fit it into a garment without making the garment much larger or smaller than was originally intended. In such a case you can either accept the change in size, choose another color pattern, or adapt the existing color pattern. Sometimes it is possible to extend a pattern at the sides to less than a full repeat. You must still ensure that there will be an acceptable match at seams and that the pattern is centered. Distribute the extra stitches evenly on both sides to serve as edge stitches (illustration 1).

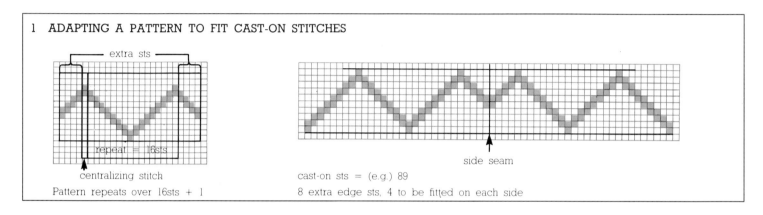

1 ADAPTING A PATTERN TO FIT CAST-ON STITCHES

extra sts

repeat = 16sts

centralizing stitch

Pattern repeats over 16sts + 1

side seam

cast-on sts = (e.g.) 89

8 extra edge sts, 4 to be fitted on each side

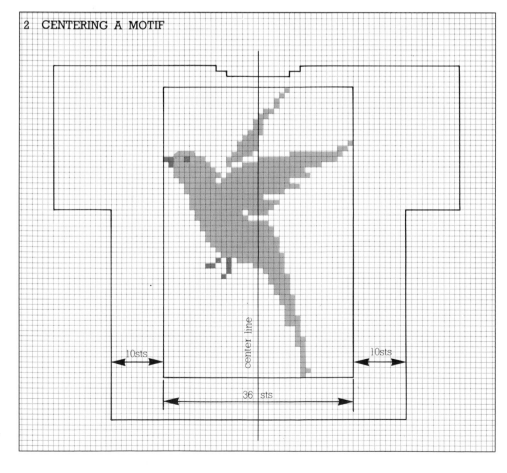

2 CENTERING A MOTIF

center line

10sts

10sts

36 sts

USING SINGLE MOTIFS

Single motifs can be used in many ways on garments, accessories, and furnishings: a flower on the bodice of a child's dress, a large initial or numeral on the back of a bomber jacket, a star in the middle of a pillow cover, a huge exotic bird on the front of a bulky sweater. The two most important considerations are the scale of the motif—how large or small it should be—and where on the garment or object it is to be placed.

If you are using a motif that has already been charted, check that the number of squares, both horizontally and vertically, can be fitted into the relevant area of the garment. If the motif is very large it may be advisable to make a chart representing the whole of that section of the garment (front, back, or sleeve, for example) and transfer the motif to the new chart in the appropriate position.

Centering a motif, especially an asymmetrical one, can sometimes be tricky. Match the vertical center line of the motif (not necessarily the same as the middle of the first row of motif stitches) to the center line of the background (illustration 2).

Where the motif is strongly asymmetrical, draw the garment shape on one grid and the motif on another, as shown, and move the motif around until you are satisfied.

COLOR PATTERNS AND GAUGE

The gauge of color patterns is directly related to the way in which the different yarns are handled. If colors are worked intarsia (that is, if the yarns are crossed or twisted together at each color change—see p. 115), the resulting fabric will be of single thickness and the gauge will not differ greatly from a normal stockinette stitch gauge.

If the yarns are carried across the back of the work, however, and either woven in or stranded (see pp. 116–117), the fabric will be double thickness, with far less sideways stretch, and the stitch gauge will be much tighter in relation to the row gauge. It is most important, therefore, not to mix these methods—intarsia and stranding or weaving—in the same piece of knitting, or the fabric may be badly distorted. When following a pattern you must use the method specified. When designing your own garments, knit the gauge swatch using the method to be used in the garment. The rules governing the choice of method are given on p. 114.

DESIGNING COLOR PATTERNS

There are many sources of charted patterns which you can use in your knitting designs. Dictionaries of stitch patterns often include charts that are specifically designed for knitting. (See also the Fair Isle patterns on pp. 68–69.) You may already have some charts in old knitting patterns that can be adapted for new designs. Other crafts, such as rug-making, cross stitch and needlepoint, and bead work, frequently use charted designs similar to those used for knitting; the craft book shelves of your local library may yield useful material.

If no suitable ready-made chart can be found, you can easily design your own. Books of photographs, printed fabric, wallpaper, tiles, calendars, postcards, and inexpensive reproductions of paintings are just a few of the many sources of pictorial ideas that you can adapt for color-patterned knitting. You could trace one motif from a picture and use it on its own or as a repeating pattern. Or you could chart a whole picture. Although the fashion for picture knitting in adults' garments tends to come and go quite frequently, it is always a popular style with children. Abstract motifs are fairly easy to design "from scratch"; however, you may find it helpful to use a book of decorative patterns as inspiration.

Whether you are designing an original motif or adapting one from another source, you will need some graph paper on which to chart the design. Ordinary graph paper, with about 10 squares to the inch, is perfectly suitable for small-scale repeating patterns and motifs. Large motifs and all-over picture knitting are best represented on a gauge grid (see p. 9); this reflects the true shape of the knitted stitches, which are wider than they are tall. A motif knitted from a graph paper chart will look a little more squat than it does on the chart, and this distortion increases with the size of the motif or pattern. If the motif is charted on a gauge grid, it will be a more faithful representation of the finished effect. If you cannot obtain a ready-made gauge grid of the correct size, you can construct your own, as explained on p. 42.

In addition to graph paper or a gauge grid you will also need colored pencils or felt-tipped pens.

When charting the design you should bear in mind the special characteristics of yarn and knitting and how they will affect the finished result. Scale is obviously a significant factor: if the yarn used for the knitting is fine, the pattern will appear much smaller than if it were knitted in bulky yarn. Fine and medium-weight yarns are better suited than bulky yarns to picture knitting, for they make it possible to incorporate more detail in the design. Unless the picture is very simple, a bulky yarn can look crude and ungainly.

For your first attempts at designing color-patterned knitting, however, it is best to try something simple. If possible, limit the colors to two or three in a row, and avoid making the design too "busy." Although single dots of color show up perfectly well, if there are too many of these too close together, it can be difficult to keep the fabric smooth. If you need to use very small amounts of one color—for flower centers, for example—it may be better to work these in Swiss darning or in other forms of embroidery.

Narrow lines in a design are handled in various ways. Horizontal lines present no problem; they are simply stripes. Diagonal lines and curves have to be stepped (illustration **3**). The more stitches in each horizontal step, the shallower the angle of the diagonal. The more stitches in each vertical step, the steeper the angle of the diagonal. With horizontal and diagonal lines you can make all kinds of geometric patterns—diamonds, triangles, and stars, to name only a few. Long, narrow vertical lines can be difficult to work neatly. Any single-stitch vertical lines are more easily Swiss-darned than knitted in.

If your design is a repeating pattern, mark the repeat on the chart along with any edge stitches needed to balance or center the pattern (illustration **4**). Try to place the repeat lines at logical points on the chart—immediately before the beginning of a motif, for example, not halfway through it. When you are marking repeat lines and edge stitches, bear in mind the desirability of patterns' matching neatly at seams and openings. If the chart is to be worked in the round there should be no edge stitches, since only the repeat will be worked.

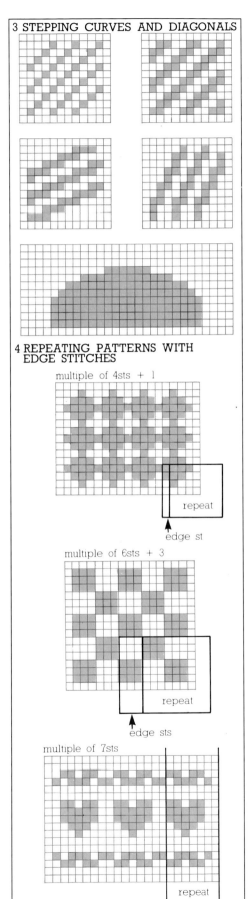

3 STEPPING CURVES AND DIAGONALS

4 REPEATING PATTERNS WITH EDGE STITCHES

multiple of 4 sts + 1

repeat

edge st

multiple of 6 sts + 3

repeat

edge sts

multiple of 7 sts

repeat

MAKING AND USING A GAUGE GRID

If you are transferring a design on to a gauge grid—the recommended method for large motifs and picture knitting—you must first establish the gauge of the proposed garment. Knit a sample in the chosen yarn or yarns, working an approximation of part of the motif and using the chosen method (either intarsia, stranding, or weaving).

Block or press the sample and measure the gauge; for this example suppose it is 25 stitches and 32 rows to 4 in. You may be able to buy a ready-made grid for this gauge. If not, you can construct your own grid. Take a large sheet of paper—either large enough to cover the area of the design or a convenient size for photocopying. (If you are copying the design in its existing size, use tracing paper.) Divide the sheet into 4 in squares, then divide the 4 in squares into 32 horizontally, to give the correct number of rows, and 25 vertically, to give the correct number of stitches. Construct the new grid along these divisions (illustration **5**). If necessary, make copies of the grid and tape them together—aligning the grid lines—to make a grid large enough to cover the whole design.

If the design, or design source, is the same size as the proposed knitting, place the grid over the design and trace it directly on to the paper. (If the grid is not on tracing paper, tape the design and the grid to a window to make the design visible.) If the design is not the same size, you can either have it enlarged, or scale it up as described on p. 39, or draw it freehand on to the gauge grid.

5 TENSION GRID

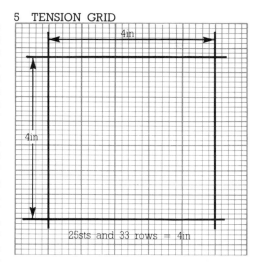

4in

4in

25sts and 33 rows = 4in

Use a very light pencil line to mark in the major features of the design (illustration **6**). Next plot the design more accurately, stepping the curves and diagonals in the most appropriate manner (illustration **7**). Where a line crosses a square you have to decide which of the two adjacent colors the square is to be knitted in. Finally, add the details and fill in the outlines with the suitable colors (illustration **8**). When doing an elaborate, all-over design you could plot the whole garment in this way, so ensuring that the design flows in a logical way over shoulders, across side seams, raglan seams, sleeve tops, and any other sections to be included. Allow also for the shape the garment will assume when being worn, and place significant features of the design where they will be neither

distorted nor obscured by the curvature of the body. If the garment is loose-fitting you should also take into account any folds it will adopt which might affect the design.

COMBINING COLOR AND TEXTURE

Although stockinette stitch is the most suitable background for knitted motifs and pictures, other stitches can often be used to enhance various features of a design: bobbles could suggest snowflakes, cherries, or the buttons on a clown's outfit, for example; or ribbing, a ploughed field. If a really three-dimensional effect is desired, various trimmings—such as pompoms, tufts and tassels, twisted cords, embroidery, or beads—can be added later.

Clever choice of yarns can also bring a knitted picture or motif to life: mohair or angora yarn makes fluffy clouds, sheep, or rabbits; silky yarn serves well for lakes and glitter yarn for rain or stars.

Conversely, it is possible to take an interesting texture and make it even more interesting with an ingenious use of color. Many textured stitches usually thought of as single-color patterns can be effectively worked in more than one color. Cables, for example, can combine color in several different ways. One way is simply to stripe the cabled fabric by changing colors at regular intervals. Another way is to work each half of a cable in a different color; as the cable is crossed, so too are the colors, thus emphasizing the twists and turns of the cable. This treatment can be given to complex as well as simple cables. They can look like multicolored ropes twisting all over the garment.

Bobbles also lend themselves to multi-

6 CHARTING A DESIGN: FIRST STAGE

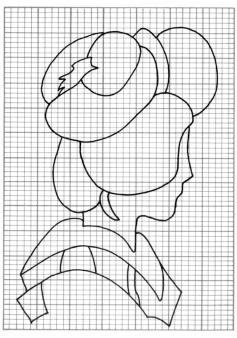

7 SECOND STAGE

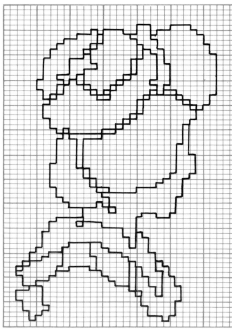

8 FINAL STAGE

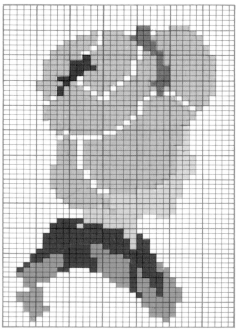

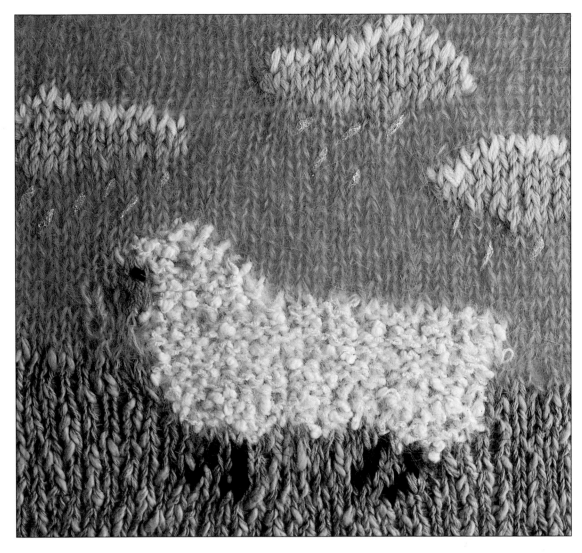

An imaginative selection of yarns (*above*), including a cream mohair blend, slubbed green linen-cotton, and silvery glitter yarn, has been used for this knitted picture (*left*) of a sheep. Bobble and cable patterns (*below*) acquire new interest when worked in contrasting colors.

colored patterns. The bobbles can be worked in a different color from the background fabric. Many different-colored bobbles on a plain background would make a wonderful fabric for a child's sweater, for example. Motifs incorporating bobbles can also be given extra impact with contrasting colors. Nosegay pattern and bunch of grapes (see p. 65), for example, are much more convincing with pink bobbles for the flowers and purple ones for the grapes.

Simpler textures can also work well in mixed colors. Even basketweave (p. 60) knitted in different blocks of color becomes much more dramatic. Ripple stitch (p. 61) could incorporate a rippling color zigzag between the textures. There is a great deal of scope for combining color and textured stitches in entirely new and exciting ways; books devoted to stitch patterns will reveal more possibilities. Don't be afraid to experiment. But first knit plenty of practice swatches to test your hunches before embarking on a complete garment.

DESIGNING SIMPLE GARMENTS

The simplest shapes to create in knitting are squares and rectangles. For these shapes you simply cast on the required number of stitches, work in whatever stitch or color pattern you choose, and bind off when the knitting is the required depth. You do not need to know any complicated shaping techniques. Even so, the elasticity of knitted fabrics makes it possible to create a surprisingly wide variety of garments and other items using combinations of these two shapes. When you incorporate interesting stitch and color patterns and exploit to the full the huge array of available yarns, then the possibilities for really stunning designs using only these simple shapes become almost infinite.

One square, for example, knitted in garter stitch using a bulky, textured yarn, could make a rug; another square, knitted in fine one-ply mohair in a delicate, lacy pattern, makes an exquisite shawl for evening wear. (Run a strand of glitter yarn along with the mohair and edge the square with a long tasseled fringe.) A single rectangle of ribbing in a firmly twisted yarn could be a tube dress, or a sun top, or a string bag, or a pull-on ski hat, or one half of a pair of leg-warmers; in a soft baby-yarn it could be a cozy sleeping bag for

a new baby. Long thin rectangles—that is strips—make marvelous edgings, braids, belts, even jewelry. Take advantage of the inward curl of stockinette stitch to make thin tubes in different colors, and twist, braid, or knot them together to make unusual chokers, bracelets, and hair ornaments.

With two squares you have even more scope—summer tops, skirts, and dresses in cotton, silk, and linen yarns; winter slipovers, tunics, and ponchos in wools. Three, four, or five squares or rectangles enable you to make jackets, coats, cardigans and pullovers. With more rectangles you can add the finishing touches: pockets, collars, and ties.

THE DESIGN PROCESS

Whatever design method you use, the stages involved remain roughly the same. All designs, whether for garments or other objects, begin with an idea. This idea could come from the designer or from another person or source; it might be vague ("I really need something new for my summer vacation") or precise ("Can you make a school sweater? It has to be plain, gray, and with long sleeves and a V-neck").

At this stage it is helpful to put your ideas

down on paper, so make a sketch. Even if you cannot draw particularly well, a rough sketch will help to fix the idea in your mind and to sort out exactly what is required. Add to the sketch any relevant information. Who is the garment for? Does that person have any preferences as to colors or yarns, or any allergies to particular yarns? How and when is the garment intended to be worn: on the beach in summer, or for a Christmas party? What about fit? Should it be tight fitting or loose? Does it have to accommodate a growing child? If it is for a child, make sure that you allow for putting it on and taking it off easily.

Writing as much information as possible on the sketch will be a great help when it comes to choosing yarns and stitch patterns. You will also find out whether some of your aims are incompatible early enough so that you can make sensible changes. Having made the sketch, do not become trapped by it; at any stage the design could—and, in many cases, should—change. Do not be afraid to reject something that is obviously not working. At this stage there is nothing to lose.

The next stage is to choose the yarn and the stitch pattern. These two choices have to be made simultaneously, since the yarn

and stitch pattern must be compatible (see p. 16). Both yarn and stitch pattern must also be appropriate for the purpose of the design. A bathmat, for example, would be better made in a thick cotton yarn and in garter stitch than in knitting worsted and stockinette stitch. Refer to the notes on your sketch, which may help you to eliminate unsuitable choices. Many children and some adults object to hairy yarns such as mohair, so do not use them for anything that will be worn next to the skin unless you are sure that it will be acceptable.

Next, do some experimenting with stitches and yarns. Knit small swatches to check that the stitch and yarn work well together. If the design uses more than one stitch pattern, make swatches in all of them. Similarly, if you are using two or more colors, knit them both to see if they will combine successfully: yarn colors often look quite different when knitted.

Next, decide how the garment will be constructed. This may be partly determined by the chosen stitch or color pattern. Vertical stripes, for example, are much easier to achieve if worked sideways—i.e., horizontally. A cable pattern could look good either way. Fishtail lace must run vertically.

Having decided on the direction of the knitting, dissect the garment into its component parts. How many pieces do you need? Can the garment be made in one piece? One simple rule of thumb in knitting is that the fewer the seams needed to finish the garment, the better. Make a flat plan of the garment showing all the separate pieces. Remember to include any pockets or separate edgings.

Now you can mark on the flat plan all the relevant measurements. First take the appropriate body measurements, and add on an allowance for ease (see pp. 22–23). This allowance will, of course, be related to the styling of the garment, so your original sketch will again be useful. In the case of garments based on squares and rectangles, the number of measurements needed is minimal. The most important is the width of each shape—the length can easily be adjusted later. You will also need to mark the dimensions of armholes and neck opening and the required depth of any edgings.

The next stage is to make the gauge swatch in the chosen yarn and stitch pattern (see pp. 20 21). If there are two or more stitch patterns involved, you must make a gauge swatch in each one.

The gauge swatch will enable you to calculate the cast-on stitches for each piece. Mark these figures on the flat plan and the pattern is basically ready. If the design includes a color pattern or one of the larger stitch patterns, it may also be necessary to work out exactly where on the garment motifs or cables, for example, are to be placed (see pp. 40 and 56). In such cases, and where it is essential to a design that there be a definite number of repeats of a pattern, you will need to use the row gauge to calculate the number of rows in each piece.

In the following pages you will find three examples of designing with squares and rectangles worked out in detail. The designs are for a sleeveless top and skirt, a lacy sweater, and a hooded coat for a child. By simply reading the examples you will come to understand the design process— the decisions involved and the calculations used to implement the decisions. But you can also use the examples in a practical way, either to make garments resembling those described or as an inspiration for similar garments to suit your own needs and tastes. In either case, they will provide a framework for your first ventures in designing.

dropped shoulder

slash neck

ribbing

SLEEVELESS TOP AND SKIRT

It is possible to design a simple top and a skirt using just two squares or rectangles for each garment. In theory, the skirt could be made from only one square, but unless it is full, or the seam can be run invisibly down the back, two squares are preferable. Even within this narrow format there are many possibilities for variation. The size and/or proportions of the rectangle can be altered to give a wide range of styles. The top, for example, could be huge, baggy, and knee length or skimpy and body hugging. The skirt could be straight and pencil slim, or full, or mini.

MAKING THE SKETCH
Imagine that the garments are intended for a small, slim teenage girl to take with her on her summer holiday. The outfit should be cool and comfortable, young looking but not too young, stylish but not outrageous, and for daytime wear.

Large, baggy garments tend to "drown" small people, so a fairly close-fitting top, slightly boxy and finishing just below the waistline, might be most suitable. A long knitted skirt is obviously unsuitable for summer daywear—it has to be cool. Since the wearer is slim and young, a mini skirt may be appropriate.

CHOOSING THE YARN AND STITCH
The coolness of linen and cotton yarns makes them ideal for summer wear. Both are fairly heavy yarns, but since the garments are quite skimpy this will not be a disadvantage. Since linen is rather expensive and available only in a limited range of colors, a cotton or cotton mixture yarn is probably a better choice.

The mini skirt will hang better if it is ribbed; a two-by-two (knit two, purl two) rib will also give a faint impression of pleats. In order for the ribs to show up crisply, the yarn for the skirt should be a smooth one. Cotton is not normally the ideal choice for ribbing because it lacks elasticity; however, in this case, the ribbing is not meant to cling. A mixture of cotton and wool, if one is available, would be ideal. Otherwise, a mercerized, tightly twisted cotton, such as the one shown here, is a good choice. This type of yarn wears better than the loosely twisted, soft, matte-finish cottons.

You can be a lot more adventurous with the yarn for the top. There are many fancy cotton yarns from which to choose. A flecked slub or bouclé yarn, for example, would provide instant textural and color interest. A tubular cotton ribbon yarn

knitted in a loose tension would be marvelously cool, as well as quick to knit. Such yarns are quite expensive, but since relatively little is required for the top, and the skirt is plain, the higher cost is justifiable. Some cotton ribbon yarns, such as the one shown here, are space-dyed, giving a striped effect at no extra cost or effort.

Assuming that a space-dyed cotton ribbon will be used for the top, the stitch pattern should be simple, since the yarn itself provides the excitement. A "busy" stitch pattern would be ineffective. Either garter stitch or stockinette stitch would be suitable, but garter stitch has the advantage of not curling under at the edges, eliminating the need for hems or other edgings on the armholes, neck, and lower edges.

CONSTRUCTION
Two rectangles for each garment have already been decided on. The ribbed skirt must be knitted vertically—either from the bottom up or from the top down. There is no particular reason for knitting the top sideways, so it might as well also be worked from the bottom up. Both squares for the top will be exactly the same width and length. The same is true of the skirt.

space-dyed cotton ribbon

garter stitch
loose gauge

2 x 2 rib

side slits

cotton
worsted-weight

mini-length

MEASUREMENTS

For the skirt you will need a hip measurement. Add to this an amount for ease. (See pp. 22–23.) Because of the lack of stretchiness in cotton yarn a close-fitting skirt—even worked in ribbing—would not wear well. A standard fitting, with about 2 in of ease included, is probably the best choice. Divide the total (hip measurement plus ease) by 2 to find the required width of each square for the skirt. For example: 34 in (hip measurement) + 2 in (ease) = 36 in; 36 in ÷ 2 = 18 in (width of one rectangle).

For the skirt length, measure from the waist to the chosen hemline between the knee and the hip, and add on 1 in for a cased elastic waistband. This will give you the required depth of the skirt rectangles.

For the top you will need a bust measurement, length measurement, and measurements for the armhole depth and the neck opening. Add to the bust measurement an allowance for ease. The top should hang comfortably straight down, so 2 in should be sufficient (add 4 in for a baggy top). Divide the total (bust measurement plus ease) by 2 to find the required width of the pieces for the top. For example: 32 in (bust measurement) + 2 in (case) = 34 in; 34 ÷ 2 = 17 in (width of one rectangle).

Mark the required width of the top squares and skirt squares on the flat plan. (Note that on the flat plan given here, the measurements have not been supplied; fill in your own, using a separate sheet of paper if you prefer.)

MAKING THE GAUGE SWATCH

Make one gauge swatch in two-by-two rib using the smooth cotton yarn and another in garter stitch using the ribbon yarn. Begin with the recommended needle size for the weight of each yarn (see p. 14), and adjust this if necessary. The ribbed fabric should be fairly tight, so that the ribs are sharply defined. The ribbon can be much looser. Keep on making gauge swatches using different sizes of needle until the fabric has the correct handle. Label each square with the needle size used.

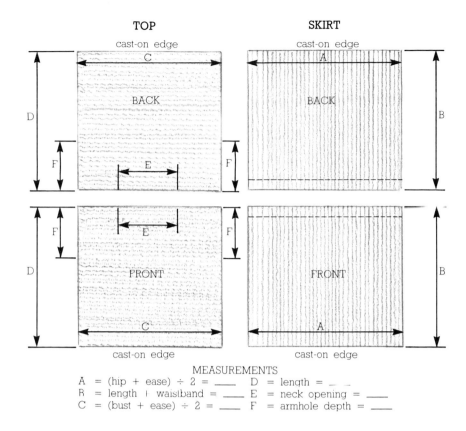

	TOP	SKIRT
	cast-on edge	cast-on edge
	C BACK	A BACK
	FRONT	FRONT
	cast-on edge	cast-on edge

MEASUREMENTS

A = (hip + ease) ÷ 2 = ____   D = length = ____
B = length + waistband = ____   E = neck opening = ____
C = (bust + ease) ÷ 2 = ____   F = armhole depth = ____

Now measure the number of stitches there are to 4 in across the width and the number of rows there are to 4 in across the depth of the best swatch. This gives the gauge measurement. In the case of the top, say, for example, that it is 16 stitches and 30 rows to 4 in over garter stitch on size 5 needles. For the skirt: 40 stitches and 40 rows to 4 in over two-by-two rib (unstretched) on size 3 needles.

CALCULATING THE CAST-ON STITCHES

For the top, divide the stitch gauge by 4 to give the number of stitches per inch (16 sts ÷ 4 in = 4 sts) and multiply the result by the required width of the top: 4 sts × 17 in = 68 sts. Add two selvage stitches for seams (see p. 105). The number of cast-on stitches for the top rectangles is 70.

To find the required number of rows, divide the row gauge (30) by 4 (in) and multiply this figure (7½) by the required length.

For the skirt the process is basically the same, except that there is the added complication of a stitch pattern that must be worked over a definite multiple of stitches. Two-by-two rib (see p. 59) can be worked either over a multiple of 4 stitches or over a multiple of 4 stitches, plus 2 extra. In this case, as the garment will be seamed, the pattern must be worked over a multiple of 4 stitches in order to match neatly at the side seams. Each piece will have 2 knit stitches at the right-hand edge and 2 purl stitches at the left (not including selvage stitches). Where seams are joined, the rib pattern will flow around the skirt without a break.

To begin, repeat the process given for the top: divide the stitch gauge by 4 and multiply the answer by the required width of the piece: 40 sts ÷ 4 in = 10 sts; 10 × 18 in = 180 sts. Check whether the result is a multiple of 4 (in this case it is). If so, add 2 selvage stitches (180 sts + 2 = 182 sts). If not, the nearest multiple of 4 (plus 2 selvage stitches) is the number of stitches to be cast on.

MAKING THE GARMENTS

For the top, cast on the correct number of stitches for one piece and work in garter stitch to the required length. Make another piece in the same way. For the skirt, make two squares in two-by-two rib. Do not press the square for either garment, since neither garter stitch nor rib should be pressed. Instead, block and gently steam each piece (see p. 133).

Join the side seams of the top, leaving an opening at the top of each seam for armholes and 3 in at the bottom of each seam for slits, if desired. Join the shoulder seams, leaving a neck opening.

Join the side seams of the skirt. Turn the top edge over to a depth of 1 in and sew it in place using slipstitch. Cut a piece of ¾ in-wide elastic to the waist measurement, plus 1 in for joining. Thread it through the waistband and sew the ends together firmly.

VARIATIONS ON THE TOP AND SKIRT

Just by changing the yarn or stitch pattern, you can make an entire wardrobe of tops and skirts using squares or rectangles. For example you could make the skirt a little longer and tighter and in wool for the winter (leave a slit in one side). Alternatively, try a long, full skirt, striped with all your left-over yarns in lots of different colors and textures.

If you are really ambitious, you could make a mid-length, full skirt in a fine, tweedy yarn, knitted in panels of textured stitches—a beautiful addition to your wardrobe. The main thing to remember with skirts is not to make them so heavy that they drop or hang badly. Do not use yarns thicker than sport weight; if you want to use a relatively heavy cotton or wool yarn, combine it with a light acrylic yarn.

The basic design of the top is also versatile. Try a top in a fine glitter yarn in lace, perhaps, for evenings; instead of seaming the shoulders, tie them together with fine twisted cords and leave deep armhole openings, or make the neck opening wide enough to fall off one shoulder. Or lengthen and widen the shape and knit it in wool bouclé to make a warm jumper to wear over blouses and sweaters in winter.

Or make it in stockinette stitch and hem or blanket stitch the edges and Swiss darn a huge initial on the front for a child's tunic. Stripe it for a neat T-shirt in plain cotton or wool. Knit in some cables, working the top sideways so that they go across instead of up the garment. Work it in rib in a fine glitter yarn and make it ankle length for a sinuous evening dress; tie it over one shoulder and let the other corner just drop down (leave a slit up the side so that you can walk!). These are just a few of the possibilities. Once you start experimenting with shapes, yarns, and stitch patterns, you will find hundreds more.

EVENING SWEATER

A sweater can be made from a minimum of four squares or rectangles; one each for the back and front and two for the sleeves. Again, by varying the proportions of the shapes and using different combinations of yarn and stitch pattern it is possible to make styles to suit all occasions.

MAKING THE SKETCH

The first step, as always, is to clarify the purpose of the design—whom it is for and where or when is it meant to be worn? This one is for a woman who likes clothes that are elegant but neither severe nor flashy. It is to be worn on autumn or winter evenings, possibly to the theatre or a dinner party, and it should be impressive but not too dressy. She will probably wear it with some fine wool pants or a heavy silk skirt. A loose-fitting lacy sweater could be the answer, perhaps one with some light beading. The sleeves could also be loose, finishing just below the elbow. If the neck is wide enough, the sweater could be worn either on or off the shoulder.

CHOOSING THE YARN AND STITCH PATTERN

A lacy sweater in a fine glitter yarn could look wonderful, but it might be a little too cool and over-dressy for the purpose. However, a special yarn with a luxurious feel to it does seem appropriate. Most mohair yarns would be too bulky, although a fine kid mohair might work well. Alternatively, a fine angora-wool blend would look pretty with, for example, seed pearls or small crystal beads, as well as being warm enough for cool evenings. There is a good range of colors available in angora, so it would probably be possible to find it in black or dark gray or purple, as well as in soft pastels.

Before buying enough yarn and beads for the whole garment, check that they are compatible with each other and with the stitch pattern. If you intend to knit the beads in (see p. 122), knit them in on your gauge swatch. Some angora yarns are too soft for bead knitting and will break if beads are strung on to them; if you cannot find suitable angora yarn, choose a fine kid mohair instead.

Lacy stitch patterns tend to give a garment a "special occasion" look, particularly when combined with a luxury yarn. Since the keynote of this sweater is subtlety, and the angora and the beads provide a measure of glamour, it might be wise to choose a fairly restrained eyelet pattern. Quatrefoil eyelet (see p. 71) is a pretty, easy-to-knit eyelet stitch that will not compete with the yarn or beads for attention. Its motif, composed of four eyelets clustered together, is also the perfect "frame" for one bead in the center (you can knit the bead in on the 6th and 14th pattern rows).

Since the eyelet pattern is based on stockinette stitch, it will be necessary to work a non-curling border on the garment edges. A few rows of garter stitch at the lower edges of the body and sleeves and at the neck edge will do the trick.

CONSTRUCTION

You will need two rectangles the same size for the front and back and two rectangles, also the same size, for the sleeves. In both cases there is no advantage to be gained by knitting sideways, so all the pieces can be knitted from the bottom (that is, the lower edge and the sleeve edge) to the top. Mark the direction of knitting on the construction diagram.

wide slash neck

angora colors? — dark

garter stitch borders

quatrefoil eyelet with beads

deep armholes

FRONTS

BACK

SLEEVES

MEASUREMENTS

For the back and front a bust measurement and a length from back neck measurement (see p. 23) will be needed; the neck width measurement can be decided later. For the sleeve you will need measurements of the armhole depth and of the back neck to sleeve edge.

When working out a series of interrelated measurements it is often helpful to make a scale drawing of the plan of your design. It is easy to do this using graph paper (especially the kind divided into 10 squares per inch) and it will help you to check and cross-check your calculations as you go along. For example, you will realize at a glance that if you increase the body width you must shorten the sleeve length; otherwise the sleeves will end farther down on the arm.

Front and back Suppose that the bust measurement is 36 in. To this must be added a certain amount of ease (see p. 23). Since the body is to be very wide, you will need to add a generous amount—say $7\frac{1}{2}$ in—to achieve the desired proportions. Draw the rectangles for the front and back to scale with a width of 22 in (36 in + $7\frac{1}{2}$ in = $43\frac{1}{2}$ in; $43\frac{1}{2}$ in ÷ 2 = $21\frac{3}{4}$ or 22 in) and a chosen length of $23\frac{1}{2}$ in.

Sleeves Suppose that the measurement from the back neck to a sleeve length of just below the elbow is $23\frac{1}{2}$ in. The depth of the rectangle for the sleeve will be this measurement minus half the width of the back: $23\frac{1}{2}$ in − 11 in = $12\frac{1}{2}$ in. Mark the center back on your scale drawing and measure off $23\frac{1}{2}$ in to one side to cross-check your calculation. The sleeve width in this design is a matter of styling and will be considerably deeper than the body's armhole measurement. Measure around the shoulder to the point on the body where you want the sleeve and side seams to meet to find the total sleeve width—say, 24 in.

MAKING THE GAUGE SWATCH

Make a gauge swatch in angora or fine mohair in quatrefoil eyelet, including beads if desired. Use a larger needle, if necessary, to achieve an appropriately open look for the eyelet pattern and a suitable stitch size for the fluffy yarn. Measure the gauge carefully. Suppose in this case it is 24 stitches and 32 rows to 4 in.

CALCULATING CAST-ON STITCHES

Divide the stitch gauge by 4 to give the number of stitches per inch: 24 sts ÷ 4 in = 6 sts. To find the number of cast-on stitches

for the front and back, multiply the chosen width by this figure: 22 in × 6 sts = 132 sts. Check that this figure can be divided evenly by the stitch multiple of the eyelet pattern: 132 sts ÷ 8 sts = 16.5 (repeats). Since it cannot, you will have to adjust the number of cast-on stitches to the nearest multiple of 8: make it 136 stitches (136 sts ÷ 8 sts = 17). This will give you an extra half inch or so on the back and front, so reduce the sleeve length to $12\frac{1}{4}$ in. Add 2 selvage stitches. So the number of cast-on stitches for the back and front is 138.

Proceed in the same way for the sleeves: multiply the stitch gauge by the required width: 6 sts × 24 in = 144 sts. Check the result against the stitch multiple: 144 sts ÷ 8 sts = 18 sts). Add 2 selvage stitches: 144 sts + 2 sts = 146 sts. The number of cast-on stitches for the sleeves is 146.

MAKING THE SWEATER

For the back and front, cast on 138 stitches and work, for example, six rows in garter stitch for a border. Continue in quatrefoil eyelet until the piece is the required length, less the depth of the top border. Work six rows in garter stitch and bind off. For the sleeves, cast on 146 stitches and work six rows in garter stitch. Continue in quatrefoil eyelet until the sleeve measures $12\frac{1}{4}$ in, then bind off.

Join the shoulder seams, leaving the desired neck opening. Set in the sleeves by matching the center of the bound-off edge of the sleeve to the shoulder seam, and sewing the sleeve to the upper 12 in of the back and the front.

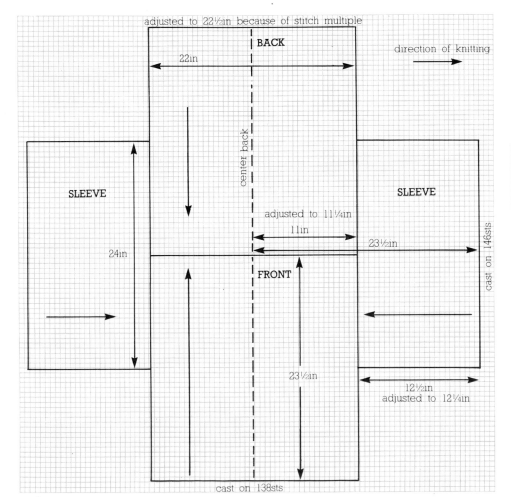

adjusted to $22\frac{1}{2}$in because of stitch multiple

BACK

direction of knitting

22in

center back

SLEEVE

SLEEVE

adjusted to $11\frac{1}{4}$in

11in

$23\frac{1}{2}$in

cast on 146sts

24in

FRONT

$23\frac{1}{2}$in

$12\frac{1}{2}$in
adjusted to $12\frac{1}{4}$in

cast on 138sts

ESTIMATING NUMBERS OF BEADS

To calculate the number of beads needed to complete the sweater, divide the total number of rows in each piece by the row repeat of the pattern and multiply the answer by the number of beads in each repeat. Add about five per cent to this figure to allow for variations in row gauge and for broken or unusable beads. In this example, assuming 33 beads per pattern repeat (one in each eyelet motif) and allowing for the garter stitch borders, the total number of beads needed would be about 1,300. The number of beads or sequins needed for this kind of work is often surprisingly high. However, it is often cheaper to buy such trimmings in bulk, especially if you go to a specialist store or dealer.

VARIATIONS ON THE SWEATER

The length and width of the body and the sleeves can be altered in many ways to change the styling of this sweater dramatically and make anything from a skimpy T-shirt to a voluminous sweater dress. Made in thick yarn and bold cable and Aran stitch patterns, it could be a snug winter pullover.

Alternatively, try knitting the sweater on big needles, using garter stitch and a matte soft cotton yarn for a beach cover-up (run a drawstring around the bottom). Make it very long and narrow in an openwork mesh pattern, with long, tight sleeves, for a slinky evening dress (belt it with metallic twisted cords).

Instead of sewing in the sleeves, you could work a row of eyelets on the armhole and sleeve top edges and lace the pieces together. Instead of garter stitch borders, work picot hems or ribbing, or trim the lower edge with a thick fringe. Instead of beads, use ribbon to embellish the knitting: choose a vertical eyelet pattern and thread the ribbon through the holes. Or Swiss-darn a huge cabbage rose on a plain stockinette stitch background.

Knitted in baby yarn, in stripes or simple color patterns, these T-shaped sweaters are perfect for babies and small children, whose clothes normally require only simple shaping. The shoulders can be fastened with ties or with buttons and button loops, so that they can be put on and taken off easily.

CHILD'S COAT

At least five squares or rectangles are needed for a coat, jacket, or cardigan: one for the back, two for the fronts, and two for the sleeves. With more pieces the garment can also have a collar, pockets, a hood and a belt, or special trimmings such as epaulettes, cuffs and borders. Since there is no scope for neat, tailored shaping in these rectangle-based designs, it is best to aim for a fairly casual, roomy look, as in a duffel coat or kimono. A close-fitting coat would be uncomfortable.

MAKING THE SKETCH

This simple coat is for a child around eight or nine years old. It is to be practical enough to wear to school in cool weather and good-looking enough for weekend pleasure trips. Most children hate anything fussy that gets in the way of what they are

doing, so you should make it as simple as possible, with no trimmings or decoration, except perhaps some bright knitted-in stripes. Pockets will also be useful for the numerous objects that children collect. To make it as snug as possible, close the front edges with an open-ended zipper—adding a small tassel on the pull, just for fun; and give the coat a hood for extra warmth, instead of a collar.

CHOOSING THE YARN AND STITCH PATTERN

Many children find wool and hairy yarns such as mohair itchy and uncomfortable, especially next to the skin. It is probably wise, therefore, to choose a smooth yarn that has a good proportion of synthetic fibers. A mixture of 75 percent acrylic and 25 percent wool would be quite soft and

have good insulation properties, while also being easy to wash and dry (probably machine-washable)—an important consideration when designing children's clothes. The large synthetic component means that you can also choose a thick yarn without the garment's being uncomfortably heavy. A bulky yarn will make the coat thick and help make up in warmth for the low wool content.

Stripes can look interesting in some textured stitches—they can even be successfully worked into cables and lacy patterns. However, they are sharper and crisper worked in fairly simple stitches. Stockinette stitch shows up any color pattern particularly well because of its smooth, unbroken surface, but it also curls up at the edges. This means that it will be necessary to work another stitch along the

hood

tassel

smooth synthetic-wool blend yarn

seed stitch borders

color stripes

open-ended zipper

full length sleeves

patch pockets

unseamed edges—the lower edge of the back and fronts, the sleeve edges, and the front edge of the hood. Seed stitch will provide a firm, non-curling border as well as an interesting change of texture. The front opening edges could be left in stockinette stitch and simply given a garter stitch selvage (see p. 105), since they are to be closed with a zipper; however, for purely decorative purposes the seed stitch border could also be worked along those edges if desired.

CONSTRUCTION

One rectangle will be needed for the back, two for the fronts, one for each sleeve, one for the hood, and two for the pockets. Assuming that the stripes are to be knitted in the simplest possible way (working so many rows in color A, so many rows in color B, and so on), the direction of the knitting will determine the direction of the stripes. The first step is thus to decide in which direction you would like the stripes to run. Mark this on the construction diagram. The direction of the knitting will be in the opposite direction to that of the stripes: if the stripes are horizontal the direction of the knitting will be vertical, if they are vertical the piece should be knitted sideways.

In this case, suppose that you choose horizontal stripes. The body and the pockets will be knitted from bottom to top, the sleeves from cuff to shoulder, and the hood from one shoulder over the head to the other. Mark the direction of knitting for each piece on the construction diagram. Also mark the edges that will have seed stitch borders.

MEASUREMENTS

When measuring for a coat, it is a good idea to take the body measurements over the kind of clothes that are likely to be worn under the garment. For the back and fronts you will need to measure the chest and hips and the required length from back neck. For the sleeves, measure the armhole depth and the sleeve length from back neck. For the hood, decide on the neck width and measure loosely from center front neck around the head and back again to the center front (see p. 23). The pockets can be any convenient size; 5 in square is adequate.

Coat back Take the hip or chest measurement, whichever is the larger, add an ease allowance, and divide by 2 to give the required width of the rectangle—for example, 27 in (hips) + 6 in (ease) = 33 in; $33 \div 2 = 16\frac{1}{2}$ in. The ease allowance of 6 in will give a loose fitting and also allow a little extra for growth. An inch or two extra for growth should also be added to the back length measurement; for example, 30 in + 2 in = 32 in.

Fronts Each front should measure the same length as the back (32 in) and exactly half the width ($8\frac{1}{4}$ in). If the coat were to be fastened with buttons, it would also be necessary to allow for an overlapping button and buttonhole band, to be either knitted in or sewn on afterward; with a zipper, however, the fronts meet edge to edge and the allowance is not needed.

Sleeves To find the length of the sleeves, subtract half the coat back width from the neck-to-sleeve length; for example, $22\frac{1}{2}$ in $- 8\frac{1}{4}$ in = $14\frac{1}{4}$ in. Add about 2 in to this to allow for growth, giving a total sleeve length of $16\frac{1}{4}$ in. Measure around the armhole—say, 10 in—and add about 3 in ease to give a sleeve width of 13 in.

Hood and pockets The hood will be formed from one long rectangle folded in half widthwise and seamed down one side. This forms the center back seam of the hood; the short edges are each joined to half the back neck and the front neck. The length of the piece for the hood will be the "around the head" measurement (say, $23\frac{1}{2}$ in) and its width will be the same as that of the neck opening. To determine the neck opening, first imagine a line drawn from the ears down to the shoulders. The neck opening should be a little wider than the distance between these two points. (In this example, this is 10 in.)

The pockets must be big enough to get the hands into comfortably. In this example they measure 5 in square. Mark all these measurements on the construction diagram, or draw a new one to scale.

MAKING THE GAUGE SWATCH

Knit a gauge swatch in stockinette stitch using the chosen yarn and stripe sequence. It is unlikely in this case that the color pattern will have any discernible effect on the gauge, but it is a good idea always to knit the gauge swatch in the stitch or color pattern of the garment.

If the areas worked in seed stitch were to be extensive it would also be necessary to work another gauge swatch in this pattern, since the gauges of stockinette stitch and seed stitch are quite different; however, since the seed stitch is to be used only for narrow borders, this will not be necessary. If the border were to go along the whole width of a piece you might need to use a smaller needle to make it lie flat.

Measure the gauge of your sample carefully. In this example it is 12 stitches and 16 rows to 4 in.

CALCULATING THE CAST-ON STITCHES

Take each piece in turn and multiply the required width by the stitch gauge, then divide by 4 (in). List the calculations as follows:

Back, $(16\frac{1}{2}$ in $\times$ 12 sts) $\div$ 4 = $49\frac{1}{2}$ sts
Fronts, $(8\frac{1}{4}$ in $\times$ 12 sts) $\div$ 4 = $24\frac{3}{4}$ sts
Sleeves, (13 in $\times$ 12 sts) $\div$ 4 = 39 sts
Hood, (10 in $\times$ 12 sts) $\div$ 4 = 30 sts
Pockets, (5 in $\times$ 12 sts) $\div$ 4 = 15 sts

Although stockinette stitch can be worked over any number of stitches, every piece except the hood has a horizontal seed stitch border, which must be worked over an odd number of stitches (see p. 59), so the calculations should be rounded off to the nearest odd number. Also, one selvage stitch should be added to each front and to the hood, and 2 should be added to every other piece except the pockets, which have no selvage stitches. So the number of cast-on stitches for each piece is:

Back, 51 (49 + 2)
Fronts, 26 (25 + 1)
Sleeves, 41 (39 + 2)
Hood, 31 (30 + 1)
Pockets, 15

MAKING THE COAT

For the back cast on 51 stitches and work in seed stitch for five rows (or the preferred number). Change to stockinette stitch and work in the chosen stripe sequence until the back measures 32 in; bind off. For each front cast on 26 stitches and work the seed stitch border as for the back, then continue in stockinette stitch and the stripe sequence, but keep working a border in seed stitch—three or more stitches wide—along the right-hand edge for the right front and along the left-hand edge for the left front. Continue until the fronts are the same length as the back.

For each sleeve, cast on 41 stitches and work the seed stitch border. (You can make this deeper, if you like, to make the growth allowance into a turn-back cuff.) Continue in stockinette stitch stripes until the sleeve measures $16\frac{1}{4}$ in; bind off.

For the hood cast on 30 stitches and work in stockinette stitch stripes with a seed stitch border (3 to 5 stitches) along one vertical edge until the hood measures $23\frac{1}{2}$ in; bind off. For the pockets, cast on 15 stitches and work in stockinette stitch for 4 in, work in seed stitch for 1 in, and bind off.

Join the shoulder seams from the armhole inward for $3\frac{1}{4}$ in. Join the sleeves, matching the center of the bound-off edge of the sleeve to the shoulder seam. Fold the hood in half widthwise and seam the stockinette stitch edge. Place this seam at the center back neck and join the back of the hood (5 in to each side of the seam) to the back neck edge. Join the remaining 5 in on each side to the front neck edges. Leaving about 4 in free at the lower edge, set in an open-ended 28 in zipper (see p. 139). Position the pockets on each front and sew them neatly in place (see p. 131). Join side and sleeve seams. Make a small tassel (see p. 31) and attach it to the zipper pull.

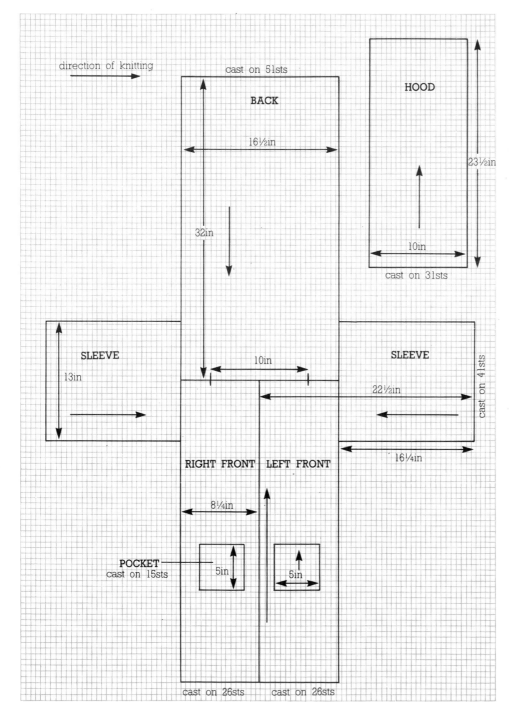

VARIATIONS ON THE COAT

This basic coat shape is endlessly versatile. Instead of the hood it could have a deep ribbed collar or a sailor collar. With a wider body, deeper sleeves, and the fronts narrowed to the shoulder width, it would take on the look of a traditional kimono. Edge it all around the hem, front opening, and back neck with one long border, knitted in stockinette stitch and folded in half lengthwise. Make a wide belt to match. Instead of a zipper, use toggle fastenings with frogging loops made from knitted cords (see p. 30). Swiss-darn a

huge motif or initial on the back, or a small one on the pockets. Instead of patch pockets, you could make vertical inset pockets (see p. 132).

Simple shapes like this one are a marvelous vehicle for bold geometric color patterns. Make a coat of many colors from leftover yarns in a variety of colors and textures. Change the stitch pattern. Work a huge central cable, Aran-style, up the back of the jacket. Or split up the basic shape into yet more squares and work each one in a different stitch to make a patchwork of knitted textures. The same patchwork idea

can work equally well with stripes—arrange the patches so that the stripes run in different directions.

Change the yarn: make a long slinky coat in silk or a glitter yarn for evenings; make a short-sleeved cardigan in a simple textured stitch (such as diamond brocade—see p. 60) in cotton or a cotton and linen blend for spring and summer. Make a hooded coat for a baby and tie it with ribbon bows, or take the coat right down to the baby's toes for a bathrobe, or seam up the lower edges and zip up the fronts for a cozy sleeping bag.

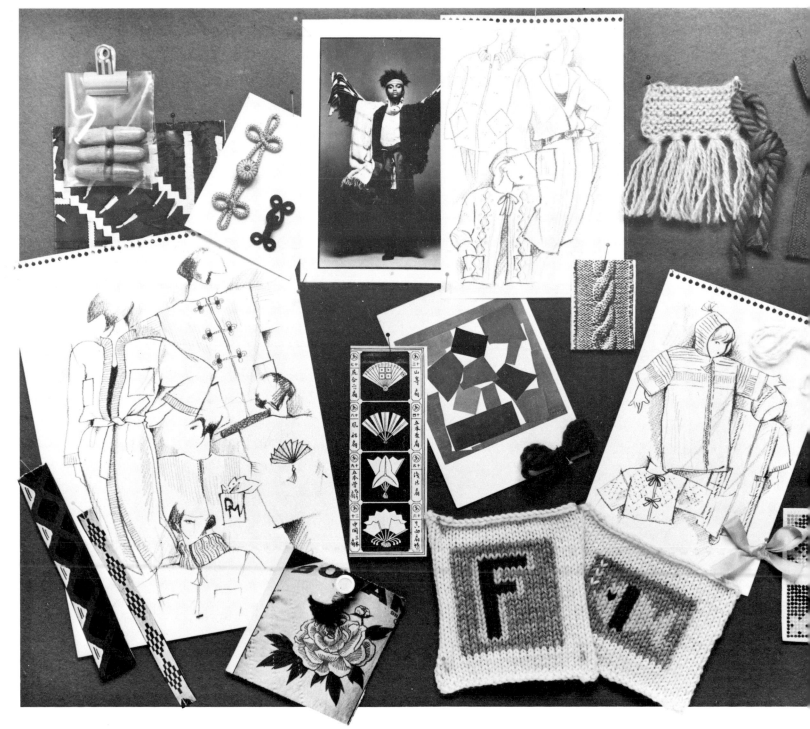

STITCH PATTERNS

Knitting is a craft of enormous versatility. This means that knitting can be almost anything, from a bulky fisherman's sweater or a thick nubbly rug to a gossamer-fine lace shawl or a coat of many colors. Two things, above all, make this possible: the immense variety of yarns (see pp. 10–17) and the equally astonishing variety of stitch patterns.

Over the hundreds of years during which knitting has developed, thousands of stitch patterns have been devised by anonymous craftsmen and women. The skill and inventiveness that have been poured into this process are enormous. This is especially true of the complex lace and cable patterns that have been handed down through generations of knitters.

The result is a legacy of great richness and diversity. The stitch pattern library available to today's knitter is versatile, adaptable, and inspiring. What is more, the patterns can be achieved with a handful of simple techniques. Once you can knit, purl, use a cable needle and make eyelets the entire library is at your disposal.

CHOOSING STITCH PATTERNS

Stitch patterns, like yarns, have their own intrinsic properties which make them particularly suitable for certain types of garment or fabric. The heavy texture of cables and Aran patterns, for example, produces thick weatherproof fabrics ideal for the fisherman knits with which they are traditionally associated. The same is true of Fair Isle patterns—the yarn carried across the back of the work creates a double-thickness fabric with effective insulation properties. Lacy stitches, by contrast, are open and cool and thus are suitable for evening and summer wear.

When choosing a stitch pattern for a particular style, make sure that it is appropriate to the nature and purpose of the garment you have in mind. It must also be compatible with your chosen yarn (see p. 16). When designing, always test the suitability of the stitch to the yarn by making samples before you come to a decision.

UNDERSTANDING STITCH MULTIPLES

Some stitch patterns—stockinette stitch and garter stitch for example—can be worked over any number of stitches. Others must be worked over a specific multiple, or repeat, such as four. There may also be extra stitches needed to balance the pattern. Thus a pattern could specify, say, "4 stitches, plus 3 extra." This means that the pattern will work on 15 stitches ($3 \times 4 = 12$; $12 + 3 = 15$) or on 19 stitches, or 23 stitches and so on. It will not work on 14, 18 or 22 stitches, for example.

When designing your own garments or other knitted items, you must allow for this in determining the number of stitches in a particular section. In other words, if the number of cast-on stitches you have arrived at as a result of body and gauge measurements (see p. 47, for example) is not the required multiple for the stitch, making allowance also for extra, balancing stitches, then either the stitch pattern or the number of cast-on stitches must be changed.

In many cases it is possible to add two or three stitches to the calculated number of cast-on stitches to make the necessary adjustment without drastically affecting the measurements. However, when the multiple is a large number such as 20 stitches, and the majority of these stitches would need to be added to those cast on, this will not be practicable. Some highly experienced knitters may be able to alter such a stitch pattern to fit, but this cannot be recommended to beginners.

HANDLING REPEATS

Most stitch patterns repeat over a certain number of rows as well as across a certain number of stitches. The balance of the stitch repeat is taken care of in the drafting of the stitch pattern instructions. This means that, if necessary, extra stitches are added at one side to ensure that the pattern is correctly centered and that where two pieces are joined the pattern will match.

The balance of the row repeats is usually less important than that of stitch repeats. The pattern can often be allowed to take its course, and the knitting ended where appropriate, irrespective of where this falls in the pattern. In some cases, however, it may be important to ensure that a specific number of row repeats is allowed for, or that the repeat ends exactly at the shoulder line, for example.

The exact placing of the row repeats is necessary in a garment such as one that is knitted in one piece, up and over the shoulder, since the patterns must match on the front and the back. When designing garments, use the row gauge to determine the number of rows you need to knit in the relevant part of the garment and adjust the length if necessary. (See the example given opposite.)

MIXING STITCH PATTERNS

Some of the most successful knitted designs are achieved by mixing several stitch patterns in one garment. Even apparently incompatible stitches such as lace and cables can be effectively combined. This is usually done by working individual stitch patterns in a series of vertical or horizontal panels, with one or two stitches dividing them. Aran sweaters are an example of this sort of design.

If panels are arranged horizontally, the greatest problem is that the gauge of the stitch patterns may be incompatible. If you are combining stitch patterns you should thus knit a test swatch that combines all the stitches you will use in the order in which they will appear. Remember that a few rows of stockinette stitch or reverse stockinette stitch worked between the different panels can even out the effect of any gauge variations. This is also aesthetically pleasing. As a rule, use reverse stockinette stitch bands to separate panels whose background is stockinette and vice versa.

Designing with vertical panels in different stitch patterns is rather more complicated. It is best to begin with no more than three panels worked, for example, on a background made up of a plain stitch such as stockinette stitch. Choose patterns in which a single stitch repeat "reads" as a design feature—that is, has a discernible, interesting shape of its own. Cables and many eyelet patterns come into this category. Your test swatch must comprise the whole width of the garment with panels and background stitches included.

If you are designing a garment with vertical panels, plan it out first of all on a piece of paper. (It need not, of course, be as finished as the sketch shown here.) Note the number of stitches in each panel, the order in which they appear, and the number of background stitches dividing them. (If the background seems too plain you can always insert single ribs at intervals to emphasize the paneled look.) Then make up a test swatch. If it is too narrow or too wide, adjust the number of background stitches, either at the side edges or evenly between the panels.

ADJUSTING LENGTH OF KNITTING TO STITCH PATTERN

If you are using a stitch pattern containing many rows in a repeat and you wish to ensure that a whole repeat will fall at a certain point (just below the shoulder seam, for example), you must plan the length of the knitting with this in mind.

Suppose, for example, that the pattern repeat contains 18 rows, and that the front and back sections of the garment are intended to measure about 18 in, not including the ribbing at the lower edge. Your row tension is 22 rows over 4 in, or 5½ rows per inch.

The first step is to ascertain how many rows of knitting will be included in 18 in:

$$5\frac{1}{2} \text{ rows} \times 18 \text{ in} = 99 \text{ rows}$$

Next, divide 99 by the number of rows in the pattern repeat:

$$99 \text{ rows} \div 18 \text{ rows} = 5\frac{1}{2} \text{ repeats}$$

In order to contain only whole repeats, the knitting must be made longer or shorter. Six repeats will make it 19½ in long (6 × 18 rows = 108 rows; 108 ÷ 5½ rows = 19½ in). Five repeats will make it 16½ in long (5 × 18 rows = 90 rows; 90 ÷ 5½ rows = approximately 16½ in).

An alternative to adjusting the length would be to begin the stitch pattern part way through the repeat. Try this on a swatch before beginning the garment.

The simplest and most basic stitch patterns involve only knit and purl stitches—or twisted knit and purl stitches. They are the most commonly used of all patterns and, as well as creating pleasing fabrics in their own right, may also form the background stitch for more complicated lacy or textured motifs. Basic stitch patterns are all-purpose and can be worked in any type of yarn. Instructions are given for working them flat unless mentioned otherwise. (For abbreviations see p. 141.)

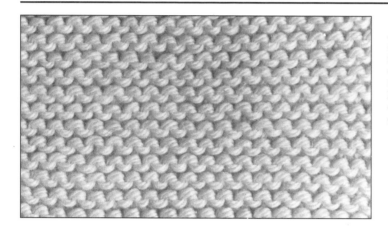

◄ GARTER STITCH

A reversible stitch which does not curl at the edges and which is ideal for both borders and larger areas of a garment. It produces a dense, firm fabric suitable for afghans and blankets. It has good sideways elasticity and was once used for garters, hence its name.

Worked over any number of sts.
1st row K.
Rep this row.
To work garter stitch in the round, K the first and every other round, P the 2nd and every other round.

REVERSE STOCKINETTE STITCH ►

The reverse, or purl, side of stockinette stitch is used as a background to many cable and embossed patterns.
Worked over any number of sts.
1st row (RS) P.
2nd row K.
Rep these 2 rows.
To work reverse stockinette stitch in the round, P every round.

STOCKINETTE STITCH ►

A stitch with good horizontal elasticity that was once used for stockings, hence its name. Stockinette stitch has a strong tendency to curl inward and thus is not usually suitable for edgings and borders unless a hem is used (see p. 128). However, the fabric is smooth and flat. Most color-patterned knitting is worked in stockinette stitch.
Worked over any number of sts.
1st row (RS) K.
2nd row P.
Rep these 2 rows.
To work stockinette stitch in the round, K every round.

◄ TWISTED STOCKINETTE STITCH

A tighter version of stockinette stitch.
Worked over any number of sts.
1st row (RS) (K tbl) to end.
2nd row (P tbl) to end.
Rep these 2 rows.

SINGLE RIB ▶

Rib stitch patterns have great sideways elasticity. They are therefore used most in places where a garment needs to cling—for example, at waists and cuffs.

Worked over an odd number of sts.
1st row (K1, P1) to last st, K1.
2nd row (P1, K1) to last st, P1.
Rep these 2 rows.
To work single rib in the round, cast on an even number of sts.
1st round (K1, P1) to end.
Rep this round.

◀ DOUBLE RIB

Worked over a multiple of 4 sts, plus 2 extra.
1st row (K2, P2) to last 2 sts, K2.
2nd row (P2, K2) to last 2 sts, P2.
Rep these 2 rows.
To work double rib in the round, cast on a multiple of 4 sts.
1st round (K2, P2) to end.
Rep this round.

SEED STITCH ▶

Sometimes called "moss stitch," this is a tight, reversible fabric suitable for borders and edgings as well as for the main parts of garments.

Worked over an odd number of sts.
1st row (K1, P1) to last st, K1.
Rep this row.
To work seed stitch in the round, cast on an even number of sts.
1st round (K1, P1) to end.
2nd round (P1, K1) to end.
Rep these 2 rounds.

◀ DOUBLE SEED STITCH

Worked over a multiple of 4 sts, plus 2 extra.
1st row (K2, P2) to last 2 sts, K2.
2nd row (P2, K2) to last 2 sts, P2.
3rd row As 2nd.
4th row As first.
Rep these 4 rows.
To work double seed stitch in the round, cast on a multiple of 4 sts.
1st and 2nd rounds (K2, P2) to end.
3rd and 4th rounds (P2, K2) to end.
Rep these 4 rounds.

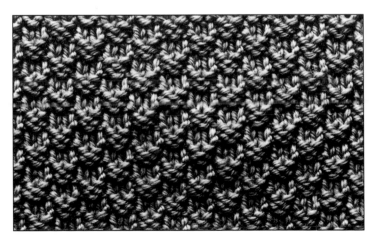

Using only knit and purl stitches it is possible to produce some interesting, if subtle, textures in knitted fabrics. The effect often relies on the fact that single purl stitches stand out against a plain knit background, so that lightly embossed repeating patterns and motifs can be worked.

To make the most of such patterns, choose a plain, smooth yarn and a gauge that is fairly tight. It is also preferable for the fabric to be in a single color throughout, since the introduction of contrasting colors can completely obscure the textures.

(For abbreviations, see p. 141.)

◄ DOUBLE BASKETWEAVE

This pattern clearly demonstrates how purl stitches in horizontal rows stand out and purl stitches in vertical rows recede.

Worked over a multiple of 18 sts, plus 10 extra.

1st row (RS) *K11, P2, K2, P2, K1; rep from * to last 10 sts, K10.
2nd row P1, K8, P1, *P1, (K2, P2) twice, K8, P1; rep from * to end.
3rd row *K1, P8, (K2, P2) twice, K1; rep from * to last 10 sts, K1, P8, K1.
4th row P10, *P1, K2, P2, K2, P11; rep from * to end.
5th–8th rows As first–4th rows.

9th row K to end.
10th row (P2, K2) twice, P2, *P10, (K2, P2) twice; rep from * to end.
11th row *(K2, P2) twice, K2, P8; rep from * to last 10 sts, (K2, P2) twice, K2.
12th row (P2, K2) twice, P2, *K8, (P2, K2) twice, P2; rep from * to end.
13th row *(K2, P2) twice, K10; rep from * to last 10 sts, (K2, P2) twice, K2.
14th–17th rows As 10th–13th rows.
18th row P to end.
Rep first–18th rows.

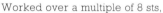

◄ EVEN BASKETWEAVE

Worked over a multiple of 8 sts, plus 4 extra.

1st row (RS) K4, (P4, K4) to end.
2nd row P4, (K4, P4) to end.
3rd–4th rows As first–2nd rows.
5th and 7th rows As 2nd row.
6th and 8th rows As first row.
Rep first–8th rows.

◄ DIAMOND BROCADE

This is one of the patterns on the knitted shirt worn by King Charles I of England at his execution in 1649. He is said to have asked specifically for a woolen garment in case the cold morning air caused shivers which the onlookers might mistake for fear.

Worked over a multiple of 12 sts, plus 1 extra.

1st row (RS) K1, *P1, K9, P1, K1; rep from * to end.
2nd row K1, *P1, K1, P7, K1, P1, K1; rep from * to end.
3rd row K1, *P1, K1, P1, K5, (P1, K1) twice; rep from * to end.

4th row P1, *(P1, K1) twice, P3, K1, P1, K1, P2; rep from * to end.
5th row K1, *K2, (P1, K1) 3 times, P1, K3; rep from * to end.
6th row P1, *P3, (K1, P1) twice, K1, P4; rep from * to end.
7th row K1, *K4, P1, K1, P1, K5; rep from * to end.
8th row As 6th row.
9th row As 5th row.
10th row As 4th row.
11th row As 3rd row.
12th row As 2nd row.
Rep first–12th rows.

◄ SEEDED RIB

This is a reversible all-over pattern. Unlike other ribs it is not suitable for cuffs, neckbands, and so on.

Worked over a multiple of 4 sts, plus 3 extra.
1st row K3, *P1, K3; rep from * to end.
2nd row K1, *P1, K3; rep from * to last 2 sts, P1, K1.
Rep first–2nd rows.

◄ WAGER WELT

The "wager" referred to in the name of this stitch is to guess how many purl rows there are in each pattern repeat.

Surprisingly, the answer is only one.

Worked over any number of sts.
1st row (RS) K to end.
2nd row P to end.
3rd–8th rows As first row.
Rep first–8th rows.

◄ RIPPLE STITCH

Worked over a multiple of 8 sts, plus 6 extra.
1st row (RS) K6, *P2, K6; rep from * to end.
2nd row K1, *P4, K4; rep from * to last 5 sts, P4, K1.
3rd row P2, *K2, P2; rep from * to end.
4th row P1, *K4, P4; rep from * to last 5 sts, K4, P1.
5th row K2, *P2, K6; rep from * to last 4 sts, P2, K2.
6th row P6, *K2, P6; rep from * to end.
7th row P1, *K4, P4; rep from * to last 5 sts, K4, P1.

8th row K2, *P2, K2; rep from * to end.
9th row K1, *P4, K4; rep from * to last 5 sts, P4, K1.
10th row P2, *K2, P6; rep from * to last 4 sts, K2, P2.
Rep first–10th rows

◄ TRIANGLE STITCH

Like many similar patterns (including the diamond brocade, opposite) triangle stitch is often found on the traditional British fisherman's sweater known as a "gansey" or Guernsey. It can be worked in vertical panels of one or two repeats or as an all-over pattern.

Worked over a multiple of 7 sts.
1st row (RS) *P6, K1; rep from * to end.
2nd row *P2, K5; rep from * to end.
3rd row *P4, K3; rep from * to end.
4th row *P4, K3; rep from * to end.
5th row *P2, K5; rep from * to end.
6th row *P6, K1; rep from * to end.
Rep first–6th rows.

Cabling involves moving stitches from their usual position in a row and working them in a different order. Some simple "mock" cables (see p. 119) can be created with only two needles, but most cable patterns require the use of a cable needle.

The simplest cable patterns are those in which a set of stitches (four, six, or eight) are cabled, or crossed, at regular intervals (see p. 118) forming a twisted, ropelike effect, but there are many more complex variations. Most of them are "panel" patterns, which means that they are worked over a set number of stitches once only, but there are a few all-over cable patterns.

When designing using cable patterns it is customary to arrange the vertical panels on a plainer background or in combination with other panel patterns. A background of reverse stockinette stitch throws the cables into relief. Where the background is in stockinette stitch it is advisable to work at least two purl stitches on each side of the cable to make it stand out.

The gauge of cable patterns is usually much tighter than that of simple knit and purl textured stitches. The pulling-in effect of cables is quite dramatic and must be allowed for, or your garment will be far too narrow. For this reason, remember to measure the gauge of the cable panel as well as that of the background stitches when calculating your gauge. Subtract the width of the proposed panel or panels from the total required width to find the total width of background fabric. Use this measurement to calculate the number of background stitches. Add the number to the panel stitches to find the total number of stitches.

Cables are so crisp that they can be successfully worked in many types of yarn. Smooth, thick yarns will greatly enhance the three-dimensional effect. Worked in a finer or a lightly textured yarn such as mohair, angora, or thin bouclé, the cables will be more subtle.

(For abbreviations see p. 141.)

◀ DEER CABLE
Worked over 20 sts.
1st and every other row (WS) K2, P16, K2.
2nd row P2, K4, C4B, C4F, K4, P2.
4th row P2, K2, C4B, K4, C4F, K2, P2.
6th row P2, C4B, K8, C4F.
Rep first–6th rows.

HORSESHOE CABLE ▶
Worked over 12 sts.
1st and every other row (WS) K2, P8, K2.
2nd row P2, C4B, C4F, P2.
4th, 6th and 8th rows P2, K8, P2.
Rep first–8th rows.

RIBBED CABLE ▲
Worked over 11 sts.
1st, 3rd and 5th rows (RS) P2, K1 tbl, (P1 tbl, K1 tbl) 3 times, P2.
2nd and every other row K2, P1 tbl, (K1 tbl, P1 tbl) 3 times, K2.
7th row P2, sl next 4 sts on to cable needle and hold at front of work, K1 tbl, P1, K1 tbl, sl 4th st from cable needle back onto LH needle and P1, then (K1 tbl, P1, K1 tbl) from cable needle, P2.
9th, 11th, 13th, and 15th rows As first row.
16th row As 2nd row.
Rep first–16th rows.

LOBSTER CLAW ▶

Worked over 12 sts.
1st row (WS) K.
2nd row P2, K1, P6, K1, P2.
3rd, 5th and 7th rows K2, P2, K4, P2, K2.
4th and 6th rows P2, K2, P4, K2, P2.
8th row P2, sl next 2 sts on to cable needle and hold at front of work, P2, yo, K2 tog tbl from cable needle, sl next 2 sts on to cable needle and hold at back of work, K2 tog, yo, P2 from cable needle, P2.
Rep first–8th rows.

EYELET CABLE ▼

Worked over 10 sts.
1st and every other row (WS) K2, P6, K2.
2nd row P2, K6, P2.
4th row P2, C6B, P2.
6th row As 2nd row.
8th row P2, K1, yo, K2 tog, K3, P2.
10th row P2, sl 1, K1, psso, yo, K4, P2.
12th row As 8th row.
14th, 16th and 18th rows As 2nd, 4th and 6th rows.
20th row P2, K3, sl 1, K1, psso, yo, K1, P2.
22nd row P2, K4, yo, K2 tog, P2.
24th row As 20th row.
Rep first–24th rows.

BASKET CABLE ▲

Worked over a multiple of 6 sts, plus 4 extra (minimum of 6 sts).
1st and 3rd rows (WS) K2, P to last 2 sts, K2.
2nd row K to end.
4th row K2, (C6B) to last 2 sts, K2.
5th and 7th rows As first row.
6th row As 2nd row.
8th row K5, (C6F) to last 5 sts, K5.
Rep first–8th rows.

◀ CHEVRON CABLE

Worked over a multiple of 12 sts, plus 2 extra.
1st and every other row (WS) P to end.
2nd row K1, (C6B, C6F) to last st, K1.
4th, 6th and 8th rows K to end.
Rep first–8th rows.

Bobbles are small round clusters of stitches that appear to "sit" on the surface of the knitted fabric. They are extremely versatile and are often combined with other embossed or textured patterns (as in many Aran designs), or with lace and openwork stitches, or as part of a multicolored, multi-textured scheme, or even in picture knitting. The bobbles can be worked either in the same yarn and color as the background fabric or in a different yarn.

Technically bobbles are easy to work (see p. 120): you simply increase a number of times into one stitch, then turn and work several rows on the increases before de-creasing again to a single stitch. (Less often, the bobble is completed along with the background fabric over several rows.)

Single bobbles can be placed anywhere on a background fabric so long as there is a single "free" stitch—not otherwise required for the pattern—to anchor them. Because of this, it is very easy to add bobbles to almost any existing stitch pattern without affecting the structure or gauge of the underlying stitches. It is worth experimenting with new combinations to try to create new fabrics and an original style for your designs. When placing bobbles, try to frame them in some motif of the pattern—the hollow of a cable, for example, or the apex of a triangular eyelet motif. When placing bobbles on a plain background, arrange them in a definite order rather than randomly. In an all-over arrangement, rows of bobbles look more pleasing if they are staggered above each other, rather than ranged in columns.

The choice of yarn can be crucial. Bobbles are often associated with heavily textured garments, but if the yarn is too thick the over-all effect can be ungainly.

Note The bobble in all the following stitch patterns is made thus: (K1, yo, K1, yo, K1) all into next st, turn, P5, turn, K5, turn, P2 tog, P1, P2 tog, turn, sl 1, K2 tog, psso. (For abbreviations, see p. 141.)

◀ LACY BOBBLE
Worked over a multiple of 10 sts, plus 1 extra.
1st row (RS) P1, *yo, sl 1, K1, psso, P5, K2 tog, yo, P1; rep from * to end.
2nd row K1, *K1, P1, K5, P1, K2; rep from * to end.
3rd row P1, *P1, yo, sl 1, K1, psso, P3, K2 tog, yo, P2; rep from * to end.
4th row K1, *K2, P1, K3, P1, K3; rep from * to end.
5th row P1, *P2, yo, sl 1, K1, psso, P1, K2 tog, yo, P3; rep from * to end.
6th row K1, *K3, P1, K1, P1, K4; rep from * to end.
7th row P1, *P3, yo, sl 2 K-wise, K1, p2sso, yo, P3, make bobble; rep from * ending last rep P4.
8th row K1, *K3, P3, K3, P1 tbl; rep from * ending last rep K4.
9th row P1, *P2, K2 tog, yo, P1, yo, sl 1, K1, psso, P3; rep from * to end.
10th row K1, *K2, (P1, K3) twice; rep from * to end.
11th row P1, *P1, K2 tog, yo, P3, yo, sl 1, K1, psso, P2; rep from * to end.
12th row K1, *K1, P1, K5, P1, K2; rep from * to end.
13th row P1, *K2 tog, yo, P5, yo, sl 1, K1, psso, P1; rep from * to end.
14th row K1, *P1, K7, P1, K1; rep from * to end.
15th row K2 tog, *yo, P3, make bobble, P3, yo, sl 2 K-wise, K1, p2sso; rep from * to last 9 sts, yo, P3, make bobble, P3, yo, sl 1, K1, psso.
16th row P1, *P1, K3, P1 tbl, K3, P2; rep from * to end.
Rep first–16th rows.

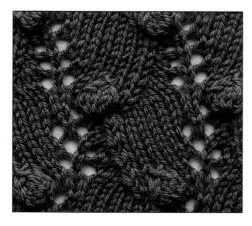

◀ FIELD OF WHEAT
Worked over 11 sts, plus 2 extra.
1st row (RS) K1, *K5, yo, K1, yo, K3, K2 tog; rep from * to last st, K1.
2nd, 4th, 6th and 8th rows P1, *P2 tog, P10; rep from * to last st, P1.
3rd row K1, *K6, yo, K1, yo, K2, K2 tog; rep from * to last st, K1.
5th row K1, *K7, (yo, K1) twice, K2 tog; rep from * to last st, K1.
7th row K1, *K8, yo, K1, yo, K2 tog; rep from * to 1st st, K1.
9th row K1, *sl 1, K1, psso, K4, yo, K1, yo, K2, make bobble, K1; rep from * to last st, K1.
10th row P1, *P1, P1 tbl, P8, P2 tog tbl, rep from * to last st, P1.
11th row K1, *sl 1, K1, psso, K3, yo, K1, yo, K5; rep from * to last st, K1.
12th, 14th, 16th and 18th rows P1, *P10, P2 tog tbl; rep from * to last st, P1.
13th row K1, *sl 1, K1, psso, K3, yo, K1, yo, K5; rep from * to last st, K1.
15th row K1, *sl 1, K1, psso, (K1, yo) twice, K7; rep from * to last st, K1.
17th row K1, *sl 1, K1, psso, yo, K1, yo, K8; rep from * to last st, K1.
19th row K1, *K1, make bobble, K2, yo, K1, yo, K4, K2 tog; rep from * to last st, K1.
20th row P1, *P2 tog, P8, P1 tbl, P1; rep from * to last st, P1.
Rep first–20th rows.

◀ CHEVRON BOBBLE
Worked over a multiple of 20 sts, plus 1 extra.
1st row K1, *yo, sl 1, K1, psso, K15, K2 tog, yo, K1; rep from * to end.
2nd row P2, *yo, P2 tog, P13, P2 tog tbl, yo, P3; rep from * to last 19 sts, yo, P2 tog, P13, P2 tog tbl, yo, P2.
3rd row K3, *yo, sl 1, K1, psso, K11, K2 tog, yo, K5; rep from * to last 18 sts, yo, sl 1, K1, psso, K11, K2 tog, yo, K3.
4th row P4, *yo, P2 tog, P9, P2 tog tbl, yo, P7; rep from * to last 17 sts, yo, P2 tog, P9, P2 tog tbl, yo, P4.
5th row K5, *yo, sl 1, K1, psso, K3, make bobble, K3, K2 tog, yo, K9; rep from * to last 16 sts, yo, sl 1, K1, psso, K3, make bobble, K3, K2 tog, yo, K5.
6th row P6, *yo, P2 tog, P5, P2 tog tbl, yo, P11; rep from * to last 15 sts, yo, P2 tog, P5, P2 tog tbl, yo, P6.
7th row K7, *yo, sl 1, K1, psso, K3, K2 tog, yo, K6, make bobble, K6; rep from * to last 14 sts, yo, sl 1, K1, psso, K3, K2 tog, yo, K7.
8th row P8, *yo, P2 tog, P1, P2 tog tbl, yo, P15; rep from * to last 13 sts, yo, P2 tog, P1, P2 tog tbl, yo, P8.
9th row K9, *yo, sl 1, K2 tog, psso, yo, K17; rep from * to last 12 sts, yo, sl 1, K2 tog, psso, yo, K9.
10th row P to end.
Rep first–10th rows.

◄ SIMPLE BOBBLES

The arrangement of these bobbles can be endlessly varied. Work them closer together or farther apart, depending on the desired effect. The background, too, can be changed from the stockinette stitch shown here to reverse stockinette stitch, or garter stitch or a fancy pattern.

Worked over a multiple of 6 sts, plus 5 extra.

1st and 3rd rows (RS) K to end.
2nd and every other row P to end.
5th row K5, *make bobble, K5; rep from * to end.
7th and 9th rows K to end.
11th row K2, *make bobble, K5; rep from * to last 3 sts, K3.
12th row As 2nd row.
Rep first–12th rows.

◄ HOLLOW OAK

This is arranged as a panel pattern, but it could easily be adapted to repeat across the fabric.
Worked over 15 sts.

1st, 3rd, 5th and 7th rows (WS) K5, P5, K5.
2nd row P5, K2, make bobble, K2, P5.
4th row P5, make bobble, K3, make bobble, P5.
6th row As 2nd row.
8th row P4, Tw3B, P1, Tw3F, P4.
9th row K4, P2, K1, P1, K1, P2, K4.
10th row P3, Tw3B, K1, P1, K1, Tw3F, P3.
11th row K3, P3, K1, P1, K1, P3, K3.
12th row P2, Tw3B, (P1, K1) twice, P1, Tw3F, P2.
13th row K2, P2, (K1, P1) 3 times, K1, P2, K2.
14th row P2, K3, (P1, K1) twice, P1, K3, P2.
15th, 17th and 19th rows As 13th, 11th and 9th rows.
16th row P2, Tw3F, (P1, K1) twice, P1, Tw3B, P2.
18th row P3, Tw3F, K1, P1, K1, Tw3B, P3.
20th row P4, Tw3F, P1, Tw3B, P4.
Rep first–20th rows.

◄ NOSEGAY PATTERN

This is a panel pattern.
Worked over 16 sts.

1st row (WS) K7, P2, K7.
2nd row P6, C2B, C2F, P6.
3rd row K5, Cr2F, P2, Cr2B, K5.
4th row P4, Cr2B, C2B, C2F, Cr2F, P4.
5th row K3, Cr2F, K1, P4, K1, Cr2B, K3.
6th row P2, Cr2B, P1, Cr2B, K2, Cr2F, P1, Cr2F, P2.
7th row (K2, P1) twice, K1, P2, K1, (P1, K2) twice.
8th row P2, make bobble, P1, Cr2B, P1, K2, P1, Cr2F, P1, make bobble, P2.
9th row K4, P1, K2, P2, K2, P1, K4.
10th row P4, make bobble, P2, K2, P2, make bobble, P4.
Rep first–10th rows.

◄ BUNCH OF GRAPES

Worked over a multiple of 20 sts, plus 1 extra.

1st row (RS) K1, *(P4, K1) twice, P4, make bobble, P4, K1; rep from * to end.
2nd row P1, *K4, P1 tbl, (K4, P1) 3 times; rep from * to end.
3rd row K1, *(P4, K1) twice, P3, make bobble, P1, make bobble, P3, K1; rep from * to end.
4th row P1, *K2, (K1, P1 tbl) twice, K3, P1, (K4, P1) twice; rep from * to end.
5th row K1, *(P4, K1) twice, P2, make bobble, (P1, make bobble) twice, P2, K1; rep from * to end.
6th row P1, *K2, P1 tbl, (K1, P1 tbl) twice, K2, P1, (K4, P1) twice, rep from * to end.
7th row K1, *P4, make bobble, (P4, K1) 3 times; rep from * to end.
8th row P1, *(K4, P1) twice, K4, P1 tbl, K4, P1; rep from * to end.
9th row K1, *P3, (make bobble, P1) twice, P2, K1, (P4, K1) twice; rep from * to end.
10th row P1, *(K4, P1) twice, K3, P1 tbl, K1, P1 tbl, K3, P1; rep from * to end.
11th row K1, *P2, make bobble, (P1, make bobble) twice, P2, K1, (P4, K1) twice; rep from * to end.
12th row P1, *(K4, P1) twice, K2, (P1 tbl, K1) twice, P1 tbl, K2, P1; rep from * to end. Rep rows 1–12.

The Aran Islands, off the west coast of Ireland, have become associated with some highly distinctive, heavily textured stitch patterns. Whether these patterns originated in the Arans is unclear; in any case, it is unlikely that the Aran style of knitting is more than a century old. The use of a variety of cables and traveling stitches is reminiscent of other fisherman knits from elsewhere in the British Isles, but Arans are usually much more heavily textured with embossed stitches and lattice patterns.

Although these stitches can be applied to many types of garment and to furnishings such as rugs and throws, for example, they still look their best on the traditional Aran sweater. Typically this is a crew-neck or polo-neck style with set-in sleeves, creating an unbroken expanse of front and back divided into a series of vertical panels. In most commercial patterns the front and back are the same, but when the islanders were knitting for themselves these would often be different and the panels improvised as the work progressed. In your own designs you can do the same.

Like cables, Aran patterns fall into two categories, panel patterns and all-over patterns. The panel patterns tend to be the main features of a design, with all-over patterns being used in between the panels or at the sides. Sometimes a wide, complex panel will be edged with one or more narrow cables or with a twisted-stitch rib. Occasionally there is a wide panel of an all-over stitch (Irish moss stitch, trinity stitch, or honeycomb, for example) down the center, with more elaborate lattices or lozenges on each side.

When planning an Aran design it is important to remember that the gauges of the various panels and all-over patterns will be different. The width of the panel patterns is usually fixed, but the all-over stitches can often be finely adjusted to give the required measurements.
(For abbreviations, see p. 141.)

◀ TRINITY STITCH

Many traditional stitch patterns are said to have a religious inspiration or symbolism. Because of the way it is worked (making three stitches from one, then working three together) this pattern represents the Holy Trinity ("Three in One and One in Three").
Worked over a multiple of 4 sts.
1st and 3rd rows (RS) P to end.
2nd row * (K1, P1, K1) into first st, P3 tog, rep from * to end.
4th row * P3 tog, (K1, P1, K1) into next st, rep from * to end.
Rep first–4th rows.

INTERLACED CABLE ▶

This pattern is reminiscent of the interlaced stone carving on Celtic crosses.
Worked over 17 sts.
1st row (WS) (K2, P2) twice, K1, (P2, K2) twice.
2nd row P2, K2, P2, sl next 3 sts on to cable needle and hold at back of work, K2, sl P st from cable needle back on to LH needle and P it, K2 from cable needle, P2, K2, P2.
3rd row As first row.
4th row P2, Tw3F, Tw3B, P1, Tw3F, Tw3B, P2.
5th row (K3, P4) twice, K3.
6th row P3, C4B, P3, C4F, P3.
7th row As 5th row.
8th row P2, Tw3B, Tw3F, P1, Tw3B, Tw3F, P2.
9th row As first row.
10th row P2, K2, P2, sl next 3 sts on to cable needle and hold at front of work, K2, sl P st from cable needle back on to LH needle and P it, K2 from cable needle, P2, K2, P2.
11th–16th rows As 3rd–8th rows.
Rep first–16th rows.

TREE OF LIFE ▲

The Tree of Life symbol is found in many different craft traditions, from Islamic carpet weaving to Chinese embroidery. In knitting it takes the form of a highly stylized tree skeleton worked either in raised traveling ribs, as here, or in purl stitches on a plain ground, as in Guernsey patterns. Working the stitches through the back of the loop enhances the embossed effect. These twisted stitch motifs are also a marked feature of some German and Austrian knitting traditions.
Worked over 11 sts.
1st row (RS) P4, K3 tbl, P4.
2nd row K4, P3 tbl, K4.
3rd row P3, Tw2B, K1 tbl, Tw2F, P3.
4th row K3, (P1 tbl, K1) twice, P1 tbl, K3.
5th row P2, Tw2B, P1, K1 tbl, P1, Tw2F, P2.
6th row K2, P1 tbl, (K2, P1 tbl) twice, K2.
7th row P1, Tw2B, P1, K3 tbl, P1, Tw2F, P1.
8th row K1, P1 tbl, K2, P3 tbl, K2, P1 tbl, K1.
9th row P3, Tw2B, K1 tbl, Tw2F, P3.
Rep 4th–9th rows.

IRISH MOSS STITCH ▶

Worked over an even number of sts.
1st row (RS) (K1, P1) to end.
2nd row As first row.
3rd–4th rows (P1, K1) to end.
Rep first–4th rows.

MOSS DIAMOND ▲

Panels of diamonds are extremely common on Aran sweaters. Sometimes the diamonds are filled with Irish moss stitch, as here, or with popcorn or bobble motifs or a small cable; or they can be left open with a background of reverse stockinette stitch.
Worked over 17 sts.
1st row (RS) P6, K2, P1, K2, P6.
2nd and every other row K all the P sts of previous row and P the K sts.
3rd row P6, sl next 3 sts on to cable needle and hold at back of work, K2, sl P st from cable needle back on to LH needle and P it, then K2 from cable needle, P6.
5th row P5, Tw3B, K1, Tw3F, P5.
7th row P4, Tw3B, K1, P1, K1, Tw3F, P4.
9th row P3, Tw3B, (K1, P1) twice, K1, Tw3F, P3.
11th row P2, Tw3B, (P1, K1) 3 times, K1, Tw3F, P2.
13th row P2, Tw3F, (P1, K1) 3 times, P1, Tw3B, P2.
15th row P3, Tw3F, (P1, K1) twice, P1, Tw3B, P3.
17th row P4, Tw3F, P1, K1, P1, Tw3B, P4.
19th row P5, Tw3F, P1, Tw3B, P5.
20th row As 2nd row.
Rep 3rd–20th rows.

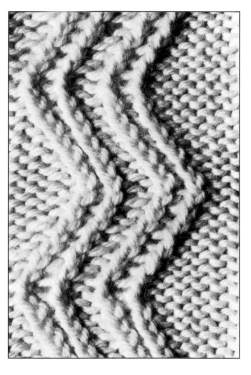

MARRIAGE LINES ▼

This pattern is said to represent the ups and downs of married life, and was traditionally worked only on sweaters for married men.
Worked over 13 sts.
1st row (RS) P5, (K1 tbl, P1) twice, (P1, K1 tbl) twice.
2nd and every other row P tbl the K tbl sts of the previous row and K the P sts.
3rd row P4, Tw2B twice, P1, Tw2B twice.
5th row P3, (Tw2B twice, P1) twice.
7th row P2, (Tw2B twice, P1) twice, P1.
9th row (P1, Tw2B twice) twice, P3.
11th row (P1, Tw2F twice) twice, P3.
13th row P2, (Tw2F twice, P1) twice, P1.
15th row P3, (Tw2F twice, P1) twice.
17th row P3, (P1, Tw2F twice) twice.
Rep 2nd–17th rows.

◀ HONEYCOMB STITCH

Worked over a multiple of 8 sts.
1st row (RS) K to end.
2nd and every other row P to end.
3rd row (C4F, C4B) to end.
5th row As first row.
7th row (C4B, C4F) to end.
8th row As 2nd row.
Rep first–8th rows.

Fair Isle is a small island between the Orkneys and Shetlands, off the northeast coast of Scotland. It has given its name to a distinctive type of color-patterned knitting which is native not only to Fair Isle but also to the Shetlands.

Various legends have grown up surrounding the origins of Fair Isle patterns. According to the best known of these, the islanders copied the patterns from the clothes of Spanish sailors who were shipwrecked there following the defeat of the Spanish Armada in 1588. There are, in fact, some similarities between Spanish and Fair Isle patterns. However, these are no stronger than the ones between Fair Isle and Norwegian knitting traditions, and since trading and cultural links between the Scottish islands and Scandinavia go back to the time of the Vikings, it seems reasonable to assume that this influence is the more significant one.

The distinguishing characteristics of Fair Isle knitting are a two-colors-a-row structure and the yarn used for it: a loosely twisted Shetland wool called "fingering," dyed in a range of beautifully soft colors. Originally, natural dyes were used for this purpose; nowadays chemical dyes reproduce, as closely as possible, the authentic mellow hues.

In spite of using only two colors to a row, Fair Isle patterns look exceedingly complex. This is partly because of the dense nature of the motifs (there are rarely more than seven stitches between color changes—usually less than five) but also because of the frequency of the vertical color changes. In other words, although there are only two colors to a row, these colors may change after two, four, six, or eight rows.

The choice of colors is also important to the over-all effect. Soft colors are usually more successful than bright ones. You can choose a scheme of light colors on a dark ground or dark colors on light. If you mix tones, the motifs may not "read" well.

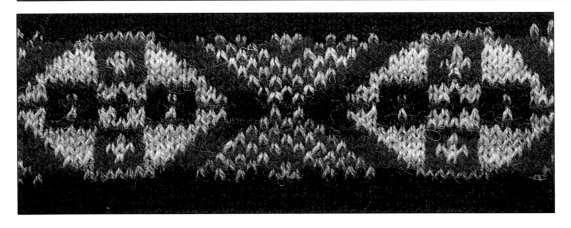

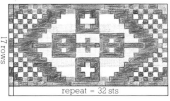

◄ LOZENGE AND CROSS
Worked over 17 rows and a multiple of 32 sts, plus 1 extra.
Patterns combining the lozenge and Maltese cross are known as "OXO" patterns. The stitch to the left of the repeat is the centralizing stitch which balances the pattern.

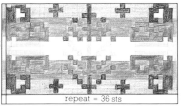

◄ TREE OF LIFE AND ROSETTE
Worked over 19 rows and a multiple of 36 sts, plus 1 extra.
The rosette is another version of Norwegian star (*below*). Single rosettes and stars are often worked on the backs of mittens and gloves or in the center of berets.

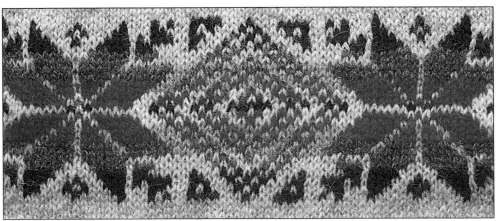

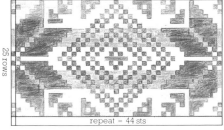

◄ NORWEGIAN STAR
Worked over 25 rows and a multiple of 44 sts, plus 1 extra.
This version of a Fair Isle motif can also be worked as an all-over pattern by staggering the stars.

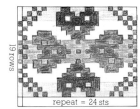

HEARTS ROSETTE ▶

Worked over 19 rows and 24 sts, plus 1 extra.

Hearts are often found either in this rosette formation or in rows. They are separated here by a simple Maltese cross.

A peerie pattern (see below) has been used above and below the band.

ALL-OVER DICE PATTERN ▶

Worked over a multiple of 36 sts and 32 rows.

In some versions of this and similar checked patterns the background color is kept the same throughout, with shading introduced only into the motif colors. This is a favorite type of pattern for stockings and scarves (this type of scarf would be worked in the round).

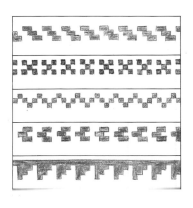

PEERIE PATTERNS ▶

"Peerie" means "small" in the local Shetland dialect. These tiny patterns are used to separate other larger motifs. There are hundreds of different kinds. On the whole they do not occupy more than four or five rows. The ones shown here repeat over four or eight stitches. One of them has been used along with the hearts rosette patterns given here. Besides serving as "fillers" they are also useful for edgings and borders, and for small areas such as the fingers of gloves. Most Fair Isle knitters invent their own peerie patterns as they go along.

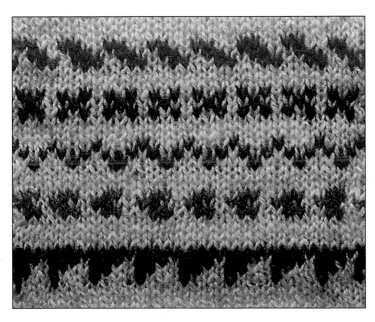

The distinction between eyelet and lace patterns is not a hard and fast one. Both are based on arrangements of holes, or eyelets, on a background fabric. In eyelet patterns the holes tend to be more separate and scattered on a fairly solid background; lace patterns are usually much more open, with the proportions of holes and background being about equal.

In eyelet patterns the wrong-side rows are always composed entirely of knit or purl (or knit and purl) stitches. In lace patterns the holes can be formed on wrong-side as well as right-side rows. The holes are formed by "yarn over" techniques (see p. 112), in which a yarn-over increase is matched by a decrease. In most lace patterns (excluding edgings) the number of loops on the needle, including the yarn-overs, should remain the same at the end of every row.

The charm of lace and eyelet patterns lies in their delicate, fragile appearance, and they are rarely successful worked in heavy yarns. Fingering yarns and fine crochet cottons and silks display them at their best. The needles should be small enough to maintain the structure of the pattern but not so thin that the holes close up. Lace and eyelet patterns benefit from being well stretched, so when you knit a gauge swatch for a design, make sure it is blocked and pressed—if appropriate for the yarn—before taking the gauge measurement.

Lace is perfect for evening wear and for cool summer clothes. It also makes pretty accessories, such as scarves, shawls, and even gloves. It is a traditional favorite, also, for many kinds of home furnishings. A "sampler" cushion, using a variety of lace patterns, would be an excellent way of practising these stitches. Like cables, lace stitches are often worked in panels—horizontal as well as vertical—either set into a plain background or combined with other lacy or textured stitches. (For abbreviations, see p. 141.)

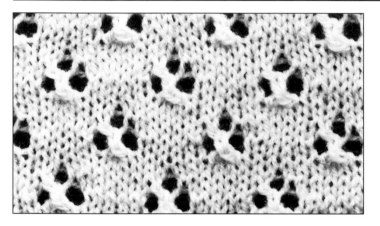

◀ CLOVERLEAF EYELET
Worked over a multiple of 8 sts, plus 7 extra.
1st and every other row (WS) P to end.
2nd row K to end.
4th row K2, yo, sl 1, K2 tog, psso, yo, *K5, yo, sl 1, K2 tog, psso, yo; rep from * to last 2 sts, K2.
6th row K3, yo, sl 1, K1, psso, *K6, yo, sl 1, K1, psso; rep from * to last 2 sts, K2.
8th row K to end.
10th row K1, *K5, yo, sl 1, K2 tog, psso, yo; rep from * to last 6 sts, K6.
12th row K7, *yo, sl 1, K1, psso, K6; rep from * to end.
Rep first–12th rows.

◀ VINE LACE
Worked over a multiple of 9 sts, plus 4 extra.
1st and every other row (WS) P to end.
2nd row K3, *yo, K2, sl 1, K1, psso, K2 tog, K2, yo, K1; rep from * to last st, K1.
4th row K2, *yo, K2, sl 1, K1, psso, K2 tog, K2, yo, K1; rep from * to last 2 sts, K2.
Rep first–4th rows.

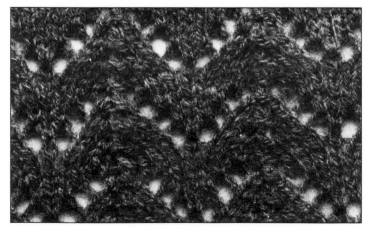

◀ FISHTAIL LACE
This is an old Shetland lace pattern, traditionally knitted in very fine one-ply or two-ply laceweight yarn to make delicate shawls, scarves, and christening gowns.

Worked over a multiple of 10 sts, plus 1 extra.
1st row (RS) K1, *yo, K3, sl 1, K2 tog, psso, K3, yo, K1; rep from * to end.
2nd and every other row P to end.
3rd row K1, *K1, yo, K2, sl 1, K2 tog, psso, K2, yo, K2; rep from * to end.
5th row K1, *K2, yo, K1, sl 1, K2 tog, psso, K1, yo, K3; rep from * to end.
7th row K1, *K3, yo, sl 1, K2 tog, psso, yo, K4; rep from * to end.
8th row As 2nd row.
Rep first–8th rows.

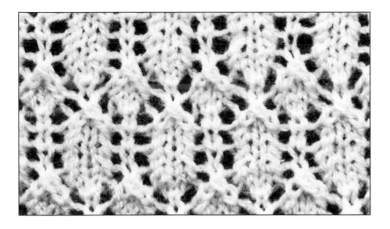

◄ SIMPLE LACE

Worked over a multiple of 6 sts, plus 1 extra.

1st and every other row (WS) P to end.

2nd, 4th and 6th rows K1, *yo, sl 1, K1, psso, K1, K2 tog, yo, K1; rep from * to end.

8th row K2, *yo, sl 1, K2 tog, psso, yo, K3; rep from * ending last rep K2 instead of K3.

10th row K1, *K2 tog, yo, K1, yo, sl 1, K1, psso, K1; rep from * to end.

12th row K2 tog, *yo, K3, yo, sl 1, K2 tog, psso; rep from * to last 5 sts, yo, K3, yo, sl 1, K1, psso. Rep first–12th rows.

◄ QUATREFOIL EYELET

Worked over a multiple of 8 sts.

1st and every other row (WS) P to end.

2nd row K to end.

4th row K3, *yo, sl 1, K1, psso, K6; rep from * ending last rep K3 instead of K6.

6th row K1, *K2 tog, yo, K1, yo, sl 1, K1, psso, K3; rep from * ending last rep K2 instead of K3.

8th row As 4th row.

10th row K to end.

12th row K7, *yo, sl 1, K1, psso, K6; rep from * to last st, K1.

14th row K5, *K2 tog, yo, K1, yo, sl 1, K1, psso, K3; rep from * to last 3 sts, K3.

16th row As 12th row.
Rep first–16th rows.

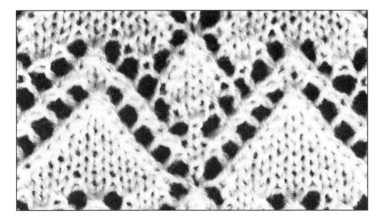

◄ CHEVRON LACE

Worked over a multiple of 12 sts, plus 1 extra.

1st and every other row (WS) P to end.

2nd row K4, *K2 tog, yo, K1, yo, sl 1, K1, psso, K7; rep from * ending last rep K4.

4th row K3, *K2 tog, yo, K3, yo, sl 1, K1, psso, K5; rep from * ending last rep K3.

6th row K2, *(K2 tog, yo) twice, K1, (yo, sl 1, K1, psso) twice, K3; rep from * ending last rep K2 instead of K3.

8th row K1, *(K2 tog, yo) twice, K3, (yo, sl 1, K1, psso) twice, K1; rep from * to end.

10th row K2 tog, *yo, K2 tog, yo, K5, yo, sl 1, K1, psso, yo, sl 1, K2 tog, psso; rep from * ending last rep sl 1, K1, psso, instead of sl 1, K2 tog, psso.

12th row K1, *K2 tog, yo, K1, yo, sl 1, K1, psso, K1; rep from * to end.

14th row K2 tog, *yo, K3, yo, sl 1, K2 tog, psso; rep from * ending last rep sl 1, K1, psso instead of sl 1, K2 tog, psso.
Rep first–14th rows.

◄ ZIGZAG EYELET

Worked over a multiple of 11 sts, plus 2 extra.

1st and every other row (WS) P to end.

2nd row K6, *yo, sl 1, K1, psso, K9; rep from * ending last rep K5.

4th row K7, *yo, sl 1, K1, psso, K9; rep from * ending last rep K4.

6th row K3, *K2 tog, yo, K3, yo, sl 1, K1, psso, K4; rep from * ending last rep K3.

8th row *K2, K2 tog, yo, K5, yo, sl 1, K1, psso; rep from * to last 2 sts, K2.

10th row K1, *K2 tog, yo, K9; rep from * to last st, K1.

12th row *K2 tog, yo, K9; rep from * to last 2 sts, K2.
Rep first–12th rows.

The intricate appearance of many slip-stitch color patterns is deceptive, since they are easy to knit. Unlike Fair Isle and other color-pattern knitting, in which several yarns must be handled simultaneously, these patterns use only one color in any one row. The patterns are achieved by slipping stitches (see p. 111).

When working slipstitch patterns always slip the stitches purlwise. The pattern will tell you whether the yarn should be held in front (wyf) or at the back (wyb) of the work when the stitches are slipped.

If you are slipping stitches with yarn in front of the work, return the yarn to the back of the work before any following knit stitch. When slipping stitches with yarn at the back, return the yarn to the front before any following purl stitch.

Always be careful when counting rows on gauge samples in slipstitch color patterns. In many of them it takes two pattern rows to make one row of knitting. (For abbreviations, see p. 141.)

◀ SLIPSTITCH CHECKS

Worked over a multiple of 4 sts and in two colors (A, B).

1st row (RS) With A, K to end.
2nd row With A, P to end.
3rd row With B, K3, * sl 2 wyb, K2; rep from * to last st, K1.
4th row With B, P3, * sl 2 wyf, P2; rep from * to last st, P1.
5th–6th rows As first–2nd rows.
7th row With B, K1, * sl 2 wyb, K2; rep from * to last 3 sts, sl 2 wyb, K1.
8th row With B, P1, * sl 2 wyf, P2; rep from * to last 3 sts, sl 2, P1.
Rep first–8th rows.

RIDGE CHECK ▶

Worked over a multiple of 4 sts, plus 3 extra, and in two colors (A, B).

1st row (WS) With A, P to end.
2nd row With B, K3, * sl 1 wyb, K3; rep from * to end.
3rd row With B, P3, * sl 1 wyf, P3; rep from * to end.
4th row As 2nd row.
5th row With B, P to end.
6th–8th rows With A, as 2nd–4th rows.
Rep first–8th rows.

◀ THREE-COLOR STRIPE

Worked over a multiple of 4 sts, plus 3 extra, and in three colors (A, B, C).

1st row (RS) With A, K to end.
2nd row With A, P to end.
3rd row With B, K3, * sl 1 wyb, K3; rep from * to end.
4th row With B, P3, * sl 1 wyf, P3; rep from * to end.
5th row With C, K1, * sl 1 wyb, K3; rep from * to last 2 sts, sl 1 wyb, K1.
6th row With C, P1, * sl 1 wyf, P3; rep from * to last 2 sts, sl 1 wyf, P1.
7th–8th rows With B, as 3rd–4th rows.
9th row With A, as 5th row.
10th row With A, P1, * sl 1 wyf, P3; rep from * to last 2 sts, sl 1, P1.
Rep first–10th rows.

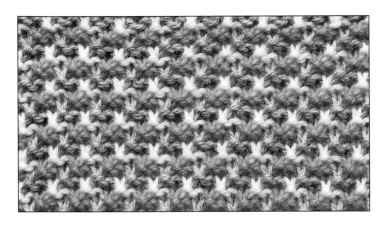

◄ THREE-COLOR TWEED

THREE-COLOR TWEED

Worked over a multiple of 3 sts, plus 1 extra, and in three colors (A, B, C).

1st row (WS) With A, K to end.
2nd row With B, K3, * sl 1 wyb, K2; rep from * to last st, K1.
3rd row With B, K3, * sl 1 wyf, K2; rep from * to last st, K1.
4th row With C, * K2, sl 1 wyb; rep from * to last st, K1.
5th row With C, K1, * sl 1 wyf, K2; rep from * to end.
6th row With A, K1, * sl 1 wyb, K2; rep from * to end.
7th row With A, * K2, sl 1 wyf, rep from * to last st, K1.
Rep 2nd–7th rows.

CHAIN STITCH ►

Worked over a multiple of 8 sts, plus 6 extra, and in three colors (A, B, C).

1st row (RS) With A, K to end.
2nd row With A, P to end.
3rd–4th rows With B, K to end.
5th row With A, K6, * sl 2 wyb, K6; rep from * to end.
6th row With A, P6, * sl 2 wyf, P6; rep from * to end.
7th row With B, as 5th row.
8th row With B, K to end.
9th–10th rows As first–2nd rows.
11th–12th rows With C, K to end.
13th row With A, K2, * sl 2 wyb, K6; rep from * to last 4 sts, sl 2 wyb, K2.
14th row With A, P2, * sl 2 wyf, P6; rep from * to last 4 sts, sl 2 wyf, P2.
15th row With C, as 13th row.
16th row With C, K to end.
Rep first–16th rows.

◄ TWO-COLOR TWEED

TWO-COLOR TWEED

Worked over a multiple of 4 sts, plus 3 extra, and in two colors (A, B).
Cast on in B.

1st row (WS) K to end.
2nd row With A, K3, * sl 1 wyb, K3; rep from * to end.
3rd row With A, K3, * sl 1 wyf, K3; rep from * to end.
4th row With B, K1, * sl 1 wyb, K3; rep from * to last 2 sts, sl 1 wyb, K1.
5th row With B, K1, * sl 1 wyf, K3; rep from * to last 2 sts, sl 1 wyf, K1.
Rep 2nd–5th rows.

MULTICOLORED STRIPES ►

Worked over a multiple of 4 sts, plus 3 extra, and in four colors (A, B, C, D).

1st row (WS) With A, P to end.
2nd row With B, K2, * sl 1 wyb, K1; rep from * to last st, K1.
3rd row With B, P2, * sl 1 wyf, P1; rep from * to last st, P1.
4th row With C, K1, * sl 1 wyb, K1; rep from * to end.
5th row With C, P to end.
6th row With D, K1, * sl 1 wyb, K3; rep from * to last 2 sts, sl 1 wyb, K1.
7th row With D, P1, * sl 1 wyf, P3; rep from * to last 2 sts, sl 1 wyf, P1.
8th row With B, K2, * sl 3 wyb, K1; rep from * to last st, K1.
9th row With B, * P3, sl 1 wyf; rep from * to last 3 sts, P3.
10th row With A, K1, * sl 1 wyb, K3; rep from * to last 2 sts, sl 1 wyf, K1.
Rep first–10th rows.

Knitted fabrics often need edgings. Only a few stitch patterns have a firm enough edge to be left as they are. Among these are garter stitch, seed stitch, and rib patterns. These can also be used to edge other stitch patterns, either by being worked as part of the fabric or by being knitted in strips and sewn on.

There are many other more decorative edgings that can be knitted and sewn on to hems, necklines, armholes, and cuffs, or along the edges of shawls, rugs, pillows, and other home furnishings. These include simple ruffles as well as the most exquisite lace. Lace edgings knitted in fine cotton have traditionally been used to trim white household linen and lingerie.

Edgings fall into two groups: those that are knitted sideways and those that are knitted from the bottom up or the top down. Those in the first group are always made separately from the main fabric: you simply work the edging until it is long enough to fit the corresponding edge. Those in the second group can be made separately, but they can also be knitted on to the main fabric. The length of these edgings is determined by the number of stitches on the needle, so this must be calculated by means of a gauge swatch.

Edgings can be made either in the same yarn and color as the main fabric or in a contrasting yarn. Lacy edgings look their most delicate and beautiful when worked in fine cotton yarns, but they can also be very effective in soft brushed yarns, mohair, or angora. Ruffles work best in plain, smooth yarns, but they can also be striped or color-patterned if desired. Avoid thick yarns, which tend to give edgings a stiff, clumsy appearance.

Some edgings lend themselves to additional decoration in the form of tiny beads, crystals, or touches of embroidery. In general, if the garment or furnishing is rather ornate it is best to go for a more restrained edging.
(For abbreviations, see p. 141.)

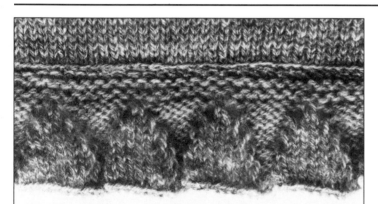

◄ BELL EDGING
This is a pretty edging which is made from the inner edge outward. It can be made longer by continuing to increase on each side of the bells as set.
Worked over a multiple of 6 sts, plus 1 extra.
1st–5th rows K to end.
6th row K3, *P1, K5; rep from * ending last rep K3.
7th row P3, *yo, K1, yo, P5; rep from * ending last rep P3.
8th row K3, *P3, K5; rep from * ending last rep K3.
9th row P3, *yo, K3, yo, P5; rep from * ending last rep P3.
10th row K3, *P5, K5; rep from * ending last rep K3.
11th row P3, *yo, K5, yo, P5; rep from * ending last rep K3.
12th row K3, *P7, K5; rep from * ending last rep K3.
13th row P3, *yo, K7, yo, P5; rep from * ending last rep K3.
14th row K3, *P9, K5; rep from * ending last rep K3.
15th row P3, *yo, K9, yo, P5; rep from * ending last rep P3.
16th row K3, *P11, K5; rep from * ending last rep K3.
Bind off in patt.

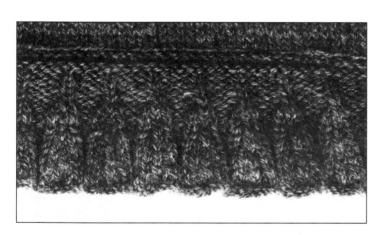

◄ RUFFLED EDGING
This edging is made from the outer edge inward.
Worked over a multiple of 10 sts, plus 3 extra.
1st and 3rd rows (WS) K3, *P7, K3; rep from * to end.
2nd row P3, *K7, P3; rep from * to end.
4th row P3, *K2, sl 2, K1, p2sso, K2, P3; rep from * to end.
5th and 7th rows K3, *P5, K3; rep from * to end.
6th row P3, K5, P3; rep from * to end.
8th row P3, *K1, sl 2, K1, p2sso, K1, P3; rep from * to end.
9th and 11th rows K3, *P3, K3; rep from * to end.
10th row P3, *K3, P3; rep from * to end.
12th row P3, *sl 2, K1, p2sso, P3; rep from * to end.
13th and 15th rows K3, *P1, K3; rep from * to end.
14th and 16th rows P3, *K1, P3; rep from * to end.
17th and 18th rows K to end.
Bind off.

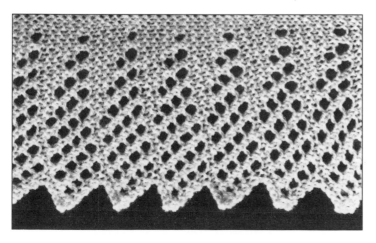

◄ GODMOTHER'S EDGING
This is an openwork edging and should be well stretched and pressed, if appropriate for the yarn (if worked in fine cotton it can also be starched). It is worked sideways.

Cast on 20 sts.
1st row K to end.
2nd row Sl 1, K3, (yo, K2 tog) 7 times, yo, K2.
3rd, 5th, 7th and 9th rows K to end.
4th row Sl 1, K6, (yo, K2 tog) 6 times, yo, K2.
6th row Sl 1, K9, (yo, K2 tog) 5 times, yo, K2.
8th row Sl 1, K12, (yo, K2 tog) 4 times, yo, K2.
10th row Sl 1, K23.
11th row Bind off 4 sts, K19.
Rep 2nd–10th rows.

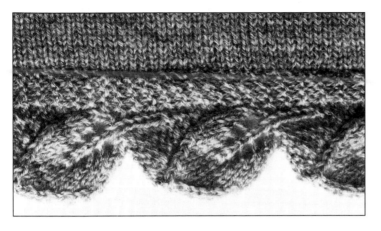

◄ LEAF EDGING

This edging is worked sideways. Cast on 8 sts.

1st row (RS) K5, yo, K1, yo, K2.
2nd row P6, K into front and back of next st, K3.
3rd row K4, P1, K2, yo, K1, yo, K3.
4th row P8, K into front and back of next st, K4.
5th row K4, P2, K3, yo, K1, yo, K4.
6th row P10, K into front and back of next st, K5.
7th row K4, P3, K4, yo, K1, yo, K5.
8th row P12, K into front and back of next st, K6.
9th row K4, P4, sl 1, K1, psso, K7, K2 tog, K1.
10th row P10, K into front and back of next st, K7.
11th row K4, P5, sl 1, K1, psso, K5, K2 tog, K1.
12th row P8, K into front and back of next st, K2, P1, K5.
13th row K4, P1, K1, P4, sl 1, K1, psso, K3, K2 tog, K1.
14th row P6, K into front and back of next st, K3, P1, K5.
15th row K4, P1, K1, P5, sl 1, K1, psso, K1, K2 tog, K1.
16th row P4, K into front and back of next st, K4, P1, K5.
17th row K4, P1, K1, P6, sl 1, K2 tog, psso, K1.
18th row P2 tog, bind off 5 sts using P2 tog to bind off first st, P3, K4.
Rep first–18th rows.

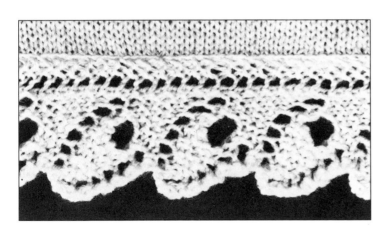

◄ RUFFLES

Knitted ruffles can be made in two ways: either from the base of the ruffle outward or from the edge inward. In the first method you should cast on the number of stitches needed to fit the edge; in the second method, cast on twice the number of stitches needed to fit the edge. In both methods the principle is the same: the stitches are rapidly gathered by mass increasing or decreasing on one row. To make deeper or more flouncy ruffles, work more than one increase or decrease row.

1st method
Worked over any number of sts.
1st row K into front and back of every st.
Work in st st to required depth of ruffle, ending with a K row.
K 2 rows.
Bind off.

2nd method
Worked over an even number of sts.
1st–3rd rows K to end. Work in st st to required depth of ruffle, ending with a P row.
Next row (K2 tog) to end.
Bind off.

◄ EYESPOT EDGING

This edging is worked sideways. Cast on 10 sts.

1st row K to end.
2nd row Sl 1, K1, (yo, K2 tog) twice, yo 4 times, K2 tog, yo, P2 tog.
3rd row Yo, P2 tog, K1, (K1, P1) twice into yo 4 times of previous row, (K1, P1) twice, K2.
4th row Sl 1, (K1, yo, K2 tog) twice, K4, yo, P2 tog.
5th row Yo, P2 tog, K5, (P1, K2) twice.
6th row Sl 1, K1, yo, K2 tog, K2, yo, K2 tog, K3, yo, P2 tog.
7th row Yo, P2 tog, K4, P1, K3, P1, K2.
8th row Sl 1, K1, yo, K2 tog, K3, yo, K2 tog, K2, yo, P2 tog.
9th row Yo, P2 tog, K3, P1, K4, P1, K2.
10th row Sl 1, K1, yo, K2 tog, K4, yo, K2 tog, K1, yo, P2 tog.
11th row Yo, P2 tog, K2, P1, K5, P1, K2.
12th row Sl 1, K1, yo, K2 tog, K5, yo, K2 tog, yo, P2 tog.
13th row Bind off 3 sts, sl st on RH needle back on to LH needle, yo, P2 tog, K5, P1, K2.
Rep 2nd–13th rows.

◄ LACY EDGING

This edging is worked sideways. Ribbon can be slotted through the eyelets if desired.
Cast on 18 sts.

1st row (WS) K6, P7, K5.
2nd row Sl 1, K2, yo, K2 tog, K2, K2 tog, yo, K5, yo, K2 tog, (yo, K1) twice.
3rd row K6, yo, K2 tog, P7, K2, yo, K2 tog, K1.
4th row Sl 1, K2, yo, K2 tog, K1, (K2 tog, yo) twice, K4, yo, K2 tog, (yo, K1) twice, K2.
5th row K8, yo, K2 tog, P7, K2, yo, K2 tog, K1.
6th row Sl 1, K2, yo, K2 tog, (K2 tog, yo) 3 times, K3, yo, K2 tog, (yo, K1) twice, K4.
7th row K10, yo, K2 tog, P7, K2, yo, K2 tog, K1.
8th row Sl 1, K2, yo, K2 tog, K1, (K2 tog, yo) twice, K4, yo, K2 tog, (yo, K1) twice, K6.
9th row Bind off 8 sts, K3, yo, K2 tog, P7, K2, yo, K2 tog, K1.
Rep 2nd–9th rows.

DESIGNING CLASSIC SHAPES

Most garments are based on an assortment of classic body, sleeve, and neckline shapes. By combining these shapes in different ways it is possible to construct an infinite variety of garments. In knitting, unlike dressmaking, the fabric itself is created, as well as shaped and pieced together; and the shaping has to be done as the knitting progresses, since there is little possibility of altering the shape once the fabric is completed. You cannot simply snip bits off to make the garment fit more accurately. To shape a knitted fabric you simply increase or decrease (see p. 108) at the sides of the work. You can also shape by working increases and decreases within the fabric, but this is usually rather more complicated.

The initial stages in the design process are the same whether you are designing with squares and rectangles or with classic shapes: you begin with an idea, which you put down on paper in the form of a sketch; you choose a suitable yarn and stitch pattern; and you decide how your garment can be constructed (see pp. 44–45). With shaped garments, however, you have far more choices than are possible with squares and rectangles, at least so far as the shaping and the construction are concerned.

CHOOSING THE BASIC SHAPE

The extraordinary variety of knitted garments depends less on shape than on the choice of yarn and stitch or color pattern and on embellishments such as collars, edgings, and borders. If you look carefully at the garments you see in magazines, books, and pattern leaflets you will see that the number of basic shapes is quite limited. Most garments are composed of shapes drawn from the following categories.

BODY SHAPES

Straight As the name suggests, this kind of body is the same width from the lower edge to the armhole. The elasticity of knitting makes this shape practical for many types of garment.

Bloused This is a variation on the straight-sided body. Above the edging, which is usually ribbed, there is a mass increase, which brings the width to the chest width; from this point on there is no shaping.

Tapered Here the side edges are decreased or increased at regular intervals to produce tapering either inward to the armholes or outward. The former shaping is often used for flared dresses, coats, and jackets; the latter for close-fitting sweaters and tops.

SLEEVES

Set-in The armhole is shaped to fit a curved sleeve cap. For a puff sleeve the sleeve cap is gathered at the finishing stage to fit the armhole.

Dropped shoulder The armhole is unshaped. The sleeve cap is straight and is set in flat. Sometimes a few stitches are bound off the armhole and the sleeve set deeper into the body (known as French shaping).

Saddle shoulder The sleeve cap is finished with a flap, which is set into the shoulder.

Raglan The body and sleeve cap are shaped at an acute angle into the neck.

Batwing Here the sleeve forms an extension of the body, and the sleeve and side seams are continuous.

Straight The sleeve is not shaped between the wrist and the armhole, which means that the wrist will inevitably be quite wide.

Bloused The sleeve is increased above the wrist to achieve the necessary width at the armhole.

Tapered The sleeve is tapered inward or outward from lower edge to armhole.

NECKLINES

An endless variety of necklines can be devised; common shapes are round (crew-neck), scooped, square, boat, slash, and V-neck (back or front). When choosing a particular collar, make sure to work the correctly shaped neckline for it (see p. 96).

GARMENT CONSTRUCTION

Once the garment shapes have been chosen, the next step—as with simple garments—is to decide how they will fit together and how they are best worked. Some garments can be worked from cuff to cuff (so long as they do not have set-in sleeves) and in one piece. The advantages of this method are that you have fewer seams to interrupt the flow of the work and that you have the possibility of working stitch or color patterns sideways, so producing unusual effects. These gains must be weighed against the disadvantages of sometimes having a great many stitches on your needles.

You can also work a garment in one piece from the bottom upward, so long as the sleeves are not set in and the shoulders are not shaped. Alternatively, work just the back and front in one piece and add the sleeves later. If you are making a jacket with set-in sleeves and shaped shoulders, you can work the back and fronts in one piece by casting on for all of them at the same time and then splitting the work at the armholes. In this way you eliminate side seams, which enables you to carry a stitch or color pattern smoothly across the whole garment.

Working garments in the round (see p. 123) can also have advantages. Some accessories—gloves, hats, socks and stockinette-stitch scarves—are much better knitted in the round: seams on these items are always ugly and uncomfortable. Other knits, such as Guernseys, have tradi-tionally been knitted in the round and still seem to work better that way. It can also be helpful to knit intricately color-patterned garments in the round, since you will thus always be looking at the right side of the work. You can knit the body in the round up to the shoulders, splitting the work at the armholes as shown in the illustration on p. 79.

If the shoulders are dropped, you can also knit the sleeves in the round, picking up the stitches around the armhole edge and working down to the wrist (any color pattern will, of course, be inverted). Alternatively, knit the sleeves in the conventional way on two needles and set them in as usual. Skirts should also, if possible, be knitted in the round to avoid seaming.

Garments can also be worked diagonally—that is, beginning at the lower right-hand or left-hand corner of a shape and working to the top left-hand or right-hand corner. For this, you cast on about three stitches at the corner and steadily increase at the sides to the desired width before decreasing again to the opposite corner. This method would enable you to work stitch and color patterns in a diagonal formation (imagine the effect it would have on cables, for example). It is advisable to work out the shaping for diagonal knitting on a gauge grid (see p. 42).

MEASUREMENTS

After choosing a shape and deciding on the construction of your garment the next step is to take the necessary measurements (see pp. 22–23). The number and nature of these measurements obviously depend greatly on exactly what you have in mind for your design. You may well have to add other measurements to the basic ones. List the appropriate body measurements plus the amounts to be added for ease where relevant. Make a plan of the garment, broken down into its separate parts, and put on it the dimensions of the various sections, based on the body measurements plus ease. It is also useful at this stage to mark the depth of edgings, ribbing, button bands, and any other trimmings.

CHOOSING A DESIGN METHOD

There are several approaches to designing classically-shaped knitwear—all varying in complexity and likely degree of success. The simplest thing you can do is to take an existing pattern and adapt it (see p. 24). Although this may save you much laborious measurement and calculation, it is ultimately rather limiting and, of course, dependent on finding a suitable pattern.

Another easy approach is to use a garment you already own, and which you know has the correct dimensions and fit, as a model. Take all the relevant measurements from this garment and carry on from there. However, this way of doing things will not gave you a true understanding of knitting design. Nor will it give you much scope for originality.

Another method often recommended is to take a dressmaking pattern and construct a gauge grid on the pattern shapes (remembering to exclude seam allowances, darts, and such). If you have some highly complex shaping in mind—such as a huge leg of mutton sleeve, for example, this method has something to recommend it, at least for parts of a garment. Some professional knitwear designers will first construct a "toile" (a muslin prototype of the garment) to make sure that a complicated garment will fit together accurately.

However, for classic shapes the best method, even for comparative beginners, is to combine some straightforward mathematical calculations with working out parts of the shaping on graph paper. (If you want a really accurate visual representation of the proportions of the garment, you can substitute a gauge grid—see p. 9—for

the graph paper, but this is not strictly necessary.) In this way you can best acquire an understanding of what you are doing, of how garments are shaped and constructed, and of how a reasonable fit can be obtained.

Knitting design is not an exact science, and there are many occasions on which you will need to use your judgment in working out shaping lines and details. You can only develop this judgment through the experience of working things out from scratch for yourself. The math involved is all basic and simple (addition, subtraction, multiplication, and division) and there is no need even to attempt to work it out on paper if you have a pocket calculator on hand.

In the following pages this method has been used to design three classic shapes: a crew-neck pullover, a raglan dress, and a cardigan. In each example you are taken step by step through the design process, including all the necessary calculations, and with shaping worked out on a graph

where necessary. The basic principles of constructing various sleeve shapes (set-in, raglan, dropped), necklines (round, V-neck, front opening), and body shapes (straight, bloused) are explained.

The stitch pattern chosen for each garment is basic stockinette stitch, but the same principles apply to any stitch pattern, and it would be relatively easy to adapt these shapes for other stitches once these principles are grasped (see p. 56). The measurements are based on hypothetical body measurements and are *not* intended to provide an actual pattern. If you wish to make these garments you should substitute your own measurements and use the example to work out a pattern that will fit you (or the intended wearer) perfectly.

Simple body shapes such as these can be endlessly varied by using different collars or edgings or by adding extras such as pockets. On pp. 92–97 you will find suggestions and instructions for working some additional features to vary these basic shapes.

BODY SHAPES

straight

bloused

tapered

NECKLINE SHAPES

round

square

V-neck

scooped

wide square

wide V

slash

boat

back V

WORKING IN THE ROUND

SLEEVE SHAPES

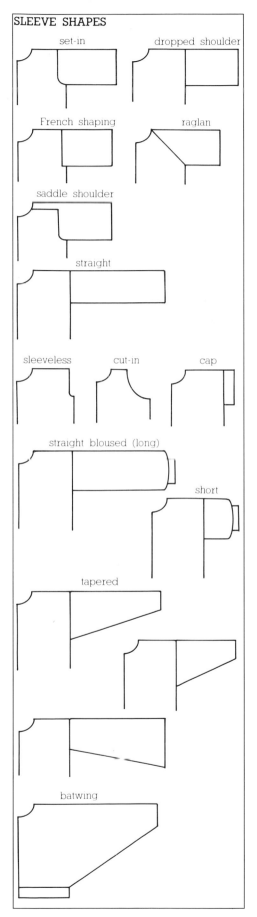

set-in

dropped shoulder

French shaping

raglan

saddle shoulder

straight

sleeveless

cut-in

cap

straight bloused (long)

short

tapered

batwing

WORKING GARMENTS IN ONE PIECE

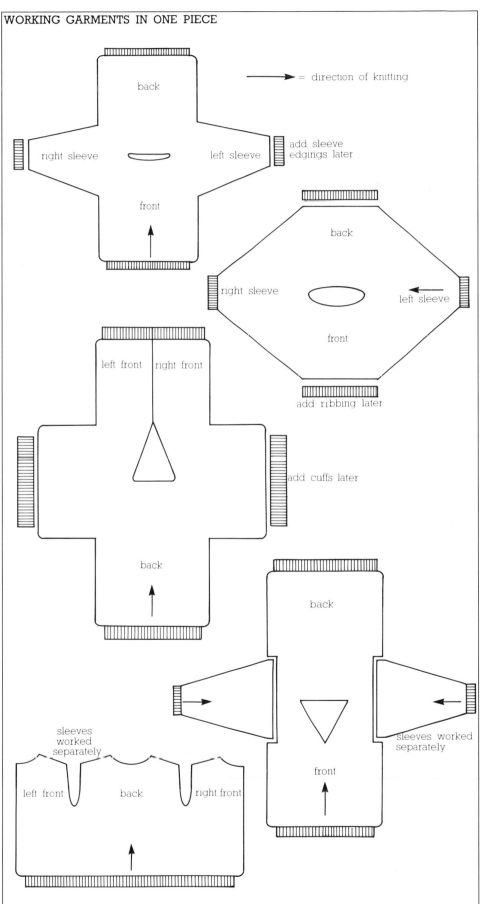

back

→ = direction of knitting

right sleeve

left sleeve

add sleeve edgings later

front

back

right sleeve

left sleeve

front

add ribbing later

left front   right front

add cuffs later

back

back

sleeves worked separately

sleeves worked separately

left front   back   right front

front

CREW-NECK PULLOVER

The most basic of all sweater shapes, a crew-neck pullover is also one of the most versatile. It has a straight body, round neck, and tapered sleeves set into shaped armholes. The neckband can be single or double thickness—only one of the countless variations that can be achieved with this simple shape.

The look of the garment depends a great deal on the choice of yarn and stitch pattern. The sweater can vary from an absolutely plain stockinette stitch garment to an intricate color-patterned one (most classic Fair Isle pullovers have this shape) or something heavily textured or lacy. If the stitch is a simple one, this shape can be an excellent vehicle for fancy yarns, especially slubbed or bouclé types, which can often be difficult to use in more complicated stitches or shapes.

For a first attempt at designing a classic pullover, it is advisable to choose a simple stitch pattern, such as stockinette stitch, and a medium-weight yarn that is easy to handle. Knitting worsted is the obvious choice, although you could try a tweedy yarn, such as the one shown, or possibly a fine mohair. Make things as simple as possible to begin with, since you will have enough to do coping with the shaping.

For this garment you will need to shape the armholes, the shoulders, the front neck, the sleeves, and the sleeve cap. The side edges of the front and back are straight. The shape of this sweater determines its construction: set-in sleeves can only be worked from the bottom upward. Four pieces are required: a back, front, and two sleeves—the neckband being worked afterward as part of the finishing.

Having chosen the yarn and stitch pattern and established the method of construction, you now need to make a gauge swatch (see p. 20) in stockinette stitch. For this example, suppose that the gauge is 22 stitches and 28 rows to 4 in on size 5 needles. Plan to use single ribbing for the waistband and cuffs. For this you will need to use needles two sizes smaller than the main size—that is, size 3.

MEASUREMENTS

The next step is to take the relevant measurements (see p. 22). Make a flat plan of the sweater (illustration 1) and put on it all the measurements as you take them, adding ease allowance where necessary. For this shape you will need the following measurements: bust/chest (if the sweater were long-line you would also need the hip measurement), length from shoulder, shoulder to shoulder, back neck width, front neck depth, wrist, upper arm, shoulder point to wrist, and armhole.

Bust/chest (a) Suppose that the sweater is to fit a $32\frac{1}{2}$ in bust/chest. To this add 2 in for ease and divide the result by 2 to get the width of the back and the front: $32\frac{1}{2}$ in + 2 in = $34\frac{1}{2}$ in; $34\frac{1}{2}$ in ÷ 2 = $17\frac{1}{4}$ in. So the back and front should be $17\frac{1}{4}$ in wide.

Length from shoulder (b) Since this is a classic sweater it should sit just above the hips; make the length 22 in.

Shoulder to shoulder (c) This should be an actual body measurement with nothing added for ease—say $13\frac{1}{4}$ in.

Back neck (d) Measure the required finished width of the neck (say $4\frac{1}{2}$ in) and add an allowance for the neckband width **(e)** on each side. If the neckband is to measure $\frac{3}{4}$ in, the back neck should be 6 in.

Front neck depth (f) This should be the full depth of the front neck at its lowest point (say $2\frac{1}{4}$ in). Add $\frac{3}{4}$ in to allow for the neckband: $2\frac{1}{4}$ in + $\frac{3}{4}$ in = 3 in.

Wrist (g) Assume this to be $6\frac{1}{2}$ in, to which you must add $\frac{1}{2}$ in for ease, giving 7 in.

Upper arm (h) Assume 12 in, to which $1\frac{1}{4}$ in must be added for ease, giving $13\frac{1}{4}$ in.

Shoulder point to wrist (i) This body measurement—here $23\frac{1}{4}$ in—is used for the sleeve length.

Armhole (j) To this measurement—here 15 in—add 1 in ease. Divide the result by 2 to get the armhole depth for front and back: (15 in + 1 in) ÷ 2 = 8 in.

For the sleeve seam length subtract the armhole depth from the sleeve length: $23\frac{1}{4}$ in − 8 in = $15\frac{1}{4}$ in.

For the side seam length subtract the armhole depth from the length from shoulder: 22 in − 8 in = 14 in.

You should now have a complete plan of your garment with all the relevant measurements marked on it. Also mark the depth of the ribbing on each piece. This is mainly a matter of choice, but $2\frac{1}{2}$ in is about average on this type of garment.

The next step is to work out the pattern. It is advisable to complete the calculations for all the separate pieces before beginning to knit the garment, in case adjustments have to be made or problems arise at a later stage. You can either write down your conclusions as a conventional pattern, or map the entire garment on graph paper. It is usual to begin with the back, so that you can work out the shoulder shaping before tackling the front neck shaping.

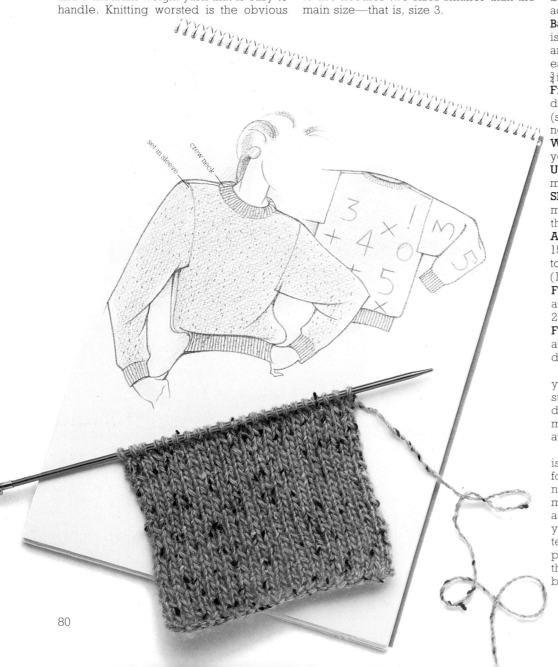

1 MEASUREMENTS AND FLAT PLAN

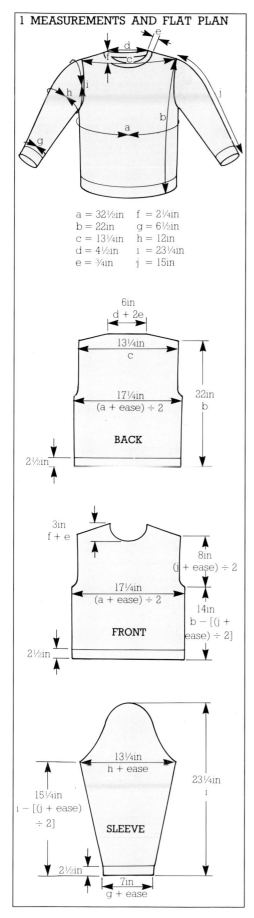

a = 32½in   f = 2¼in
b = 22in   g = 6½in
c = 13¼in   h = 12in
d = 4½in   i = 23¼in
e = ¾in   j = 15in

6in
d + 2e

13¼in
c

17¼in
(a + ease) ÷ 2

22in
b

BACK

2½in

3in
f + e

8in
(j + ease) ÷ 2

13¼in

17¼in
(a + ease) ÷ 2

14in
b − [(j + ease) ÷ 2]

FRONT

2½in

13¼in
h + ease

23¼in
i

15¼in
i − [(j + ease) ÷ 2]

SLEEVE

2½in

7in
g + ease

BACK

Multiply the back width by the stitch gauge and divide by 4 in (the gauge measurement): 17¼ in × 22 sts = 379½ sts; 379 ÷ 4 in = 94¾ sts. You need an odd number of stitches for single rib, so the first instruction should read, "Using size 3 needles, cast on 95 sts. Work in K1, P1 rib for 2½ in. Change to size 5 needles and work in stockinette stitch until the work measures 14 in." This takes you to the beginning of the armhole shaping; it is usual to end this section on a wrong-side row.

Shaping the armholes The armhole shaping for set-in sleeves should be completed within approximately 2 in (that is, 14 rows in this case). Use graph paper to plan the shaping if you find it easier (see illustration 2). To find the number of stitches that must be decreased, first calculate the number of stitches that should be left at the shoulder-to-shoulder line: 13¼ in (shoulder width) × 22 (stitch gauge) = 291½ sts; 291 ÷ 4 in = 72¾, or 73 sts. Subtract these stitches from the chest width stitches to get the number to be decreased: 95 − 73 = 22. Therefore, 11 stitches must be decreased at each armhole. Always take off at least ¾ in at each side in the first row of shaping; the remaining stitches are taken off more gradually, usually on every other row.

The instructions for the armhole shaping should thus read, "Bind off 5 stitches (that is, about ¾ in) at the beginning of the next 2 rows, then decrease 1 stitch at each end of the next and every other row 5 times." This leaves 73 stitches on the needle.

Now you work straight up to the beginning of the shoulder shaping, so the next instruction should read, "Work even in stockinette stitch until the work measures 8 in from beginning of armhole shaping." Again, it is usual to end this section on a wrong-side row.

Shaping the shoulders First work out the number of stitches there should be in the back neck: 6 in × 22 sts = 132 sts; 132 ÷ 4 in = 33 sts. Subtract these stitches from the shoulder stitches: 73 − 33 = 40. Divide the result by 2 to find the number of stitches to be decreased on each shoulder: 40 sts ÷ 2 = 20 sts. It's advisable to try to decrease this amount as evenly as possible and within about ⅝–¾ in at the most, in order to achieve the desirable gentle slope on the shoulder. In this case you should bind off the shoulder stitches within four to six rows. (For an extra-smooth shaping on the shoulder, use the bias bind-off method shown on p. 109.)

The instructions for the shoulder shaping should thus read, "Bind off 10 stitches at the beginning of the next 4 rows," leaving 33 stitches on the needle for the back neck. These can either be bound off or left on a length of yarn or stitch holder until the neckband is worked. Leave them on a stitch holder unless the main stitch

pattern is very loose and open (lace, for example), in which case they should be bound off. This completes the pattern for the back.

FRONT

The sweater front is worked in exactly the same way as the back until the beginning of the neck shaping. So the first step is to work out the distance between the beginning of the armhole shaping and the beginning of the neck shaping. Add the armhole depth (8 in) to the depth of the shoulder shaping (4 rows = ⅝ in—say ½ in for convenience) and subtract the front neck depth: 8½ in − 3 in = 5½ in. So the first instruction for the front should read, "Work as for back until front measures 5½ in from beginning of armhole shaping, ending on a wrong-side row."

At this point there are 73 stitches on the needle. To shape a round neck you must divide the front in two and work each side of the neck separately. The base of the curve for the neck is virtually a straight line, so a number of stitches must either be bound off at the center front or left on a stitch holder. This number is usually about a third of the stitches left for the back neck, which in this case is 33: so the number bound off or left at the front neck should be 11, leaving 31 stitches on each side: 73 sts − 11 sts = 62 sts; 62 ÷ 2 = 31 sts. So to divide for the front neck you should "work across the first 31 stitches, then turn, leaving the remaining stitches on a spare needle. Complete left side first."

Use graph paper to work out the rest of the neck shaping. There are 11 stitches to be decreased on each side (the remaining two-thirds of the original 33 stitches), and it is advisable to complete these decreases before the beginning of the shoulder shaping, so that the last few rows of the neck shaping are straight. Subtract the shoulder depth from the front neck depth to get the distance to the beginning of the shoulder shaping: 3 in − ½ in = 2½ in. This represents 17½, or 18 rows. If you decrease one stitch on every row there will be 7 rows left before the shoulder shaping (that is, 1 in).

The next instructions for the front should thus read, "Decrease 1 stitch at neck edge on the following 11 rows, leaving 20 stitches on the needle. Work even until the armhole measures 8 in from the beginning, ending at the armhole edge." Now shape the shoulders as for the back: "Bind off 10 stitches at the beginning of the next row. Work one row. Bind off the remaining 10 stitches."

The next step is to return to the stitches left on the spare needle, bind off the center 11 stitches (or leave them on a stitch holder) and complete the second side of the neck to match the first one. This completes the pattern for the front.

2 SHAPING THE FRONT AND BACK

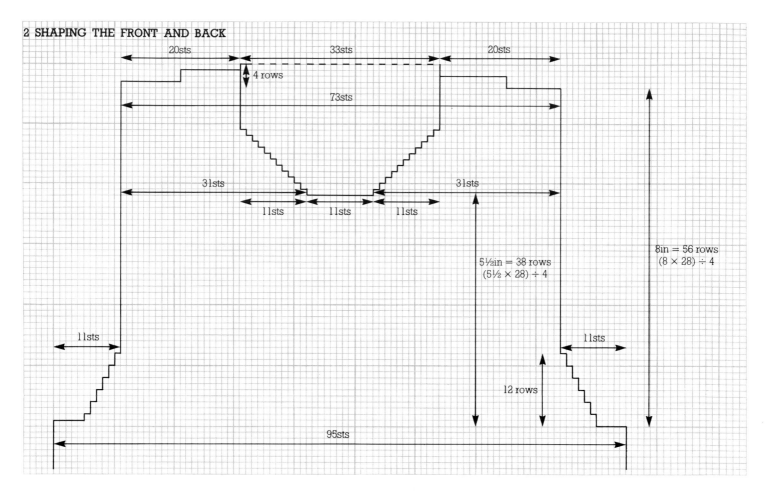

SLEEVES

The wrist measures 7 in, including ease, so the number of cast-on stitches should be 39: 7 in × 22 sts (gauge) = 154 sts; 154 ÷ 4 in = 38½ sts; single rib works over an odd number of stitches, so make it 39. So the first instruction for the sleeve should read, "Using size 3 needles cast on 39 stitches. Work in K1, P1 rib for 2½ in. Change to size 5 needles."

Now you must plan the sleeve shaping (see illustration **3**). The sleeve has to be increased from 7 in at the wrist to 13¼ in at the armhole, but this width should really be reached about 2 in before the beginning of the sleeve cap shaping to give enough room for movement at the crucial point. First subtract the depth of the ribbing from the sleeve seam length: 15¼ in − 2½ in = 12¾ in; then subtract another 2 in, which leaves 10¾ in, the length within which the increases must be made. Calculate the number of rows in 10¾ in: 10¾ in × 28 rows (gauge) = 301 rows; 301 ÷ 4 in = 75¼ rows. Therefore, the increases must be completed within 76 rows.

To find the number of increases that must be made, subtract the cast-on stitches from the number of stitches there should be in the upper arm: 73 sts − 39 sts = 34 sts. Therefore, it is necessary to increase 34 stitches evenly over 76 rows, half on each

side of the sleeve. So there will be 17 increase rows (34 sts ÷ 2). Divide 76 rows by 17 increase rows to get the interval between the increase rows: 76 ÷ 17 = 4.47 rows.

The next instruction should thus read, "Work in stockinette stitch, increasing 1 stitch at each end of every 4th row until there are 73 stitches. Work even until sleeve measures 13¼ in from cast-on edge, ending with a wrong-side row."

Shaping the sleeve cap The sleeve cap shaping must be worked out on graph paper (or on a gauge grid if you prefer). The bound-off stitches in the first 2 rows of the sleeve cap shaping should match those bound off on the body. The bound-off edge of the sleeve cap should measure about 2 in. These rules are generally applicable to set-in sleeves, but the curve in between the beginning and end of the shaping must be carefully judged in each separate case. As a rule of thumb, it should begin steeply and level off toward the end, but the frequency of decreases depends on precisely how many rows and stitches are involved in the shaping.

First find the number of rows in the sleeve cap. Subtract half the sleeve bound-off edge (1 in) and another ¾ in to achieve a neat fit over the shoulder from the armhole depth on the body: 8 in − 1 in − ¾ in = 6¼ in.

Multiply the result by the row gauge and divide by 4 in to get the number of rows in the sleeve cap: 6¼ in × 28 rows = 175 rows; 175 ÷ 4 in = 43¾ rows. You need an even number of rows for the shaping, so round this down to 42.

Next, subtract the number of stitches in the bound-off edge (2 in × 22 sts = 44 sts; 44 ÷ 4 in = 11 sts) from the number of stitches at the armhole: 73 sts − 11 sts = 62 sts. Thus, 62 stitches are to be decreased in the sleeve cap. Subtract the 5 stitches to be bound off on the first 2 rows (to match those bound off on the body): 62 sts − 10 sts = 52 sts. So 52 more stitches must be decreased gradually over the sleeve cap—half on each side. Divide 52 by 2 to get 26 decrease rows, each having 1 stitch decreased at each end.

Start plotting the shaping on graph paper. Mark off the 73 stitches and the 42 rows, then draw lines to represent the bound-off stitches in the first 2 rows and the final bound-off stitches. The remaining decreases must be plotted between these points. Begin at the top by decreasing one stitch on every row. (This is the safest method, although the decreases at this point are often accomplished more rapidly by binding off two or more stitches at a time.) At the same time, work up from the bottom with a steeper line by decreasing

3 SHAPING THE SLEEVES

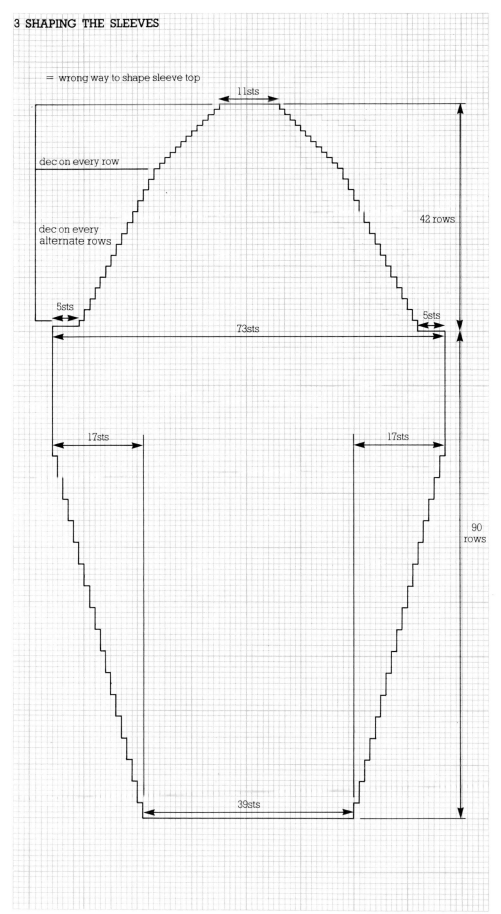

= wrong way to shape sleeve top

11sts

dec on every row

dec on every
alternate rows

42 rows

5sts

5sts

73sts

17sts

17sts

90 rows

39sts

on alternate rows. Aim for a rounded cap and a gentle curve down to the underarm point. If you cut into the sleeve cap stitches too early, the sleeve cap will be too narrow and will pull across the upper arm. If the curve is too convex, you will have to gather it into the armhole. This is, of course, desirable for a puffed sleeve, but in that case you would also have to make the sleeve cap a little deeper. The diagram shows both right and wrong ways of curving the sleeve cap; you really must experiment on the graph until you obtain a suitable curve. In this case, a solution could be as follows: to shape the sleeve cap, "Bind off 5 stitches at the beginning of the next 2 rows, then decrease 1 stitch at each end of next and every other row until 33 stitches remain, then decrease 1 stitch at each end of every row until 11 stitches remain. Bind off." This completes the pattern for both sleeves.

NECKBAND
One or both of the shoulder seams must be joined before the neckband is worked. If only one is joined, the neckband can be worked on two needles, but will then have to be seamed. Otherwise it is worked in the round, on double-pointed needles. Either way, the number of stitches to be picked up is approximately the same. There are 33 stitches along the back neck and 11 stitches along the front neck. To work out how many stitches to pick up on the sloping edges of the front neck, work out the number of rows on each side and subtract about 20 per cent, or one-fifth. There are 18 rows up to the beginning of the shoulder shaping and 2 rows from there up to the back neck (3 rows on the right side)—that is 20 (21) rows altogether, so pick up 17 stitches on each side of the front neck (21 rows × .20 = 4.2 rows; 21 − 4.2 = 16.8 or 17 rows). If the neck is too loose or too tight, unravel and adjust the number of stitches.

The instruction for the neckband should thus read, "Using set of double-pointed size 3 needles and beginning at left shoulder seam, with right side of work facing, pick up and knit 17 stitches down left side of neck, 11 stitches across front neck, 17 stitches up right side of neck and 33 stitches across back neck, making 78 stitches in all. Work in K1, P1 rib for $\frac{3}{4}$ in. Bind off in rib." (If you prefer, you can work a double neckband, making it twice as deep; then turn the band to the wrong side and sew it in place.)

MAKING THE PULLOVER
Having worked out your pattern in detail, you can proceed to knit the garment. When all the individual pieces are completed, block or press them, as appropriate for the yarn. Join the shoulder seams and work the neckband; join the side and sleeve seams. Finally, set in the sleeves.

RAGLAN DRESS

Raglan sleeves are a prominent feature of many knitted garments. They can be used on coats, jackets, and cardigans as well as on pullovers and dresses, and they combine well with a variety of necklines—turtleneck, crew-neck, and V-neck, in particular. The garment used here to illustrate raglan shaping is a woman's dress. The basic design could easily be adapted to make a pullover, simply by making it shorter and working a deeper, clinging waistband at the lower edge. And the same pattern could be used for a girl's dress or pullover.

The shaping lines of a raglan design are always fairly conspicuous, so it is important that they be worked as neatly as possible. Unless the yarn used is a highly textured one, which would hide any unevenness, it is advisable to work "fully-fashioned" shaping along the decrease lines of the sleeve top and armholes. This means that the decreases are worked within a border (see p. 109). The border can be as narrow as one stitch, but sometimes incorporates narrow cables or eyelet patterns. In this example, for simplicity the decreases can be worked within a two-stitch border—that is, on the third and fourth stitches from the edge.

In order to concentrate on the problems involved in raglan shaping, make the rest of the dress as simple as possible. It will have a straight body, straight sleeves gathered into the cuff, and a V-neck. Make it in a medium-thick yarn, such as knitting worsted. Also for simplicity, work the main fabric in stockinette stitch. Once you have grasped the basic principles of this type of garment you can try it in many other stitch patterns or yarns. The important lessons to be learned in designing this garment are the shaping of the raglan armholes and sleeve and of the V-neck. The shaping of a long bloused sleeve is also included.

Having chosen a yarn and stitch pattern and decided on the basic shape, you must work out how the dress should be constructed. In this case, you will need four pieces: a back, front, and two sleeves, all of which should be worked from the bottom upward. Obtain a suitable gauge on the chosen yarn (see p. 20). Suppose that it is 18 stitches and 22 rows to 4 in over stockinette stitch on size 8 needles. You will need smaller needles—size 6—for the cuffs and neckband, to be worked in K1, P1 rib.

stockinette stitch

MEASUREMENTS

Put all your measurements on a flat plan (illustration 1). For this garment you will need the following measurements: bust, hip, length from back neck, back neck width, front neck depth, wrist, upper arm, neck to wrist, and armhole (see p. 22).

Bust (a) Suppose that the bust measurement is 32 in. However, since the dress is going to be straight from the armholes to the hem, the over-all width must also accommodate the hip measurement—whichever is the greater.

Hips (b) Assuming that the hips measure 34 in, you will need to base the width of the dress on this measurement. Add a suitable amount for ease. The dress is a standard fitting, but the yarn is fairly thick, so about 3 in would be appropriate: 34 in + 3 in = 37 in. Now divide by 2 to find the width for the back and front: 37 in ÷ 2 = 18½ in.

Length from back neck (c) This is entirely a matter of choice and styling. Assume in this case that it is 38 in.

Back neck (d) Measure the required finished width of the back neck (it should be a little wider than for a crew-neck) and add the width of the neckband (e) on each side. Suppose that the finished width will be about 5 in and add 1¼ in to each side for a neckband. So the back neck should measure 7½ in.

Front neck depth (See "Armhole depth" below.) This is also a matter of styling and personal choice. V-necklines can be as shallow or deep as you like. For a classic V-neck, however, it is usual (and a useful rule of thumb) to begin the neck shaping at the same time as the armhole shaping. Thus the depth of the front neck is dependent on the calculations for the armhole.

Wrist (g) A standard fitting cuff is required, so measure as for the crew-neck pullover (see p. 80): 5½ in plus 1½ in ease, or a total of 7 in.

Upper arm (i) Assume 12 in, to which 2 in must be added for ease (more ease is required if the yarn is fairly thick; 1 in would be adequate for a sport yarn. This makes 14 in.

Neck edge to wrist (h) This, less the neckband width, represents the sleeve length. Suppose that it is 27 in.

Armhole depth (f) You need to add a little more ease for a raglan than for a set-in sleeve; about 2½ in should be enough. Divide the body measurement plus ease by 2: for example 14½ in + 2½ in = 17 in; 17 ÷ 2 = 8½ in, which is the armhole depth. Since the raglan sleeve goes right up to the neck edge, you must add the shoulder depth (say 1 in) to this measurement to give a total raglan depth of 9½ in. Subtract this from the sleeve length to get the sleeve seam length: 27 in − 9½ in = 17½ in. Subtract it from the length from back neck to get the side seam length: 38 in − 9½ in = 28½ in.

Mark all these measurements on your plan. Mark on the depth of the ribbing—say 1¼ in for the lower edge of the dress and the neckband, and 3 in for the cuffs. Now you can begin to work out your pattern. The dress and sleeves up to the raglan shaping can be worked out mathematically, but you will need graph paper for all the raglan shapings and for the V-neck shaping.

When working fully-fashioned shaping on a textured or lacy stitch pattern, maintain the two-stitch border in stockinette stitch throughout.

If the point of a ribbed V-neckline consists of a single stitch, work the ribbing so that this center stitch is knitted, rather than purled.

1 MEASUREMENTS AND FLAT PLAN

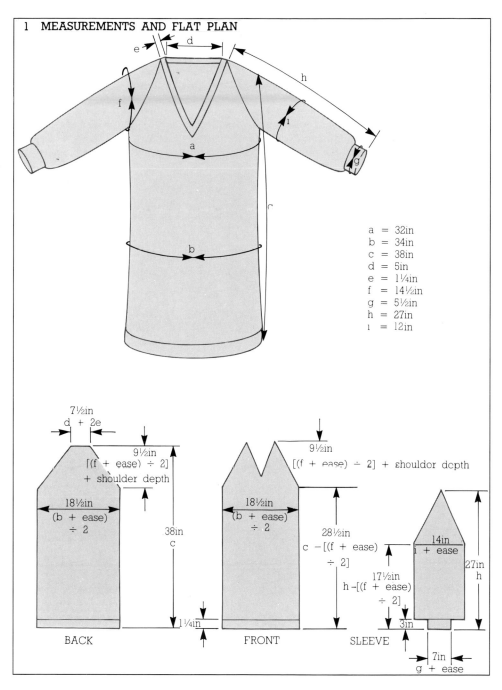

a = 32in
b = 34in
c = 38in
d = 5in
e = 1¼in
f = 14½in
g = 5½in
h = 27in
i = 12in

7½in
d + 2e

9½in
[(f + ease) ÷ 2] + shoulder depth

18½in
(b + ease) ÷ 2

38in
c

1¼in

BACK

9½in
[(f + ease) ÷ 2] + shoulder depth

18½in
(b + ease) ÷ 2

28½in
c −[(f + ease) ÷ 2]

17½in
h −[(f + ease) ÷ 2]

3in

FRONT

14in
i + ease

27in
h

3in

SLEEVE

7in
g + ease

BACK

To find the number of cast-on stitches, multiply the width by the stitch gauge and divide by 4 in (the gauge measurement): 18½ in × 18 sts = 333 sts; 333 ÷ 4 in = 83¼, or 84 sts. The ribbing at the lower edge of a dress should not pull in, as it does on a pullover or jacket, so use the larger size needles for the ribbing on the back and front. The first instruction should thus read, "Using size 8 needles, cast on 84 stitches. Work 1¼ in in K1, P1 rib. Work in stockinette stitch until back measures 28½ in from cast-on edge, ending with a wrong-side row."

Shaping the raglan armholes (illustration 2). This must be worked out on graph paper. Mark out an area representing the number of rows and stitches in the dress top. The number of stitches is 84. To find the number of rows, multiply the armhole depth by the row gauge and divide by 4 in: 9½ in × 22 rows = 209 rows; 209 ÷ 4 in = 52¼ rows. The shaping must be worked over an even number of rows, so make this 52 rows to the back neck.

Next mark the number of stitches in the back neck on the graph paper. Multiply the width of the back neck by the stitch gauge and divide by 4 in: 7½ in × 18 sts = 135 sts; 135 ÷ 4 in = 33¾ sts. Therefore the number of stitches that should be left at the back neck is 34. The total number of stitches to be decreased is 50 (84 sts − 34 sts). You will need to decrease 25 stitches on each side.

Raglan shaping must be worked as evenly as possible over the entire depth of the armhole. The shaping must go right to the top in as straight a line as possible. There are two ways you can do this. You can plot the line on the graph paper as for a set-in sleeve top (see p. 81), using trial and error until you reach a satisfactory solution, or you can draw a straight line between the beginning of the armhole shaping and the back neck and plot where it crosses the grid lines. To begin, divide the number of rows by the number of decreases to get a rough idea of the kinds of intervals that will be necessary: 52 rows ÷ 25 sts = 2.08 rows. Therefore, decreases will need to be worked approximately every two rows.

Whichever method you use, it is best to begin at the top and work downward, because it is much more important that the shaping be smooth at the upper end of the seam. Also, if it helps, you can bind off several stitches on the first two rows. In this case, the most satisfactory solution is to decrease one stitch at each end of the first row, then on the following 4th row, and then on all the following alternate rows. These decreases must be placed within a two-stitch border and they must also be matched (see p. 109); that is, you work different types of decreases at the begin-nings and ends of rows to make the shaping line neat and attractive. So the first row of the shaping for the raglan armholes will read as follows: "Next row: K2, sl 1, K1, psso, K to last 4 sts, K2 tog, K2."

This row is repeated at the appropriate intervals (see above) until 34 stitches remain. Always end the decreases with a wrong-side row, so that the stitches can be left on a stitch holder in the correct position for knitting into the neckband. This completes the pattern for the back.

FRONT

The front is worked in exactly the same way as the back up to the beginning of the raglan armhole shaping. The armhole shaping is also the same as on the back, but the V-neck must be worked at the same time. This can be plotted on the same graph as was used for the armhole shaping (illustration 2).

Find the center of the front and mark it. In this case there is an even number of stitches, so the point of the V can either consist of two stitches or lie between two stitches (if there is an odd number of stitches across the front, the point of the V consists of a single stitch). The shoulder must end in a point—that is, a single stitch.

The neck shaping should go as smoothly as possible toward the top, losing half the number of back neck stitches minus 2 (the top shoulder stitches) on each side of the V: 34 sts − 2 sts = 32 sts; 32 ÷ 2 = 16 sts. Begin at the point of the V, since this is where the shaping must be smoothest. Divide the number of rows by the number of decreases to provide a starting point: 52 rows ÷ 16 sts = 3.25 rows. Or work on the graph by trial and error until you find a satisfactory solution. In this case, if you leave your center 2 stitches on a safety pin and decrease one stitch at the neck edge on every 3rd row, you will have several rows straight at the top of the neck, which will help the neckline to lie flat at that point. The neckline decreases can be fully fashioned, like the armhole decreases, or they can be worked on the last two stitches of the row. Naturally, the armhole shaping (already worked out for the back) must be maintained at the same time as the neck shaping is worked.

SLEEVES

To find the number of cast-on stitches, multiply the wrist width plus ease by the stitch gauge and divide by 4 in (the gauge measurement): 7 in × 18 sts = 126 sts; 126 ÷ 4 in = 31½ sts. So you need to cast on 32 stitches, this time using the smaller size needle: "Using size 6 needles, cast on 32 stitches and work 3 in in K1, P1 rib." Since the sleeve is to be bloused above the cuff, the stitches must be increased at this point to make up the upper arm width. Multiply the upper arm width plus ease by the stitch gauge and divide by 4 in: 14 in × 18 sts = 252 sts; 252 ÷ 4 in = 63 sts. However, you need to have an even number of stitches to begin shaping the raglan top, so make it 64 stitches.

To increase 32 stitches to 64 stitches you can simply work into the front and back of each stitch. (For working increases that are separated by intervals, see p. 91.) Then change to size 8 needles and work in stockinette stitch until the sleeve measures 17½ in, again ending with a wrong-side row.

Shaping the raglan sleeve top (illustration 3) This is worked over the same number of rows as the back and front, so mark out an area 52 rows by 64 stitches on graph paper. For a neat effect, the sleeve top can be decreased up to the last 2 stitches, which are slipped on to a safety pin and later picked up for working the neckband. Altogether, then, you need to lose 62 stitches over the 52 rows, half of them on each side of the sleeve top.

You should begin with the same pattern of decreases as for the back and front (especially if you have bound off several stitches). Again, plot a suitable decrease line, keeping it as smooth as possible. In this case you can decrease in the same way as on the back until there are 26 stitches left, then decrease on every row until 2 stitches remain.

As on the back and front, these decreases must be worked within a border and matched. On wrong-side rows work purlwise decreases as follows: "P2, P2 tog, P to last 4 sts, P2 tog tbl, P2." Leave the last 2 stitches on a safety pin. This completes the pattern for the sleeve. Both sleeves are made in the same way.

NECKBAND

Three of the raglan seams must be joined before the neckband is worked; the left back seam is left open. To work out approximately how many stitches to pick up along the sloping sides of the neck, subtract about 20 per cent from the number of rows: 52 rows × .20 = 10.4 rows; 52 rows − 10.4 rows = 41.6 or 42 rows. Therefore, you should pick up 42 stitches along each side. If the neckband is too loose or too tight you can unravel and re-knit it.

Instructions for working the neckband should thus read, "Using size 6 needles, with right side of work facing, K the 2 stitches left on a pin at the top of the left sleeve, then pick up and K 42 stitches down the left side of the neck, K the 2 stitches left on a pin at center front (mark these stitches), pick up and K 42 stitches up the right side of the neck, K the 2 stitches left on a pin at the top of the right sleeve, then K across the 34 stitches left for back neck, making 124 stitches in all." (To obtain an odd number of stitches for single rib, reduce the stitches on one side of the V to 41.)

2 RAGLAN ARMHOLE AND V-NECK SHAPING

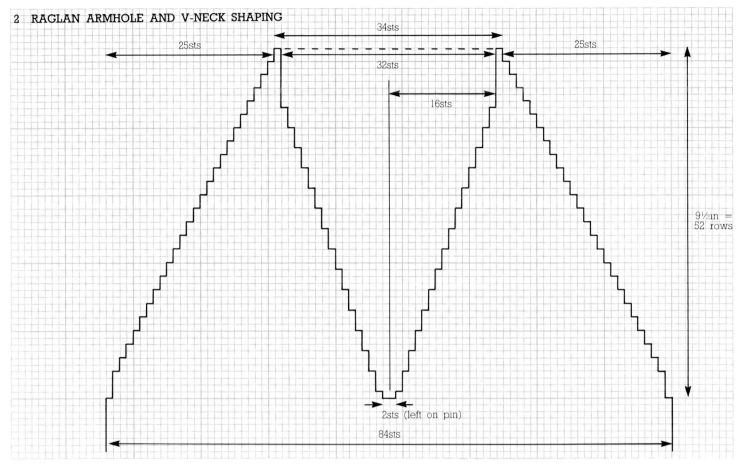

34sts

25sts

25sts

32sts

16sts

9½in = 52 rows

2sts (left on pin)

84sts

The neckband is worked in K1, P1 rib, but in order for it to lie flat it must be shaped at the center front by decreasing on each side of the point as follows: "1st row (WS): Rib to within 2 sts of marked sts, P2 tog, P2, P2 tog tbl, rib to end. 2nd row: Rib to within 2 sts of marked sts, sl 1, K1, psso, K2, K2 tog, rib to end."

These two rows should be repeated until the neckbank measures 1¼in. Bind off in rib, working decreases on the bound-off row as before.

MAKING THE DRESS

Knit the sections of the dress, following your instructions. Block or press the completed sections. Join three of the raglan seams, leaving the back left seam open, and work the neckband. Finally, join the left back raglan seam, then the side and sleeve seams.

3 RAGLAN SLEEVE TOP SHAPING

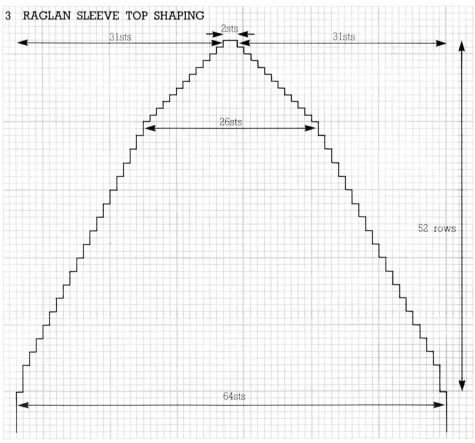

2sts

31sts

31sts

26sts

52 rows

64sts

CLASSIC CARDIGAN

A cardigan is a useful and versatile garment. It is basically a sweater with a front opening of some kind, usually placed centrally. Sometimes the opening goes straight up to the neck (closed with buttons or a zipper, for example), but often the upper part of the opening slopes outward to form a V-neck. Exactly where this slope begins is a matter of choice and styling. It can begin as far down as the waist or only an inch or two below the neck. More often it begins at about the same level as the armhole shaping.

The woman's cardigan used as an example here has a V-neck that begins about ¾ in below the armhole. The sleeves are set in with French shaping, which makes them slightly dropped. The body and sleeves are slightly bloused above the ribbing, and the front opening is closed with buttons.

Because this cardigan is intended to be a light-weight garment that can be worn indoors, over a blouse, for example, it is designed for a sport yarn. The stitch pattern is stockinette stitch, with K1, P1 rib used along the bottom and for button and buttonhole bands. The key problems to solve in this garment are: shaping the front neck, working French shaping on the sleeves, working button and buttonhole bands, and increasing above the ribbing.

After choosing the yarn and stitch pattern, the next step, as usual, is to make a gauge swatch and work out the construction of the garment. Assume that the gauge in this case is 28 stitches and 36 rows to 4 in over stockinette stitch worked on size 4 needles. Use size 2 needles for the ribbing.

There are four main pieces to the garment: a back, two fronts and two sleeves. The button and buttonhole bands will be begun as part of the ribbing on the two fronts and completed separately after the back and front shoulder seams have been joined. All the pieces will be worked from the bottom up.

MEASUREMENTS

Make a flat plan and put all the measurements on it (illustration 1). For this garment they should include: bust/chest, length from back neck, back neck width, front neck depth, wrist, neck to wrist, and armhole.

Bust/chest (a) Suppose that this measurement is 32½ in. The cardigan should be a standard fitting, which—given a fine yarn —would normally mean adding about 1½ in for ease. However, cardigans are usually worn over other garments, so a little more ease will be required. About 3 in should be enough. The total width will therefore be 35½ in. Divide by 2 to find the width of the back: 17¾ in.

Length from back neck (b) This is very much a matter of choice; however, classic cardigans are usually a little longer than pullovers. In this case, make it 23 in.

Back neck (c) The neck of a cardigan should be about the same width as that of an ordinary V-neck pullover—that is, slightly wider than a crew-neck pullover. Make the finished width 5¼ in and add 1¼ in to each side for the neckband **(d)**, making a total neck width of 7¾ in.

Front neck depth This will be ¾ in longer than the armhole depth (see p. 89).

Back neck to wrist (g) For a dropped sleeve take this measurement from the center of the back neck with the arm outstretched. Suppose that it is 28 in. Subtract half the width of the back to find the length of the sleeve seam: 28 in − (17¾ in ÷ 2) = 19⅛ in—say 19 in.

Wrist (e) Assume that this is 5½ in. Add 1½ in for ease, which makes 7 in.

Armhole (f) Assume that the body measurement is 15 in, to which ease must be added. On a dropped sleeve the ease should be a little greater than for a raglan or set-in sleeve, or the sleeve will be too narrow around the upper arm. In this case, about $4\frac{1}{2}$ in ease should be enough, making a total measurement of $19\frac{1}{2}$ in. Divide this by 2 to get the armhole depth: $9\frac{3}{4}$ in.

The total armhole measurement equals the width of the bound-off edge of the sleeve. This type of armhole shaping involves setting the straight edge of the sleeve about 1 in into the body, so the sleeve will be 1 in longer than the sleeve seam: 19 in + 1 in = 20 in.

To find the length of the side seam, subtract the armhole depth from the total length: 23 in − $9\frac{3}{4}$ in = $13\frac{1}{4}$ in. The neck shaping will begin $\frac{3}{4}$ in below this, so that the center front edge will measure $12\frac{1}{2}$ in.

Mark the depth of the ribbing on the flat plan: 3 in for the back, fronts, and sleeves and $1\frac{1}{4}$ in for the button and buttonhole bands. You will need graph paper to work out the front neck shaping and possibly also the sleeve shaping.

BACK

The body of this cardigan, unlike that of the crew-neck pullover and raglan dress, is slightly bloused, rather than straight, so the number of cast-on stitches will be correspondingly fewer. To calculate the number of stitches to cast on, take the width of the back, minus ease (the ease will be added by the increases above the ribbing), multiply it by the stitch gauge and divide by 4 in (the gauge measurement): $16\frac{1}{4}$ in (back width) × 28 sts = 455 sts; 455 ÷ 4 in = $113\frac{3}{4}$ sts. Make this 114 (an even number will make it easier to calculate the fronts). So the first instruction in your pattern will read, "Using size 2 needles, cast on 114 stitches and work 3 in in K1, P1 rib.' (Ideally, single rib should be worked over an odd number of stitches. So you might prefer to subtract one stitch when casting on for the back and fronts and increase one stitch when beginning the main fabric.)

On the next row you must increase by enough stitches to make up the total width of the back, and the increases should be placed as evenly as possible across the row. To calculate the number of increases, take the total ease and divide by 2 to find the amount of ease for the back: 3 in ÷ 2 = $1\frac{1}{2}$ in. Multiply this figure by the stitch gauge and divide by 4 in: $1\frac{1}{2}$ in × 28 sts = 42 sts; 42 ÷ 4 in = $10\frac{1}{2}$ sts. Therefore you need to increase 10 stitches on the increase row. Use the method shown on p. 91 to determine the placement of the increases. In this case—assuming that you are working simple increases—the instruction would read as follows: "Increase row (wrong side): Rib 7, (inc 1, rib 10) 9 times,

inc 1, rib 7. 124 sts."

Next, change to size 4 needles and work in stockinette stitch until the work measures $13\frac{1}{4}$ in, ending with a wrong-side row. **Shaping the armholes** The amount you bind off for the armholes on this type of shaping is mainly a matter of judgment. It depends on the size of the garment and the precise styling of the sleeve. The main thing to watch for is that you do not cut too deeply into the body sections; otherwise the armhole seam makes an unattractive square shape. If in doubt, cut in less rather than more. In this case about 1 in will be adequate. Multiply this figure by the stitch gauge and divide by 4 in to find the number of stitches to be bound off at this point: (1 in × 28 sts) ÷ 4 in = 7 sts. So bind off 7 stitches at the beginning of the next 2 rows, leaving 110 stitches on the needle. Now work straight up to the shoulder (that is, until the work measures 23 in from the cast-on edge).

Shaping the shoulders With this type of

armhole the shoulder seam is not normally tapered, so a straight bind-off is worked on the stitches on each side of the back neck. First work out the number of stitches in the back neck: $7\frac{3}{4}$ in × 28 sts = 217 sts; 217 ÷ 4 in = $54\frac{1}{4}$ sts. Make this 54, since you have an even number on the needle.

To find the number of stitches to bind off, subtract the back neck stitches from the total (110 sts − 54 sts = 56 sts) and divide the result by 2, giving 28 stitches in each shoulder. So to complete the back, "Bind off 20 stitches at the beginning of the next 2 rows. Bind off the remaining 54 stitches.''

LEFT FRONT

First work out the number of stitches in the front band. Either measure the gauge over the ribbing on the back, or make up a new gauge swatch in rib. Suppose that there are 36 stitches to 4 in over K1, P1 rib. In a $1\frac{1}{4}$ in-wide front band there will thus be 11 stitches ($1\frac{1}{4}$ in × 36 sts = 45 sts; 45 ÷ 4 in = $11\frac{1}{4}$ sts).

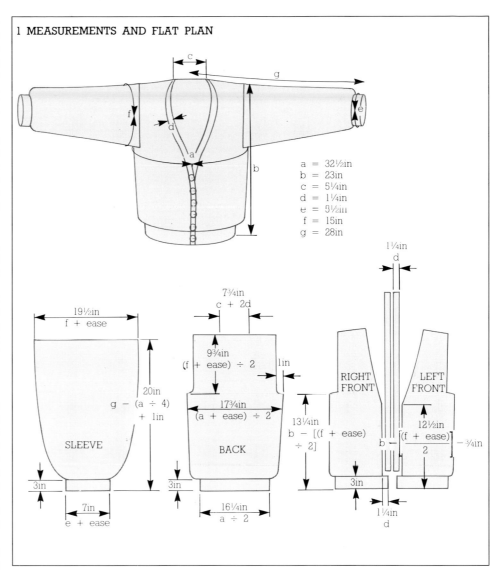

1 MEASUREMENTS AND FLAT PLAN

a = $32\frac{1}{2}$ in
b = 23 in
c = $5\frac{1}{4}$ in
d = $1\frac{1}{4}$ in
e = $5\frac{1}{2}$ in
f = 15 in
g = 28 in

SLEEVE
$19\frac{1}{2}$ in
f + ease
20 in
g − (a ÷ 4) + 1 in
3 in
7 in
e + ease

BACK
$7\frac{3}{4}$ in
c + 2d
$9\frac{3}{4}$ in
(f + ease) ÷ 2
1 in
$17\frac{3}{4}$ in
(a + ease) ÷ 2
3 in
$16\frac{1}{4}$ in
a ÷ 2

RIGHT FRONT
$13\frac{1}{4}$ in
b − [(f + ease) ÷ 2]
3 in
$1\frac{1}{4}$ in
d

LEFT FRONT
$1\frac{1}{4}$ in
d
$12\frac{1}{2}$ in
b − $\dfrac{[(f + ease)}{2}$ − $\frac{3}{4}$ in

CLASSIC CARDIGAN/2

2 SHAPING THE LEFT FRONT NECK AND ARMHOLE

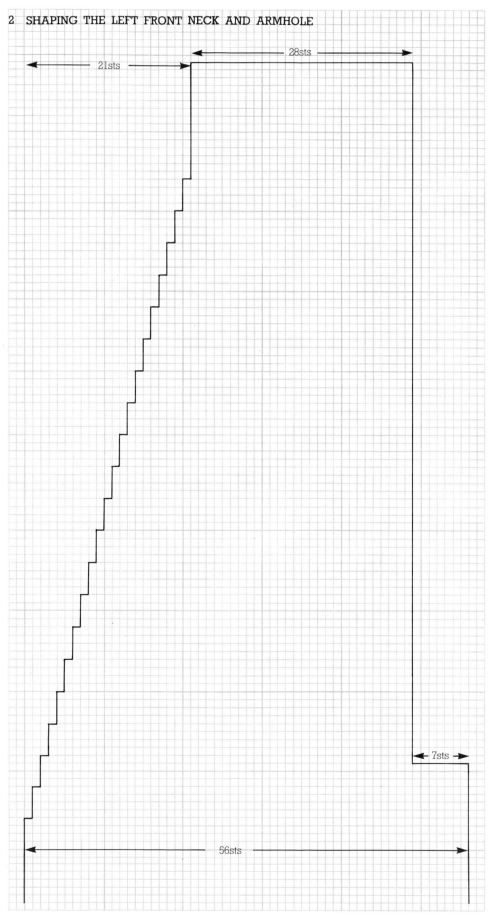

Next, find the number of stitches to cast on for each front, *not* including the front band stitches. Take the number of cast-on stitches for the back (114) and subtract the number for *one* front band (since the bands overlap each other): 114 sts − 11 sts = 103 sts. Now divide by 2 to get the basic number of stitches for each front: 51.5, or 52 stitches. This would be the number to cast on if the bands were to be worked separately. However, in this case the front bands are worked along with the fronts up to the top of the ribbing, so now it is necessary to add the 11 band stitches on to each front, making the total number of stitches to cast on for each front 62.5, or 62, to make an even number.

Thus the first instruction for the left front will be, "Using size 2 needles, cast on 62 stitches and work 3 in in K1, P1 rib." On the next row you must increase half the number of stitches that were increased at the same point on the back, but before doing so you must slip the 11 stitches for the band on to a safety pin. Since this increase row is a wrong-side row, the left front band stitches are at the beginning of the row and must be worked first before being slipped on to the pin. So, on the increase row, rib 11 stitches, then slip them on to a safety pin; then work as follows: "rib 5, (inc 1, rib 9) 4 times, inc 1, rib 5. 56 sts." (See method for placing increases on p. 91.)

Now work in stockinette stitch (on size 4 needles) straight up to the beginning of the front neck shaping ($12\frac{1}{2}$ in from the cast-on edge), ending at the front edge.

Work out the front neck shaping on graph paper (illustration **2**). Mark out the width of the left front section (56 stitches) and the remaining length: $9\frac{3}{4}$ in (armhole depth) + $\frac{3}{4}$ in (additional neck depth) = $10\frac{1}{2}$ in; $10\frac{1}{2}$ in × 36 rows (gauge) = 378 rows; 378 ÷ 4 in = $94\frac{1}{2}$ or 94 rows. Mark the beginning of the armhole shaping $\frac{3}{4}$ in, or 7 rows, above the point where the neck shaping will begin. Also mark the width of the shoulders (28 sts).

Now subtract the number of stitches bound off at the armhole and the number of stitches bound off at the shoulder from the total number of stitches to find the number of decreases in the front neck: 56 sts − 7 sts − 28 sts = 21 sts). Divide this figure into the number of rows to find the interval between the decreases: 94 rows ÷ 21 (decreased stitches) = 4.47 rows. So if you decrease on the next and 20 following 4th rows, there will be several rows straight at the top of the neck opening, which will help it to lie flat.

Of course, the armhole shaping must be carried out at the same time as the front neck shaping and at the same point as on the back. When the decreases for the neck have been completed, work even until the front matches the back to the shoulder, then bind off.

RIGHT FRONT

The right front is worked in exactly the same way as the left front but in reverse and incorporating buttonholes in the part of the waistband that forms the beginning of the buttonhole band. (If you are making a cardigan or jacket for a man, these buttonholes are usually worked on the left side rather than the right.) On a waistband 3 in deep you need two buttonholes, one about $\frac{1}{2}$ in above the cast-on edge and another near the top of the waistband to prevent the fronts from gaping at that point.

The lower edge of a buttonhole must be worked on a right-side row (see p. 138 for how to work buttonholes). The number of stitches bound off depends on the thickness of the yarn, the width of the buttonhole band, and the size of the buttons. In this case, 3 stitches will be enough for each buttonhole. As a rule of thumb, buttonholes should be placed in the middle of the buttonhole band; or, if the button is large, slightly farther in from the edge. This 3-stitch buttonhole can be placed in the center of the 11-stitch band, leaving 4 stitches on each side.

Make one buttonhole $\frac{1}{2}$ in above the ribbing and another 2 in above that, working them 4 stitches in from the beginning of right-side rows. Instructions for the buttonhole rows should read: "1st buttonhole row: rib 4, bind off 3 sts, rib to end; 2nd buttonhole row: rib to last 7 sts, cast on 3 sts over those bound off on the previous row, rib 4."

The rest of the right front is worked as for the left, reversing the front and armhole shaping and slipping the 11 stitches for the front band on to a safety pin at the end of the increase row rather than the beginning (this time the stitches are not worked before being slipped).

SLEEVES

Calculate the number of cast-on stitches by multiplying the wrist width by the stitch gauge and dividing by 4: 7 in × 28 sts = 196 sts; 196 ÷ 4 in = 49 sts. Work 3 in in K1, P1 rib.

There are various ways in which you can shape a dropped sleeve, but since this armhole is fairly deep, it is a good idea to make some of the increases immediately above the ribbing and taper the sleeve outward to make up the rest (illustration **3**). First work out the total number of increases necessary. Multiply the width of the bound-off edge by the stitch gauge and divide by 4: 19$\frac{1}{2}$ in × 28 sts = 546 sts; 546 ÷ 4 in = 136$\frac{1}{2}$, or 137 sts. Subtract the number of cast-on stitches: 137 sts − 49 sts = 88 sts—the number to be increased.

The number of increases you make above the cuff depends on the degree of fullness you want in the lower part of the sleeve. For this garment the sleeve should not be too full around the wrist, so increase by about a quarter of the stitches in the cast-on edge—say 12. These should be worked evenly across the next (rib) row to give a total of 61 stitches. Change to size 4 needles and continue in stockinette stitch.

To taper the sleeve edges, divide the 76 remaining increases (88 sts − 12 sts) into the number of rows to the underarm, less about 2 in (18 rows) to make the sleeve the full width for this distance up to the underarm. The length of the sleeve seam is 19 in. Subtract the upper and lower unshaped parts—2 in and 3 in respectively: 19 in − (2 in + 3 in) = 14 in. Multiply the result by the row gauge and divide by 4 in: 14 in × 36 rows = 504 rows; 504 ÷ 4 in = 126 rows.

Next, divide the number of increases by 2: 76 sts ÷ 2 = 38 sts—the number to be increased on each side, or the number of increase rows. Divide this into the number of rows in the shaping to get the interval between increases: 126 rows ÷ 38 rows = 3.3 rows. So increase one stitch at each end of every following 3rd row until there are 137 stitches. Work even until the sleeve measures 20 in and bind off.

MAKING THE CARDIGAN

Having worked out your pattern in detail, knit the back, two fronts, and sleeves. Block or press the pieces, as appropriate for the yarn. Join the shoulder seams.

Next, work the front bands, beginning with the button band. Pick up the 11 stitches left on the left front safety pin and, using size 2 needles, work in K1, P1 rib until the button band reaches the center of the back neck. The band should be slightly stretched to cover the distance so that it will lie flat. It can help to sew the band in place as you go (see p. 139). When the band is the correct length, bind off.

Next, mark the positions of the buttons on the button band. They should be spaced evenly, with the last one positioned just before the beginning of the front neck shaping. You already have two buttonholes in the waistband; since the remaining center front edge measures 10 in, you will be able to have another 5 buttons, placed 2 in apart. Work the buttonhole band to match the button band, working buttonholes opposite the markers.

Sew the button and buttonhole bands to the front edges (or complete the sewing if already begun). Join the short ends of the bands. Set the sleeves in flat, matching the last 1 in of the sleeve to the bound-off stitches at the underarm and the center of the bound-off edge of the sleeve to the shoulder seam. Join the side and sleeve seams. Sew on the buttons.

WORKING OUT A MASS INCREASE

When you need to increase a number of stitches in one row—called a "mass increase"—you should distribute the increases fairly evenly across the row. It is not necessary to place them with mathematical precision; however, you may find the following method useful. (The figures used are those for the back of the cardigan described here.)

1 Divide the number of stitches on the needle by the number of stitches to be increased: 114 ÷ 10 = 11.4. This means that one increase will be worked for every 11 stitches. (Ignore the .4 left over.) Put another way, there are 10 stitches between each increased stitch (a simple increase formed by making 2 stitches from 1; see p. 108).

2 The number of groups between increases is one less than the number of stitches to be increased; that is, there will be 9 groups of 10 stitches each between the increases. Multiply the number of stitches in a group by the number of groups: 10 × 9 = 90. Add the increased stitches: 90 + 20 = 110. Subtract this from the total number of stitches after increasing: 124 − 110 = 14. Divide this figure by 2. The result, 7, is the number of stitches to be added to each end of the row, before the first increase and after the last one. (In some cases an odd number will be left, so that, for example, you might have 6 stitches at one end and 7 at the other.)

3 Write out the instructions for the increase row: In this example, they read: "Rib 7, (inc 1, rib 10) 9 times, inc 1, rib 7, 124 sts."

You may find it helpful to draw a diagram of the increase row.

V = 2 sts

7 V 10 V 10 V 10 V 10 V 10 V 10 V 10 V 10 V 7

If you are working raised increases instead of simple ones, the method of expressing the problem is slightly different. Using the same example, follow step 1, as for a simple increase, but do *not* count 1 stitch from each group of 11 as part of the increase; the increased stitch is made from a strand lying between stitches. Before adding the end stitches, you will have 10 "made" stitches (called "M1") separated by 9 groups of 11 stitches, making a total of 109. Subtract this figure from 124, leaving 15 stitches, to be divided between the ends of the row. So the instructions in this case might read: "Rib 8, (M1, rib 11) 9 times, M1, rib 7. 124 sts."

Deep single rib collar can be worn turned down or buttoned up.

Ribbed button and buttonhole bands worked horizontally give a firm finish.

Apart from yarn and stitch pattern, the features that contribute most to the individuality of a garment are details such as the precise shape of a collar or the type of edging used for front openings, or the size and shape of a pocket. It is often possible to identify the work of a particular designer by the use of such features. Some will favor crocheted neck edgings, others picot hems or striped ribbing. Others are particularly fond of ruffles, for example, or pompom ties, or wing collars.

You, also, can develop an individual style. Once you have learned the basic principles and techniques involved in shaping the main sections of a garment, you can apply these techniques, and the ones described in this section, to working the details that will give your designs a truly professional look.

EDGINGS

Most knitted fabrics need the addition of an edging to any edge that is to be open—that is, not joined to another piece of knitting. Some stitch patterns, notably garter stitch, seed stitch, and ribs, are firm enough not to need a separate edging. These—especially rib patterns—are often used as edgings on garments made in a different stitch pattern. By contrast, stockinette stitch has a pronounced tendency to curl back upon itself at the edges. Although this is not usually desirable, it can sometimes—depending on fashion—be exploited to good effect. A soft roll of reverse stockinette stitch may provide an interesting variation in texture and shape at a neckline, for example.

Normally, however, the edges of a stockinette stitch fabric—and most other fabrics—must be treated in some way to

Single rib collar is worked in contrasting color to match the smocking on the yoke.

Contrasting cuffs are worked in single rib.

Picot hem adds a delicate touch to the lower edge.

Stockinette stitch worked on the neck edge curls naturally to give a soft finish.

Deep single rib cuff sets off batwing sleeve.

make them either fit the body or hang smoothly.

Ribbing Patterns composed of ribs have the particular quality of elasticity, which makes them perfect for edges that need to grip the wrist, waist, or ankle. They are also by far the most common edging used for neckbands. Ribbing is usually worked to a single thickness and to whatever depth is required. Neckbands and button and buttonhole bands are not usually more than 1¼ in wide, whereas waistbands and cuffs may vary from 2 to 4 in or more.

Waistbands and cuffs are generally knitted into a garment (unless it is worked from side to side or all in one piece (see p. 79); neckbands and button bands are worked after the main garment pieces are finished. You either pick up stitches along the corresponding edge and knit the band on to these stitches (see p. 135) or you work it separately and then sew it on. A ribbed front band worked on picked-up stitches, will, of course, have horizontal ribs. For vertical ribs, you must work the band separately. For a neat effect, work the lower part of such a band as an extension of the waistband (see p. 90) so that no seam is required here.

Ribbed edgings are generally unobtrusive parts of a garment; however, if you wish you can emphasize them in various ways: by choosing an unusual rib pattern instead of the familiar single or double rib; by working the ribbing in a contrasting color, or even in a stripe pattern; or perhaps by incorporating narrow cables in the basic rib—a common feature in traditional Guernsey sweaters. (The cables can, if desired, be continued up into the main part of the garment.)

Borders Unlike rib patterns, garter stitch and seed stitch do not cling, which makes them well-suited for use as borders on edges that must lie, or hang, flat. They also provide an interesting change of texture on a garment knitted in stockinette stitch.

A more unusual border to experiment with is the single cable. Simply work a plain six- or eight-stitch cable and sew it carefully around a neck edge or the brim of a cap, for example, or all around the edges of a Chanel-style jacket.

Crocheted edgings are frequently used on knitted garments. Their use on adults' knitwear goes in and out of fashion, but they are often appropriate on garments for small children and on lingerie. Basic crochet techniques are given on p. 140; you can find patterns for crocheted edgings in books devoted to this craft.

Binding It is also possible to bind the edges of knitted garments. Simply knit a long strip of stockinette stitch twice the required finished depth of the edging (about 1¼ in should be enough for a fabric worked in a medium-weight yarn) and apply it to the edge more or less as you would a fabric bias binding: fold it over the edge, baste it in place, then slipstitch the edges to the main fabric using fine yarn or thread. The binding can be worked in a color matching the garment or in a contrasting color.

Ruffles Knitted ruffles are easy to make (see p. 75). They can be narrow or deep, gently flared or full, depending on the frequency of increasing (or decreasing, if worked from the outer edge inward). A ruffle can be made in stockinette stitch or in an elaborate lace pattern.

Ruffles can be used in various ways. They are especially pretty used to trim round or scooped necklines. A short ruffle can serve as the cuff of a sleeve; a longer one might form the sleeve itself on a summer sweater. You might try adding a narrow ruffle to the inner edge of a wrap-around cardigan.

Clothes for little girls lend themselves especially well to ruffled edgings. For example a ruffle about 1½ in deep could be sewn just under the hem of a toddler's dress to suggest a petticoat.

Hems If you wish an edge to be smooth and fairly firm, a hem (see p. 128) is the usual solution. This type of edging is especially suitable for the lower edges of boxy, straight-sided shapes and of ones that tend to flare, such as skirts. However, they can also be worked as neckbands and as button and buttonhole bands. (When working a hem as a buttonhole band, you must, of course, work buttonholes in both the outer fabric and the hem fold.)

Stockinette stitch is always used for the hem fold and usually for the main fabric as well, although this could be worked in a different stitch, provided the gauge is similar. It can be rather difficult to prevent a rigid, bulky effect in a knitted hem; you might, instead, prefer to emphasize the hem (and so conceal the variation in thickness) by working it in a contrasting color.

When used on a horizontal edge, a hem is normally worked as part of the main fabric. When working hems as button, buttonhole, or neckbands, you must first pick up stitches (see p. 135) along the vertical or curved edge. Any shaping on the top part of the hem must be reversed on the hem fold; that is, decreases must be matched with corresponding increases and *vice versa*.

A hem can also be used as a casing on the lower edge of a full sleeve, for example. Work a couple of eyelets in the top fabric for a cord or ribbon.

Picot hems form a decorative edge ideally suited to delicate, lacy garments and baby clothes. They also lend themselves to further decoration in the form of tiny beads worked into the points (not advisable on baby clothes) or embroidery stitches. Work the embroidery before turning and sewing the hem in place.

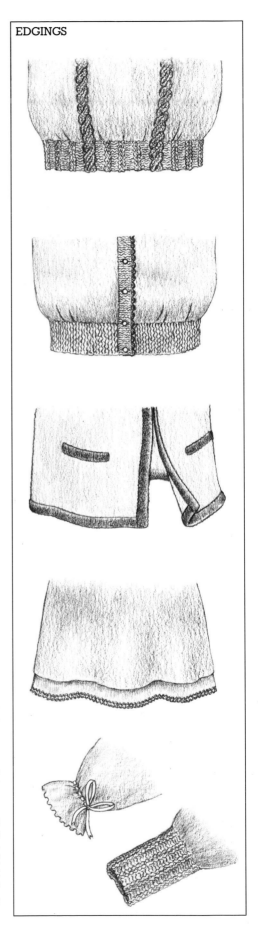

EDGINGS

OPENINGS

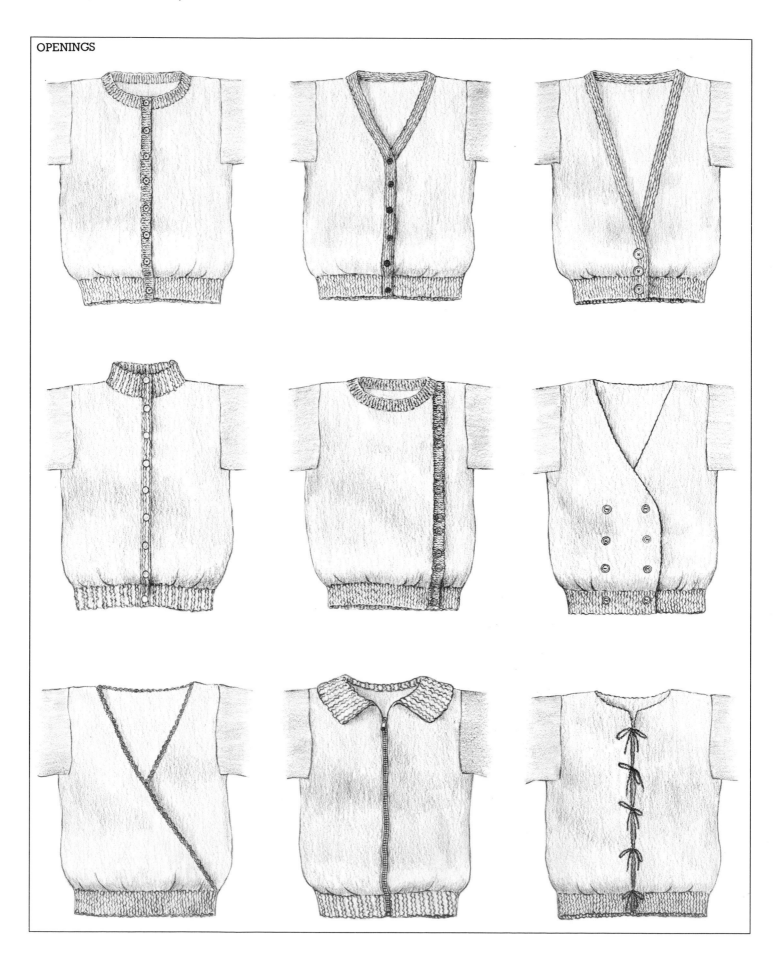

OPENINGS

Many garments have an opening of some kind, in addition to those for the head and arms. Cardigans, jackets, and coats are the obvious examples, but pullovers and similar garments may have partial neck or shoulder openings, either so that they can be put on and removed easily (especially important in children's clothes) or simply as a design feature. Children's garments are often designed with openings along the shoulders and sometimes also at the sides. These may be buttoned, but you could instead use snaps, or Velcro, or possibly ribbon ties. When making clothes for babies, it is important not to include any features that could cause the baby harm—glass or metal buttons or beads, for example.

On jackets, cardigans, and coats the opening is usually in the front of the garment (although back-buttoned cardigans occasionally come into fashion). However, even in front-opening garments there is a degree of choice in the exact placement of the opening. Double-breasted garments have the advantage of a double front layer, which is useful in a winter coat. A Russian-style, off-center opening is another alternative, as are wrap-over fronts, either buttoned at the sides or tied at the back.

The choice of fastening presents another opportunity for diversity. Buttons are the usual type of fastening for knitwear and an excellent—and easy—way to add individuality to a garment (see p. 33). When you are designing the garment yourself, you need to plan the placement of buttons and buttonholes carefully, making sure, for example, that they hold the edges together at key points, such as the top of a ribbed waistband on a cardigan.

Apart from such practical considerations, you have considerable scope in using buttons. Normally they are spaced equally, but you might prefer to place small buttons in pairs up the front of a cardigan. A single, huge button could be used to fasten a dashing coat (if additional fastenings are necessary, use a few large snaps, or waist ties, on the underside). On a deep rolled collar, you might take the buttons and buttonholes on up through the collar edges, so that it can be worn fastened if desired. If you want to use glittery or sharp-edged buttons that might snag the fabric, sew them to what would otherwise be the buttonhole band and apply snaps or Velcro underneath.

A zipper is a practical alternative to buttons, particularly on children's clothes and heavy cardigans intended for outdoor wear. The zipper can be inserted inconspicuously or in a way that exposes it, making it a design feature (see p. 139). Openings can also be tied with a cord, either sewn to the edges or laced, peasant-style, through a series of eyelet holes.

COLLARS

Seed stitch turtle-
neck collar can be
worn high or low on
the neck.

Stockinette stitch
knitted to the sleeve
edge produces a
rolled-back effect.

Striped patch pockets
have deep flaps.

Hem is worked in
stockinette stitch
and slipstitched on
the wrong side.

Ties knitted in
garter stitch to the
same width as the
edging are sewn in
place.

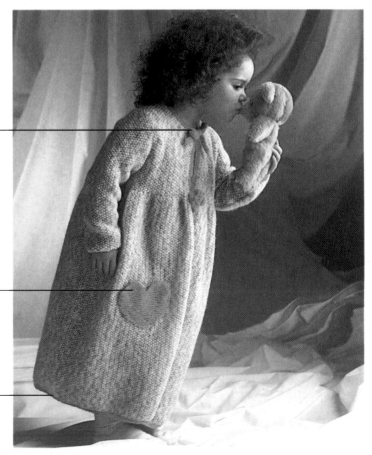

Heart-shaped patch
pocket is knitted in
garter stitch to
match the garment
edging.

Narrow garter stitch
edging is worked in
contrasting color.

COLLARS

A collar is essentially an extension of an edging. With a few exceptions the function of a collar is purely decorative. It exists simply to add style and individuality to a garment. Many people have fairly strong opinions regarding collars, finding certain styles uncomfortable or unflattering. Turtlenecks, for example, tend to look best on people with reasonably long necks.

Besides being comfortable and becoming to the wearer, a collar must also suit the general style of a garment. You would not normally, for example, work a deep shawl collar on a slinky evening dress or a tie collar on an Aran sweater. Some collars are also trickier to shape than others, and this may present problems for a beginner. If you have something complicated in mind, find a pattern with the same design and analyze how the collar has been shaped. Don't forget to look at the neckline; a collar must be matched to the appropriate neckline if it is to fit and lie properly. In some cases the best approach may be to use a suitable shape from a dressmaking pattern (see p. 77), then transfer it to the appropriate gauge grid. Normally, however, your measurements and calculations will serve as an adequate guide in charting a collar shape.

The simplest collars to work are those based on a plain round neckline. For a turtleneck, simply pick up the stitches as for a neckband and work to the required depth. The basic turtleneck can be varied in several ways. Apart from using different rib patterns you can shape the collar gently by means of subtle increasing and/or changing to larger needles. A split turtleneck collar is an interesting variation: pick up stitches around the neck as usual, starting at the place where the collar is to divide; then, when you reach the end, cast on a few extra stitches for an underlap. Work the collar in rows until it is the desired depth, then bind off. Sew the cast-on stitches to the neckline on the wrong side.

A straight collar can also be worked on a round neck. It is shaped like a rectangle and can either be made separately and sewn on or knitted on to the neck edge after the shoulder seams have been joined. A straight collar is sometimes combined with a placket opening at the center front.

The shape of this collar is improved if you taper the points. This can be done either by increasing while working from the neck edge outward or by decreasing, if working from the outer edge inward. As usual, you must first decide on the measurement of the finished edge and find your gauge in order to calculate the number of increases or decreases.

A shawl collar is also easy to work. It can be deep enough to roll over or (less often) it can lie flat. The neckline is normally square or rectangular, and the collar is worked as a long rectangle by one of two methods. In the first method the cast-on and bound-off edges should fit the base of the front neck, and the collar should be long enough to fit up the side of the neck, across the back, and down the side again. The cast-on and bound-off edges are lapped; the remaining edge folds over naturally.

In the second method the cast-on edge is long enough to fit the sides and back of the neck, and the side edges are lapped at the front. The intended direction of the stitch pattern will determine the method.

A shawl collar can also be fitted into a V-neckline with the ends lapped on each side of the V. You may need to shape the ends to make them fit the angle of the neck.

A square neckline can also be fitted with a square collar. The collar is made separately and has a square hole which fits the neckline exactly. After the shoulders are joined the collar and neck are placed together, right sides upward, and stitches for a neckband are picked up through both thicknesses. When working the neckband, miter the corners by decreasing one stitch on each side of the corner stitch on every other row (this may need to be adjusted).

Another simple collar that can be adapted to fit various necklines is a tie collar. Simply knit a strip of fabric as wide or narrow as you like, but considerably longer than the neckline. Sew the strip to the neck edge, placing the ends at the front—or perhaps at the shoulder, or center back. Tie the ends as you please.

Coats and cardigans can also take a variety of collars, ranging from slightly deeper versions of a neckband to huge cape-like structures. A deep button-through, roll-over collar provides extra warmth, as well as style, on a winter coat.

A V-necked cardigan can be finished with a shawl collar, but this is somewhat more difficult to shape than the versions used on a pullover. The collar is begun as the button or buttonhole band and increased from the beginning of the V at the neck edge side of the band to the desired width of the collar, then worked straight across the back neck and decreased down to the band by the point of the V.

Another way of working a shawl collar on a cardigan is used where a rib pattern is to run perpendicular to the edge. Cast on the required number of stitches for the outer edge of the entire front band and collar (use a circular needle to accommodate the large number of stitches). Work in the chosen rib pattern until the band is the required depth for the front edges, then bind off the stitches for the bands and gradually shape the collar by binding off a few stitches at a time on subsequent rows until the maximum depth has been reached. Bind off the remaining stitches. Sew the bound-off edge to the garment.

POCKETS

Pockets can be inserted into garments in various ways (see p. 130). The most common are those in which the pocket opening is either horizontal or vertical. The two other main categories of pocket are patch pockets, which consist of a pocket shape sewn on to the garment either invisibly or decoratively, and side seam pockets, which consist of a pocket "bag" inserted into the side seam of a garment.

Pockets can be worked on many types of garment including dresses and pullovers, but they appear most commonly on jackets, coats, and cardigans. Most coats and jackets need pockets of one kind or another (for hands, purses, handkerchiefs, and so on). On a short cardigan a pocket is more decorative than functional, but a cardigan that reaches below the hip bone will usually benefit from a pocket.

Your approach to pockets can be either restrained or extravert. A pocket itself can be a striking, or amusing, decorative feature, or it can be barely visible. The most inconspicuous pocket is the side seam pocket. Without an edging this is hardly noticeable. The pocket "bag," which is usually rectangular but can be shaped, should not descend below the top of the rib. If it is rectangular, knit it in one piece and fold it in half, thus eliminating one seam.

Pockets that are inserted into the body of the garment, whether vertically or horizontally, are much more visible by virtue of the pocket edgings. It is usual to link these edgings visually with those on the front opening, and possibly also with the cuffs and waistband, by working them in the same stitch and/or color pattern. Sometimes these edgings are buttoned on to the main fabric. A flap can be worked on the pocket edge or worked separately and sewn to the main fabric so as to cover the pocket. Or the pocket opening can be closed with a short zipper.

Patch pockets are the most obviously decorative kind of pocket. These can be made in an entirely different yarn or stitch pattern from the rest of the garment. Or they can incorporate motifs, initials, or color patterns. On a horizontally-striped garment, work vertical stripes on the pocket and vice versa. Patch pockets need not be square or rectangular: try circles, hexagons, diamonds, or triangles. Work animal or flower pockets for children's garments. The way the pocket is attached can be another decorative feature. The Swiss darning method shown on p. 37 is one possibility; others include cross stitch, and blanket stitch (see p. 34). Use thick yarn for a bold effect and, if you like, work the same stitch along the open edge.

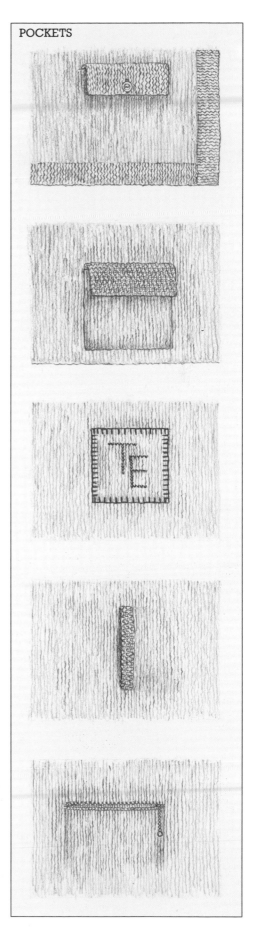

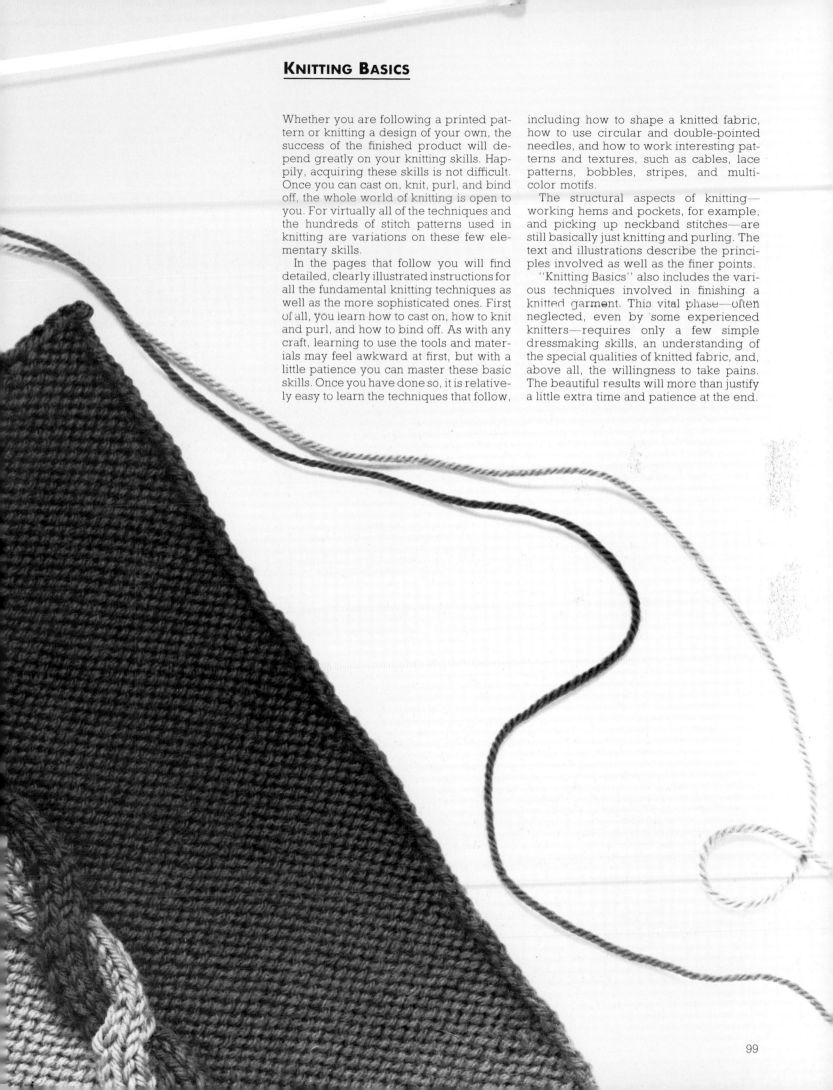

KNITTING BASICS

Whether you are following a printed pattern or knitting a design of your own, the success of the finished product will depend greatly on your knitting skills. Happily, acquiring these skills is not difficult. Once you can cast on, knit, purl, and bind off, the whole world of knitting is open to you. For virtually all of the techniques and the hundreds of stitch patterns used in knitting are variations on these few elementary skills.

In the pages that follow you will find detailed, clearly illustrated instructions for all the fundamental knitting techniques as well as the more sophisticated ones. First of all, you learn how to cast on, how to knit and purl, and how to bind off. As with any craft, learning to use the tools and materials may feel awkward at first, but with a little patience you can master these basic skills. Once you have done so, it is relatively easy to learn the techniques that follow,

including how to shape a knitted fabric, how to use circular and double-pointed needles, and how to work interesting patterns and textures, such as cables, lace patterns, bobbles, stripes, and multicolor motifs.

The structural aspects of knitting—working hems and pockets, for example, and picking up neckband stitches—are still basically just knitting and purling. The text and illustrations describe the principles involved as well as the finer points.

"Knitting Basics" also includes the various techniques involved in finishing a knitted garment. This vital phase—often neglected, even by some experienced knitters—requires only a few simple dressmaking skills, an understanding of the special qualities of knitted fabric, and, above all, the willingness to take pains. The beautiful results will more than justify a little extra time and patience at the end.

The first step in knitting is to cast on—that is, to place a given number of stitches on the needle. These serve as the foundation for the following rows of knitting. There are many different methods of casting on. The choice is usually a matter of personal preference; however, since the different methods produce slightly different edges, it is a good idea to become familiar with several of them, so that you can choose an appropriate one for a particular piece of knitting. Five popular and widely useful methods are explained and illustrated here.

All of these methods except double casting on and single (which is not so generally useful) require that you hold the yarn as for knitting (see p. 103). If you are a beginner, you may prefer to ask someone to cast on some stitches to get you started, then practice knitting until you can handle

yarn and needles easily before you try casting on. Or begin with double casting on, then learn other methods later.

The cable method uses two knitting needles and produces a strong edge; it is used mainly with fairly thick yarns.

The thumb method uses only one needle, and is so called because the thumb of the left hand does most of the work. It produces a fairly elastic edge.

The double cast-on method produces the same kind of edge as the thumb method, but it is slightly more elastic since it is worked over two needles. It is especially well suited to left-handed knitters, because nearly all the work is done by the left hand.

The single cast-on method is very simple, but knitting into the cast-on stitches requires a little skill. It is a good method to use where a fine edge is required.

The invisible cast-on method uses an extra length of yarn, which is later removed, leaving a smooth edge of stitches that can be picked up or grafted on to another piece of knitting.

Practice these methods and see which you prefer. For normal use it is best to choose the method with which you can produce the neatest edge, with the stitches not too tight. Make sure to maintain an even tension, so that the stitches are evenly spaced.

MAKING A SLIP KNOT

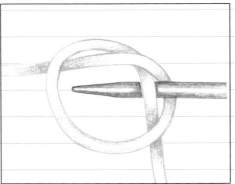

1 Make a loop in the yarn as shown, about 8 in from the end. Slip the point of a knitting needle into the loop and under the short end of yarn.

2 Holding both ends of yarn with one hand, pull the needle upward to tighten the knot.

If you tend to cast on very tightly, use a needle one size larger than you are using for the knitting itself. After casting on, change to the correct size needles.

Occasionally a skein or hank of yarn will contain a knot or imperfection. You can avoid coming upon these in the middle of a row by always rewinding the yarn before you begin to knit. Wind it around a few fingers, changing direction occasionally to form a ball and always winding over a couple of fingers to avoid winding too tightly. If you encounter a knot, simply cut the yarn and begin a new ball. (See also, joining in new yarn, p. 124.)

CABLE METHOD

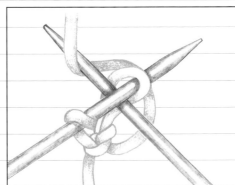

1 Make a slip loop on one needle, then take this needle in your left hand. Take the other needle in your right hand and insert the point through the loop so that it rests under the left-hand needle, forming a cross. Take the main yarn under and over the point of the right-hand needle as shown.

2 With the right-hand needle, pull the yarn through the slip knot on the left-hand needle, making a new stitch. Transfer this stitch on to the left-hand needle, making sure that each loop is facing in the same direction.

3 Insert the right-hand needle between the two stitches on the left-hand needle. Take the yarn under and over the point of the right-hand needle. Draw the yarn through between the first two stitches to make a new stitch, then transfer the new stitch on to the left-hand needle.

THUMB METHOD

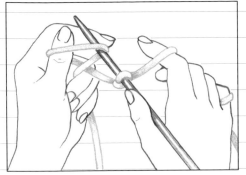

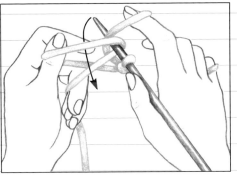

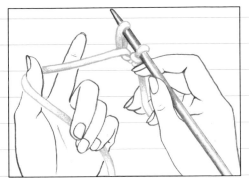

1 Measure off approximately 1 in for each stitch to be cast on, and make a slip knot a short distance beyond this point. Place the loop on a needle and hold the needle and the yarn from the ball in your right hand.

2 Wind the free end of yarn around the thumb of the left hand and hold it in place with three fingers as shown. Insert the needle upward through the loop on the thumb.

3 Take the yarn from the ball under and over the point of the needle. Draw the yarn through the loop on the thumb to form the new stitch. Slip the thumb out of the loop and use it to tauten the free end of the yarn.

DOUBLE CAST-ON METHOD

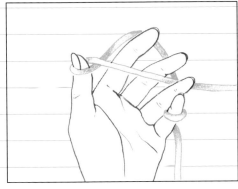

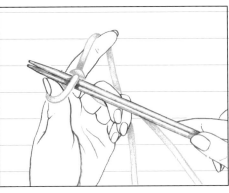

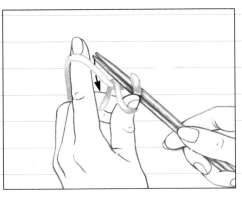

1 Measure off enough yarn for the stitches, as for the thumb method. Wind the yarn around the fingers of your left hand as follows: between the third and little fingers, behind all four fingers, under and around the thumb and back over itself between the second and third fingers.

2 Extend the thumb and index finger to hold the yarn taut. Take both needles together in the right hand and slip them up through the loop on the thumb.

3 Rotate the left hand toward you and at the same time take the needles over and under the thumb-to-finger yarn. Bring this yarn forward through the loop.

SINGLE CAST-ON METHOD

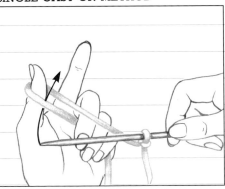

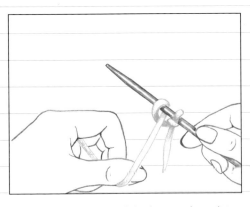

4 Slip the thumb out of the loop and use it to pull the free yarn downward, so tightening the knot on the needles. Repeat steps 2–4 the necessary number of times. To begin knitting, remove one needle, taking care that the stitches do not slip off.

1 Make a slip knot a short distance from the end of the yarn, and hold the working end in the left hand as shown, with the thumb pulling it taut. Bring the needle upward through the loop.

2 Slip the thumb out of the loop and use it to pull the yarn downward, tightening the loop and pulling it close to the slip knot. Form another loop over the thumb, as in step 1, and repeat the movements to cast on another stitch. Keep the stitches evenly spaced and not too tight.

INVISIBLE CAST-ON METHOD

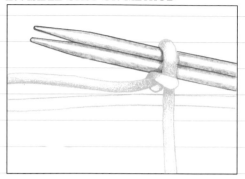 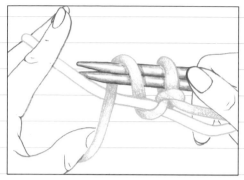 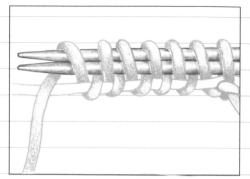

1 Cut a length of extra yarn (the foundation yarn) about four times as long as the knitting will be wide. Make a slip loop a few inches from the end of the main yarn and place it on two needles. Hold the needles in the right hand with the foundation yarn below them.

2 Take the main yarn under the foundation yarn, then up in front of the needles, around the back of the needles, and in front of foundation yarn.

3 Repeat step 2 as many times as necessary to cast on the required number of stitches. Withdraw one of the needles, but leave the foundation yarn in place until work has to be added at a later stage. (See grafting, p. 137.)

CAST ON EDGES

Cable method The finished edge is firm and hard wearing. This is a good method to use when adding stitches part of the way through a piece of knitting (see multiple increasing, *right*).

Thumb method The edge produced by this method is the same as that produced by the double cast-on method.

 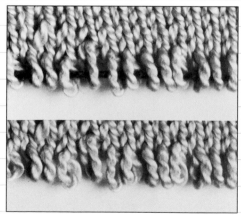

Single cast-on method The edge is flexible, which makes it well suited to a lacy pattern such as this one.

Invisible cast-on method The foundation yarn (here in a contrasting color) can easily be seen in the upper photo. The lower photo shows the edge with the foundation yarn removed.

MULTIPLE INCREASING

Extra stitches may need to be cast on while working a piece of knitting—to make a sleeve shaping, for example, on a simple T-shaped garment. In this case, you must either use a single-strand method of casting on, such as the cable method, or attach a separate length of yarn to the point where the shaping begins, if you want to use a two-strand method.

If you are increasing at the right-hand edge of the work, you cast on immediately after working a wrong-side row. Tie the extra yarn (if required) to the first stitch on the needle. If you are using the cable method, use this stitch to make the first new stitch. Cast on the required number of stitches. Then work across these cast-on stitches and the original stitches to the end of the row.

If you are increasing at the left-hand edge, you cast on immediately after working a right-side row.

The process of knitting consists essentially of working stitches off the left-hand needle onto the right-hand needle. There are two basic stitches: knit and purl. All the hundreds of stitch patterns are produced by combining and varying these stitches in different ways.

Before learning to knit and purl, however, you must learn how to hold the yarn and needles. Various methods are used in different parts of the world; in some countries, for example, very long needles are used and held tucked under the arms. You can hold the needles in whatever position feels comfortable and enables you to knit smoothly, and you can hold the yarn in either your right hand or your left.

The right-hand method, which is used in the United States, Britain, and some other Western European countries, involves looping the yarn around the right-hand needle with the index finger of the right hand.

The left-hand method, which is also used in the United States and in German-speaking countries, among others, is sometimes misleadingly called the "Continental" method. The yarn is picked up from the left hand with the right hand needle. Because the work is more evenly divided between the two hands, left-handed knitters may find this method easier.

It is a good idea to learn both methods, since some multicolor patterns require you to work with two yarns simultaneously, one in each hand.

Note that for either method the yarn must be wrapped around the fingers in some way to keep it at the correct tension—that is, so that it will slip easily, but not too loosely, through the fingers. The methods shown here are among the most popular, but you may find or devise another way that is more comfortable for you. The important factors are ease of knitting and the evenness of the finished work.

In the illustrations below, the yarn is shown held behind the needles, in position for the knit stitch. Only a slight shift of the hands is necessary to bring the yarn forward for the purl stitch. Both of these stitches are explained and illustrated on the following page.

Once you have learned to knit and purl, you can work dozens of different stitch patterns. A collection of these is given in the Stitch Pattern Library (see pp. 36–75). On the following page you will find the three simplest, most common patterns: garter stitch, stockinette stitch, and single rib.

HOLDING THE YARN—RIGHT-HAND METHOD

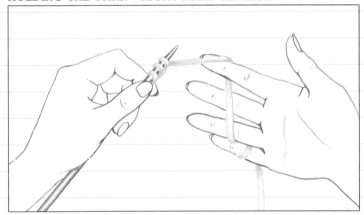

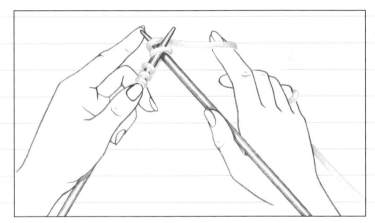

1 Hold the needle with the cast-on stitches in the left hand (taking care that the stitches do not slip off). Wind the yarn around the little finger of the right hand and then under and over the remaining three fingers as shown.

2 When starting to knit, hold the needle with the stitches firmly in the left hand, with the thumb at the front and the fingers at the back. The right-hand needle rests at the base of the thumb, while the index finger and hand slide forward to the needle point to work each stitch. The index finger takes the yarn around the right-hand needle.

HOLDING THE YARN—LEFT-HAND METHOD

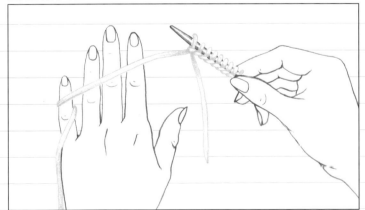

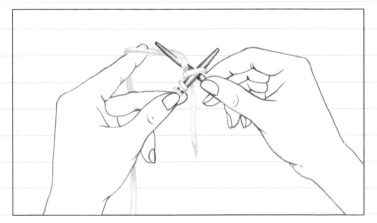

1 Hold the needle with the cast-on stitches temporarily in the right hand, and wrap the yarn around the left-hand fingers as shown: around the little finger, then over the remaining fingers.

2 Transfer the needle with stitches to the left hand and raise the left index finger to tension the yarn. Hold the other needle in the right hand with the thumb at the front and fingers at the back. As the right-hand needle slides upward, the left hand pivots forward to bring the yarn around the needle.

THE KNIT STITCH

1 Take the needle holding the stitches in the left hand. Keeping the yarn at the back of the work, insert the right-hand needle through the front of the first stitch, from left to right. (The needle actually points from right to left, because the yarn twists immediately to accommodate it.)

2 Take the yarn under and over the point of the right-hand needle. Draw the yarn back through the stitch on the left-hand needle.

3 Slip this stitch off the needle on to the right-hand needle. This completes one stitch. Repeat steps 1–3 to the end of the row.

THE PURL STITCH

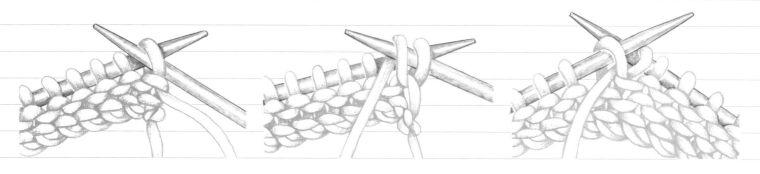

1 Hold the needle with the stitches in the left hand. With the empty needle in the right hand, insert the point from right to left through the front of the stitch.

2 Take the yarn over and under the point of the right-hand needle. Draw the yarn through the stitch on the left-hand needle, still leaving the yarn at the front of the work.

3 Slip this stitch off the left-hand needle on to the right-hand needle. This completes one purl stitch. Repeat steps 1–3 to the end of the row.

BASIC STITCH PATTERNS

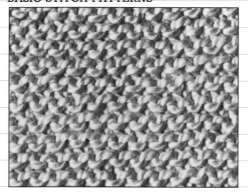

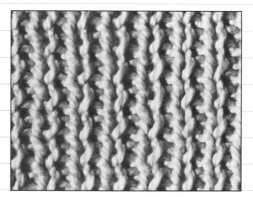

Garter stitch is the easiest of all patterns: you simply knit every row. (Purling every row also produces garter stitch, though knitting usually makes a more even fabric.) Garter stitch is a dense, ridged fabric and is used for borders, hems, and simple garments.

Stockinette stitch is probably the most common of all patterns. To work this pattern, knit every right-side row and purl every wrong-side row. The fabric is smooth on the right side (*left*) and ridged on the wrong side (*right*). Sometimes a design will use the purled side as the right side; this is called "reverse stockinette stitch."

Single rib is the simplest of the various rib stitch patterns, which all have raised vertical lines and, usually, a degree of elasticity. To produce single rib, knit one stitch and purl one stitch alternately across the row. On the following row, knit the stitches that were purled in the previous row and purl the knitted stitches.

The term "selvage" refers to various kinds of edges worked on a piece of knitting while it is being knitted. The selvage may serve a decorative or a practical purpose, or sometimes both. For example, where an edge will be left exposed—such as on a scarf—it is important that it be neat and not curl back upon itself. In this case, a decorative, two-stitch selvage will solve the problem.

Even if the edge will be joined into a seam or worked into later, it may be easier to handle if you work a simple, one-stitch selvage as you knit. On a plain fabric, such as stockinette stitch, it is not usually necessary to add extra stitches for the selvage, since taking one edge stitch into the seam will not interrupt a pattern. However, when working some stitch patterns it is advisable to add an extra stitch to each edge, so that when seams are joined the

pattern will flow across them without interruption. In this case you simply add a knit stitch to each edge on the right side of the work and purl these stitches on the wrong side.

The three selvages shown below are simple ones, used mainly for stockinette stitch, garter stitch, and similar fabrics.

Stockinette stitch single edge On every RS row, slip the first stitch knitwise off the LH needle. Knit to the end of the row in the usual way. On the WS row, slip the first stitch purlwise off the LH needle. Purl to the end of the row. Repeat these two rows throughout.

Garter stitch single edge Holding the yarn at the front of the work, slip the first stitch purlwise. Take the yarn to the back of the work and knit to the end of the row. Repeat this row throughout.

Double garter stitch edge On every row slip the first stitch knitwise off the LH needle. Knit the second stitch in the usual way, work to the last two stitches in the fabric stitch pattern and knit these two stitches.

KNITTING LANGUAGE
Like any other craft, knitting has its own special vocabulary. You will pick up most of these terms gradually as you learn the techniques to which they refer. Many of the terms are normally abbreviated, especially in patterns, where writing out every word and procedure would produce formidably long instructions. A list of commonly used abbreviations is provided on p. 141. Although the instructions in the pages that follow are written mainly in normal English, they do contain some terms and abbreviations you will need to know.

For the sake of brevity and ease of recognition, "right side" and "wrong side" are abbreviated to RS and WS, respectively; "right-hand" and "left-hand" to RH and LH.

The term "knitwise" in an instruction means to insert the needle into a stitch as if you were going to knit it; similarly, "purlwise" means inserting the needle as if to purl (see p. 104).

An asterisk * is used to mark the beginning of some instructions that are to be repeated. At the end of the instructions you will be told to "repeat from * to the end of the row" or to another specified point. Some knitting patterns use asterisks in groups of two or more to indicate repeats within repeats.

Parentheses ( ) are used sometimes to enclose instructions that are to be repeated a given number of times and sometimes to mark off a combination of steps worked into a single stitch, as in: "(knit 1, purl 1, knit 1) into next stitch."

Two terms of crucial importance in knitting are "gauge" and "tension."

"Gauge" refers to the number of stitches and rows produced over a given measurement using specified yarn, needles, and stitch pattern. A full explanation of gauge is given on pp. 20–21; but the important thing to remember when following a pattern is that in order for the garment to be the correct size you *must* obtain the same gauge as that obtained by the designer of the pattern. Any difference is due to a difference in "tension"—that is, the degree of tautness with which the yarn is held and the stitches worked. Tension varies considerably from one knitter to another; however, it is a relatively easy matter to compensate for any deviation between your own tension and that of the pattern designer—and so obtain the correct gauge—by using smaller or larger needles as required.

When a piece of knitting is completed, the remaining stitches must usually be bound off—a process that links them together, preventing the work from unraveling. Stitches are also bound off at the beginning of armhole and neckband shapings and when working buttonholes.

Care must be taken that the stitches are not cast off tightly, for this will pucker the fabric and could easily break the stitches. A loose bind-off is especially important on a neckband, for the stitches need to stretch every time the garment is put on or removed. If you tend to bind off tightly, you should change to a larger needle when binding off.

Several methods of binding off are shown here. In plain binding off, all the stitches are first knitted before being bound off—unless you are working on a purl row, in which case they are purled.

Ribbing bind-off is used on a ribbed fabric—for example on a neckband—and produces a less conspicuous edge than would a plain bind-off. For a professional touch, single ribbing can be finished with invisible bind-off, using a tapestry needle. Practice this method first on a sample piece of ribbing to make sure that you can work it smoothly.

Bias bind-off is a technique used to prevent the "stepped" effect that results when an edge—on a shoulder for example—is bound off in the usual way in several stages. This jagged edge is usually acceptable, for it is hidden in the seam; but the bias bind-off is not difficult and produces an extra-neat finish.

PLAIN BIND-OFF

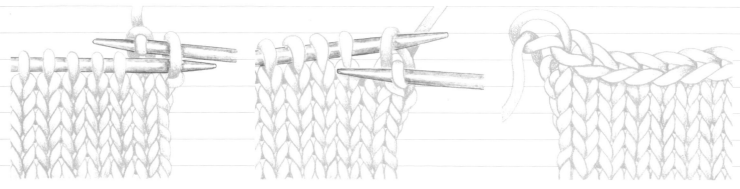

1 With the RS of the work facing, knit the first 2 stitches from the LH needle in the usual way. Insert the point of the LH needle through the front of the first knitted stitch on the RH needle as shown.

2 Lift this stitch over the second knitted stitch and off the needle. One stitch has been bound off. Knit the next stitch, then lift the first stitch on the RH needle over the second stitch and off the needle. The first 2 stitches have now been bound off.

3 Continue binding off the stitches until 1 stitch remains on the RH needle. Unless other stitches remain to be worked (e.g. on an armhole shaping), cut off the yarn, leaving a short end. Thread this through the stitch and pull the end tightly.

RIBBING BIND-OFF

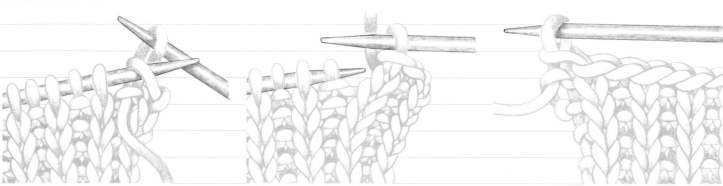

1 This example is worked in single rib, beginning with a knit stitch. Knit the first stitch from the LH needle and purl the second stitch in the usual way. Now bind off the first stitch as in step 2 of "Plain bind-off."

2 Knit the next stitch from the LH needle. Lift the purl stitch over the knit stitch to bind it off.

3 Continue to bind off, remembering to knit or purl the stitches as if you were continuing in the rib pattern, before binding them off. The same technique can be adapted for other types of ribbing; you simply continue in the pattern. Finish as in step 3 of "Plain bind-off."

INVISIBLE BIND-OFF

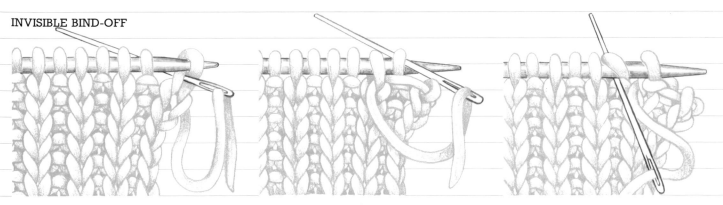

1 Cut the yarn at least four times the length of the row, and thread it into a tapestry needle. * Insert the tapestry needle knitwise through the first stitch and slip the stitch off the needle.

2 Skip the purl stitch and insert the tapestry needle purlwise through the next knit stitch. Draw the yarn through. Return to the skipped purl stitch and insert the needle into it purlwise as shown. Draw the yarn through and slip the stitch off the needle.

3 Take the yarn behind the knit stitch, bring it forward and insert the tapestry needle knitwise through the next purl stitch as shown. Pull the yarn through.
Repeat from * to the end of the row.

BIAS BIND-OFF

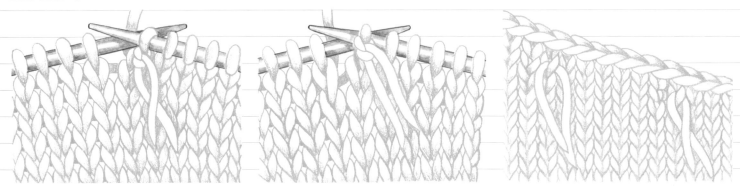

1 Work to the first row on which stitches are to be bound off. Work across the stitches to be bound off on that row—*without binding them off*. Mark the last of these stitches with a contrasting thread. Insert the needle into the next stitch and slip it off the needle.

2 Work to the end of the row. Turn and work across the next row, up to, but not including, the marked stitch. Turn and work across the next set of stitches to be bound off and mark the last stitch. Slip the next stitch and work to the end of the row.

3 Continue in this way until you have worked across all the stitches to be bound off. Work one row. Now bind off all the stitches, using the plain bind-off method. Fasten off securely.

SHAPING A SHOULDER

The plain bind-off method can be used to shape a shoulder, but the resulting edge will have a "stepped" effect.

The bias bind-off method produces a smooth shaping, which makes seaming easier and gives the work a professional finish on the underside.

Before working a ribbing bind-off, it is a good idea to practice it first on a sample piece of ribbing, for it is difficult to achieve a rhythmic, even tension that will give the necessary elasticity without a rippled effect. If you try to loosen up or tighten up part of the way along the row, the ribs will slant in different directions.

In most knitting patterns it is necessary to increase or decrease the width of the fabric at one or more points. For example, a sleeve must usually be gradually increased from cuff to underarm, then decreased from underarm to shoulder point in order to fit the armhole—which must itself be shaped by decreasing.

There are various methods of increasing and decreasing stitches. The choice of method in a given case depends mainly on the number of stitches to be added or subtracted, and whether the shaping is intended to be decorative or inconspicuous. Increasing and decreasing techniques are also used in creating certain stitch patterns, notably lace and bobble fabrics (see pp. 112 and 120). The following are the methods most often used in shaping a fabric.

A simple increase—known also as a bar increase because of the horizontal thread produced on the knit side of the fabric—is the usual method employed when a single stitch needs to be added at one or both edges of the fabric. If the side edge needs to be smooth, the increase can be worked one or two stitches in from the edge. The bar will then be visible; but if repeated over several rows, this will have a decorative effect.

A raised increase is inconspicuous and is the usual choice where a number of stitches must be increased across a row—for example just above the ribbing of a waistband or a cuff.

The simplest method of decreasing is to knit or purl two stitches together. This is the method normally used in shaping the side edge of the fabric. It can also be used across the row to decrease a number of stitches. In some cases stitches are knitted

or purled together through the back of the loops. Three stitches can also be knitted or purled together in order to decrease two stitches, although if two stitches must be decreased at the edge, the usual method is to bind them off.

Decorative decreasing is sometimes used when shaping a raglan armhole or a V-neck. This shaping is normally worked only on the knit side of the fabric and involves two different methods: a slip stitch decrease at the right-hand edge and a simple "knit two together" decrease at the left. The decreases have a noticeable slant, as can be seen in the photograph opposite.

SIMPLE INCREASE

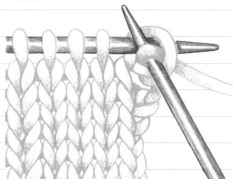 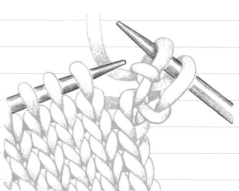 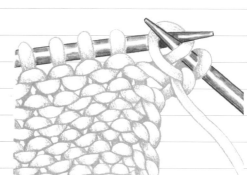

Increase into a knit stitch: 1 With the knit side facing, insert the RH needle knitwise into the front of the first stitch on the LH needle. Knit this stitch in the usual way, but do not slip it off the needle.

2 Insert the needle knitwise into the same stitch, this time through the back of the loop. Knit the stitch in the usual way and slip it off the needle. Two stitches have been made from one stitch.

Increase into a purl stitch With the purl side facing, purl the next stitch, but do not slip it off the needle. Now insert the needle purlwise into the same stitch, through the back of the loop. Purl the stitch and slip it off the LH needle.

RAISED INCREASE

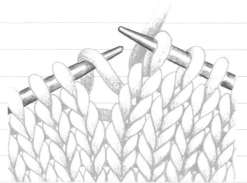 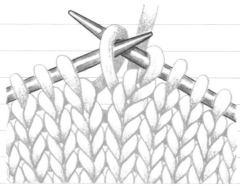 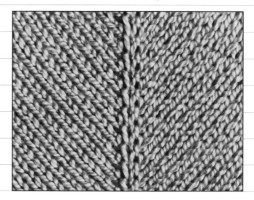

1 With the knit side of the work facing, insert the point of the LH needle from front to back under the horizontal strand lying between the next stitch and the one just worked.

2 Insert the RH needle through the back of the loop and knit this stitch. (It is important to work into the back, unless you want to make a small hole in the fabric.)

Raised increases are sometimes used in pairs, on each side of a single knit stitch, producing a decorative, flared effect, as shown here. The increase is worked into the strands just before and after the center stitch.

SIMPLE DECREASE

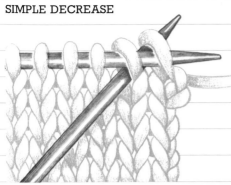

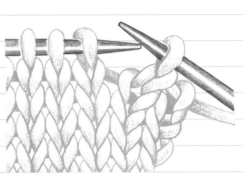

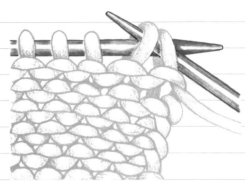

Decreasing a knit stitch: 1 With the knit side of the work facing, insert the RH needle knitwise through the second stitch, then the first stitch on the LH needle.

2 Knit these stitches together and slip them off the LH needle. One stitch has been made from 2 stitches. The decrease slants to the right.

Decreasing a purl stitch With the purl side facing, insert the RH needle purlwise into the front of the next 2 stitches. Purl them together and slip them off the LH needle. The decrease slants to the right on the knit side of the work.

SLIP STITCH DECREASE

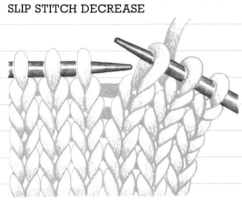

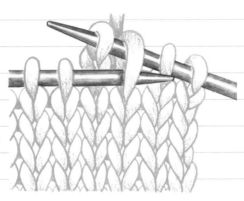

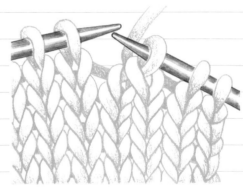

1 This decrease is usually worked two or three stitches in from the edge, and is intended to be visible on the RS. With the knit side of the work facing knit to the stitch to be decreased. Insert the RH needle knitwise into the next stitch and slip it off the LH needle.

2 Knit the next stitch. Now insert the LH needle from left to right through the front of the slipped stitch.

3 Lift this stitch over the knitted stitch and over the point of the RH needle. One stitch has been decreased. The slipped stitch slants to the left.

PURLING THROUGH BACK OF LOOPS

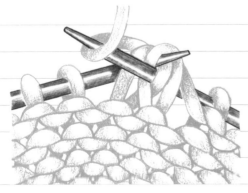

This decrease is used, when required, on the purl side of the work. The decrease slants to the left on the knit side.

Insert the needle purlwise through the back of the second, then the first stitch, twisting them as shown, and purl them together.

Paired decreases The sample (*above*) shows the effect of paired decreases worked 2 stitches in from the right and left side edges. The decreases have been worked on the RS only: slip stitch decreases at the right edge, and 2 stitches knitted together at the left. For a sharper decrease, stitches can also be decreased on the purl side.

Every knitter occasionally drops a stitch or makes a mistake. Learning how to correct such errors is not difficult. Practice the techniques shown here on a sample piece of knitting, so that when a mistake really occurs you can deal with it effectively.

Picking up a dropped stitch is a relatively simple matter. If the dropped stitch is not picked up immediately, it will cause a run, which must be picked up row by row with the help of a crochet hook. This is best done with the knit side of the work facing, since picking up a purl loop is more awkward than picking up a knit loop. In the case of garter stitch, however, this is unavoidable, because rows of knit and purl loops alternate on each side.

If you discover a mistake several rows down, you can either make a deliberate run, correct the mistake, and then pick up the run, or unravel the work.

When unraveling and picking up stitches to correct a mistake, use a needle one or two sizes smaller than those you are using for knitting. The smaller needle will slip into the loops more easily and will not stretch them.

When unraveling a mohair or other hairy yarn, keep a pair of manicure or embroidery scissors handy, so that you can snip any hairs that cause stitches to stick together. Be very careful, however, to cut only where necessary, since this tends to weaken the yarn.

PICKING UP A RUN

1 Slide the stitches on both needles away from the points, to prevent further loss of stitches. Whichever row is being worked, turn the fabric so that the knit side is facing. Insert a small crochet hook through the stitch immediately below the run from front to back and under the first loose strand.

PICKING UP A DROPPED STITCH

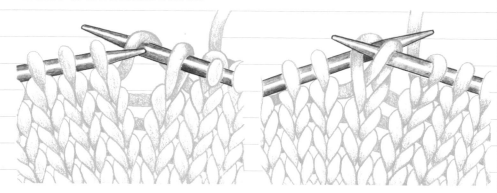

Picking up a dropped knit stitch: 1 Insert the RH needle through the dropped stitch from front to back, then insert it under the strand lying above the dropped stitch, as shown.

2 Insert the LH needle into the dropped stitch from left to right. Lift this stitch over the strand of yarn and off the RH needle. Slip the stitch on the RH needle back on to the LH needle, making sure it lies correctly. Continue working across the row.

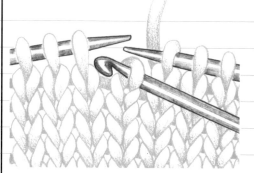

2 Turn the hook counter-clockwise to catch the strand, then draw it toward you through the stitch. Repeat to draw the next strand through and continue in this way to the top of the run. Slip the remaining stitch from the crochet hook back on to the LH needle.

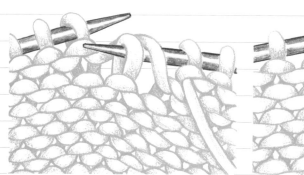

Picking up a dropped purl stitch: 1 Insert the RH needle through the dropped stitch and under the strand from back to front.

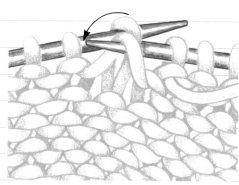

2 Insert the LH needle through the front of the dropped stitch (behind the strand) as shown. Lift this stitch over the strand and off the RH needle. Slip the stitch back on to the LH needle, making sure it lies correctly. Continue working across the row.

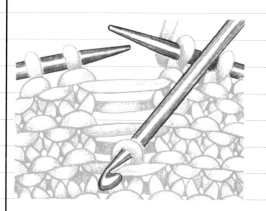

In a garter stitch run the purl loops are the ones lying toward the front of the work. To pick up one of these, first remove the hook, then reinsert it from back to front, pulling it up under the purl loop. Draw the purl loop back through the stitch as shown.

MISTAKE SEVERAL ROWS BELOW

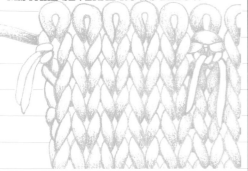

Mark the incorrect stitch with a contrasting thread. Also mark each end of the row in which it occurs. Carefully unravel the stitches until one complete row is left above the markers.

Many patterns require that stitches be slipped from one needle to the other without being knitted. Sometimes they are slipped on to an extra needle, such as a cable needle (see p. 19), or on to a stitch holder, which keeps them from unraveling while other parts of that piece are completed.

Stitches can be slipped either knitwise or purlwise. Unless otherwise instructed, you should slip them purlwise, whether the other stitches in the row are being knitted or purled. This ensures that the stitch lies in its original position after being slipped; if slipped knitwise, it will twist to the right. The illustrations show the yarn held in the normal position in each case; however, pattern instructions may specify holding it differently.

Where stitches need to be held in readiness for picking up later (at the front of a neck shaping, for example), you can use one of several implements for holding them. If only one or a few stitches must be held, a safety pin will do. If more stitches are involved, use either a stitch holder (which resembles a giant safety pin), a double-pointed needle, or a spare ordinary needle. The double-pointed needle has the advantage of allowing knitting to be resumed at either end, whereas otherwise they must sometimes first be slipped on to yet another needle. To prevent stitches from sliding off accidentally, use stitch stoppers, or wind rubber bands around the points.

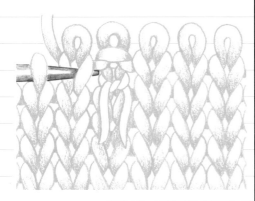

If the mistake is in a knit row, hold the yarn behind the work. Insert the LH needle from front to back into each stitch in the marked row, at the same time pulling out the stitch above it. Correct the mistake.

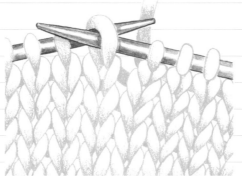

To slip a stitch purlwise on a knit row, keep the yarn at the back and insert the RH needle purlwise into the stitch. Slip it off the LH needle.

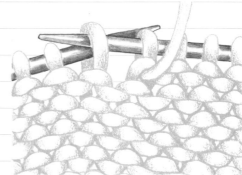

To slip a stitch purlwise on a purl row, keep the yarn at the front and insert the RH needle purlwise into the stitch. Slip it off the LH needle.

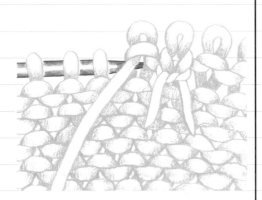

If the mistake is in a purl row, hold the yarn in front of the work. Insert the LH needle from front to back into each stitch in the marked row, at the same time pulling out the stitch above it. Correct the mistake.

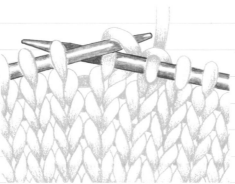

To slip a stitch knitwise, insert the RH needle knitwise into the stitch and slip it off the LH needle. Hold the yarn at the back of the work, as shown, unless otherwise instructed.

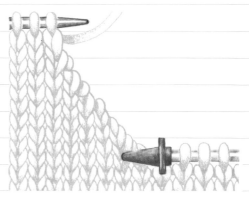

Holding stitches A spare needle can be used for holding stitches left unworked at the base of a neck shaping while the left and then the right side (*shown*) are completed.

Wrapping the yarn around the needle to form an extra loop or stitch makes a hole in the fabric. This technique, known as "decorative increasing," is used to work lace patterns. The increase is always paired with a decrease in order to maintain the existing number of stitches; this decrease may come immediately before or after the increase, elsewhere along the row, or on the following row.

Decorative increasing may look complicated, but it is really quite easy. The technique varies slightly, depending on the type of stitch (knit or purl) that precedes and follows the increase. The different techniques are collectively known as "yarn-over" increases.

An individual decorative increase followed immediately by a decrease produces an eyelet hole. Eyelets can be worked in a row to form a series of holes for a drawstring. If placed close together, they can be used to make a decorative picot hem (see p. 128).

A similar technique is used to make elongated stitches, producing dropped stitch patterns. The yarn is taken twice around the needle, forming an extra loop. Sometimes two or more loops are formed in this way. In the following row, only one loop is worked and the other(s) allowed to drop off the needle. A row of elongated stitches produces a band of vertical threads across the fabric.

DECORATIVE INCREASES

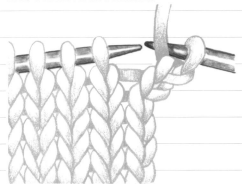

Between two knit stitches: 1 Bring the yarn forward under the RH needle, then over it, so that it is once more at the back of the work, in position for knitting.

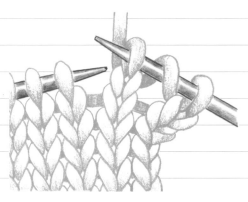

2 Insert the RH needle into the next stitch and knit it. In all these techniques the process is essentially the same: make an extra loop on the needle, bringing the yarn to the correct position for the next stitch.

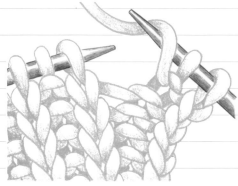

Between a purl and a knit stitch Take the yarn (which is at the front of the work) over the RH needle, so that it is at the back. Knit the next stitch.

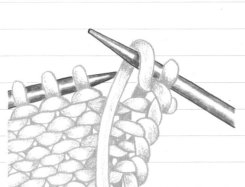

Between two purl stitches Take the yarn back over the RH needle, then under it, so that it is once more at the front. Purl the next stitch.

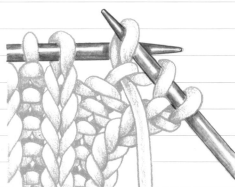

Between a knit and a purl stitch Bring the yarn forward under the RH needle, then take it over the needle and forward again so that it is at the front. Purl the next stitch.

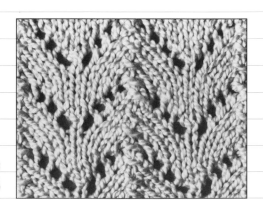

One of the most popular of lace patterns, fishtail is also relatively simple. The double decrease that forms the central rib is worked by slipping a stitch, knitting 2 together, and passing the slipped stitch over them. The pattern is also sometimes called "horseshoe." (For complete instructions see p. 70.)

EYELETS

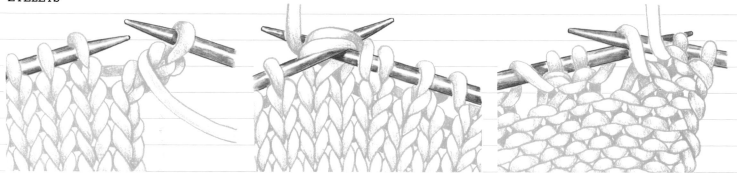

1 To work a row of eyelets in stockinette stitch: with the RS facing, * knit the first stitch. Now bring the yarn forward as shown and then over the needle.

2 Knit the next 2 stitches together to decrease 1 stitch. Continue knitting to the position for the next eyelet (in this example, only 1 stitch). Repeat from * to the end of the row.

3 On the following row, purl every stitch, taking extra care when working the increased stitches. A series of small holes is formed in the work.

ELONGATED STITCHES

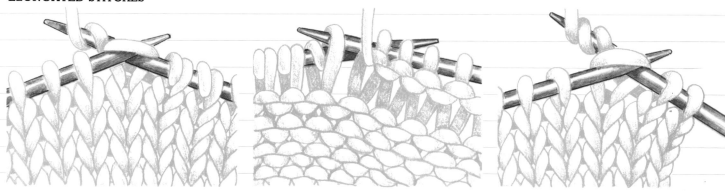

1 Insert the RH needle knitwise into the next stitch. Wrap the yarn around the needle, not once, as for an ordinary knit stitch, but twice. Draw both loops through the stitch and slip the stitch off the LH needle.

2 On the WS row, work only into the first loop of each stitch. Slip the new stitch off the LH needle, allowing the extra loop to drop off and unwind.

Longer stitches can be produced by wrapping the yarn three or more times around the needle. Take care to keep the loops as even as possible.

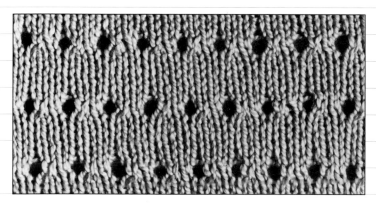

These rows of eyelets were made by the method shown above, with one knit stitch worked between each decrease and increase. An eyelet row should not be placed immediately above the cast-on edge, for this will distort the fabric; a few rows of stockinette stitch, or other fabric stitch, must be worked first.

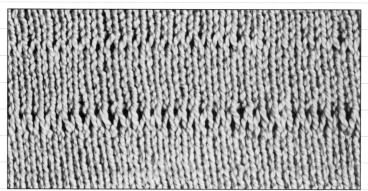

The upper row of elongated stitches in this sample was worked by wrapping the yarn twice around the needle; the one below it was produced by wrapping the yarn 3 times. Elongated stitches are also often worked in garter stitch and reverse stockinette stitch fabrics.

Some of the most attractive knitting patterns use two or more colors. Fair Isle designs, horizontal and vertical stripes, chevrons, and jacquard patterns are among the most familiar examples of multicolor knitting.

Various different techniques are required in creating these effects. The simplest kind of multicolor design, horizontal stripes, uses only one color in a row. (Chevron stripes are essentially horizontal: the zigzag effect results from decreasing two stitches at the downward point and increasing two stitches at the upward point.)

Vertical and diagonal stripes, and all others using two or more colors in the row (except for slipstitch patterns—see p. 72), entail either working with two or more balls of yarn or working with two yarns together, stranding or weaving them into the wrong side of the work.

A simple way of producing a fabric with many vertical stripes in several colors is to knit it sideways, so that you are actually working horizontal stripes; however, this method is not always appropriate to the style of the garment.

Some confusion surrounds the terms "Fair Isle" and "jacquard." Strictly speaking, "Fair Isle" patterns are traditional motifs such as those shown on pp. 68–69. Although a Fair Isle pattern may contain several colors, only two colors are used in any one row, and the term "Fair Isle" is consequently often applied to any design worked in this way.

Jacquard patterns may use more than two colors in a row, and are knitted using the intarsia method shown opposite. They may be geometrical or pictorial, a single motif or a repeating pattern.

Narrow vertical stripes in two colors can be worked by the stranding method shown on p. 116, instead of the intarsia method, if you prefer. However, care should be taken to keep the tension fairly loose on the stranded yarn to avoid drawing the stripes together. Also, work a sample first to make sure that the darker color does not show through the lighter one.

HORIZONTAL STRIPES

Patterns composed of horizontal stripes are the simplest of all multicolor patterns, since only one color is used within a row. If the stripes use only two colors, the color that is not being used can be carried up the side and worked into the edge as shown in step 2, then picked up when needed. In this way you avoid having to darn in the numerous loose ends that result if the yarn for each stripe is rejoined at the edge. If several colors are used, they must be fastened off and rejoined; otherwise the edge would be too bulky.

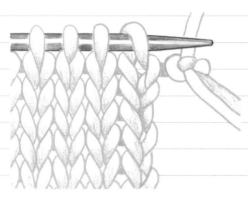

1 To introduce the new color, tie it to the first color at the edge, using a double knot. Do not cut off the first color. Work in the new color for the required number of rows.

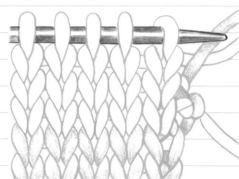

2 On every alternate row, twist the two colors together as shown. This weaves the unused yarn into the edge, keeping it neat. When changing back to the first color, bring it up in front of the other one. If the stripes are very wide, fasten off and rejoin yarns as needed.

SIMPLE STRIPE PATTERNS

In a garter stitch fabric, solid stripes result if the colors are changed only at the RH edge. In the stripes at the top of this sample, new colors were introduced at the LH edge—that is, on WS rows, so that the two colors interlock.

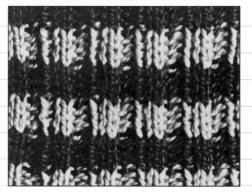

On this 2 × 2 ribbed fabric the stripes are each 4 rows deep. The purled stitches illustrate the broken stripe effect that results on the purl side of the work when a new color is introduced.

BOBBINS

If colors must be changed frequently in a row, bobbins should be used instead of balls of yarn, which easily become tangled. Wind the various colors of yarn around the bobbins, and tie them to the back of the work.

To make a bobbin cut a rectangle about 2 × 1¼ in from thin cardboard. In each short end cut a notch. Wind the yarn through the notches.

INTARSIA METHOD

A pattern that includes wide vertical stripes or several colors in a row is generally worked using separate balls, or bobbins, of yarn—one for each color and for each subsequent repeat of that color across the row. This method of color-patterned knitting is sometimes called "intarsia," a word derived from an Arabic word meaning "mosaic."

The essential point to remember when working with separate balls or bobbins of yarn is that every time a new color is picked up it must be crossed over the first color. This technique—called "twisting" the yarn—links the stitches. If this is not done, a slit forms between the two colors.

The illustrations here show the formation of a vertical stripe. The same technique is used when changing colors for motifs and jacquard patterns.

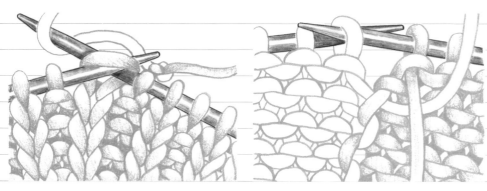

1 Work to the position of the stripe. Tie the second color (B) to the first color (A), leaving a short end of B, to be darned in later. (Do not cut off A.) Knit the required number of stitches in B. Tie a new length of A to B, and continue working in A.

2 On the following purl row, when changing color, let the first color fall down to the left and bring the new color under and around it as shown. In the illustration the stripe is partially completed, to show the linking of the stitches.

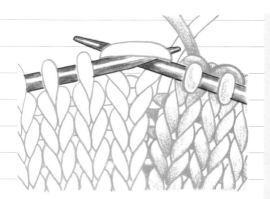

3 On a knit row, cross the yarns as shown. Let the first color drop down to the left, over the new color.

On both RS and WS rows, work the stitches tightly on each side of the change to prevent the formation of a gap.

FOLLOWING A CHART

Color patterns are often given in the form of a chart. This is easier to follow than line-by-line instructions, which would be lengthy and confusing.

Each square represents one stitch. The different colors are indicated either by symbols, as in the examples given here, or by colors corresponding to those to be used for the knitting.

A chart is worked from bottom to top. The rows are often numbered, with odd numbers on the right and even numbers on the left. The odd-numbered rows are knit rows and are read from right to left; the even-numbered are purl rows and are read from left to right (except when working in the round: see p. 123).

If a design consists of a repeating motif, the chart will normally show only the motif itself, plus, in some cases, a partial repeat to be used at the side edges. The Fair Isle chart (*below left*) shows a motif presented in this way, with the repeat marked off with a bracket. Pattern instructions will specify how many repeats are to be worked.

You may find it a good idea to draw a line in pencil through each row as it is completed; this will help you to keep track of the rows you have worked.

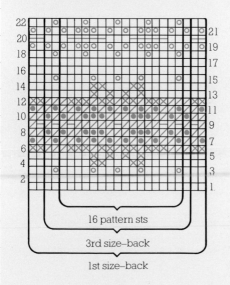

16 pattern sts

3rd size–back

1st size–back

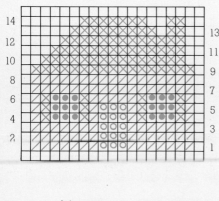

Key   ✕ =red   ○ =blue
       ╱ =white   ● =green

STRANDING AND WEAVING

Designs that use only two colors in a row but repeat them at frequent intervals are best worked with the two yarns together, rather than with many separate lengths of yarn. There are two different methods of working with two yarns: "stranding," in which the yarn not in use is carried loosely across the wrong side of the work until it is needed again, and "weaving," in which the unused yarn is joined into the stitches on the wrong side.

Both methods produce a double-thickness fabric. The stranding method is suitable where the yarns are picked up at intervals of no more than five stitches; if yarn is stranded over more stitches it is difficult to keep the guage correct, and the fabric may be puckered. Also, the long strands may be snagged when the garment is put on or removed.

The weaving method is slightly more difficult than stranding, but it helps to keep the gauge correct and produces a sturdy fabric which is neat on the wrong side.

For both stranding and weaving it is easier to keep the gauge even if you work with one yarn held in the right hand and the other held in the left. This takes some practice, but will eventually result in smoother, more efficient work than if one hand were to pick up each yarn in turn.

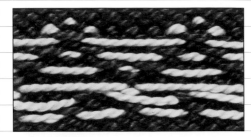

These photographs show the wrong sides of the stranding method (*top*) and the weaving method (*below*). The two methods can be combined where yarn is taken across only a few stitches in some parts of the design and over six or more in others.

STRANDING

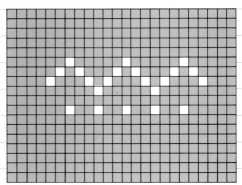

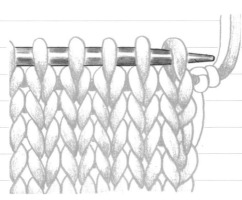

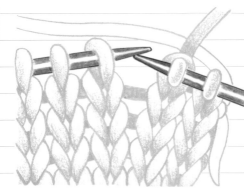

In this example the pattern is a simple zigzag and dot motif. Notice that the widest distance that the contrasting yarn must cover is 5 stitches; if more stitches had to be spanned, the weaving method would be preferable.

1 Join the contrasting yarn with a knot at the RH edge. In this example the main color is referred to as "A," the contrasting as "B."

2 Holding yarn A in one hand and B in the other, knit in A up to the first stitch in B. (These illustrations show A coming from the right hand; some knitters may prefer to work with the main color in the left hand.) Yarn B is held loosely below the stitches.

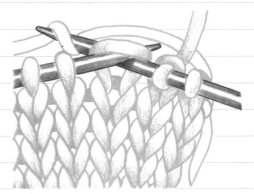

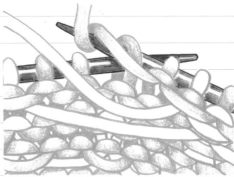

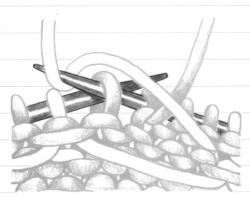

3 Now hold yarn A out of the way and knit 1 stitch with B, as shown. Knit 2 more stitches in A. Continue knitting 1 stitch in B and 2 in A to the end of the row, remembering to hold the stranded yarn loosely to avoid puckering the fabric.

4 The second row of this motif is purled in A, so B is cut off and rejoined on the third row. Work the third row using the techniques described above. On the fourth row the yarns are stranded on the front (WS) of the work. Hold B loosely while purling with A.

5 When purling with B, hold A out of the way. When A is next needed, take it loosely across the front (WS) of the work.

Check the work frequently to make sure it is not puckered.

WEAVING

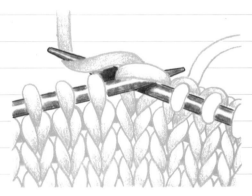

This Greek key motif is a good one on which to practice weaving techniques. In this example the light yarn, held in the right hand, is "A" and the dark one, held in the left hand, "B."

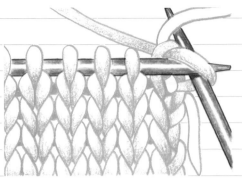

1 Using B, cast on 20 stitches and work a few rows before beginning the pattern. Join in A. Knit a stitch with A, holding B slightly below it as shown. This weaves the *LH yarn below the stitch*.

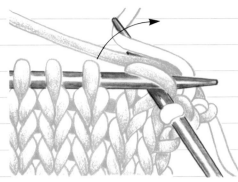

2 Knit the next stitch, again with A, but weave the *LH yarn above the stitch* as shown: insert the needle; take B over the needle from back to front, but not around it. Knit with A; then before pulling the stitch through, slip B back off the needle.

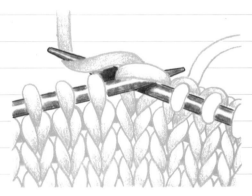

3 Weave B alternately under and over A for 6 more stitches. Knit the next stitch in B, holding A out of the way as shown. This weaves the *RH yarn below the stitch*.

Knit 9 stitches in A, weaving B above and below it as before, then knit 1 stitch in B and 1 in A.

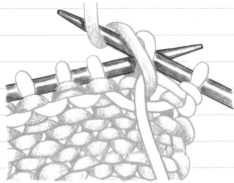

4 On the WS, purl the first stitch with A in the usual way, holding B out of the way.

Purl the next stitch with B as shown, holding A out of the way. This weaves the *RH yarn above the stitch*.

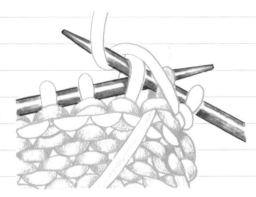

5 Purl the next stitch with A, holding B slightly below it. This weaves the *LH yarn below the stitch*.

Purl the next stitch with B, as shown in step 4.

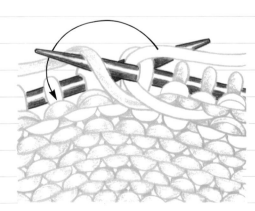

6 Purl the next stitch, again with B, but weave the *RH yarn below the stitch* as shown: insert the needle; take A under and over the needle. Purl with B; then, before completing the stitch, bring A back under the needle toward you. Complete the purl stitch in B.

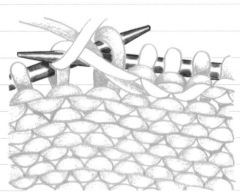

7 Continue following the chart, practicing these six techniques.

For other charts you may need two more techniques. To weave the *LH yarn above a purl stitch*: insert the needle; take B back over the needle. Purl with A; pull B toward you before completing the stitch in A.

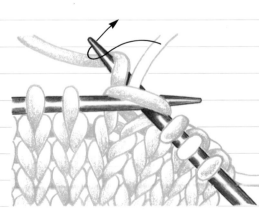

8 To weave the *RH yarn above a knit stitch*: insert the needle; knit with A. Knit with B; then bring A toward you and under the needle before completing the stitch in B.

117

Many interesting stitch patterns are formed by crossing stitches—that is, altering the sequence in which they are worked, and so moving them to the left or to the right.

The crossover is often accomplished with the help of a cable needle, which holds stitches at the front or back of the work while other stitches are worked. The stitches on the cable needle are then worked back into the fabric. The illustrations on this page show how to work a simple cable that twists to the left (called "cable forward") and one that twists to the right (called "cable back"). Other popular cable patterns are shown on pp. 62–63.

A cable is worked in stockinette stitch and is usually placed against a background of reverse stockinette stitch to enhance its texture. The example given here is worked over six stitches, and the cable row is repeated every sixth row. If the cable is worked over more stitches, more rows should be included between the cable rows in order to keep the cable a graceful shape and to minimize the tendency of the cable to distort the fabric.

Similar effects can be produced by the technique of crossing stitches on an ordinary pair of needles. This method, which can be worked over two, three, or four stitches, can be used to produce a great variety of effects, including lattice and basketweave textures, coiled ribs, and mock cables. When three or more stitches are involved, the technique can be awkward to execute; it will be easier if you keep your tension fairly loose at this point on both the preceding row and the crossover row. Also keeping a loose tension on the following row will avoid placing a strain on these stitches.

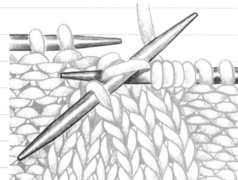 When working cables, use a cable needle that is the same size, or smaller than the needles you are using, so as to avoid stretching the stitches.

Use a row counter when working a cable pattern to ensure that the cable row is worked at regular intervals.

CABLE FORWARD

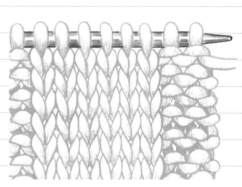

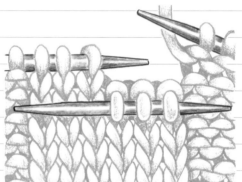

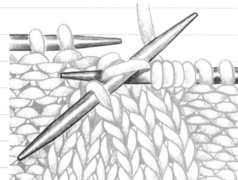

1 Work the specified number of ordinary rows before the cable row: on the RS the background is purled and the cable knitted; on the WS this is reversed.

2 On the cable row: purl the background stitches as before. Then slip the first 3 cable stitches on to the cable needle. Leaving these at the front of the work, as shown, knit the next 3 stitches.

3 Now knit the stitches from the cable needle. Work to the end of the row. On the WS, work as on other WS rows, purling the crossed cable stitches. The result is a cable that twists to the left.

CABLE BACK

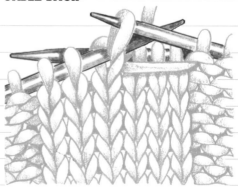

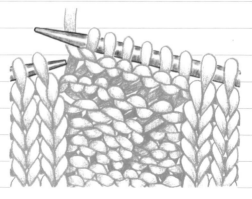

1 Establish the position of the cable as in step 1 of "Cable forward." On the cable row, slip the first 3 stitches on to the cable needle and place this at the back of the work. Knit the next 3 stitches.

2 Now knit the stitches from the cable needle. On the WS (*shown*), work as on other WS rows, purling into the crossed cable stitches. The result is a cable that twists to the right.

CROSSING STITCHES RIGHT

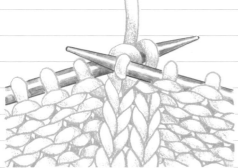

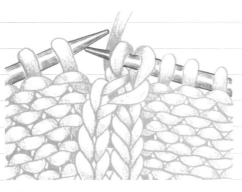

1 Insert the RH needle from left to right into the front of the second stitch on the LH needle. Knit the stitch but leave it on the needle.

2 Now knit the first stitch and slip both stitches off the needle.

To cross 3 stitches in this way, work step 1 into the third stitch on the needle, then the second, then knit the first stitch and slip all 3 stitches off the needle.

CROSSING STITCHES LEFT

Work as for a cross right, but knit the second stitch through the back of the loop, as shown. Now knit the first stitch, also through the back of the loop. If 3 stitches are involved, knit the third, then the second, then the first.

MOCK CABLE FORWARD

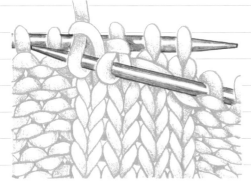

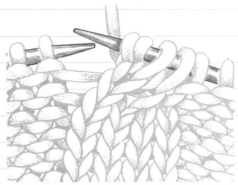

1 This mock cable is worked over 4 stitches. Knit the third stitch on the LH needle through the front, then knit the fourth stitch, still keeping all stitches on the needle. (In the illustration the third and fourth stitches have been knitted.)

2 Knit the second, then the first stitch, then slip all 4 stitches off the LH needle. Work to the end of the row. On the WS row purl the twisted stitches, keeping a fairly loose tension.

MOCK CABLE BACK

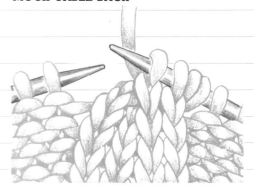

Work this mock cable as for the mock cable forward, but knit the third and fourth stitches through the back of the loop. Then knit the first and second stitches through the front of the loop in the usual way.

CROSSED STITCHES AND CABLES

This sample shows the finished effects produced by the techniques described on these pages. From left to right: cable forward over 6 stitches, mock cable forward, 2 stitches crossed left, 2 stitches crossed right, mock cable back, and cable back over 6 stitches. The crossed stitches at the center and the mock cables are worked on every fourth row. The true cables are worked on every sixth row.

Attractive three-dimensional effects can be achieved in knitting by working bobbles and loops into the fabric.

There are various kinds of bobble, but they all involve making several stitches out of one stitch, working a few rows on these stitches, then decreasing back to one stitch. Sometimes the bobble is worked gradually, along with the rows of background fabric, and sometimes—as shown here—the bobble rows are worked separately, with the work being turned until the bobble is completed. This produces a bobble that stands out sharply against the background.

For extra emphasis bobbles can be worked in a contrasting yarn. With the addition of embroidery stitches, contrasting bobbles can be used to create simple motifs such as flowers and cherries.

The size of the bobble is determined by the number of increases made and the number of rows worked on these stitches. The bobble shown below consists of four stitches worked over five rows and is worked in reverse stockinette stitch on a stockinette stitch background. For a smoother bobble you could follow the same instructions but work the bobble in stockinette stitch—purling the bobble stitches on the wrong side and knitting them on the right side.

Knots are similar to bobbles, but smaller. They, too, are formed in various ways. Some knots are used to make an entire fabric: trinity stitch (see p. 66) is an example. The knot shown opposite is a simple one that is formed without turning the work, by making five stitches out of one and then immediately decreasing the stitches back to one. This kind of knot is sometimes called a "popcorn."

Loops can be worked either in isolated rows on a fabric to give decorative interest, or all over the fabric to produce a thick "furry" pile. The loops can be left uncut or trimmed for a shaggy effect. In either case, the fabric is both warm and reasonably light-weight, ideal for coats and jackets.

Forming the loops takes a little practice. Knitters who hold the yarn in the left hand may find it easier in the long run to learn the right-hand method (see p. 103) for this stitch, since this method leaves the left thumb free for use in forming the loops. An alternative is to use the right thumb.

If the loops are being worked thickly for a mock-fur fabric, it is not vital to make them exactly the same length—especially if the loops will be cut later. However, a single row of loops should be worked as evenly as possible.

MAKING A BOBBLE

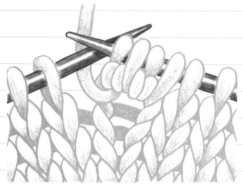

1 With the RS facing, work up to the position of the bobble. Knit the next stitch, but do not slip it off the needle. Purl, then knit, then purl into the same stitch, and slip it off the needle, thus making 4 stitches out of 1.

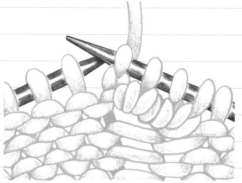

2 Turn the work so that the WS is facing. Knit the first 4 stitches on the LH needle, working the first and last stitches fairly tightly.

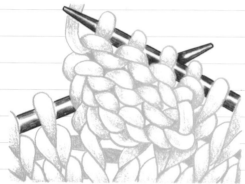

3 Turn the work again and purl these 4 stitches. Work 2 more rows in reverse stockinette stitch on the bobble stitches only, ending with the RS facing.

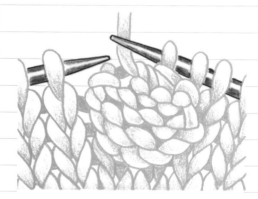

4 Use the LH needle to lift the second, third, and fourth stitches over the first one, thus decreasing the 3 stitches increased in step 1 and completing the bobble.

Continue knitting to the position for the next bobble.

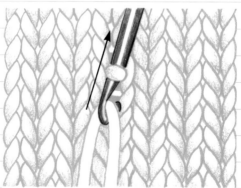

To work a contrasting bobble in a completed fabric: 1 Insert a crochet hook, as shown, into the stitch in which the bobble is to be worked, and pull a loop through. Holding the short end of yarn with the free hand, make 4 stitches as in step 1 (*above*). Complete the bobble as for an ordinary bobble.

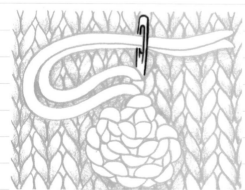

2 Cut the yarn and draw it through the remaining stitch. Thread both ends into a tapestry needle, take them to the WS, and darn them in securely.

MAKING A KNOT

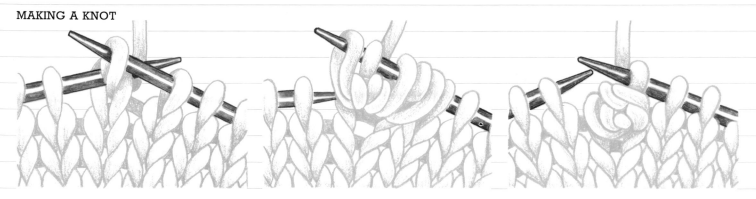

1 Work to the position of the knot. Knit into the next stitch, but do not slip the stitch off the needle.

2 Purl, then knit, then purl, then knit into this same stitch, thus making 5 stitches out of 1, and slip the original stitch off the needle.

3 Use the LH needle to lift the second, third, fourth, and fifth stitches over the first, so decreasing the 4 stitches increased in step 2.
Continue working to the position for the next knot.

WORKING LOOPS

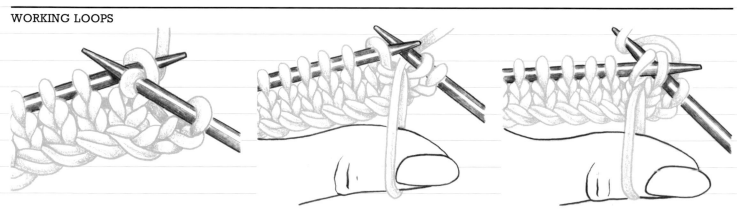

1 Work 2 rows of stockinette stitch to begin the fabric. With the RS facing, knit the first stitch. * Knit the second stitch, but do not slip the stitch off the needle.

2 Bring the yarn forward, between the needles, under the left thumb from back to front, then back between the needles as shown. Knit into the stitch again and slip the stitch off the needle, without removing the thumb from the loop.

3 Still keeping the thumb in the loop, insert the LH needle into the 2 stitches just worked, then knit these stitches together through the back of the loops as shown. Slip the thumb out of the loop *

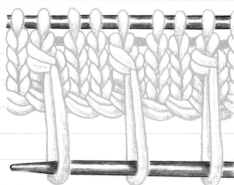

4 Knit to the position for the next loop. (In this example 2 stitches are worked between each loop.) Repeat from * to * to form another loop. Continue in this way to the end of the row.

5 Work one row. Slip the free needle through the loops, making sure they are aligned the same way, and pull gently downward.

On this sample of loop stitch the loops have been worked on every RS row, with one ordinary knit stitch between each loop and the positions of the loops alternated on each loop row. The RH side shows the effect produced by cutting the loops.

For added textural interest beads or sequins can be worked into a knitted fabric. You can sew them on individually after the knitting is completed, but if there are many, or if they are to be used in a regular pattern, it is better to add them while knitting.

When choosing a bead for knitting, make sure that its hole is large enough for the yarn to slip through it without stretching; otherwise either the yarn or the bead (if fragile) might break. Most sequins have very small holes, and thus can be used only with fine yarns. When washing a garment decorated with beads or sequins, use a mild soap and handle the garment gently to avoid damaging them.

Two methods for knitting in beads are shown here. The slip stitch method is suitable for designs in which beads are separated by at least one stitch. It is worked on the right side and the bead, or sequin, is held securely on the surface of the work by a horizontal strand of yarn.

The yarn-over-needle method must be used if beads are to be worked into consecutive stitches—to form a cluster, for example. This method can also be used on wrong side rows. It requires a little more skill to keep the beads at the front of the work.

Before beginning the knitting for either method, thread all the beads or sequins you will need on to the yarn as shown (*right*). While knitting, move the beads back up the yarn as required.

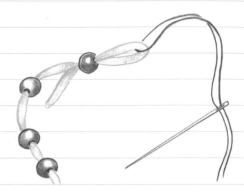

To thread beads on to yarn, thread a sewing needle with a doubled strand of strong thread, preferably silk. Slip the yarn through the loop of thread and turn one end back to form another loop. Thread beads as shown, always keeping one bead on the yarn loop to hold it in place.

SLIP STITCH METHOD

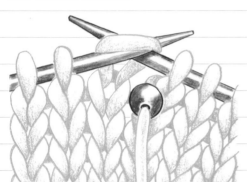

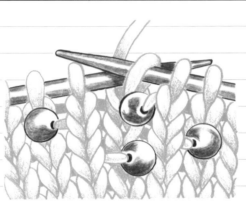

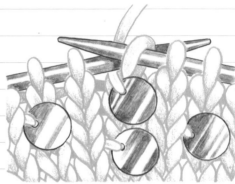

1 Work at least two rows of knitting before adding beads. With the RS facing, work up to the position for the first bead. Bring the bead up to the knitting, then bring the yarn forward and slip the next stitch knitwise.

2 Take the yarn back and knit the next stitch. The bead lies on the front of the work, held by a horizontal strand. Continue placing the beads as required.

Sequins are knitted in using the same method. Each time you add a sequin, turn it so that it lies as flat as possible against the fabric.

YARN-OVER-NEEDLE METHOD

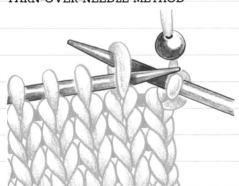

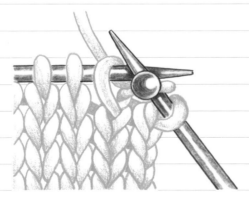

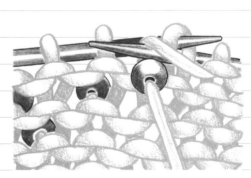

1 Complete several rows of knitting. With the RS facing, work up to the position for the first bead (in this example, the second stitch). Insert the needle through the back of the loop and draw a bead up to the back of the work.

2 Take the yarn over the needle and push the bead through the stitch on the LH needle to the RS. Complete the knit stitch. Continue working in beads as required along the row. Work the stitches on the WS fairly tightly to keep the beads in place.

3 To work in beads on a purl row, insert the needle through the back of the loop as shown. Push the bead through the loop to the RS as you complete the purl stitch.

Often it is necessary or desirable to knit a fabric in rounds, rather than in rows, producing a seamless, tubular piece of knitting. Small items such as socks are normally knitted partly or entirely in the round. A turtle-neck collar is best knitted in this way, for a seam at one side might be noticeable. Similarly, a circular yoke is knitted in the round, on stitches picked up from the front, back, and sleeves. The body of a sweater can also be knitted in the round, thus eliminating side seams.

Two different kinds of needles can be used for knitting in rounds: a circular needle or a set of double-pointed needles (see p. 19). Double-pointed needles are generally used for small items, a circular needle for larger ones.

A circular needle can also be used for flat knitting. Because it distributes the weight of the work evenly between the hands and can hold more stitches than a single-pointed needle, it is well suited to knitting large, heavy items.

Working in rounds differs from flat knitting in two important ways. First of all, the right side of the work is always facing you. This means that in order to work stockinette stitch you must *knit every round*, rather than alternately knitting and purling, as when working in rows. Conversely, for garter stitch you must knit one round and purl the next. For reverse stockinette stitch, purl every round; for a rib pattern, repeat the first (right side) row throughout.

The other main difference between tubular and flat knitting is that, because the work is seamless, no edge stitches are required. Only whole pattern repeats are included in the round. For example, if you decide to work a two-by-two rib neckband in the round, you must make sure that the number of stitches you pick up is a multiple of four, so that if you start the round with "K2" you will end with "P2."

The instructions in the following pages are for working tubular knitting from cast-on stitches; however, in the case of a neckband, for example, the knitting is worked on stitches picked up from completed sections. The method used is the same as that shown on p. 135 except for the different type of needle that is used.

If you are working from cast-on stitches, it is vital to make sure, before knitting the first round, that the stitches are not twisted around the needle(s); otherwise the work will have to be unraveled.

Place a marker at the end of the cast-on stitches and slip it before beginning each new round. This enables you to keep track of the rounds.

WORKING IN ROUNDS—CIRCULAR NEEDLE

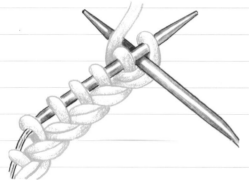

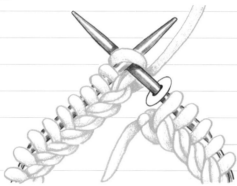

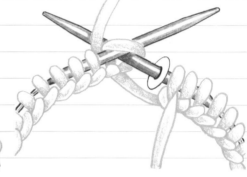

1 Cast on the required number of stitches. You can use a two-needle method, such as cable cast-on (*shown*), or a one-needle method, casting on to either point of the needle. Wind a rubber band around the other point to prevent the stitches from slipping off.

2(a) Make sure that none of the cast-on stitches are twisted around the needle. Place a marker next to the first cast-on stitch (on the RH point). Insert the RH point into the last cast-on stitch and knit it, pulling the yarn firmly.

2(b) If you use the thumb or double cast-on method, both ends of yarn will be attached to the last cast-on stitch. In this case, you hold the point with the first cast-on stitch in your left hand and work the first stitch into it as shown.

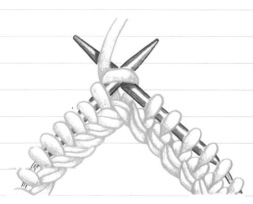

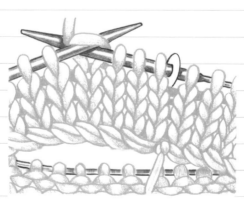

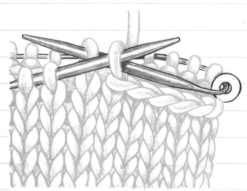

3 Continue knitting the cast-on stitches until you reach the marker. Slip the marker on the RH point and continue as before, always knitting the first stitch of a round firmly to make the join as inconspicuous as possible.

4 For a stockinette stitch fabric, as shown, knit every round. To produce garter stitch, knit one round and purl the next throughout the fabric. For a rib pattern, repeat the first row throughout, knitting the knitted stitches and purling the purled ones.

5 When the work is the required length, bind off the stitches, as on a piece of flat knitting, beginning with the first stitch after the marker. Work the bind-off rather loosely.

FLAT KNITTING WITH A CIRCULAR NEEDLE

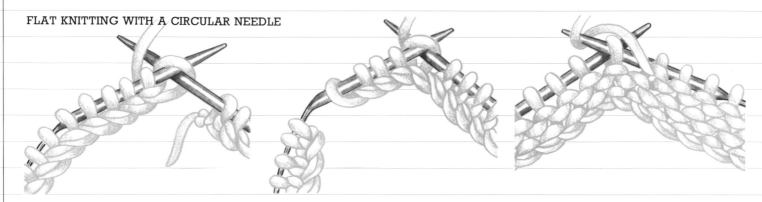

1 Cast on the required number of stitches. (The cable method has been used for this illustration, but another method could be used.) Hold the point with the last cast-on stitch in your left hand, and use the RH point to knit the first stitch.

2 Continue knitting to the end of the cast-on stitches. Note that the first and last stitch are *not* joined, as in tubular knitting.

3 For the next row, turn the needle so that the point holding the last stitch worked is in your left hand and the WS of the work is facing. Purl the next row. Continue in this way to work stockinette stitch, as for the normal two-needle method.

JOINING IN NEW YARN

In flat knitting yarn should always, if possible, be joined at a side edge. A simple double knot joins the new yarn to the old, and the ends are later darned into the work (see p. 136). By rewinding new yarn as suggested on p. 100, you can avoid having to break off and rejoin yarn in mid-row because of a knot or imperfection.

To avoid running out of yarn in the middle of a row, check the yarn when you are nearing the end of the ball and estimate how many rows can be worked with the remaining yarn. Lay the work flat, with the stitches spread evenly along the needle. (If the work is wider than the needle is long, stop in the middle of a row and spread the stitches over both needles.) Take the remaining yarn back and forth loosely across the work to see how many widths it covers. Allow at least four times the width for one row of an ordinary stitch pattern—proportionately more for a dense fabric, such as one including bobbles.

If you think you may have enough yarn left for two more rows, double the yarn and fix a paper clip at the mid-point. Work one row. If four or more inches remain before the paper clip, you can work another row; if not, cut the yarn and join in a new ball.

In tubular knitting, yarn cannot, of course, be joined at a side edge, but must be joined within a round—preferably at a place where the join will be least noticeable. Either of the following two methods can be used, although the double-strand method is slightly more conspicuous and thus better suited to fuzzy yarn or a textured stitch. Splicing is preferred for a smooth yarn worked in stockinette stitch.

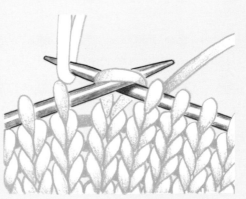

Double-strand method: 1 After working the last stitch in the old yarn, let this yarn fall to the back of the work, insert the needle into the next stitch and wrap the new yarn around it, leaving a tail a few inches long. Knit the stitch with the new yarn.

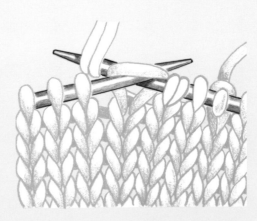

2 Knit the next two or three stitches using the new yarn doubled, then continue knitting with the single strand. On the following round, treat the double strands as single stitches. Trim the short end of new yarn. Thread the old yarn into a yarn needle and darn it into the WS.

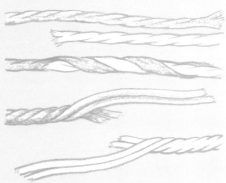

Splicing method: Trim the old yarn to measure about 3 in and place the new yarn alongside the old. Twist the yarns around each other, then quickly rub the twisted section between the palms of your hands. Gently pull at the joining; if it feels loose, dampen it and repeat the rubbing process. Continue knitting, using the spliced yarn and taking extra care over the next few stitches.

If the yarn is bulky, eliminate the extra bulk by trimming each piece of yarn as shown.

WORKING IN ROUNDS—DOUBLE-POINTED NEEDLES

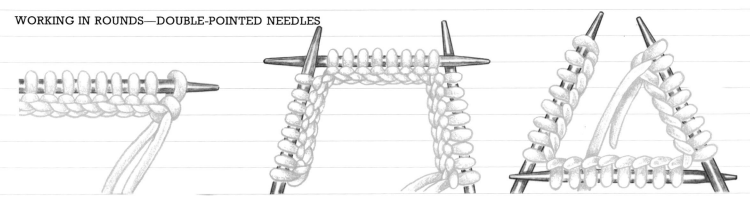

1 Cast the required number of stitches on to a single-pointed needle the same size as the double-pointed needles (or larger, if you cast on tightly). The thumb method has been used for this example, but another method could be used instead.

2 Slip the cast-on stitches on to the double-pointed needles, dividing them evenly and leaving one needle free for working the stitches. (A set of 4 needles is used for this example.)

3 Arrange the needles as shown so that they cross each other. Make sure that the stitches lie smooth and are not twisted around the needles.

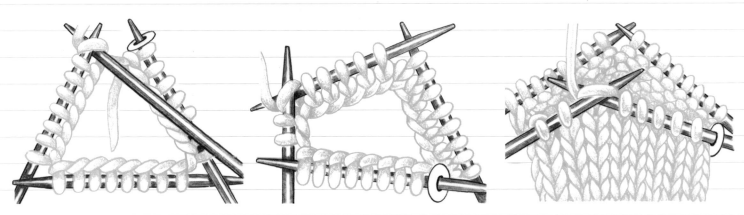

4 Place a marker next to the last cast-on stitch to mark the beginning of the round. Insert the free needle into the first cast-on stitch and knit it, pulling the yarn tightly across from the adjacent needle to prevent a gap at this point.

5 Continue knitting all the stitches from the first needle. Then use this needle to knit all the stitches from the second needle, and the second to knit the stitches from the third, slipping the marker on to the needle to mark the end of the round.

6 Continue working in this way until the work is the required length, taking extra care to pull the stitches at the corners tightly to prevent a "run" effect at these points. Bind off in the normal way.

WORKING MEDALLIONS

Double-pointed needles are also used for working flat, symmetrical motifs, such as those sometimes used for patchwork bedspreads and pillow covers. These are normally knitted from the center outward. Because the number of stitches at the center is very small—perhaps eight or fewer—a different method of casting on is used.

Begin by crocheting a chain (see p. 140), working one chain for each stitch required, including the slip loop. For eight stitches, for example, work seven chains. Join the first and last chain with a slip stitch. Insert one double-pointed needle into the remaining loop (the first stitch of the round), then insert the needle through the first chain and wrap the working yarn around it to pick up one stitch. Pick up another stitch in the same way.

Using another needle, pick up three

more stitches; with the third needle, pick up two more stitches, making a total of eight stitches. Slip a marker on to the third needle to denote the end of the round.

Work the stitches as for tubular knitting (*above*), increasing as instructed by the pattern to form a flat motif.

A circular needle is usually bought tightly wound in a packet. To smooth out the coils, immerse the needle in hand-hot water for about five minutes. Dry it and pull it gently between your fingers.

When putting away a piece of knitting being worked on a circular needle, pull the rigid points out of the stitches so that the points cross each other and the stitches are held securely on the wire without stretching.

The steps involved in turning a heel can look rather daunting, even to an experienced knitter, but the method shown in these pages—known as a "Dutch heel"—is not really difficult.

This method has the advantage of being worked in the round, so that the completed sock is seamless. No finishing is required, and the sock is smooth and comfortable to wear.

The example given here uses 42 cast-on stitches, increased to 48 over the instep, then decreased over the length of the foot. If worked in a knitting worsted yarn it would fit an average-size eight- or nine-year-old child. For a larger-sized sock, cast on more stitches, making sure that the total number is divisible by three. The number of stitches remaining in step 8 must also be divisible by three.

The heel is shaped by first working it separately from the instep, knitting in rows on the center eight stitches and gradually working in and decreasing the stitches on either side. Then the heel is rejoined to the instep stitches and the shaping completed.

Instructions for completing the sock are given on p. 127.

If you are working a single rib cuff on the sock, make sure that the number of cast-on stitches is divisible by two. For double ribbing the number must be divisible by four.

Single-pointed needles can be used, if you prefer, to work steps 2–6 of the heel shaping.

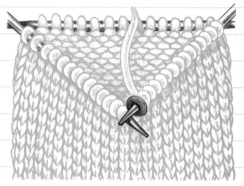

1 Cast on 42 stitches as shown in step 1, p. 125, and divide the stitches equally on to 3 double-pointed needles. Work in rounds until the work is the required length (from top of sock to bottom of heel). Fasten off the yarn.

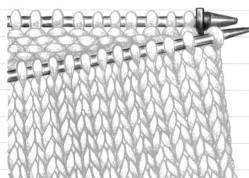

2 Slip the first and last 11 stitches of the round on to one needle. These 22 stitches will be used for the heel. Slip the remaining 20 stitches on to a spare needle. These will be picked up when working the instep.

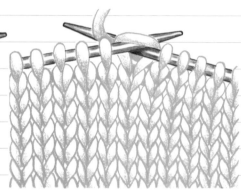

3 Rejoin the yarn to the RH side of the heel stitches. Using a spare needle, knit across these stitches. Continue working in stockinette stitch for approximately 2 in, ending with a purl row.

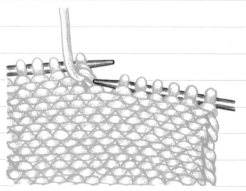

4 With the RS facing, knit 14 stitches, then slip 1, knit 1, and pass the slipped stitch over to decrease 1 stitch. Leave the last 6 stitches unworked; turn. The RH needle holds 6 unworked stitches from the previous row; the LH needle, 15 stitches.

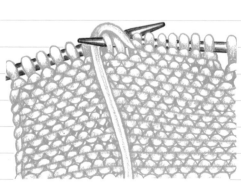

5 Purl the next 7 stitches, then purl the next 2 stitches together. Turn the work, leaving the last 6 stitches unworked.

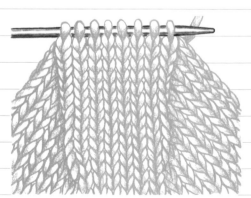

6 On the next row, knit 7 stitches, then decrease 1 stitch as instructed in step 4; turn. Purl 7 stitches, then purl 2 together; turn. Repeat these last 2 rows until 8 stitches remain on the needle, ending with a WS row; turn.

7 Now resume working in rounds. First knit across the 8 heel stitches, then pick up and knit (see p. 135) 10 stitches along the side of the heel. Using a second needle, knit across the 20 instep stitches.

8 Using a third needle, pick up and knit 10 stitches along the remaining side of the heel, then knit across 4 of the stitches on the first needle. Place a marker after the last stitch. There should be a total of 48 stitches on the needles.

9 Knit one round. On the second round knit to the third stitch from the end on the first needle, then knit 2 together as shown. Knit the last stitch from the first needle.

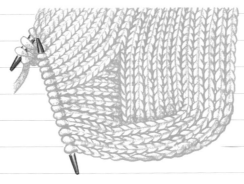

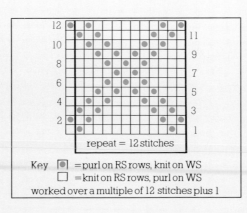

To complete the sock When the sock is the required length to fit the foot up to the point where it narrows, work the toe shaping as follows: on the next round, decrease 1 stitch at the end of the first needle and the beginning of the third needle, as instructed in steps 9 and 10. Repeat this round 4 more times. There should be 30 stitches on the needles. Divide the stitches equally among the 3 needles and continue the shaping, knitting 2 stitches together at the beginning and end of each needle on every round until there are 2 stitches on each needle, Bind off. Darn in the loose ends.

10 Knit across the 20 instep stiches. Knit 1 stitch from the third needle, slip 1, knit 1, and pass the slipped stitch over as shown. Knit to the end of the round.

11 Repeat this decrease round 3 more times, so that 40 stitches remain on the needles. This completes the shaping of the heel.

CHARTED STITCH PATTERNS

Symbols are normally used to represent multicolor stitch patterns such as Fair Isle and jacquard designs, but they can also be used for one-color stitch patterns. One or more repeats of the pattern will be shown, with each symbol standing for a particular technique: "knit," "purl," "knit 2 together through back of loops," and so on.

A visual representation of the pattern often takes less space than row-by-row instructions; it also has the advantage of needing no adjustment if the work is to be done in the round, for the chart shows the work as seen from the right side. In the example (*right*), a blank square indicates a knit stitch (on right-side rows) and a purl stitch (on wrong-side rows). If working in the round, you would knit all the blank squares. A dot indicates a purl stitch.

Key ◉ = purl on RS rows, knit on WS
☐ = knit on RS rows, purl on WS
worked over a multiple of 12 stitches plus 1

Although symbolic pattern instructions are widely used in some countries there is, unfortunately, no internationally-accepted set of symbols and meanings. However, the key provided with the pattern can usually be learned quickly.

As with multicolor charts, stitch pattern charts are read from bottom to top, starting at the lower right-hand corner.

For practice in following a stitch pattern chart, try the simple textured pattern shown here. Line-by-line instructions are on p. 60.

Where the edge of a knitted garment is intended to lie flat, rather than cling to the body, it must be finished either with a knitted or crocheted edging or with a hem. The lower edge of a skirt is normally finished with a hem, which helps it to hang well. Coats and jackets, also, may be hemmed.

Although they are not difficult to work, hems require a little care if they are not to appear bulky. The fold should be worked in stockinette stitch—whatever the main fabric stitch—for this is the smoothest of stitch patterns. It should also be worked on needles one or two sizes smaller than those used for the main fabric.

Three methods of working a hem are shown here. The ordinary sewn-in hem is fairly elastic and thus suitable for skirts. The knitted-in hem is firmer and is recommended for jackets, which need a strong

edge. The picot hem, which is normally sewn in, gives a decorative edge.

It is possible to work a waistband in the same way as a hem. A length of elastic is inserted into the waistband before the stitching holding the band in place is completed. For an extra-snug fit the fold can be worked in single rib; this is especially well suited to clothing for babies and toddlers, who have no natural waistline to help keep the garment in place. On adults' garments it may be preferable to use a herringbone-stitch waistband, which has only one layer of knitting and thus prevents excess bulk.

Since most knitting is worked from the lower edge upward, the hem fold is usually knitted first. However, if you are working from top to bottom (some skirts are knitted in this way), you can easily adapt the instructions here, working the hem fold at the end. After the last right-side row of the main fabric, work the fold line as described in step 1 of "Sewn-in hem." Then change to smaller needles, work the appropriate number of rows for the hem fold, and bind off.

If you are working in the round, a slightly different technique must be used to work the hem fold line: simply purl one row instead of knitting. This produces a ridge virtually identical to that produced by knitting through the backs of the loops, although it is not quite as firm.

SEWN-IN HEM

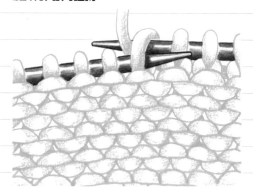 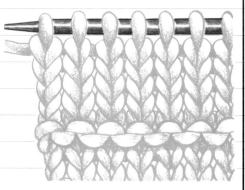

1 Using the smaller needles, cast on the required number of stitches and work in stockinette stitch for the appropriate depth, ending with a RS row. On the next row, change to the larger needles and knit all stitches through the backs of the loops.

2 The last row forms the ridged fold line for the hem. Now proceed with the main fabric, using the larger needles. (In this example, the main fabric is stockinette stitch.)

PICOT HEM

This type of hem is ideal for baby clothes, lingerie, and some dressy garments. It is most effective worked in a fine yarn—such as fingering. As for the other types of hem, it should be worked on needles a size or two smaller than those used for the main fabric.

Using the smaller needles, cast on and work in stockinette stitch for the depth of the hem, ending with a WS row. On the next row, work eyelets as follows: knit 1, * yarn over, knit 2 together, repeat from * to the last stitch, yarn over, knit 1.

Change to the larger needles and continue with the main fabric.

When the work is completed and any seams joined, turn the hem to the WS along the row of eyelets and whipstitch it in place.

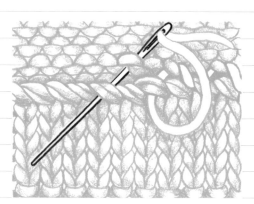 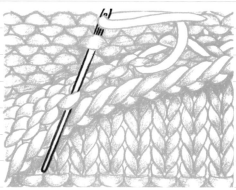 

3 After the pieces are completed and seamed, turn up the hem along the fold line and pin it in place. Using matching yarn, sew the hem in place with whipstitch, taking the needle through one stitch of the garment and one of the hem each time.

4 If the yarn used for the garment is thick, a blind hem is preferable to whipstitch, since it does not draw the cast-on edge into the garment. Separate the yarn into one or two plies to work the stitching; this will further help to reduce bulk.

KNITTED-IN HEM

This method of working a hem involves picking up stitches along the cast-on edge and knitting these stitches into the main fabric. The hem is firm, but it can look bulky unless it is worked carefully.

In the example shown here, one less row is worked in the main fabric than in the hem fold. The looser stitches produced by the larger needles make up the depth. If the yarn is fine, however, you may need to work an extra row in the main fabric to align it with the picked-up stitches. The best procedure is always to work a small sample before starting the main fabric. If either side of the hem pulls on the other, adjust the number of rows accordingly.

The double cast-on method (see p. 101) has been used in the example, since it gives a flexible edge; however, another method can be used if preferred.

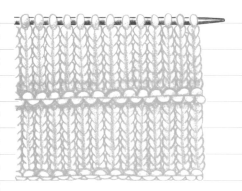

1 Cast on the required number of stitches and work the hem fold and fold line as in step 1 of "Sewn-in hem" (*opposite*). Work the main fabric until it contains 1 row less than the hem fold (excluding fold line), ending with a WS row.

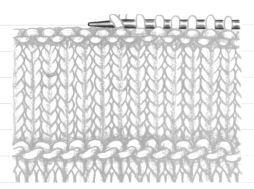

2 Leaving the needle in the work, return to the cast-on edge. With the RS facing, fasten a spare length of yarn to the RH edge (contrasting yarn is used here for clarity), and pick up and knit (see p. 135) the *farther loop only* of each cast-on stitch.

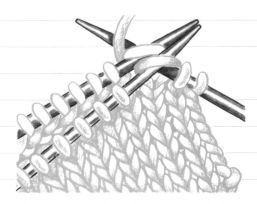

3 Fasten off the extra yarn. Bring the two edges together and, using the main yarn, knit 1 stitch from the main fabric together with 1 stitch from the hem fold to the end of the row.

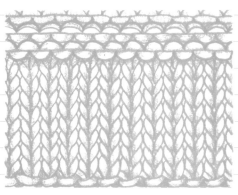

4 Continue working the main fabric. On the WS of the work the stitches picked up along the cast-on edge are securely knitted into the fabric. When joining seams, use the edge-to-edge method (see p. 136), working through the main fabric only.

RIBBED WAISTBAND

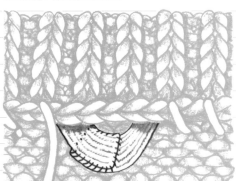

Work the fold and fold line as for a sewn-in hem (*opposite*), but use 1 × 1 rib for the fold. When the work is complete, sew the fold in place, leaving a 2 in gap. Thread elastic through the casing, sew the ends together firmly, and close the gap.

HERRINGBONE CASING

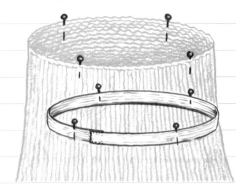

1 Cut the elastic 1½ in longer than the waist measurement, lap the ends, and sew them together. Divide the elastic and the garment edge into quarters and mark them with pins as shown.

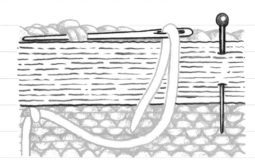

2 Matching corresponding points, pin the elastic to the WS of the garment. Insert a few more pins at intermediate points.

Secure the yarn with a backstitch just below the elastic. Insert the needle 3 stitches to the right, above the elastic, from right to left.

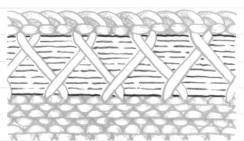

3 Now insert the needle 3 stitches to the right, below the elastic, again from right to left.

Continue working in this way back to the starting point, completely enclosing the elastic. Fasten off.

There are various ways of working pockets. The three types most often used are the patch pocket, the horizontal inside pocket, and the vertical inside pocket.

The patch pocket is the simplest in its construction, but care must be taken in sewing it on to the garment; otherwise it will have a "home-made" appearance. The Swiss-darned method shown below can be used on a stockinette stitch pocket; if the pocket is worked in another stitch, sew it on using the overcasting method. To make a feature of the pocket, make it in a contrasting color. A patch pocket can also be sewn on leaving the side edge—rather than the top edge—free, so forming a vertical patch pocket.

If a patch pocket is to be placed immediately above the ribbing, work it on stitches picked up from the main fabric. Sew the edges in place using the chosen method.

A separate patch is also worked for a horizontal or vertical inside pocket, but for these types of pocket the patch serves as the lining. The process of incorporating the lining into the main fabric may look complicated but it is really quite simple.

Wherever possible, the pocket or pocket lining and the main fabric should be blocked or pressed (see p. 133) before being joined; this makes it easier to sew down the edges.

You can easily add a flap to a patch pocket: simply continue working until the pocket, including the flap, is the desired depth. If the fabric is not reversible, you must reverse the method of working at the fold line. For example, if the pocket is in stockinette stitch, work reverse stockinette stitch from the fold line onward, so that the knit side will form the right side of the flap.

SWISS-DARNED PATCH POCKET

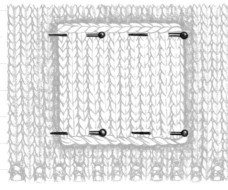

1 Make the pocket by casting on the appropriate number of stitches and working to the required depth. Bind off.

Block or press the pocket and main section, making sure that the pocket corners are square. Pin the pocket to the main fabric.

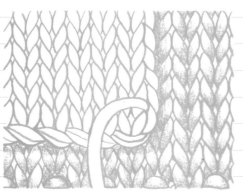

2 Secure the yarn on the WS of the main fabric, under the lower RH corner of the pocket. Bring the yarn up 1 stitch in from the edge as shown.

3 Take the yarn down into the base of the stitch, through both fabrics, covering one side of the stitch, and bring it up at the upper LH corner as shown. Finally, take it down again into the base of the stitch.

4 Work across the row in this way, taking care to keep the lower edge of the pocket aligned with a row of stitches in the main fabric.

5 Now work in the same way, but vertically, into the line of stitches lying just in from the LH edge, keeping the work aligned with the main fabric stitches.

Fasten off the yarn, then rejoin it at the starting point and work vertically up the RH edge of the pocket.

HORIZONTAL INSIDE POCKET

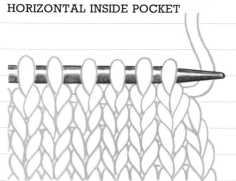

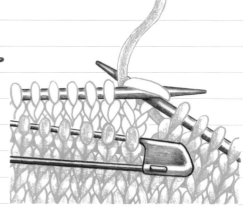

1 Cast on the required number of stitches for the lining (2 more than for the opening), and work until it is the desired depth. Decrease 1 stitch at each end of the second-to-last row, and slip the last row of stitches on to a spare needle.

2 Knit the main fabric up to the top edge of the pocket, ending with a WS row. Turn and work back to the position for the pocket opening; fasten off. Slip the pocket opening stitches on to a stitch holder, rejoin yarn, and continue to the end of the row.

3 Work back across the main fabric to the pocket opening, then work across the pocket lining stitches. Then work across the main fabric stitches to the left of the pocket opening.

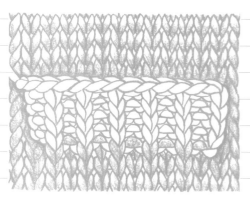

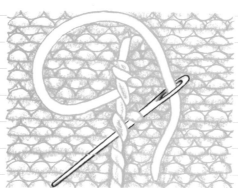

PICKING UP STITCHES FOR A POCKET

4 When the section is complete, rejoin the yarn to the stitches on the holder, at the RH side. Using smaller needles, and increasing 1 stitch at each end of the first row, work in 1 × 1 rib until the border is the desired depth. Bind off.

5 Using matching yarn, whipstitch the lining to the WS of the garment, working from the top downward on each side and making sure that the stitching does not show on the RS. Slipstitch the edges of the ribbed border in place.

1 After completing the main fabric piece, pick up stitches just above the ribbing, using a crochet hook. Slip the hook under a stitch, catch the yarn, then pull the yarn through the stitch. Slip the point of a spare knitting needle through each loop.

OVERCAST PATCH POCKET

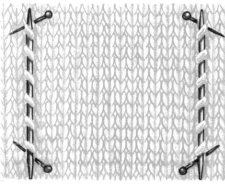

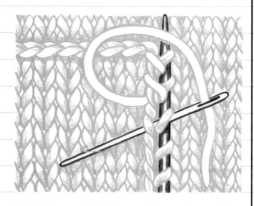

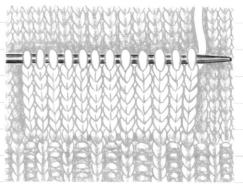

1 Place the pocket on the main section and insert a pin just outside each corner. Remove the pocket. Using two fine, double-pointed needles, pick up alternate stitches between each set of pins, making sure that the stitches are aligned.

2 Pin the pocket between the needles and sew it in place as shown, picking up a stitch from the pocket edge and one from the needle along each side. Sew the lower edge in place, working into alternate stitches.

2 Beginning with a purl row, work in stockinette stitch until the pocket is the desired depth. Bind off evenly.
   Sew the side edges in place, using either the Swiss darning method or the overcasting method.

VERTICAL INSIDE POCKET

Working a vertical pocket involves working on one side of the garment section, while incorporating the pocket lining, then working on the other side until it is the same depth. Work then continues on the rejoined parts of the main section.

The instructions given here show a pocket being placed in the left-hand side of a garment. To work a vertical pocket in the right-hand side, follow the same basic procedure, but in reverse: in step 2 end with a right side row—that is, at the right-hand edge of the garment (in relation to the body); on the next (wrong side) row, work back toward the center, picking up the lining stitches and placing the lining at the *front* of the work. Work the two sides separately and then rejoin them, reversing the direction of working as necessary.

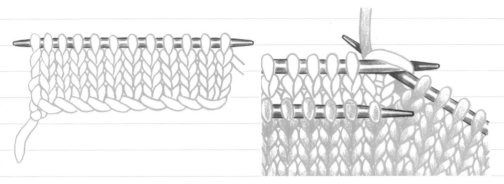

1 Cast on the required number of stitches for the lining and work for a few rows. (This part of the lining extends a short way below the opening.) End with a WS row and slip the stitches on to a spare needle or stitch holder.

2 Work the main section up to the position for the pocket opening, ending with a WS row. Now work across to the opening and slip the remaining stitches on to a spare needle. Continue working across the lining stitches.

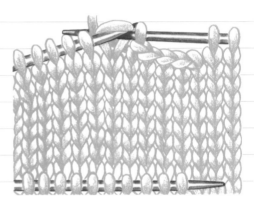

3 Work on the lining stitches and the left side of the main section only, until the work—from the held stitches upward—is the correct measurement for the pocket opening, ending with a WS row. Work across the main fabric and bind off the lining stitches.

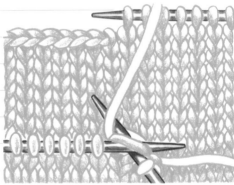

4 Return to the stitches on the spare needle. Rejoin the yarn at the RH side and work to the end of the row. Work on these stitches until the work is level with the top of the lining, ending with a RS row.

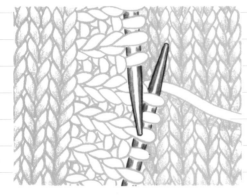

5 On the next (WS) row, work across all the main section stitches, thus completing the pocket opening. When the main piece is complete, pick up stitches along the opening (see p. 135) and work a border. Sew the lining and border edges in place.

POCKET STYLES

This patch pocket, worked in seed stitch, adds contrasting texture to a garment in stockinette stitch.

A contrasting color has been used here for the ribbed border of a horizontal inside pocket, in order to make it a styling feature.

The border on this vertical pocket has been worked in seed stitch. A single or double rib could be used instead if preferred.

Before you join the sections of a knitted garment or accessory, you must usually either block or press the pieces. This may be necessary to bring the pieces into the correct shape, to smooth the texture of the knitting, or to prevent the edges from curling and thus being difficult to seam. In some cases blocking or pressing may be necessary for all three reasons—in others, neither process should be used.

Two factors must be considered when deciding whether to block or press: the fiber content of the yarn and the stitch pattern. A highly textured stitch should never be pressed, whatever yarn is used, although it may respond well to blocking. Ribbing should not even be blocked, for the essential characteristic of rib patterns (with very few exceptions) is their elastic quality. On the other hand, stockinette stitch usually needs blocking or some-

times—if worked in wool or cotton— pressing. Some synthetic yarns require neither blocking nor pressing, whatever the stitch pattern.

The yarn label normally includes information on the care of the yarn (see the chart on p. 134). If you are in any doubt about blocking or pressing, experiment with a sample piece to see the effect.

Materials you will need for blocking and pressing include: a large, flat surface (preferably a board about 24 by 60 in, but the kitchen table or even the floor will do), one or more thick towels or an old blanket, some rustproof pins, a spray bottle, an iron, and a pressing cloth.

BLOCKING

Pin each piece to a flat, padded surface, RS up, placing the pins at intervals of about 1 in. Avoid the ribbed areas; when pinning a ribbed neckline or armhole, place the pins in the main fabric, just beside the ribbing.

Place the first pins at key points, such as just below the armhole shaping and at each end of the shoulder edge. Check occasionally with a ruler to make sure that the piece fits the measurements specified in the pattern and that rows of stitches run straight. It may be possible at this stage to correct *slight* deviations in size—making the garment slightly wider, for example. If two front sections of a cardigan or two sleeves need to be blocked, place them side

by side and check each measurement on both pieces as you pin; this will save time and will also ensure (barring mistakes in the knitting) that the pieces are the same size and shape.

Fill the spray bottle with cold water and spray the knitted pieces evenly. Allow them to dry thoroughly, away from direct heat.

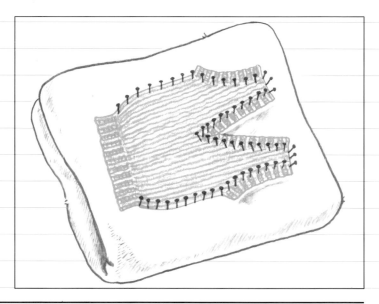

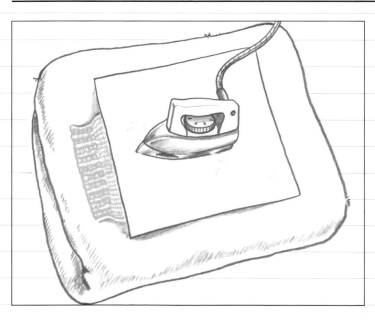

PRESSING

If the pieces need to be pressed, pin them to a padded surface, as for blocking, but pin them RS down. Use pins with ordinary heads (making sure they are rustproof) and insert them at an angle, all the way into the padding.

A pressing cloth should be used between the knitting and the iron.

On wool, cotton, linen, or silk, use either a dry cloth and a steam iron, or a damp cloth and dry iron, with the iron set at a temperature appropriate for the fiber (hot for linen or cotton, warm for wool or silk). Synthetics should be blocked, rather than pressed; but a natural–synthetic blend can be pressed using a cool iron over a dry cloth.

Never slide the iron over the

surface of the work. Place it on the cloth for a moment—without letting its full weight rest on the work—then lift it off and reapply it to another area.

Some highly textured stitches and yarns—notably mohair and angora—should be steamed rather than pressed. Pin the work RS up and lay a wet cloth over it. Hold a moderately hot iron just above the cloth for a moment to create steam.

Just as the individual sections of knitting must be treated in a suitable way before joining (see p. 133), so the completed garment requires careful treatment if it is to retain its shape, color, and texture.

Many synthetics and even some specially-treated wools can be machine washed, but in most cases hand washing is the preferred method. A liquid soap or mild detergent, manufactured especially for knits, is recommended; the water should be cool to lukewarm. Do not use bleach.

Gently squeeze the suds through the fabric—do *not* wring. Rinse well (adding a water softener to the last rinse if necessary), drain out the water, and squeeze the garment gently to remove as much water as possible.

Lift the garment carefully on to a thick towel and roll it up for a few minutes so that the towel can absorb as much moisture as possible. Then place the garment on another towel on a flat surface and pull it gently into shape. Leave it to dry naturally, away from direct heat.

Although most knits can be safely dry-cleaned, this process is not recommended for hand knits, because it tends to take the resilience out of the fabric.

RE-BLOCKING A GARMENT
Some garments need to be blocked every time they are washed. This is especially true of those worked in Fair Isle patterns, particularly if the strands on the wrong side were pulled rather tightly. Pull the garment into shape when it is still slightly damp, and pin it to the towel around the edges as shown, avoiding the ribbing. When the garment is dry, it may be pressed lightly—if the fiber content permits.

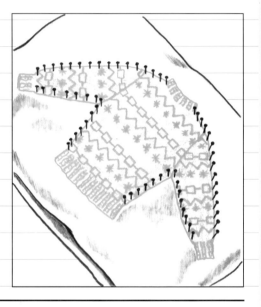

 After washing a garment made in a fluffy yarn, such as angora or mohair, allow it to dry flat. Then put it into a plastic bag and place this in the refrigerator overnight; this will restore the soft, fluffy texture.

 Never hang up a knitted garment, or it will sag out of shape. Store it carefully folded in a drawer or on a shelf. If it becomes creased, drape it over a drying rack placed over the bathtub and run a little hot water into the tub. The rising steam should remove the creases.

 If you need to unravel a piece of knitting and re-use the yarn, wind the yarn on to a wire coathanger bent to the shape shown here and covered with a cloth to avoid rust. Hold the hanger over steam from a boiling kettle to smooth out the kinks. Leave the yarn—still on the hanger—to dry naturally.

FIBER CARE SYMBOLS
Most yarns carry, on the label, instructions for after-care. These instructions are sometimes given in the form of symbols, eliminating the need for translation in different countries. Below are the symbols most often used for knitting yarns.

 Machine/Hand wash warm (40°C) Medium machine wash, normal rinse and spin Do not rub or wring Dry flat

 Machine/Hand wash warm (40°C) Minimum machine wash, cold rinse, short spin Do not wring

 Machine/Hand wash warm (40°C) Minimum machine wash, spin Do not rub or wring Dry flat

 Hand wash only warm (40°C) Do not rub or wring Dry flat

 Do not bleach

 Cool iron

 Warm iron

 Hot iron

 Do not iron

 Dry-clean only

 Dry-cleanable in all solvents

 Dry-cleanable in certain solvents; consult cleaner

 Do not dry-clean

It is often necessary to pick up stitches along an edge—in order to knit a neckband, for example. This technique involves attaching a new length of yarn and drawing loops through to the right side of the fabric.

Sometimes the new stitches are picked up vertically, along the side edge; this technique would be used, for example, when working a buttonhole band. In other cases, such as the front of a neck shaping, stitches may need to be picked up horizontally, just below the bound-off edge. (For a smoother finish the main fabric stitches are not bound off, but left on a stitch holder or spare needle and then knitted with the new yarn in the usual way.) Working a neckband also usually involves picking up stitches along a curved or diagonal edge.

Picking up stitches is not difficult, but if the results are to be neat it must be done with care. The stitches must be spaced as evenly as possible. This can be tricky on a curved or diagonal edge; dividing the edge into small sections, as shown at right, will help to ensure even spacing. Even so, you will often need to pull out a few stitches and pick them up again more evenly.

The pattern will usually specify the number of stitches to be picked up along each edge. If you are doing your own design, consult the guidelines given on p. 83.

SPACING STITCHES EVENLY

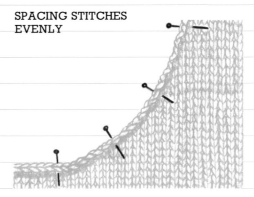

Where a number of stitches are to be picked up (irrespective of the number of rows in the edge), mark the edge into even sections, using pins or contrasting threads. Divide the stitches into equal groups and pick up each group within the corresponding section.

ON A VERTICAL EDGE

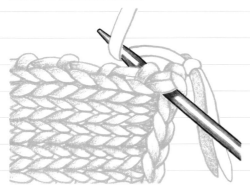

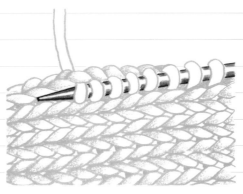

1 With the RS of the work facing, fasten the yarn at the RH corner. Insert the needle into the fabric, 1 stitch in from the edge. Take the yarn around the needle as for a knit stitch. Pull the new stitch through to the RS.

2 Continue in this way, always inserting the needle 1 stitch in from the edge and spacing the stitches evenly as required. In the illustration, 1 stitch has been picked up for each row, but in many cases a row must be skipped at regular intervals.

ON A HORIZONTAL BOUND-OFF EDGE

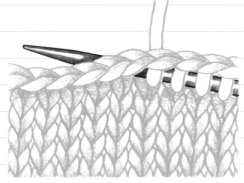

Work as for a vertical edge, but insert the needle into the last row of stitches before the bind-off.

One stitch is normally picked up for each stitch in the main fabric.

ON A CURVED OR DIAGONAL EDGE

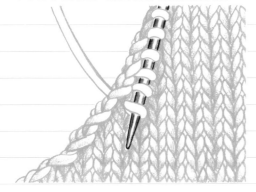

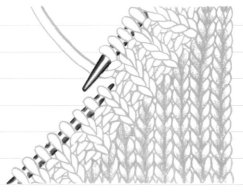

The decreases that shape the curve produce long loops along the edge of the fabric. These must be covered by the picked-up stitches if the RS is to look neat. Work slightly in from the edge, taking care to follow the shape of the curve.

After picking up stitches, work in the specified stitch pattern—in the example this is 1 × 1 rib. A slightly jagged line is almost inevitable on a curve; however, this is not readily apparent, especially if a matching yarn is used.

CROCHET HOOK METHOD

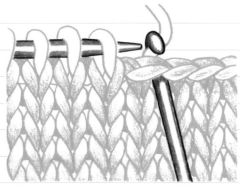

A crochet hook can be used to pick up the stitches. Pull each loop through with the crochet hook, then place it on the needle. Take care that the loops are evenly tensioned and slant correctly. Left-handed knitters can work on the WS, from right to left.

Finishing a garment requires care and patience; carelessly joined seams can ruin the appearance of a garment that has been beautifully knitted.

Several different types of seams are used for knitting. The choice of method depends on various factors, including the position of the seam, the stitch pattern, the type of yarn, and the type of garment.

A flat seam, for example, is the preferred seam for ribbing, but can be used wherever a smooth finish on the underside is desirable and extra strength is not necessary. The edges to be joined must contain the same number of rows and must not be shaped.

A somewhat firmer seam is obtained with the edge-to-edge, or "invisible" seam. This seam is particularly recommended where the wrong side needs to be as smooth as possible—on baby clothes,

for example. It is a good seam to use for attaching button and buttonhole bands.

A backstitch seam is the strongest type of seam. It is often used for side, shoulder, and sleeve seams and always for an armhole seam.

Grafting is a method of joining two edges with stitches that imitate a row of knitting, thus eliminating a seam. It is best worked on a stockinette stitch fabric, knitted in a smooth yarn; textured yarns do not lend themselves well to this technique.

When stitching seams, always use a blunt-pointed needle, such as a yarn needle or large tapestry needle, to avoid splitting the strands of yarn. Use the yarn in which the garment was knitted, unless this is bulky, highly textured, or rather weak; in such cases you should use a smooth light- to medium-weight yarn in a matching color.

Fasten the yarn with two or three backstitches—that is, stitches worked on top of each other—*not* with a knot. Fasten off in the same way, then darn the thread through several stitches in the selvage before cutting it.

Other yarn ends from the knitting should also be darned in; one or two backstitches worked along the way will prevent their slipping out.

If a seam needs to be pressed, use the point of the iron only and work over a pressing cloth, with the iron set at the appropriate temperature (see p. 133).

EDGE-TO-EDGE SEAM

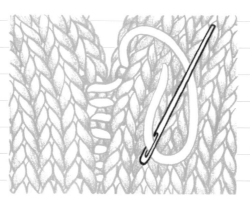

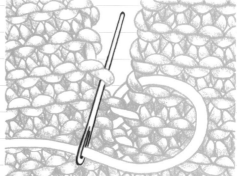

1 Fasten the yarn to the WS at the lower edge of one piece and bring it to the RS. Place the pieces side by side, RS upward. Take the needle across to the other piece and take it under the strand lying between the first and second stitches in the first row.

2 Return to the other piece and take the needle through the edge one row up, between the first and second line of stitches. Continue in this way to the end of the seam, pulling the yarn to bring the edges close together.

On a garter stitch fabric, work through the lower loop on one edge, then through the upper loop of the corresponding stitch on the other edge.

FLAT SEAM

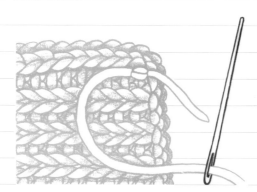

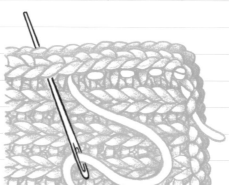

When pinning edges together for seaming, use color ball pins, which are less likely to slip out than ordinary ones. Always place pins at a right angle to the fabric edges.

For extra strength, on a coat or jacket the shoulder seam can be reinforced with a length of seam binding. Baste the pieces together with the binding on the underside, then sew through all three layers.

This seam is often used on ribbing. If worked carefully, it produces little extra bulk.
1 Place the two pieces together with RS facing and secure the thread at the RH corner of the top piece.

2 Take the needle straight through to the other side, then bring it up 1 stitch to the left. Take it down another stitch to the left. Continue in this way, working in a straight line close to the edge, and taking the needle straight through each pair of stitches.

BACKSTITCH SEAM

1 Place the pieces together with RS facing. Secure the thread on the upper piece. Take the needle through both pieces at the RH edge, then up 2 stitches to the left.

2 Take the needle down again, 1 stitch to the right, then up 2 stitches to the left. Continue in this way to the end.

Where possible, keep the stitches in a straight line, 1 stitch in from the edge. Make sure the other side is as neat as possible.

GRAFTING

This method of joining is invisible, if worked carefully, and results in a seamless piece of knitting. It is an ideal way to prevent the bulky effect that might result from an ordinary seam—on a shoulder, for example.

The edges to be grafted must contain the same number of stitches. The edges are not bound off but are left on the needles—one piece after completing a purl row, one after completing a knit row, so that when the pieces are positioned for grafting both needles point in the same direction.

An edge that has been cast on using the invisible cast-on method (see p. 102) can also be grafted—either to another invisibly cast-on edge or to a top edge left on the needle. Remove the contrasting foundation yarn and slip the stitches on to a knitting needle. Proceed as shown here.

1 Place the pieces RS upward as shown. Fasten a new length of yarn (about three times as long as the edge to be grafted) at the RH edge of the lower piece and thread it into a tapestry needle.

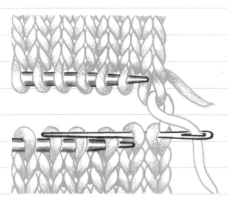

2 Take the needle purlwise through the first stitch on the lower edge, then purlwise through the first stitch on the upper edge. Insert it knitwise through the first stitch on the lower edge, then purlwise through the next stitch as shown. Remove the knitting needle from each stitch just before working it.

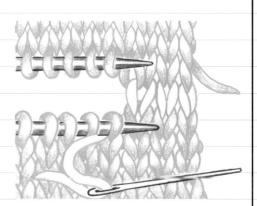

3 *Re-insert the needle knitwise into the top stitch, then insert it purlwise into the next stitch to the left, then re-insert it knitwise into the stitch immediately below, then insert it purlwise into the next stitch to the left. Repeat from * to the end.

SETTING IN A SLEEVE

Some kinds of sleeve (see p. 76) can be joined to the bodice before the side and sleeve seams are joined. A dropped shoulder sleeve, for example, is straight across the top, and this straight edge is sewn flat to the front and back of the garment after the shoulder seam is joined, so that the sleeve and garment form a "T" shape. Raglan sleeves, too, are sewn flat to the corresponding armhole edges on the front and back.

A set-in sleeve is handled somewhat differently. It is inserted into an armhole after the side and shoulder seams and the sleeve seam are sewn.

1 Press the seams lightly, if necessary, using the point of the iron. Turn the sleeve RS out. Insert a pin at the center of the cap of the sleeve and halfway between this point and the sleeve seam, on each side. Turn the garment WS out. Place pins at the halfway points along the armhole edges.

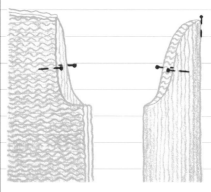

2 Insert the sleeve into the armhole and pin the two edges together, matching the top of the sleeve cap and the shoulder seam, the sleeve seam and side seam, and each midpoint on the sleeve to the two corresponding pins at each side.

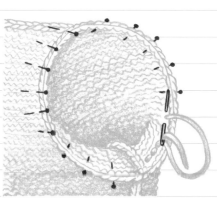

3 Add more pins around the armhole, placing them about 1 in apart. If the cap of the sleeve is larger than the armhole, ease the extra fullness to fit. A line of basting will help to hold the edges together. Join the armhole seam, using backstitch and working about ¼ in from the edge.

Many garments require a fastening of some kind—usually buttons and buttonholes, or sometimes a zipper. It is important to make these as neat as possible, for they inevitably draw the eye and are often a styling feature of the garment.

Several different methods can be used to make a buttonhole. The choice of method depends on the weight of the fabric, the intended size of the button, and the position of the buttonhole.

An eyelet (see p. 113) is the simplest kind of buttonhole. It is ideal for delicate, lacy fabrics and baby clothes, but can also be used on garments knitted in medium-weight yarns, since the hole produced using such yarns will accommodate a flat button up to ⅝in in diameter.

Horizontal buttonholes are the usual choice for fastening the front edges of a cardigan or jacket. They are often worked in a separate band. Vertical buttonholes are best restricted to a purely decorative position—such as a pocket flap—where little strain will be placed on them, for they can easily be pulled out of shape.

If you live near a store with a good selection of buttons, you can usually find ones of a suitable size and style after the garment is finished. If not, it is a good idea to select the button first, then work a sample buttonhole in a small piece of knitting to test the size in relation to the button. Reduce or enlarge the buttonhole size if necessary.

Zippers are less commonly used than buttons for fastening knitwear; however, they are well suited to some garments—particularly jackets that need to have a secure closing for warmth. Zippers are available in a wide variety of weights and lengths. Take a piece of the knitted fabric (not just the yarn) with you when buying the zipper to make sure that you select one of the appropriate color and type.

Normally a zipper should be as inconspicuous as possible; however, on a casual garment you might make a decorative feature of a zipper, using a heavy-weight one (if suitable for the fabric) in a contrasting color. Do not baste the opening edges together, as shown opposite, but baste them to the zipper tape so that they clear the teeth.

HORIZONTAL BUTTONHOLE

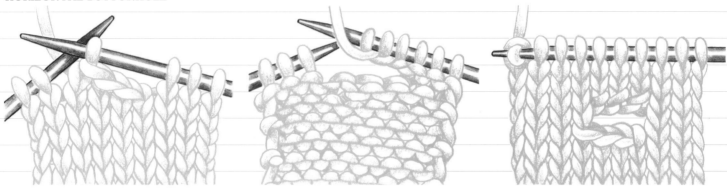

1 On the RS, work to the position of the buttonhole. Bind off the appropriate number of stitches; in the example, 3 stitches have been bound off. Work to the end of the row.

2 On the WS, work up to the bound-off stitches. Using the single cast-on method (see p. 101) cast on the same number of stitches as were bound off. Work to the end of the row.

3 On the next row, work into the back of the cast-on stitches. This helps to make the corners neat.

VERTICAL BUTTONHOLE

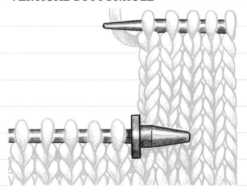
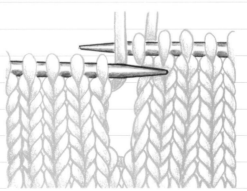
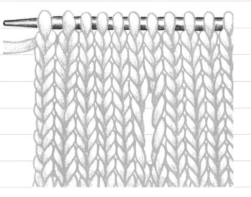

1 Work on the RS to the position of the buttonhole. Slip the remaining stitches on to a holder, turn, and work in rows on the first set of stitches until the buttonhole is the required length, ending with a RS row. Do not break the yarn.

2 Attach a new length of yarn to the held stitches, at the buttonhole edge. Work on these stitches until there is one row less than on the other side—i.e. ending with a WS row. For a neat edge, slip the first stitch on alternate rows on both sides of the buttonhole.

3 Fasten off the new yarn, then work across the second set of stitches. Continue working the fabric as before.

INSERTING A ZIPPER

The edges of the opening for the zipper should be knitted or finished so that they will lie flat and look attractive. Working a double garter stitch selvage (shown in these illustrations—see also p. 105) is one good method. Another method, which produces a less conspicuous opening, is to work crocheted slip stitch (see p. 140) along the completed fabric edges.

Always insert a zipper before finishing the garment. Block or press the section(s) in which the zipper is to be placed; if two sections are to be seamed below the zipper, sew them together and press if necessary before inserting the zipper.

If you are using an open-ended zipper, keep the lower ends joined while basting the zipper in place (step 2) to ensure that the two sides are positioned directly opposite each other.

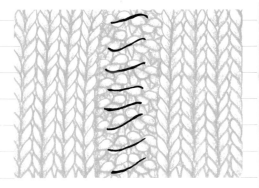

1 Place the garment section RS upward on a flat surface. Using sewing thread and a fine tapestry needle, baste the edges together with overcasting stitches.

BUTTON AND BUTTONHOLE BANDS

It takes a little skill to make and attach a button or buttonhole band so that it looks neat. Here are some techniques that will help you to give this part of a cardigan or jacket a professional finish.

Patterns will often instruct you to work the band until, "when slightly stretched," it fits from the lower edge to the center neck, then bind off. It can be difficult to judge when this length has been reached simply by pinning the band to the front edge. Instead, work until the band is one or two inches shorter than the estimated length, and slip the stitches on to a safety pin. Sew the band to the garment edge, stretching it slightly as you go. Then work a few more rows to cover the short remaining distance.

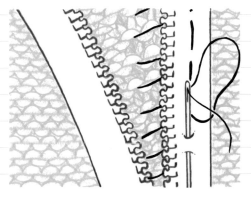

2 Turn the work WS upward. Open the zipper and place it face down, with one edge aligned exactly with the opening. Baste the tape in place as shown. Close the zipper and baste the other side.

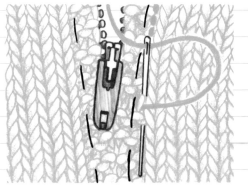

3 Turn the work RS upward. Using a single strand of matching buttonhole twist and backstitch (see p. 137), sew the zipper in place where the selvage meets the main fabric.

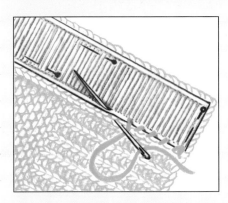

To ensure that button and buttonhole bands keep their shape, apply a ribbon facing to the wrong side. Choose a grosgrain ribbon slightly narrower than the band.
1 Pin it to the wrong side of the band, with the ends turned under, and slipstitch it in place.

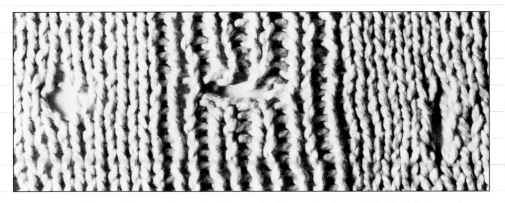

Three types of buttonhole are shown in this sample. The eyelet buttonhole (*left*) is formed by bringing the yarn over and knitting 2 stitches together. The horizontal buttonhole (*center*) is 3 stitches wide; and the vertical buttonhole (*right*) is 5 rows deep.

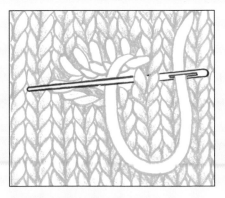

2 With the right side facing and using embroidery scissors, cut a slit in the ribbon under each buttonhole, taking care not to cut the knitting. Finish the buttonhole with buttonhole stitch.

Every knitter should know at least the simplest crochet techniques, for crochet is often used for working edgings, button loops, and ties on knitted garments and accessories. It can also be used to join seams. A good way of joining knitted patchwork motifs—to make a blanket for example—is to work a crochet edging around each motif, then join the edges with crochet.

Crochet is easy to learn: only one implement is used, and you needn't worry about "dropped" stitches or mistakes. If you make a mistake, you simply unravel the work back to the mistake and begin again.

As with knitting, however, you must work with an even tension; and you must sometimes adjust your gauge to suit the knitted fabric on which you are working. Because crochet stitches are generally larger than knitted ones, you will probably find that fewer crochet stitches are needed to edge a given number of knitted stitches. A pattern will usually specify the number of stitches to be worked along an edge, but if it does not, or if you are designing your own edging, you should experiment with a small sample of knitting in the same yarn and stitch pattern, working the edging on it and adjusting the number of stitches or the hook size, if necessary, to achieve a smooth effect—neither rippled nor puckered.

The instructions given here show crochet worked with the right hand. For left-handed people the method is essentially the same, but reversed. Holding the page to a mirror will show how crochet is worked with the left hand.

HOLDING HOOK AND YARN

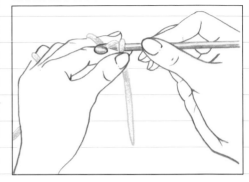

Make a slip knot (see p. 100) and place the loop on the hook. Hold the hook as shown and wrap the yarn around the fingers of the other hand: under and around the little finger, under the third, over the second and first. Extend the second finger to tension the yarn.

CHAIN STITCH

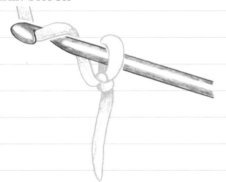

1 Place a slip loop on the hook. Hold the knot between the thumb and index finger. Slide the hook forward under the working yarn and turn it counter-clockwise, catching the yarn. Pull the hook back through the slip loop. One chain has been worked.

2 Repeat these actions as often as required, pulling each new chain stitch through the one just formed. The drawing shows both sides of a length of chain.

SLIP STITCH

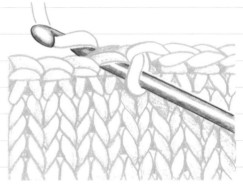

This is the shortest of crochet stitches. Here it is worked on an edge of single crochet. Insert the hook into the next stitch, turn the hook as for a chain (called "yarn over") and draw the yarn through the stitch and through the loop on the hook.

SINGLE CROCHET ON A KNITTED FABRIC

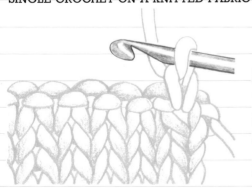

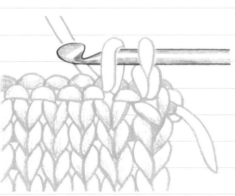

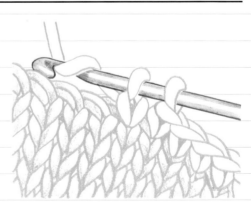

1 Fasten the short end of yarn to the edge of the knitting. Insert the hook into the fabric, (take the working yarn around the hook and draw a loop through) twice.

2 To work a single crochet stitch: *insert the hook into the next stitch, yarn over and draw through a loop, yarn over (*shown*) and draw through a loop. Two loops are now on the hook.

3 Yarn over and draw it through both loops on the hook.* This completes one single crochet stitch. (Several are shown completed in the illustration.) Repeat from * to * as often as required. At corners, work 3 single crochets into 1 stitch.

ABBREVIATIONS

The following commonly-used abbreviations are used in this book and in the Pattern Portfolio. Additional abbreviations are explained within the patterns in which they are used. See also the section on knitting language (p. 105).

approx	approximately
beg	begin(ning)
C2B	cable 2 back: sl next st on to cable needle and hold at back of work, K1, then K1 from cable needle
C4B, C6B	as C2B, but working 2 and 3 sts, respectively, at a time
C2F	cable 2 front: sl next st on to cable needle and hold at front of work, K1, then K1 from cable needle
C4F, C6F	as C2F, but working 2 and 3 sts, respectively, at a time
ch	chain(s)
cont	continu(e)(ing)
Cr2B	cross 2 back: sl next st on to cable needle and hold at back
Cr2F	cross 2 front: sl next st on to cable needle and hold at front of work, P1, then K1 from cable needle
dec	decreas(e)(ing)
foll	follow(s)(ing)
g st	garter stitch
g	gram(s)
in	inch(es)
inc	increas(e)(ing)
K	knit
K-wise	knitwise
LH	left-hand
oz	ounce(s)
P	purl
P-wise	purlwise
patt	pattern
psso	pass slipped st over
rem	remain(s)(ing)
rep	repeat(ing)
rev st st	reverse stockinette stitch
RH	right-hand
RS	right side
sc	single crochet(s)
sl	slip(ped)
st(s)	stitch(es)
st st	stockinette stitch
tbl	through back of loop(s)
tog	together
Tw2B	twist 2 back: sl next st on to cable needle and hold at back of work, K1 tbl, P1 from cable needle
Tw2F	twist 2 front: sl next st on to cable needle and hold at front of work, P1, then K1 tbl from cable needle
Tw3B	twist 3 back: sl next st on to cable needle and hold at back of work, K2, then P1 from cable needle
Tw3F	twist 3 front: sl next 2 sts on to cable needle and hold at front of work, P1, then K2 from cable needle
WS	wrong side
wyb	with yarn in back
wyf	with yarn in front
yd	yard(s)
yo	yarn over

CHOOSING A CIRCULAR NEEDLE

The table at right is a guide to selecting the correct length of circular needle for a given number of stitches, to be worked in the round.

First find your stitch gauge in the left-hand column. Then read across the line to find the last number that is *less than* the number of stitches you will be knitting. For example, if your gauge is 24 stitches to 4 in, and the knitting contains 166 stitches, you would stop at the second column and choose a needle 24 in long, which will take no fewer than 144 stitches. The next size up, 29 in, requires a minimum of 172 stitches.

Note, however, that if your knitting contains, for example, 210 stitches, you can still use the 24 in needle, or even a 16 in needle, for a circular needle will comfortably hold up to four times its minimum number of stitches. So, if you are buying a circular needle for a particular project, you might prefer to buy a shorter one than specified by the table, since it will be more versatile—accommodating narrower, as well as wider, pieces of knitting.

GAUGE	LENGTH OF NEEDLE (inches)			
(sts. to 4 in)	16	24	29	36
	Total number of sts			
16	64	96	116	144
18	72	108	130	162
20	80	120	144	180
22	88	132	158	198
24	96	144	172	216
26	104	156	186	234
28	112	168	200	252
30	120	180	214	270
32	128	192	228	288
34	136	204	242	306
36	144	216	256	324

METRIC AND AMERICAN NEEDLE SIZES

metric (European)	2mm	2¼mm	2¾mm	3mm	3¼mm	3½mm	4mm	4½mm	5mm	5½mm	6mm	6½mm	7mm	7½mm	8mm	8½mm	9mm
American (approx. equivalent)	0	1	2		3	4	5	6	7	8	9	10	10½		11		13

PATTERN PORTFOLIO

The pattern portfolio comprises 46 patterns, each with complete working instructions and a photograph of the finished article. Every one of the patterns is a designer original, and the designs have been carefully selected to provide garments for all the family and patterns to suit knitters of all abilities, including beginners.

Several of the patterns suggest "options" – ideas for altering, adapting or changing the design to suit individual needs or different yarns. Reference to both the "Design Your Own" and "Knitting Know-How" sections of the book may be helpful when following the patterns or adapting them to suit your own personal style.

A simple stripe pattern in reverse stockinette stitch takes on a whole new look and feel with a soft, bobbled novelty yarn.

SIZES

To fit 32[34:36:38]in bust, loosely
Garment measures: 39½[40½:41½:42½]in at underarm
Length from shoulder: 26[26½:27:27½]in
Sleeve seam: 12[12½:14:14½]in
Note Instructions for larger sizes are given in brackets [].

MATERIALS

Pingouin Pingostar (A)
6[6:7:7] 1¾oz/50g balls
Color shown: Noir
Pingouin Brigantin (B)
12[13:14:15] 1¾oz/50g balls
Color shown: Méphisto
Pair of size 9 knitting needles
4 large buttons

GAUGE

15sts and 18 rows to 4in over stripe patt worked on size 9 needles

To save time, take time to check gauge.

ABBREVIATIONS

See book, p. 141.

Note Sleeves are worked at the same time as each main piece, rather than separately in the usual way.
Carry contrasting yarns up side of work when not in use.

BACK

Using A, cast on 74[76:78:80]sts. K 2 rows, changing to B at end of row. Do not break off A.
Beg stripe patt:
1st patt row (WS) Using B, K.
2nd row Using B, P.
3rd row Using A, K.
4th row Using A, P.
These 4 rows form patt. Cont in patt until work measures 13[13½:13½:14]in, ending with a P row.
Shape sleeves:
Keeping patt correct, cast on 2sts at beg of next 10 rows, 5sts at beg of next 8 rows and 8[10:12:14]sts at beg of next 2 rows. 150[156:162:168]sts.
Work even in patt for 6½[6½:7:7]in, ending with a P row.
Shape shoulders:
Bind off 14[16:13:15]sts at beg of next 2 rows and 10[10:11:11]sts at beg of next 8 rows.
Next row Bind off 10[10:11:11]sts, work next 22[24:26:28]sts (including st left on needle after bind-off) and place these sts on a holder for back neck, work to end. Bind off rem 10[10:11:11]sts.

LEFT FRONT

Using A, cast on 44[45:46:47]sts. Cont in stripe patt as for Back until work measures 13[13½:13½:14]in, ending with a K row.
Shape sleeve:
Cast on 2sts at beg of next row and then every other row 5 times in all, 5sts at beg of every other row 4 times and 8[10:12:14]sts once. 82[85:88:91]sts.
Work even in stripe patt for 6½[6½:7:7]in, ending with a K row.
Shape shoulder and neck:
Next row Bind off 14[16:13:15]sts, work to end.
Next row Work 12[13:14:15]sts and place these sts on a holder, work to end.
Bind off 10[10:11:11]sts at beg of next row and then every other row 4 times in all, *at the same time* bind off 2sts at neck edge on every other row 3 times in all.
Work 1 row.
Bind off rem 10[10:11:11]sts.

RIGHT FRONT

Mark positions for 4 buttons on Left Front, first to come 2in from lower edge, 4th 2in from neck edge, with 2 more evenly spaced between.
Work Right Front as for Left Front, reversing shaping and working buttonholes as markers are reached as foll:
1st buttonhole row (WS) Work in patt to last 9sts, bind off 4sts, work in patt to end.
2nd row Work 5sts in patt, cast on 4sts, work in patt to end.

TO FINISH

Block and press lightly on WS foll instructions on yarn label.
Join shoulder seams.
Neck border Using B, and with RS of work facing, P12[13:14:15]sts from holder at right front neck, pick up and P 12sts along right front neck, P22[24:26:28]sts from holder at back neck, pick up and P 12sts along left front neck and P12[13:14:15]sts from holder at left front neck. 70[74:78:82]sts.
P 1 row. Bind off loosely.
Cuffs With WS of work facing and A, pick up and K 60[60:64:64]sts along straight edge of cuff and work in stripe patt as for Back beg with a 4th row until cuff measures approx 5[5:6:6]in, ending with a 2nd row. Bind off loosely.
Work 2nd cuff to match.
Join side and sleeve seams, sewing last 3in of cuff on RS.
Sew on buttons to correspond with buttonholes. Turn back cuffs.

Designed by Kate Jones

OPTIONS
If you prefer a smooth effect, make the jacket entirely in Pingostar, in a stripe pattern of your own devising, or in a solid color, working either in reverse stockinette stitch, as in this pattern, or in stockinette stitch. You will, of course, need to re-calculate the yarn quantities (see book, p. 17).
    Alternatively, if you prefer a regular pattern of bobbles, choose one of the many stitch patterns described on pp. 68–69 of the book.

Here is proof of just how warm and lively neutrals can look. This beautiful mohair blend is knitted in fawn and cream windowpane checks which emphasize the jacket's high-fashion boxy shape.

SIZES

To fit 34[36:38]in bust, loosely
Garment measures: 40½[44½:48½]in at underarm
Length from shoulder: 24½[24¾:25¼]in
Sleeve seam: 17in
Note Instructions for larger sizes are given in brackets [].

MATERIALS

Argyll Bedouin
14[15:16] 1¾oz/50g balls in main color A (236 – cream)
8[9:9] 1¾oz/50g balls in color B (237 – beige)
Pair each of sizes 6 and 8 knitting needles
6 buttons

GAUGE

20sts and 20 rows to 4in over check pattern in st st worked on size 8 needles
For gauge sample cast on 25sts. Work in patt from Chart 2, beg at "Start Right Front," rep 20 patt sts once on every row and working 22 patt rows once.

To save time, take time to check gauge.

ABBREVIATIONS

See book, p. 141.

Note When working patt from charts, read RS (K) rows from right to left and WS (P) rows from left to right, following the correct chart for your size. Carry yarn not in use across back of work using stranding and weaving methods (see book, pp. 116–117).

BACK

Using smaller needles and A, cast on 100[110:120]sts. Work in K1, P1 rib for 2in.
Change to larger needles and patt:
Beg with a K row, cont in st st, working 20 patt sts from Chart 1 for first and 3rd sizes and from Chart 2 for 2nd size, beg at ** and working extra 10sts on *2nd size only* at end of RS rows as shown on Chart 2.
Cont in patt until Back measures 17in, ending with a P row.
Shape armholes:
Keeping patt correct, bind off 3sts at beg of next 2 rows. Dec one st at each end of next row and then every other row twice more.
88[98:108]sts.
Work even in patt until Back measures 24½[24¾:25]in, ending with a P row. Bind off.

POCKET LININGS (make 2)

Using larger needles and A, cast on 20sts. Beg with a K row, work 18 rows st st. Leave sts on a holder.

LEFT FRONT

Using smaller needles and A, cast on 50[54:60]sts. Work in K1, P1 rib for 2in, inc one st at end of last row *for 2nd size only*. 50[55:60]sts.
Change to larger needles and patt:
Beg with a K row, cont in st st, working patt from Chart 3 for first size, from Chart 2 for 2nd size and from Chart 1 for 3rd size, beg at **, working extra 10[15]sts on first and 2nd sizes at *end* of RS rows as shown, until 18 rows have been worked in all.

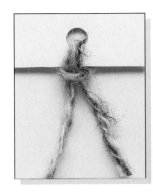

Insert Pocket Lining:
Next row (RS) Work 12[14:16]sts in patt, sl next 20sts on to a holder, patt across 20 Pocket Lining sts, work in patt to end.
Cont in patt until Front measures 17in, ending with a P row.
Shape armhole:
Bind off 3sts at beg of next row. Work 1 row. Dec one st at beg of next row and then every other row twice more. 44[49:54]sts. Work even in patt until Left Front measures 21¼[21¾:22]in, ending with a K row.
Shape neck:
Bind off 8[10:12]sts at beg of next row and 4sts at beg of every other row once. Dec one st at neck edge on next 3 rows and then every other row twice. 27[30:33]sts.
Work even until Left Front matches Back to shoulder. Bind off.

RIGHT FRONT

Work as for Left Front, working patt from Chart 3 for first size, from Chart 2 for 2nd size and from Chart 1 for 3rd size, beg at **, working extra 10[15]sts on first and 2nd sizes at *beg*, or *beg and end*, of RS rows as shown, inserting Pocket Lining as foll:

Next row (RS) Work 18[21:24]sts in patt, sl next 20sts on to a holder, work in patt across 20 Pocket Lining sts on holder, work in patt to end. Complete as for Left Front, reversing armhole and neck shaping.

SLEEVES (make 2)

Using smaller needles and A, cast on 40[44:48]sts. Work in K1, P1 rib for 2in.
Change to larger needles and patt:
Beg with a K row, cont in st st, working patt from Chart 4 for all sizes, beg at **, working extra 4[8]sts on 2nd and 3rd sizes at each end of RS rows as shown, *at the same time* inc one st at each end of every 3rd row until there are 76[80:84]sts and Sleeve measures 17in, ending with a P row.
Shape top:
Bind off 3sts at beg of next 2 rows. Dec one st at each end of next 10 rows. Bind off 5sts at beg of next 8 rows. 10[14:18]sts. Bind off.

TO FINISH

Block each piece separately, but do not press.
Pocket borders Using smaller needles, A and with RS facing, pick up 20 pocket sts from holder. Work 6 rows K1, P1 rib. Bind off in rib.
Sew pocket borders and Pocket Linings in place.
Join shoulder seams.
Neckband Using smaller needles, A and with RS facing, pick up and K 22[24:26]sts along right front neck, 30[34:36]sts from back neck and 22[24:26]sts along left front neck. 74[82:88]sts. Work 6 rows K1, P1 rib. Bind off in rib.
Button band Using smaller needles, A and with RS facing, pick up and K 108sts along left front edge. Work 6 rows K1, P1 rib. Bind off in rib.
Buttonhole band Work as for Button band, picking up sts along right front edge and making buttonholes on 3rd rib row as foll:
Next row Rib 3, *yo, K2 tog, rib 18, rep from * to last 5sts, yo, K2 tog, rib to end.
Join side and sleeve seams, matching checks.
Set in Sleeves.
Sew on buttons to correspond with buttonholes.

Designed by Brenda Sparkes

KEY
☐ = col A
▨ = col B

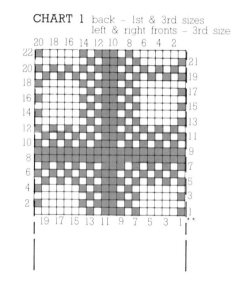

CHART 1 back – 1st & 3rd sizes
left & right fronts – 3rd size

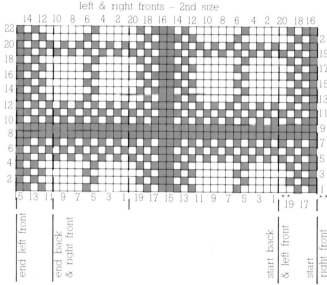

CHART 2 back – 2nd size
left & right fronts – 2nd size

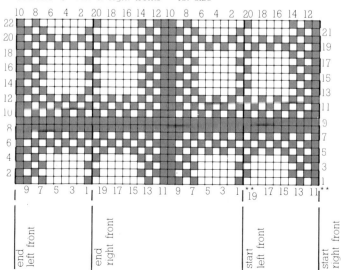

CHART 3 left & right fronts – 1st size

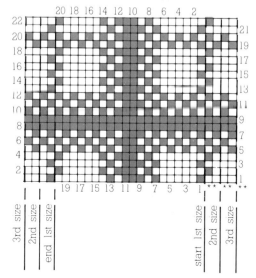

CHART 4 sleeves – all sizes

This dramatic, poncho-style wrap will serve you equally well whether you're dressed up for a night out or in jeans. It features a striking, geometric border and generous fringe.

SIZE

Wrap measures 54in × 70in, excluding fringe.

MATERIALS

Scheepjeswol Superwash Zermatt
31 1¾oz/50g balls in main color A (4808 – black)
3 1¾oz/50g balls in each of 2 contrasting colors: B (4880 – orange) and C (4822 – gray)
Pair of long size 6 knitting needles
Size 6 circular needle
Crochet hook for fringe

GAUGE

21sts and 28 rows to 4in over st st worked on size 6 needles

To save time, take time to check gauge.

ABBREVIATIONS

See book, p. 141.
Note When working in more than one color, use a separate ball of yarn for each area, twisting colors tog on WS to avoid forming holes (see book, p. 115).
When working with circular needle, work in rows rather than in rounds (see book, p. 124).

FRONT

Right side
Using pair of needles and A, cast on 150sts and work border patt as foll:
1st border row (WS) Sl 1, K to last st, P1.
2nd–6th rows As first.
7th row Sl 1, K4, P to last 5sts, K4, P1.
8th row (RS) Sl 1, K to last st, P1.
9th row As 7th.
The last 2 rows set the edge sts with center part in st st.
Rep 8th and 9th rows 5 more times, thus ending with a WS row.
Beg working from chart:
Keeping 5 edge sts at each side in A as set, work center 140sts in color patt from chart, rep 20 patt sts 7 times across each row, and reading odd (K) rows from right to left and even (P) rows from left to right until 28 chart patt rows have been completed.
Using A only, rep 8th and 9th Border patt rows 5 more times.
Keeping 5 edge sts at each side in A as set, beg with a K row, work 4 rows st st in B. **
Using A only, rep 8th and 9th Border patt rows until work measures 36in, ending with a WS row.
Next row Bind off 5sts. Cut off yarn. 145sts.
Leave rem sts on a holder.
Left side
Work as for Right side, until work measures

36in, ending with a RS row.
Next row Bind off 5sts, work in patt to end.
Sl Right side sts from holder on to same needle as Left side sts. 290sts.
Back
Transfer all sts on to circular needle and cont to work in rows.
Rep 8th and 9th Border patt rows until work measures 61in, ending with a WS row. Rep as for Right side, working from ** to **.
Rep 8th and 9th Border patt rows 5 more times.
Keeping 5 edge sts at each side in A as before, work center 280sts in color patt from chart, turning chart upside down so that 28th row will be read as a first (K) row, and rep 20 patt sts 14 times across row. Cont until 28 chart patt rows have been completed.
Using A, rep 8th and 9th border patt rows 6 times, then work 8th row again.
Rep first Border patt row 6 times. Bind off.

TO FINISH

Block, then press st st parts lightly on WS, foll instructions on yarn label.
Overlap borders in center and sew them neatly in place.
Fringe Cut 150 12in lengths of A. Using 3 strands tog, knot fringe along narrow ends of wrap, using crochet hook to pull yarn through (see book, p. 32).

Designed by Julia Howe

Scheepjeswol (UK) Ltd.

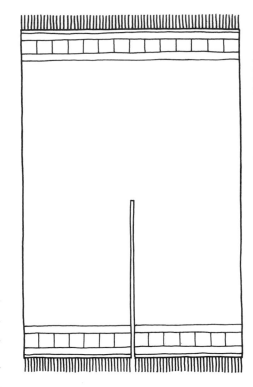

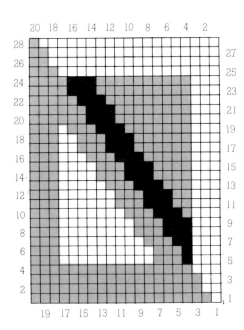

KEY
■ A = black
□ B = orange
▨ C = gray

You'll be amazed at how a cloud-light jacket could be so warm. Tiers of soft loops show off the texture of the yarn – an appealing mohair blend.

SIZES

To fit 32–34[36–38]in bust
Garment measures: 43[47]in at underarm
Length from shoulder: 24½[26]in
Sleeve seam: 17[17¾]in
Note Instructions for larger size are given in brackets [].

MATERIALS

Phildar Vizir
13[14] 1¾oz/50g balls
Color shown: Dauphin
Pair each of sizes 7 and 9 knitting needles
7[8] buttons

GAUGE

13sts and 20 rows to 4in over patt worked on size 9 needles
For gauge sample cast on at least 13sts and rep patt rows.

To save time, take time to check gauge.

ABBREVIATIONS

L1 – (loop 1) P1, but do not remove st from LH needle, yarn to back of work and around index finger of left hand, forming approx ½in loop, yo, P into same st and remove from LH needle, pass 2nd st on RH needle over first st.
For other abbreviations see book, p. 141.

BACK

Using smaller needles, cast on 72[78]sts. ** Work 2 rows in g st.
Change to larger needles and patt:
1st–12th rows Beg with a K row, work 12 rows st st.
13th row P.
14th row P1, *L1, rep from * to last st, P1.
15th row P.
16th row P.
These 16 rows form patt.
Cont in patt until Back measures 14[15]in, placing markers at each end of last row for beg of armholes. **
Cont in patt until Back measures 24½[26]in. Bind off.

LEFT FRONT

Using smaller needles, cast on 38[42]sts. Work as for Back from ** to **. Cont in patt until Left Front measures approx 21½[23¼]in, ending at center front edge with a 11th[7th] patt row.
Shape neck:
Next row Bind off 3sts, work in patt to end.
Cont in patt dec one st at neck edge on next 7[8] rows.
Cont in patt on rem 28[31]sts until Left Front measures 24½[26]in. Bind off.

RIGHT FRONT

Work as for Left Front, working 1 more row before neck shaping and *making 7[8] buttonholes at center front edge* on every 3rd and 4th patt rows by binding off 2sts, 2sts in from the edge. On the next row, cast on 2sts over those bound off in previous row to complete buttonhole.

SLEEVES (make 2)

Using smaller needles, cast on 42[46]sts and work 2 rows in g st.
Change to larger needles and patt:
Cont in patt as for Back, inc one st at each end of every 3rd row until there are 70[72]sts.
Work even until Sleeve measures 17[17¾]in, ending with a 2nd or 4th patt row. Bind off.

TO FINISH

Left front edging Using smaller needles and with RS of Left Front facing, pick up and K 89[92]sts evenly along front edge. Bind off K-wise.
Work right front edging to match.
Neck edging Join both shoulder seams.
Using smaller needles and with RS facing, pick up and K 58[62]sts evenly around neck edge.
Bind off K-wise.
Sew Sleeves in place between markers.
Join side and sleeve seams.
Sew on buttons to correspond with buttonholes.

Designed by Ruth Maria Swepson
Phildar (UK) Ltd.

OPTIONS

To make a shorter – or longer – version of this jacket, alter the length before the armholes are reached.
You could use the same basic pattern, omitting the sleeves, to make a loose, boxy vest. Edge the armholes with a garter stitch border as is described for the neck edge. You will of course need less yarn. Alternatively, work the loop pattern in strips to be used as a separate edging. Worked in fluffy mohair, this would create an unusual "fun-fur" border to liven up a plain jacket or vest.

The perennial chic of this Chanel-style suit is guaranteed for years to come. The checked jacket is complemented by a slim A-line skirt, worked in the round.

SIZES

Jacket
To fit 32[34:36:38]in bust
Garment measures: 41½[43:45:47]in at underarm
Length from shoulder: 21[21½:22½:23]in
Sleeve seam: 17[17:17½:17½]in
Skirt
To fit 34[36:38:40]in hips
Garment measures (at hem): 50[52:56:58]in
Length: 27[27:27½:27½]in
Note Instructions for larger sizes are given in brackets [].

MATERIALS

Pingouin Confortable Sport
Jacket
8[9:9:10] 1¾oz/50g balls in color A (Marine)
8[9:9:10] 1¾oz/50g balls in color B (Écru)
Skirt
9[10:11:12] 1¾oz/50g balls in color A
Pair of size 9 knitting needles
Sizes 6 and 7 circular needles
4 yards of folded, 1¼in-wide wool braid for Jacket
Waist length of 1in-wide elastic for Skirt

GAUGE

17sts and 18 rows to 4in over check patt worked on size 9 needles
For gauge sample cast on 22sts and work 4 patt rows for at least 4in.
16sts and 22 rows to 4in over st st worked on size 7 needles

To save time, take time to check gauge.

ABBREVIATIONS

M1 – lift strand running from base of st just worked to base of next st on to LH needle and work into back of it.

For other abbreviations see book, p. 141.

Note When working two-color patt, strand yarn not in use loosely across back of work. (See book, p. 116.)

JACKET

Back
Using pair of needles and A, cast on 82[86:90:94]sts. K1 row. Join in B.
Beg check patt:
1st patt row (RS) K2A, *K2B, K2A, rep from * to end.
2nd row P2A, *P2B, P2A, rep from * to end.
3rd row K2B, *K2A, K2B, rep from * to end.
4th row P2B, *P2A, P2B, rep from * to end.
These 4 rows form patt. Cont in patt until Back measures 13in, ending with a WS row.
Shape armholes:
Keeping patt correct, bind off 4sts at beg of next 2 rows. Dec one st at each end of next 7 rows.
Work 1 row.
Dec one st at each end of next row and then every other row 0[1:1:2] more times. 58[60:64:66]sts.
Work even until armholes measure 7½[8:9:9½]in, ending with a RS row.
Shape back neck:
Next row Keeping patt correct, work 20[21:22:23]sts in patt, leave these sts on a holder, bind off 18[18:20:20]sts, work in patt to end.
Complete this side first on rem 20[21:22:23]sts.
Work 1 row.
Bind off 5sts at neck edge on next row. 15[16:17:18]sts.
Shape shoulder:
Next row Bind off 8[8:9:9]sts, work in patt to end. 7[8:8:9]sts.
Work 1 row. Bind off rem sts.
With RS facing, rejoin yarn to rem sts and work in patt to end.
Complete to match first side, reversing shaping.

Pocket linings
First lining
Using pair of needles and A, cast on 24sts. Join in B.
1st and 4th sizes only
1st patt row (RS) *K2B, K2A, rep from * to end.
2nd and 3rd sizes only
1st patt row (RS) *K2A, K2B, rep from * to end.
All sizes
Cont in patt as set. Work 22 more rows, ending with a RS row. Leave sts on a holder.
2nd lining
Work as for first Lining, reversing colors so that first patt row for first and 4th sizes will read: "*K2A, K2B, rep from * to end," and so that first patt row for 2nd and 3rd sizes will read: "*K2B, K2A, rep from * to end."

Left front
Using pair of needles and A, cast on 48[50:52:54]sts. K1 row. Join in B.
Beg check patt:
1st patt row (RS) K2A, *K2B, K2A, rep from * to last 2[0:2:0]sts, (K2B) 1[0:1:0]time.
Cont in check patt as set. Work 21 more rows.
Divide for pocket:

Next row (RS) Work 10[12:12:14]sts in patt, bind off next 24sts, work in patt to end.
Next row Work 14[14:16:16]sts in patt, keeping patt correct work across 24sts of first Pocket Lining in place of those bound off, work in patt to end.
Cont in patt until Front measures 6 rows less than Back to armhole shaping, ending with a WS row.
Shape front edge:
Keeping patt correct, dec one st at end of next row and then every other row twice more.
Work 1 row.
Shape armhole:
Next row Bind off 4sts, work in patt to last 2sts, work 2 tog.
Next row Patt to end.
Cont dec at front edge on next and every other row, *at the same time* dec one st at armhole edge on next 7 rows, then on every other row 1[2:2:3] times. 27[27:29:29]sts.
Keeping armhole edge even, cont dec at front edge until 15[16:17:18]sts rem.
Work even until Front matches Back to shoulder, ending with a WS row.
Shape shoulder:
Bind off 8[8:9:9]sts at beg of next row. 7[8:8:9]sts.
Work 1 row. Bind off rem sts.

Right front
Work as for Left Front, reversing patt and shaping and noting that 2nd pocket will be worked as foll:
Next row Work 14[14:16:16]sts in patt, bind off next 24sts, work in patt to end.

Sleeves (make 2)
Using pair of needles and A, cast on 46[48:50:52]sts. K1 row. Join in B.
Beg check patt:
1st patt row (RS) K2[1:2:1] A, *K2B, K2A, rep from * to last 0[3:0:3]sts, (K2B, K1A) 0[1:0:1] time.
Cont in patt as set, inc one st at each end of 5th[7th:5th:3rd] and then every 6th[5th:5th:5th] row until there are 70[74:78:82]sts, taking extra sts into patt.
Work even until Sleeve measures 17[17:17½:17½]in, ending with a WS row.
Shape cap:
Keeping patt correct, bind off 4sts at beg of next 2 rows. Dec one st at each end of next row and then every other row until 46[50:54:54]sts rem, then one st at each end of every row until 28sts rem.
Bind off 3sts at beg of next 2 rows, and 4sts at beg of next 2 rows. 14sts. Bind off rem sts.

To finish
Block each piece separately, but do not press.
Set in Sleeves.
Join side and sleeve seams.
Pocket tops Bind top of pockets with braid and neaten ends.
Sew Pocket Linings neatly to Fronts.
Binding Beg at left side seam, sew braid around outer edge of Jacket, mitering corners and gathering in back neck slightly. Finish ends.

Sew braid around cuffs and finish ends. Press seams lightly.

SKIRT

Beg at waist, using smaller circular needle and A, cast on 116[124:132:140]sts. K6 rounds.
Change to larger circular needle.
K6 rounds.
Shape Skirt:
Next round (M1, K1, M1, K30[32:34:36]sts) 4 times. 124[132:140:148]sts. K11 rounds.
Next round (M1, K1, M1 K30[32:34:36]sts) 4 times. 132[140:148:156]sts.
Cont inc 8sts in this way, working 2 extra sts between incs, on every foll 12th round until there are 164[172:180:188]sts, ending with an inc row.
Cont inc in same way as before on every 14th[14th:13th:13th] round until there are 204[212:228:236]sts, ending with an inc row.
Work even until Skirt measures 27[27:27½:27½]in.
Make hem:
Next round P to end.
Change to smaller circular needle.
K7 rounds.
Bind off loosely.
To finish
Press lightly on WS, foll instructions on yarn label.
Turn hem to WS and slipstitch in place. Cut elastic to fit waist, join in a ring and sew to WS of waist, using herringbone st over elastic to form casing (see book, p. 129).

Designed by Barbara Clarkson
Pingouin

OPTIONS
False top pockets could be added to the jacket by sewing 5in of braid on to the Right and Left Fronts at top pocket level. Fold under ⅛in at each end of the lengths of braid. Baste, then slipstitch the braid neatly in place.

A different stitch pattern could be substituted for the check pattern used on the jacket. A slipstitch pattern, for example (see book, pp. 72–73), would be easier to work, since yarns would not have to be stranded. Work a gauge sample first, and adjust the instructions accordingly.

This wonderfully warm and easy-to-wear coat combines a slim-line silhouette with a rich bobble-and-cable texture. The luxury yarn produces subtle, random stripes.

SIZES

To fit 32–34[36–38]in bust
Garment measures: 45½[49]in at underarm
Length from shoulder: 45[45½]in
Sleeve seam: 17½in, with cuff turned back
Note Instructions for larger size are given in brackets [].

MATERIALS

Laines Plassard Harmonieuse
23[24] 2¾oz/75g hanks
Color shown: Clavecin
Pair each of sizes 10 and 10½ knitting needles
Cable needle
11 buttons

GAUGE

12sts and 14 rows to 4in over st st worked on size 10½ needles

To save time, take time to check gauge.

ABBREVIATIONS

C3B – sl next st on to cable needle and hold at back of work, K2, P st from cable needle.
C3F – sl next 2sts on to cable needle and hold at front of work, P1, K2 from cable needle.
C5B – sl next 3sts on to cable needle and hold at back of work, K2, put P st on to LH needle and P it, K2 from cable needle.
MB – (make bobble) (K1, P1, K1, P1, K1, P1, K1) all into next st, lift 2nd st on RH needle over first, then separately lift over 3rd, 4th, 5th, 6th and 7th sts.

For other abbreviations see book, p. 141.

BACK

Using smaller needles, cast on 64[68]sts.
Work 5 rows K1, P1 rib.
Next row Rib 6[8], *inc in next st, rib 3, rep from * to last 6[8]sts, inc in next st, rib 5[7]. 78[82] sts.
Change to larger needles and patt:
1st patt row (WS) P1[3], *K7, P2, K1, P2, K7, rep from * to last.1[3]sts, P1[3].
2nd row K1[3], P0[2], *P7, C5B, P7, rep from * to last 3sts, P0[2], K1[3].
3rd row As first.
4th row K1[3], *P6, C3B, P1, C3F, P6, rep from * to last 1[3]sts, K1[3].
5th and every other row K all the K sts and P all the P sts.
6th row K1[3], *P5, C3B, P1, MB, P1, C3F, P5, rep from * to last 1[3]sts, K1[3].
8th row K1[3], *P4, C3B, (P1, MB) twice, P1, C3F, P4, rep from * to last 1[3]sts, K1[3].
10th row K1[3], *P3, C3B, (P1, MB) 3 times, P1, C3F, P3, rep from * to last 1[3]sts, K1[3].
12th row K1[3], *P2, C3B, P2, K2, P1, K2, P2, C3F, P2, rep from * to last 1[3]sts, K1[3].

14th row K1[3], *P1, C3B, P3, K2, P1, K2, P3, C3F, P1, rep from * to last 1[3]sts, K1[3].
These 14 rows form patt. Cont in patt until Back measures approx 35½in, ending with an 11th patt row.
Next row (RS) P2[4], *P2 tog, P4, rep from * to last 4[6]sts, P2 tog, P2[4]. 65[69]sts.
Change to smaller needles.
K1 row. P2 rows.
Beg beaded rib patt:
1st patt row (RS) K1, *K1, yo, sl 1 P-wise, rep from * to last 2 sts, K2.
2nd row K1, *P1, K2 tog (sl st and yo), rep from * to last 2 sts, P1, K1.
These 2 rows form patt. Cont in patt until Back measures 45[45½]in, ending with a WS row.
Bind off.

LEFT FRONT

Using smaller needles, cast on 32[34]sts.
Work 5 rows K1, P1 rib.
Next row Rib 2[3], *inc in next st, rib 3, rep from * to last 2[3]sts, inc in next st, rib 1[2]. 40[42]sts.
Change to larger needles and patt:
Cont in patt as for Back, *for 2nd size only* working one st at end of RS rows and beg of WS rows instead of 3, until Left Front matches Back to yoke, ending with an 11th patt row.
Shape yoke:
Next row (RS) P1[3], *P2 tog, P4, rep from * to last 3sts, P2 tog, P1. 33[35]sts.
Change to smaller needles.
K1 row. P2 rows.
Beg beaded rib patt:
Cont in beaded rib patt as for Back until Front measures 4in less than Back, ending with a RS row.
Shape neck:
Bind off 5[7]sts at beg of next row and 3sts at beg of every other row once. Dec one st at neck edge on every other row 4 times. 21sts.
Work even until Front matches Back to shoulder, ending with a WS row.
Bind off.

RIGHT FRONT

Work as for Left Front, reversing neck shaping and *for 2nd size only* working one st at beg of RS rows and end of WS rows instead of 3.

SLEEVES (make 2)

Using smaller needles, cast on 34[36]sts.
Work in K1, P1 rib for 4½in, inc one st at end of last row. 35[37]sts.
Change to larger needles and patt:
1st patt row (WS) K15[16], P2, K1, P2, K15[16].
2nd row P15[16], C5B, P15[16].
3rd row As first.
4th row Inc in first st, P13[14], C3B, P1, C3F, P13[14], inc in last st.
5th row K all K sts and P all P sts.
6th row P14[15], C3B, P1, MB, P1, C3F, P14[15].
7th row As 5th, inc in first and last st.
8th row P14[15], C3B, (P1, MB) twice, P1, C3F,

P14[15].
9th row As 5th.
10th row Inc in first st, P12[13], C3B, (P1, MB) 3 times, P1, C3F, P12[13], inc in last st.
11th row As 5th.
12th row P13[14], C3B, P2, K2, P1, K2, P2, C3F, P13[14].
13th row As 7th.
14th row P13[14], C3B, P3, K2, P1, K2, P3, C3F, P13[14].
These 14 rows form patt. Cont in patt as set, inc one st at each end of 2nd row once and then every 3rd row until there are 69[71]sts and Sleeve measures approx 18½in, ending with a 10th patt row.
Change to smaller needles.
K1 row. P2 rows. Bind off K-wise.

TO FINISH

Block each piece separately, but do not press.
Join shoulder seams.
Collar Using smaller needles and with RS of Right Front facing, pick up and K 22[24]sts along right front neck, 24[28]sts along back neck and 22[24]sts along left front neck. 68[76]sts. Work in K1, P1 rib for 4½in. Bind off in rib.
Button band Using smaller needles and with RS of Left Front facing, pick up and K 22sts along side edge of collar, 28sts along edge of yoke and 140sts along rem edge of Left Front. 190sts. Work 8 rows K1, P1 rib. Bind off in rib.
Buttonhole band Work to match Button band, making 11 buttonholes on 4th rib row as foll:
Next row Rib 4, *yo, K2 tog, rib 16, rep from * to last 6sts, yo, K2 tog, rib to end.
Sew bound-off edges of Sleeves to sides of yoke, matching center top of Sleeve to shoulder seam.
Join side and sleeve seams, reversing seam on cuff to fold back.
Sew on buttons to correspond with button-holes.

Designed by Brenda Sparkes

Subtly-shaded autumn colors and contrasting textures contribute to the appeal of this unusual sweater. The striped seed stitch body is topped with a yoke woven in ''shoestring'' ribbon and a neat split collar.

SIZE

To fit 32–36in bust
Garment measures: 36in at underarm
Length from shoulder: 26in
Sleeve seam: 17in

MATERIALS

Rowan Yarns Double Knitting
1oz/25g in color A (613 – honey)
1¾oz/50g in color C (8 – gold)
3½oz/100g in color E (11 – light brown)
5oz/150g in color M (604 – dark brown)
7oz/200g each in colors G (86 – biscuit) and N (62 – black)
Rowan Yarns Fine Tweed
1¾oz/50g each in color B (Champagne), color D (Bamboo), color H (Autumn), color J (Ebony) and color L (Black)
5oz/150g in color F (Bracken)
Patons Cotton Ribbon
1 1¾oz/50g ball
Color shown: 2103
Pair each of sizes 3 and 8 knitting needles

GAUGE

19sts and 28 rows to 4in over seed st patt worked on size 8 needles
For gauge sample use 1 strand of A and 1 strand of B tog. Cast on 21sts. Refer to seed st patt on Back and work as foll:
1st row (K1, P1) 5 times, K1, K1V, (K1, P1) 4 times, K1.
2nd row (K1, P1) 4 times, K1, P1V, (K1, P1) 5 times, K1.
Cont in patt as set for at least 4in.

To save time, take time to check gauge.

ABBREVIATIONS

K1V – K next st in triple yarn of 1 strand M and 2 strands J tog.
P1V – P next st in triple yarn of 1 strand M and 2 strands J tog.
fwd – forward to front of work between needles.
bk – to back of work between needles.

For other abbreviations see book, p. 141.

Note Before starting, wind 6 separate balls of 1 strand M and 2 strands J for vertical lines. Use 1 strand of Double Knitting and 1 strand of Fine Tweed tog throughout for seed st panels.
When working with Cotton Ribbon, make sure that you do not pull it too tightly, to avoid puckering background fabric.
When working vertical lines keep background yarns on WS of work.

BACK

Using larger needles and 1 strand of A and B tog (see Note), cast on 88sts.
Beg seed st and vertical line patt:
1st patt row (RS) (K1, P1) 4 times, K1, K1V, (K1, P1) 4 times, K1, K1V, (K1, P1) 3 times, K1V, (K1, P1) 3 times, K1V, (K1, P1) 9 times, K1V, (K1, P1) 11 times, K1V, (K1, P1) to end.
2nd row (P1, K1) 6 times, P1V, (P1, K1) 11 times, P1V, (P1, K1) 9 times, P1V, (P1, K1) 3 times, P1V, (P1, K1) 3 times, P1V, (K1, P1) 4 times, K1, P1V, (K1, P1) to last st, K1.
These 2 rows form patt of seed st panels and vertical lines and is rep throughout. Work 2 more rows in patt. Break off A and join in C. Using C and B tog and keeping vertical lines straight, cont in color patt as foll:
Work 4 rows with B and C, 4 rows C and D, 4 rows E and D, 6 rows E and F. Break off E and join in G.**
Using F and G only, cont in patt as before until Back measures 17in. *** Break off F and join in H.
Keeping vertical lines straight, cont in color patt as foll:
Work 4 rows with G and H, 5 rows H and J, 4 rows M and J and 4 rows J and N.
Break off J and join in L.
Using N and L only, work 12 rows in patt. (Back measures approx 21in.)
Next row (WS) Using triple yarn already used for vertical lines, P to end.
Rep last row once more. K1 row with triple yarn.
Change to N and L tog. K1 row, P1 row.
Beg woven patt:
Join in Cotton Ribbon. Cont working in st st using N and L, *weave only* with ribbon as foll:
1st patt row (RS) K2, * ribbon fwd (see Note), K3, ribbon bk, K1, rep from * to last 2sts, K2.
2nd row P1, *ribbon bk, P3, ribbon fwd, P1, rep from * to last 3sts, P3.
These 2 rows form woven patt.****
Cont in patt until Back measures 26in, ending with a WS row.
Shape shoulders and neck:
Next row Work 35sts in patt, bind off 18, work in patt to end.
Complete this side first.
Next row Bind off 9sts, work in patt to last 2sts, P2 tog.
Next row K2 tog, work in patt to end.
Next row Bind off 9sts, work in patt to last 2sts, P2 tog.
Next row K2 tog, work in patt to end. 13sts. Bind off.
With WS facing, rejoin yarn to rem sts and P to end. Complete to match first side, reversing shaping.

FRONT

Work as for Back to ****. Cont in patt until Front measures 24in, ending with a WS row.
Shape neck:
Next row Work 33sts in patt, K2 tog, turn and complete this side first, leaving rem sts on a holder.
Keeping patt correct, dec one st at neck edge on every other row 3 times. 31sts.
Work even until Front matches Back to shoulder, ending with a WS row.
Shape shoulder:
Bind off 9sts at beg of next row and then every other row once. 13sts.
Work 1 row. Bind off.
With RS facing, return to rem sts, bind off 18sts, K2 tog, work in patt to end.
Shape neck and shoulder as for first side, reversing shaping.

SLEEVES (make 2)

Using larger needles and 1 strand of A and 1 strand of B tog, cast on 40sts.
Beg seed st and vertical line patt:
1st patt row (RS) (K1, P1) twice, K1V, (K1, P1) 3 times, K1V, (K1, P1) 3 times, K1V, (K1, P1) 7 times, K1V, (K1, P1) to end.
2nd row (P1, K1) 3 times, P1V, (P1, K1) 7 times, P1V, (P1, K1) 3 times, P1V, (P1, K1) 3 times, P1V, (K1, P1) to end.
These 2 rows form patt. Cont in patt as set, changing colors as for Back to ** and inc one st at each end of 5th row once and then every 4th row until there are 88sts, ending with a WS row. Work even, changing colors as for Back from *** until Sleeve measures 17in, ending with a WS row.
Bind off loosely.

TO FINISH

Block each piece separately, but do not press.
Join right shoulder seam.
Collar Using smaller needles, 1 strand of N and with RS facing, pick up and K 17sts down left side of neck, 18sts along front neck, 17sts up right side of right front, 8sts along right side of back neck, 18sts along center back neck and 8sts along left side of back neck, then cast on 12sts. 98sts.
Next row K to end, cast on 12sts. 110sts.
Work 1¼in in g st. Bind off.
Join left shoulder seam.
Fold Sleeves in half and sew in place, matching center of Sleeve to shoulder seam.
Join side and sleeve seams.
Sew extension of back collar to neck under front collar; sew front collar extension to neck over back collar.
Press seams lightly if necessary.

Designed by Edy Lyngaas

A traditional white snowflake pattern alternates with a delicate chain motif, subtly worked in pale gray and white, on this attractive pullover.

SIZES

To fit 32–34[36–38:40–42]in bust. Garment measures: 36[40:44½]in at underarm
Length from shoulder: 22½[23½:24]in
Sleeve seam: 17[18:19]in, with cuff turned back
Note Instructions for larger sizes are given in brackets [].

MATERIALS

Jaeger Luxury Spun Double Knitting
8[9:9] 1¾oz/50g balls in main color A (Roman Purple)
2[2:2] 1¾oz/50g balls in color B (White)
1[1:1] 1¾oz/50g ball in color C (Gray)
Pair each of sizes 3 and 6 knitting needles
Set of 4 size 3 double-pointed needles
(Alternative yarn: Patons Clansman Double Knitting)

GAUGE

22sts and 28 rows to 4in over st st worked on size 6 needles

To save time, take time to check gauge.

ABBREVIATIONS

See book, p. 141.

Note Carry the colors loosely across the back of the work, stranding or weaving them as appropriate (see book, pp. 116–117). Stagger the position of the weaving from row to row to prevent it from showing on RS. *Always* twist yarns tog at beg of every row.

BACK

Using smaller pair of needles and A, cast on 96[104:116]sts.
1st rib row K1, * K2, P2, rep from * to last 3sts, K3.
2nd row K1, *P2, K2, rep from * to last 3sts, P2, K1.
Rep these 2 rows 8 more times, inc 5[9:9]sts evenly across last row. 101[113:125]sts.
Change to larger needles.
Beg with a K row, work 4[6:8] rows st st. Beg working in patt.
*** 3-color patt:
1st row (RS) K1A, 1C, *2A, 4C, rep from * to last 3sts, K3A.
2nd row K1A, *P2A, 1C, rep from * to last st, K1A.
3rd row K2A, *K2B, 4A, rep from * to last 3 sts, K2B, 1A.
4th row K1A, P to last st, working in colors as set, K1A.
5th row K1A, *K1C, 2A, rep from * to last st, K1A.
6th row K1A, *P2A, 4C, rep from * to last 4sts, P2A, 1C, K1A.

7th–10th rows Using A and beg with a K row, work 4 rows st st.
Now beg working Snowflake patt from chart, reading RS (K) rows from right to left and WS (P) rows from left to right.
Snowflake patt:
1st row (RS) K4[7:10]A, *K29sts from first row of chart, K3[6:9]A, rep from * once more, K29 sts from first row of chart, K4[7:10] A.
2nd row K1A, P3[6:9]A, *P29sts from 2nd row of chart, P3[6:9]A, rep from * once more, P29sts from 2nd row of chart, P3[6:9] A, K1A.
3rd–27th rows Cont in patt, keeping colors correct and rep 29sts from chart as set.
28th–30th rows Using A and beg with a P row, work 3 rows st st.***
These 40 rows from *** to *** form patt. Rep these 40 rows once more. Cont in patt, rep from *** to *** each time until 120 patt rows have been worked in all, thus ending with 3 rows st st in A. Rep first–6th rows once more, thus ending with 6th row of 3-color patt.****
Using A and beg with a K row, work 18[20:22] rows st st.
Shape shoulders:
Cont working st st in A, bind off 8[9:10]sts at beg of next 6 rows and 7[9:11]sts at beg of next 2 rows. 39[41:43]sts.
Leave rem sts on a holder.

FRONT

Work as for Back to ****.
Using A and beg with a K row, work 8[10:12] rows st st.
Shape neck:
Next row K37[42:47]sts, turn and complete this side first.
Dec one st at neck edge on next 5 rows, then at same edge on every other row once. 31[36:41]sts. Work 2 rows st st.
Shape shoulder:
Bind off 8[9:10]sts at beg of next row then every other row twice more, using the bias bind-off method (see book, p. 107). 7[9:11]sts.

Work 1 row. Bind off rem sts.
With RS facing, sl next 27[29:31]sts on to a holder for center front neck, rejoin yarn to rem sts and K to end. Complete to match first side, reversing shaping by working 1 more row before "Shape shoulder" and working neck edge dec as sl 1, K1, psso on K rows and P2 tog tbl (see book, p. 109) on P rows.

SLEEVES (make 2)

Using smaller pair of needles and A, cast on 44[48:52]sts. Work 30 rows in rib as for Back, inc 3[5:7]sts evenly across last row. 47[53:59]sts.
Change to larger needles.
Beg with a K row, work 4 rows st st. Now work first–6th rows in 3-color patt as for Back.
Using A only, cont in st st, inc one st at each end of next and every 4th[4th:5th] row until there are 93[95:97]sts.
Work even until Sleeve measures 17[18:19]in, with cuff turned back, or desired length, ending with a P row. Bind off loosely.

TO FINISH

Block and press as instructed on yarn label. Join shoulder seams on RS using an edge-to-edge seam (see book, p. 136).
Neck border Using set of double-pointed needles and A, with RS of work facing, pick up and K 39[41:43]sts from back neck holder, 13sts along left front neck, 27[29:31]sts from holder at center front neck and 13sts along right front neck. 92[96:100]sts.
1st round * K2, P2, rep from * to end.
Rep this round 19 more times.
Bind off in rib, using a larger needle.
Using edge-to-edge seam, join Sleeves to armholes, matching center of sleeve top to shoulder seam. Join side and sleeve seams; use a fine overcasting seam on ribbing.

Designed by Betty Barnden

Triffic

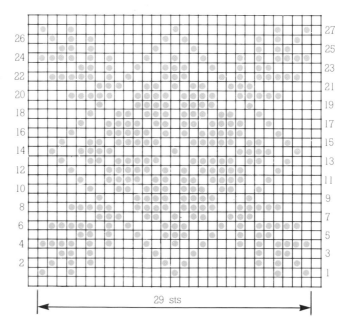

KEY

▨ = col B

☐ = col A

← 29 sts →

This lively abstract pattern, the graphic style and bright contrasting colors make this sweater an asset to any wardrobe.

SIZES

To fit 34–38in bust loosely
Garment measures: 49in at underarm
Length from shoulder: 22½in
Sleeve seam: 18in

MATERIALS

Patons Solo Double Knitting with Mohair
5 1¾oz/50g balls in main color A (2525 – blue)
1 1¾oz/50g ball in color B (2547 – green)
1 1¾oz/50g ball in color C (2500 – white)
Patons Diploma Double Knitting
1 1¾oz/50g ball in each of 3 colors: D (6736 – yellow), E (6746 – white) and F (6732 – red)
Patons Beehive Double Knitting
1 1¾oz/50g ball in color G (6147 – purple)
Pair each of sizes 6, 7 and 8 knitting needles

GAUGE

17sts and 20 rows to 4in over st st in Patons Solo worked on size 8 needles

To save time, take time to check gauge.

ABBREVIATIONS

See book, p. 141.

Note Strand – rather than weave – yarns tog behind zigzag patts (see book, p. 116), and be careful not to pull yarn tightly. Use a separate ball of yarn for each diagonal stripe.

BACK

Diagonal lines are always worked over and across zigzag patts and horizontal stripes. Diagonals in D and E take precedence over diagonals in G and F when they cross.
Once diagonal stripes have been introduced, carry them across the sweater to the other side, moving the stripes one st either to the left or to the right, as required.
Using medium-size needles and A, cast on 105sts.
1st rib row *K1, P1, rep from * to last st, K1.
2nd row *P1, K1, rep from * to last st, P1.
Rep these 2 rows twice more.
Change to largest needles.
Beg with a K row, cont working in st st throughout.
Beg color patt:
1st–8th rows Work 6 rows A, 2 rows D.
Beg first diagonal (right to left):
9th row K1A, 2D, K to end in A.
10th–21st rows Cont diagonal stripe in D as set, reading from Chart 1, with background in A.
Beg 2nd diagonal (right to left):
22nd row With background in A, and keeping first diagonal correct, work to last st, P1E. This row establishes 2nd stripe from Chart 1 in E, so that stripe runs parallel with first stripe.

23rd–27th rows Cont working stripes D and E with background in A.
Beg first single zigzag:
28th row Cont working diagonal stripes in D and E, *at the same time* work first row of single zigzag from Chart 2 in C beg with a P row (see Note).
29th–32nd rows Cont working single zigzag from Chart 2.
33rd–38th rows Cont working diagonal stripes in D and E, with background in C.
39th–40th rows Cont in diagonal stripes as before, work 2 rows background in F.
Beg 3rd diagonal (left to right):
41st row Working background in C, and

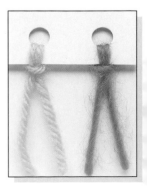

keeping diagonals correct, work to last 3sts, K2F, 1C.
This row establishes next diagonal stripe in F working from left to right instead of from right to left.
42nd–44th rows With background in C, cont working diagonal stripes in F, D and E.
Beg first double zigzag:
45th row With background in A, work first row of double zigzag from Chart 3 in C.
46th–52nd rows Keeping 3 diagonals correct, cont working double zigzag from Chart 3.
53rd 67th rows Keeping diagonals correct, cont working background in A.
68th–71st rows Keeping diagonals correct, work 4 rows with background in C.
Beg 2nd single zigzag:
72nd row With background in C and diagonals correct, work first row of single zigzag in B from Chart 2, so beg with a P row.
73rd–75th rows Complete single zigzag in B, keeping diagonals correct.
76th–84th rows With diagonals correct, cont in B only.
85th–86th rows With diagonals correct, work 2 rows with background in G.
Beg 4th diagonal (right to left):
87th row K1G, (7B, 1C) 6 times, 7B, 2F, 6B, 2E, 6B, 1C, 6B, 2D, (7B, 1C) 3 times. This row establishes next diagonal in G, *at the same time* working first row of single zigzag in C, with background in B.
88th–91st rows Keeping all diagonals correct, cont working single zigzag in C.
Work reversed single zigzag:
92nd row Keeping diagonals correct, beg with 4th row of Chart 2 and work in reverse order to first row, completing reversed single zigzag in C, with background in A.
96th–111th rows Keeping diagonals correct, work 16 rows with background in A.
Shape shoulders:
Bind off 8sts at beg of next 8 rows.
Leave rem 41sts on holder for back neck.

FRONT

Work as for Back until 92nd row has been completed.
Next row Cont working in stripes and patt as for Back, work 42sts in patt, work next 21sts in patt and sl on to a holder for front neck, work in patt to end.
Complete this side first.
*Dec one st at neck edge on every other row 9 times in all, so ending at side edge.
Shape shoulders:
Bind off 8sts at beg of next row and then every other row 3 times, *at the same time*, working one more dec at neck edge as before.
With WS facing, rejoin yarn to rem sts and work in patt to end. Complete to match first side from * to end.

SLEEVES (make 2)

Using medium-size needles and A, cast on 40sts.
Work 6 rows K1, P1 rib.
Change to largest needles.
Cont working st st, keeping background in A throughout, inc one st at each end of every 4th row until there are 80sts, then work even, working color patt (noting that stripes are carried across Sleeves from side to side) as foll:
1st–8th rows Work 6 rows A, 2 rows D. 44sts.
Beg 1st diagonal (right to left):
9th row With background in A, beg working diagonal stripe in D from Chart 1 as for Back.
10th–21st rows Cont diagonal stripe in D. 50sts.
Beg 2nd diagonal (right to left):
22nd row With background in A, beg working 2nd diagonal in E from Chart 1 as for Back.
23rd–38th rows Cont working both stripes in D and E with background in A.
39th–40th rows Keeping diagonal stripes

correct, work 2 rows with background in F. 58sts.
Beg 3rd diagonal (left to right):
41st row Keeping 2 diagonals in D and E correct and background in A, beg working 3rd diagonal in F as for Back, inc one st at each end of row. 60sts.
42nd–84th rows Keeping 3 diagonal stripes as set, work background in A. 80sts.
85th–86th rows Keeping diagonals correct, work 2 rows with background in G.
Beg 4th diagonal (left to right):
87th row Keeping diagonal stripes correct, with background in A, work to last 3sts, K2G, 1A.
88th–106th rows Keeping diagonals correct and background in A, work 19 rows.
Bind off evenly.

TO FINISH

Block and press each piece separately, foll instructions on yarn label. Join left shoulder seam.
Neckband Using smallest needles, A and with RS facing, pick up and K 31sts down left side of neck, K across 21sts on holder for front neck, pick up and K 31sts up right side of neck and K across 41sts on holder for back neck. 104sts.
Work 4 rows K1, P1 rib. Bind off in rib. Join right shoulder seam.
Fold Sleeves in half and sew in place, matching center of Sleeves to shoulder seams.
Join side seams matching stripes.
Join sleeve seams.
Press seams lightly if necessary.

Designed by Clare Johnson

KEY

☐ = background

☒ = contrast

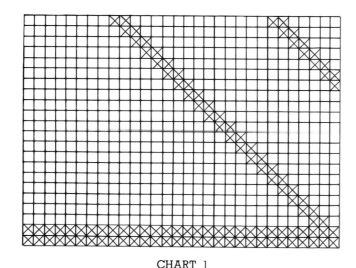

CHART 1

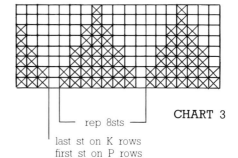

rep 8sts   CHART 2

last st on K rows
first st on P rows

rep 8sts   CHART 3

last st on K rows
first st on P rows

Modeled on the traditional fisherman's smock – with the addition of a stand-away collar – this comfortable pullover features stripes in contrasting colors and stitches.

SIZES

To fit 34–36[38–40:42–44]in bust
Garment measures: 41[46:50]in at underarm
Length from shoulder: 26½[27:30]in
Sleeve seam: 18½[18½:20½]in, unrolled
Note Instructions for larger sizes are given in brackets [].

MATERIALS

Phildar Pégase
8[9:10] 1¾oz/50g balls in color A (Véronèse)
11[12:13] 1¾oz/50g balls in color B (Roy)
Pair each of sizes 6 and 7 knitting needles

GAUGE

19sts and 26 rows to 4in over st st worked on size 7 needles
19sts and 36 rows to 4in over seed st worked on size 6 needles

To save time, take time to check gauge.

ABBREVIATIONS

See book, p. 141.

BACK

Using smaller needles and A, cast on 99[111:121]sts. Beg with a K row, work 7 rows st st.
Next row (hemline) K to end.
Change to larger needles and stripe patt:
Using A and beg with a K row, work 24[24:26] rows st st.
Break off A and join in B.
Change to smaller needles.
K1 row.
Beg seed st stripe:
Next row K1, *P1, K1, rep from * to end.
Last row forms seed st patt and is rep each time. Cont in seed st, work 32[32:34] more rows.
Last 58[58:62] rows form st st and seed st stripe patt. Rep these 58[58:62]rows throughout.
Cont in stripe patt until Back measures approx 16½[16:17¾]in from hemline, ending with a 12th [10th:12th] patt row in A.
Shape raglans:
Keeping stripe patt correct, bind off 2[2:3]sts at beg of next 2 rows. Dec one st at each end of next row and then every other row 4[5:5] more times. 85[95:103]sts.
Work 2 rows.
Dec one st at each end of next row and then next 10[10:11] 3rd rows. 63[73:79]sts.
Work 2[2:1] rows. **
Cont in patt, dec one st at each end of next row and then every other row until 41[53:57]sts rem, then one st at each end of every row until 35[39:43]sts rem.
Leave rem sts on a holder.

FRONT

Work as for Back to **.
Cont in patt, dec one st at each end of next row and then every other row until 55[63:69]sts rem, ending with a P row.
Shape neck:
Next row K2 tog, K18[20:21], K2 tog, turn and leave rem sts on a holder.
Complete this side first.
Cont dec at armhole edge on every other row 4[4:3] times, *at the same time* dec one st at neck edge on next 8[8:6] rows. 8[10:14]sts.
1st size only
Work 1 row, then dec one st at each end of next row.
Work 1 row, then dec one st at raglan edge *only* on next 4 rows. 2sts.
2nd size only
Dec one st at neck edge on every other row once, *at the same time* dec one st at raglan edge on next 7 rows. 2sts.
3rd size only
Dec one st at each end of every other row twice, then one st at neck edge on every other row once, *at the same time* dec one st at raglan edge on next 7 rows. 2sts.
All sizes
Next row K2 tog. Fasten off.
With RS facing, sl center 11[15:19]sts on to a holder, rejoin yarn to rem sts, K2 tog, K to last 2sts, K2tog. 20[22:23]sts. Complete to match first side, reversing shaping.

POCKETS (make 2)

Using larger needles and A, cast on 39[43:47]sts. Beg with a K row, work 24[24:26] rows st st.
Break off A, join in B.
Change to smaller needles.
K1 row. Cont in seed st patt as for Back, working 67[67:71] more rows. Bind off in patt.

SLEEVES (make 2)

Using larger needles and A, cast on 53[59:65]sts. Beg with a K row, work 26[28:34] rows st st, ending with a P row.
Cont in stripe patt as for Back, *at the same time* inc one st at each end of every 8th row until there are 79[87:95]sts, taking extra sts into patt.
Work even until Sleeve measures approx 18½[18½:20½]in, ending with a 12th[10th:12th] patt row in A.
Shape raglans:
Keeping stripe patt correct, work as for Back until 23[29:31]sts rem, then dec one st at each end of every row until 15[17:19]sts rem, ending with a K row.
Next row P to end, dec 2[2:3]sts evenly across row. 13[15:16]sts.
Leave rem sts on a holder.

TO FINISH

Block each piece separately.
Join raglans, leaving left back raglan open.
Collar With RS facing, using smaller needles and B, K across 13[15:16]sts from left sleeve holder, pick up and K 18[19:20]sts down left side of neck, K across 11[15:19]sts from front neck holder dec one st at center, pick up and K 18[19:20]sts up right side of neck, K across 13[15:16]sts from right sleeve holder and 35[39:43]sts from back neck holder. 107[121:133]sts.
Cont working in seed st patt as for Back, until Collar measures 12in. Bind off loosely in patt.
Join rem raglan seam and Collar, reversing seam halfway for turn-back.
Join side and sleeve seams, reversing sleeve seam at lower edge for turn-back cuff.
Turn hem to WS and slipstitch in place.
Sew Pockets in place as shown in photograph. Press seams lightly.

Designed by Elmaz Hüseyin and Barbara Clarkson

OPTIONS
You could omit the patch pockets if you prefer and make a smaller collar by working for 6in only, so that the collar is turned over only once.

Or for a softer, more draped effect you could work the collar, full size, in stockinette stitch instead of seed stitch.

A split turtleneck collar completes the asymmetrical styling of this pullover, made in an extra-luxurious kid mohair.

SIZES

To fit 32[34:36:38]in bust
Garment measures: 36[38:40:41½]in at underarm.
Length from shoulder: 23[23½:24:24½]in
Sleeve seam: 17[17:17½:17½]in
Note Instructions for larger sizes are given in brackets [].

MATERIALS

Tiber Super Kid Mohair
6[6:7:7] 1¾oz/50g balls
Color shown: 73
Pair each of sizes 3 and 6 knitting needles

GAUGE

18sts and 26 rows to 4in over st st worked on size 6 needles

To save time, take time to check gauge.

ABBREVIATIONS

M1 – lift strand running from base of st just worked to base of next st on to LH needle and work into back of it.

For other abbreviations see book, p. 141.

BACK

Using smaller needles, cast on 72[76:78:82]sts. Work in K1, P1, rib for 2½in.
Next row (WS) Rib 5[7:3:5], M1, * rib 5, M1, rib 4, M1, rep from * 6[6:7:7] more times, rib 4[6:3:5]. 87[91:95:99]sts.**
Change to larger needles and patt:
1st patt row (RS) K58[60:64:66], P1, *K1, P1, rep from * to end.
2nd row *K1, P1, rep from * 13[14:14:15] more times, K1, P58[60:64:66].
3rd row K59[61:65:67], *P1, K1, rep from * to end.
4th row *P1, K1, rep from * 13[14:14:15] more times, P59[61:65:67].
These 4 rows form patt. Cont in patt until Back measures 14½in, ending with a WS row.
Shape armholes:
Keeping patt correct, bind off 9sts at beg of next row and 10sts at beg of next row. 68[72:76:80]sts. Work even in patt until armholes measure 8½[9:9½:10]in, ending with a WS row.
Shape shoulders:
Bind off 9[10:10:11]sts at beg of next row, 10[11:11:12]sts at beg of next row, 9[9:10:10]sts at beg of next row and 10[10:11:11]sts at beg of next row. 30[32:34:36]sts.
Leave rem sts on a holder.

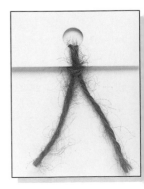

FRONT

Work as for Back to **

Change to larger needles and patt:
1st patt row (RS) P1, *K1, P1, rep from *
13[14:14:15] more times, K58[60:64:66].
2nd row P58[60:64:66], *K1, P1, rep from *
to last st, K1.
3rd row *K1, P1, rep from * 13[14:14:15]
more times, K59[61:65:67].
4th row P59[61:65:67], *K1, P1, rep from * to
end.
These 4 rows form patt. Cont in patt until
Front matches Back to underarm, ending
with a WS row.

Shape armholes:
Bind off 10sts at beg of next row and 9sts at
beg of next row. 68[72:76:80]sts. Work
even in patt until Front measures 12 rows
less than Back to shoulder, ending with a WS
row.

Shape neck:
1st row (RS) Work 27[28:30:31]sts in patt,
K2 tog, turn and leave rem sts on a holder.
28[29:31:32]sts.
Cont on these sts for first side, dec one st at
neck edge on next 6[6:8:8] rows. 22[23:23:
24]sts.
Work 1 row.
Dec one st at neck edge on next row and
then on every other row 1[1:0:0] more time.
20[21:22:23]sts.
Work 1 row.

Shape shoulder:
Bind off 10[11:11:12]sts at beg of next row.
Work 1 row.
Bind off rem 10[10:11:11]sts.
With RS of work facing, sl center
12[14:14:16]sts on to a holder for front neck,
rejoin yarn to rem sts, K2 tog, K to end.
26[27:29:30]sts.
Keeping armhole edge even, dec at neck
edge as for first side until 18[19:20:21]sts
rem.
Work 2 rows even.

Shape shoulder:
Bind off 9[10:10:11]sts at beg of next row.
Work 1 row.
Bind off rem 9[9:10:10]sts.

RIGHT SLEEVE

Using smaller needles, cast on 46[48:
50:52]sts. Work in K1, P1 rib for 2in.***
Next row (WS) Rib 4[5:4:5], M1, *rib 3,
M1, rib 3[2:2:2], M1, rep from * 5[6:7:7]
more times, rib 3, M1, rib 3[5:3:4]. 60[64:
68:70]sts.
Change to larger needles.
Beg with a K row, cont in st st, inc one st at
each end of 11th[9th:9th:9th] row once and
then every 10th[9th:9th:8th] row until there
are 76[82:88:92]sts.
****Work even until Sleeve measures
17[17:17½:17½]in. Place a marker at each
end of last row. Work another 2in, ending
with a WS row. Bind off.

LEFT SLEEVE

Work as for Right Sleeve to ***
Next row (WS) Rib 2[5:4:5], M1, *rib 2,
M1, rib 3[2:2:2], M1, rep from * 7[8:9:9]
more times, rib 2, M1, rib 2[5:4:5]. 64[68:
72:74]sts.
Change to larger needles and patt:
1st patt row (RS) *K1, P1, rep from * to end.
2nd row As first.
3rd row *P1, K1, rep from * to end.
4th row As 3rd.
These 4 rows form patt. Cont in patt inc one
st at each end of 9th[7th:7th:7th] row once
and then every 8th[8th:7th:6th] row until
there are 84[90:96:102]sts, taking extra sts
into patt. Complete as for Right Sleeve,
working from **** to end and binding off in
patt.

TO FINISH

Block each piece separately, but do not
press. Join right shoulder seam.
Collar Using smaller needles and with RS of
work facing, pick up and K 19[20:21:21]sts
down left side of neck, K12[14:14:16]sts from
front holder, inc 3sts evenly across front
neck, pick up and K19[20:21:21]sts up right
side, K30[32:34:36]sts from back holder, inc
6sts evenly across back neck, then cast on
10sts. 99[105:109:113]sts.
Next row P1, *K1, P1, rep from * to end.
Next row K1, *P1, K1, rep from * to end.
Rep last 2 rows until collar measures 1¼in.
Change to larger needles.
Cont in rib until collar measures 6in.
Bind off loosely in rib.
Join left shoulder seam.
Place 10 cast-on sts of collar at back under
front collar and slipstitch neatly around neck
edge so that front collar overlaps back
collar.
Set in Sleeves, joining seams above markers
to bound-off sts at underarm.
Join side and sleeve seams.
Press seams lightly.

Designed by Eleanor Van Zandt and
Barbara Clarkson.

OPTIONS

For a conventional turtleneck collar,
join both shoulder seams and, using a
circular needle or double-pointed
needles, pick up and knit 100[106:110:
114] stitches around the neck. Work in
single rib as instructed in the pattern,
changing to larger needles when the
collar measures 1¼in and working until
it is the desired depth.

Another textured stitch pattern could
be substituted for the Irish moss stitch
used for this sweater. First work out the
gauge of the stitch (see book, p. 20) and
make any necessary adjustments to the
sweater pattern to accommodate any
variation in gauge.

Or you could simply work the Irish
moss stitch in a contrasting color.

An interplay of triangles gives this pullover optical vitality. With its high, standing collar, and sleeves in a bright, two-tone variation of the body's tricolor theme, it's got an extra share of flair.

SIZES

To fit 30–32[34–36:38–40]in bust
Garment measures: 41½[45:48]in at underarm
Length from shoulder: 26[26¾:27½]in
Sleeve seam: 16in
Note Instructions for larger sizes are given in brackets [].

MATERIALS

Pingouin Confort
4[4:5] 1¾oz/50g balls in main color A (Bleuet)
2[3:3] 1¾oz/50g balls in color B (Pourpre)
3[4:4] 1¾oz/50g balls in color C (Souris)
Pair each of sizes 3 and 6 knitting needles
Size 5 circular needle

GAUGE

20sts and 22 rows to 4in over patt worked on size 6 needles
For gauge sample cast on 24sts and work patt rows for at least 4in.

To save time, take time to check gauge.

ABBREVIATIONS

See book, p. 141.

Note Use a combination of stranding and weaving techniques (see book, pp. 116–117) in working this pattern.

BACK

Using smaller needles and A, cast on 104[112:120]sts. Work in K1, P1 rib for 2 in.
Change to larger needles and patt:
1st patt row (RS) *K7C, 1B, rep from * to end.
2nd row *P1B, 7C, rep from * to end.
3rd row K1B, *5C, 3B, rep from * to last 7sts, K5C, 2B.
4th row P2B, *5C, 3B, rep from * to last 6sts P5C, 1B.
5th row K2B, *3C, 5B, rep from * to last 6sts, K3C, 3B.
6th row P3B, *3C, 5B, rep from * to last 5sts, P3C, 2B.
7th row K3B, *1C, 7B, rep from * to last 5sts, K1C, 4B.
8th row P4B, *1C, 7B, rep from * to last 4 sts, P1C, 3B.
9th row K3C, *1A, 7C, rep from * to last 5sts, K1A, 4C.
10th row P4C, *1A, 7C, rep from * to last 4sts, P1A, 3C.
11th row K2C, *3A, 5C, rep from * to last 6sts, K3A, 3C.
12th row P3C, *3A, 5C, rep from * to last 5sts, P3A, 2C.
13th row K1C, *5A, 3C, rep from * to last 7sts, K5A, 2C.
14th row P2C, *5A, 3C, rep from * to last 6sts,

P5A, 1C.
15th row *K7A, 1C, rep from * to end.
16th row *P1C, 7A, rep from * to end.
These 16 rows form patt. ** Cont in patt until Back measures 26[26¾:27½]in, ending with a WS row.
Shape shoulders:
Bind off 28[32:36]sts, work in patt across next 48sts (including st used in binding off, already on needle, sl these sts on to a holder, bind off rem 28[32:36]sts.

FRONT

Work as for Back to **. Cont in patt until Front measures 16 rows less than Back to shoulders, ending with a WS row.
Shape neck:
Next row Work 41[45:49]sts in patt, turn and complete this side first.
Keeping patt correct, bind off 2sts at beg (neck edge) of next row and then every other row once, one st at beg of every other row once and 2sts at beg of every other row twice. Dec one st at neck edge on next 4 rows. 28[32:36]sts.
Work even until Front measures same as Back to shoulder, ending with a WS row.
Shape shoulder:
Bind off rem sts.
With RS of Front facing, return to rem sts, sl next 22sts on to a holder, rejoin yarn to rem sts and patt to end.
Work 1 row.
Complete to match first side.

SLEEVES (make 2)

Using smaller needles and A, cast on 56sts. Work in K1, P1 rib for 2in.
Change to larger needles and patt:
Keeping patt correct, *at the same time* inc one st at each end of every 3rd row until there are 100 sts.
1st patt row (RS) *K7B, 1A, rep from * to end.
2nd row *P1A, 7B, rep from * to end.
3rd row K1A, *5B, 3A, rep from * to last 7sts, K5B, 2A.
4th row P2A, *5B, 3A, rep from * to last 6sts, P5B, 1A.
5th row K2A, *3B, 5A, rep from * to last 6sts, K3B, 3A.
6th row P3A, *3B, 5A, rep from * to last 5sts, P3B, 2A.
7th row K3A, *1B, 7A, rep from * to last 5sts, K1B, 4A.
8th row P4A, *1B, 7A, rep from * to last 4 sts, P1B, 3A.
9th row K3B, *1A, 7B, rep from * to last 5sts, K1A, 4B.
10th row P4B, *1A, 7B, rep from * to last 4sts, P1A, 3B.
11th row K2B, *3A, 5B, rep from * to last 6sts, K3A, 3B.
12th row P3B, *3A, 5B, rep from * to last 5sts, P3A, 2B.
13th row K1B, *5A, 3B, rep from * to last 7sts, K5A, 2B.
14th row P2B, *5A, 3B, rep from * to last 6sts, P5A, 1B.
15th row *K7A, 1B, rep from * to end.
16th row *P1B, 7A, rep from * to end.

These 16 rows form patt.
Work even until Sleeve measures 16in, ending with a WS row. Bind off loosely.

TO FINISH

Block and press each piece lightly on WS foll instructions on yarn label. Join shoulder seams.
Collar Using circular needle and with RS facing, pick up and K 18sts up right front neck, K across 48sts from back neck holder, pick up and K 18sts down left front neck and K across 22sts from front neck holder. 106sts.
Cont to work in rounds.
Work in K1, P1 rib for 6in. Bind off loosely in rib.
Fold collar in half to WS and sew in place.
Sew Sleeves in place, matching center of Sleeve with shoulder seam.
Join side seams.
Press seams lightly if necessary.

Designed by Fiona McTague

The check pattern on this striking pullover is created by an ingenious slip stitch technique which produces vertical ridges for both visual and textural interest.

SIZES

To fit 30–32[34–36:38–40]in bust
Garment measures: 42[45½:48]in at underarm
Length from shoulder: 23[23½:24½]in
Sleeve seam: 16in
Note Instructions for larger sizes are given in brackets [].

MATERIALS

Scheepjeswol Superwash Zermatt
8[8:9] 1¾oz/50g balls in main color A (6408 – black)
6[6:7] 1¾oz/50g balls in color B (4812 – white)
Pair each of sizes 3 and 6 knitting needles

GAUGE

21sts and 32 rows to 4in over patt worked on size 6 needles. For gauge sample cast on 23sts and rep 8 patt rows for at least 4in.

To save time, take time to check gauge.

ABBREVIATIONS

See book, p. 141.

BACK

Using smaller needles and A, cast on 110[118:126]sts. Work in K1, P1 rib for 2in, inc one st at end of last row. 111[119:127]sts.
Change to larger needles and patt:
1st patt row (WS) Using A, P.
2nd row Using B, K3, *sl 1 with yarn at back, K3, rep from * to end.
3rd row Using B, P3, *sl 1 with yarn at front, P3, rep from * to end.
4th row As 2nd.
5th row Using B, P.
6th–8th rows Using A, rep 2nd, 3rd and 4th rows.
These 8 rows form patt. Cont in patt until work measures approx 21[21½:22½]in, ending with first patt row.
Change to smaller needles and A.
Work in K1, P1 rib for 2in. Bind off loosely in rib.

FRONT

Work as for Back.

SLEEVES (make 2)

Using smaller needles and A, cast on 58sts. Work in K1, P1 rib for 2in, inc one st at end of last row. 59sts.
Change to larger needles and patt:
Cont in patt as for Back, inc one st at each end of every 5th row until there are 105sts taking extra sts into patt. Work even for a few rows until Sleeve measures approx 16in, ending with a 5th patt row. Bind off loosely.

TO FINISH

Block each piece separately.
Join shoulder seams for approx 6in from each side.
Sew Sleeves in place, matching center of Sleeve to shoulder seam. Join side and sleeve seams.
Press seams lightly if necessary.

Designed by Fiona McTague

Two sensuous yarns – a mohair-silk blend and a gleaming pure silk – have been used for this luxurious evening sweater with its soft rolled neckline and plunging back. It is worked in a single piece from cuff to cuff.

SIZES

To fit 32–34[34–36:36–38]in bust
Garment measures: 52[53½:55]in from cuff to cuff
Length from shoulder: 27[28:29]in
Sleeve seam: 17in
Note Instructions for larger sizes are given in brackets [].

MATERIALS

Anny Blatt Mohair et Soie (A)
11[11:12] 1¾oz/50g balls
Color shown: Nuit
Anny Blatt Silk'Anny (B)
3[3:4] 1½oz/40g balls
Color shown: Gris
Pair each of sizes 7 and 9 knitting needles
Sizes 7 and 9 circular needles

GAUGE

14sts and 20 rows to 4in over st st worked on size 9 needles

To save time, take time to check gauge.

ABBREVIATIONS

See book, p. 141.

SWEATER

(Worked in 1 piece from cuff to cuff)
Right Sleeve
Using pair of smaller needles and A, cast on 34[38:42]sts. Work in K1, P1 rib for 4in.
Change to pair of larger needles.
Using A and beg with a K row, cont in st st, inc one st at each end of first row and then every other row until there are 60[64:68]sts, ending with a P row.
Beg stripe patt:
Cont inc at each end of every other row as before, *at the same time* work in stripes as foll:
K2 rows B. Using A and beg with a K row, work 4 rows st st. K2 rows B. Using A and beg with a K row, work 6 rows st st. K3 rows B. P1 row B. K2 rows B. Using A and beg with a K row, work 8 rows st st. K3 rows B. P1 row B. 92[96:100]sts.
Change to larger circular needle.
Work in rows.
Shape sides:
1st row Using B, cast on 6sts, K to end.
2nd row Using B, cast on 6sts, P to end.
3rd row As first.
4th row As first.
Using A and beg with a K row, cont in st st, casting on 6sts at beg of next 4 rows and 8[10:12]sts at beg of next 2 rows. 156[164:172]sts.
Using A, work 2 rows st st. K2 rows B. Using A and beg with a K row, work 6 rows st st. K3

rows B. P1 row B. K1 row B. P1 row B. K2 rows B. Using A and beg with a K row, work 4[8:12] rows st st.
Shape front neck:
Next row Using A, K76[80:84]sts, turn and leave rem sts unworked.
Cont on these 76[80:84]sts for Front.
Using A, cont in st st, dec one st at neck edge on next 3 rows.
Using B, K3 rows, dec one st at neck edge on first and 3rd rows.
P1 row B.
Next row Using B, K to last 2sts, K2 tog.
P1 row B. 70[74:78]sts.
Using B, K2 rows. Using A and beg with a K row, work 18 rows st st. Using B, K1 row.
Next row Using B, inc in first st, K to end.
Using A and beg with a K row, work 7 rows st st, inc one st at neck edge on 2nd, 4th, 5th, 6th and 7th rows. 76[80:84]sts. Leave these sts on a holder.
With RS facing, rejoin A to rem 80[84:88]sts.
Next row Bind off 17sts, K to end.
P1 row A.
Shape back neck:
Working stripe patt as for Front, bind off 5sts at beg of next row and then every other row 3 more times.
Dec one st at neck edge on next 10 rows. 33[37:41]sts.
Work 3 rows.
Inc one st at neck edge on next 10 rows. Cast on 5sts at beg of next row and then every other row 3 more times.
P1 row.
Cast on 17sts at beg of next row. P1 row working across all sts including 76[80:84]sts from front holder. 156[164:172]sts. Using A and beg with a K row, work 20[24:28] rows st st.
Using B, K2 rows. Using A, K1 row, P1 row.
Shape sides:
Using A and beg with a K row, cont in st st, binding off 8[10:12]sts at beg of next 2 rows and 6sts at beg of next 4 rows. 116[120:124]sts.
Cont binding off 6sts at beg of each row, K2 rows B, K1 row A, P1 row A. 92[96:100]sts.
Next row Using A, K2 tog, K to last 2sts, K2 tog.
Next row Using A, P to end.
Next row Using B, K2 tog, K to last 2sts, K2 tog.
Next row Using B, K to end.
Using A and beg with a K row, work 34 rows st st, dec one st at each end of next row and then every other row. 54[58:62]sts.
Cont dec as before on every other row, K2 rows B, using A and beg with a K row, work 6 rows st st, K2 rows B, using A and beg with a K row, work 9 rows st st. 34[38:42]sts.
Change to smaller needles and work cuff:
Using A, work in K1, P1 rib for 4in. Bind off.

TO FINISH

Block pieces, but do not press.
Waist rib Using smaller needles, A and with RS facing, pick up and K 66[72:78]sts along lower edge of Front.
Work in K1, P1 rib for 4½in.
Bind off in rib.

Work back ribbing to match front ribbing.
Neckband Mark shoulder points with contrasting threads. Using smaller circular needle, A and with RS facing, beg at center back neck and pick up and K 54sts to shoulder marker, 56sts along front neck and 54sts along left back neck. 164sts.
K7 rounds.
Change to larger circular needle and K6 rounds. Bind off loosely K-wise.
Join side and sleeve seams.

Designed by Brenda Sparkes

OPTIONS
You could work many variations on the basic sweater pattern. For example, you could vary the positions and width of the stripes in different ways, or knit the whole garment in Mohair et Soie using several colors, or embellish the stripe pattern with lines of embroidery (see book, p. 34). Sew a few beads to one shoulder for extra sparkle.

This remarkably pretty cardigan features a lovely, lacy "V" motif – V for "versatile," since it's equally attractive worn buttoned up or open, over a blouse.

SIZES

To fit 30[32:34]in bust
Garment measures: 31½[34½:36]in at under-arm
Length from shoulder: 23[23½:23¾]in
Sleeve seam: 17½[17¾:18]in
Note Instructions for larger sizes are given in brackets [].

MATERIALS

Phildar Anouchka
5[6:6] 1¾oz/50g balls
Color shown: Coquelicot
Pair each of sizes 0 and 2 knitting needles
6 buttons

GAUGE

32sts and 42 rows to 4in over patt worked on size 2 needles
For gauge sample cast on 32sts. Keeping 3sts at each end of row in st st, work as for "1st patt row" from *, working patt rep twice. Cont in patt as set.

To save time, take time to check gauge.

ABBREVIATIONS

See book, p. 141.

BACK

Using smaller needles, cast on 115[123: 129]sts and work in single rib as foll:
1st rib row K1, *K1, P1, rep from * to last 2sts, K2.
2nd row K1, *P1, K1, rep from * to end.
Rep last 2 rows until Back measures 2½in, ending with a first row and inc one st in last st for *2nd and 3rd sizes only.* 115[124:130]sts.
Next row Rib 3[2:0], *rib 5[5:6], inc in next st, rib 5[6:6] rep from * to last 2[2:0]sts, rib to end. 125[134:140]sts.
Change to larger needles and patt:
1st patt row (RS) K2[0:3], *K7, K2 tog, yo, K4, rep from * to last 6[4:7]sts, K to end.
2nd and every other row P.
3rd row K2[0:3] *K6, K2 tog, yo, K1, yo, sl 1, K1, psso, K2, rep from * to last 6[4:7]sts, K to end.
5th row K2[0:3], *K5, K2 tog, yo, K3, yo, sl 1, K1, psso, K1, rep from * to last 6[4:7]sts, K to end.
7th row K2[0:3], *K4, K2 tog, yo, K5, yo, sl 1, K1, psso, rep from * to last 6[4:7]sts, K to end.
8th row As 2nd.
9th–14th rows Beg with a K row, work 6 rows st st.
These 14 rows form patt.
Cont in patt until Back measures 15½in, ending with a WS row.
Shape armholes:
Bind off 3sts at beg of next 4 rows. Dec one st at each end of next 4[5:6] rows, then one st

at each end of every other row 5 times. 95[102:106]sts.
Cont in patt on these sts until Back measures 7½[8:8¼]in from beg of armhole shaping, ending with a WS row.
Shape shoulders:
Bind off 8[9:9]sts at beg of next 4 rows and 9[9:10]sts at beg of next 2 rows. Bind off rem 45[48:50]sts for back neck.

LEFT FRONT

Using smaller needles, cast on 57[63:67]sts and work in single rib as for Back until Left Front measures 2½in, ending with a first row.
Next row Rib 2[2:1], *rib 4[4:5], inc in next st, rib 4[5:5], rep from * to last 1[1:0]sts, rib to end. 63[69:73]sts.
Change to larger needles and patt:
1st patt row (RS) K2[0:3], *K7, K2 tog, yo, K4, rep from * to last 9[4:5]sts, K to end.
2nd and every other row P.
3rd row K2[0:3], *K6, K2 tog, yo, K1, yo, sl 1, K1, psso, K2, rep from * to last 9[4:5]sts, K to end.
5th row K2[0:3], *K5, K2 tog, yo, K3, yo, sl 1, K1, psso, K1, rep from * to last 9[4:5]sts, K to end.
7th row K2[0:3], *K4, K2 tog, yo, K5, yo, sl 1, K1, psso, rep from * to last 9[4:5]sts, K to end.
8th row As 2nd.
9th–14th rows Beg with a K row, work 6 rows in st st.
These 14 rows form patt.
Cont in patt until Left Front measures 15½in, ending with a WS row.
Shape armhole:
Bind off 3sts at beg of next row and then every other row once. Dec one st at armhole edge on next 4[5:6] rows, then dec one st at armhole edge on every other row 5 times. 48[53:56]sts.
Cont in patt on rem sts until Left Front measures 21[21¼:21½]in, ending at center front edge.
Shape neck:
Bind off 6[7:8]sts at beg of next row. Dec one st at end of next row. Bind off 3[4:5]sts at beg of next row, then dec one st at end of next row. Bind off 2sts at beg of next row. Rep last 2 rows twice more.
Dec one st at neck edge on next 4[5:7] rows. 25[27:28]sts.
Work even until Left Front measures 7½[8: 8¼]in from beg of armhole shaping, ending at armhole edge.
Shape shoulder:
Bind off 8[9:9]sts at beg of next row and then every other row once.
Bind off rem 9[9:10]sts at beg of every other row once.

RIGHT FRONT

Work as for Left Front, reversing shaping and patt.

SLEEVES (make 2)

Using smaller needles, cast on 59[63:63]sts and work in single rib as for Back until Sleeve measures 2½in, ending with a first row.
Next row Rib 4[1:1], *rib 2[3:3], inc in next st, rib 2, rep from * to last 5[2:2]sts, rib to end. 69[73:73]sts.
Change to larger needles and patt:
Cont in patt as for Back, foll instructions for 2nd[1st:1st] sizes, *at the same time* inc one st at each end of every 6th row until there are 113[117:121]sts.
Work even until Sleeve measures 17¼[17¾: 18]in, ending with a WS row.
Shape sleeve cap:
Bind off 3sts at beg of next 4 rows. Dec one st at each end of next 4[5:6] rows, then one st at each end of every other row 21 times. 51[53:55]sts.
Bind off 8sts at beg of next 6 rows.
Bind off rem 3[5:7]sts.

TO FINISH

Block the pieces, but do not press.
Buttonhole band Using smaller needles, cast on 11sts and work 4 rows in single rib as for Back.
Next row Rib 5, turn and work 4 more rows on these 5sts.
Cut off yarn and rejoin to rem 6sts at inner edge. Work 5 rows on these sts.
Cont across all 11sts. *Work in rib for 43[45:47] rows, then work 1 buttonhole as before. Rep from * 3 more times, then work 39[41:43] rows rib. Leave rem sts on a holder.
Button band Work as for Buttonhole band, omitting buttonholes.
Neckband Join both shoulder seams, using small backstitch.
With RS facing and using smaller needles, rib 11 buttonhole sts from holder, pick up and K 35[37:39]sts along side of neck, 45[47:49]sts along back neck, 35[37:39]sts along side of neck and rib 11sts from Button band. 137[143:149]sts.

Work 4 rows in rib on these sts, *making a horizontal buttonhole on last row* by binding off 4sts over the previous buttonhole, 4sts in from the edge. On 5th row, cast on 4sts over those bound off previously. Cont in rib for 3 more rows. Bind off in rib.
Join side and sleeve seams, using small backstitch.
Sew Sleeves in place.
Sew front bands to front edges.
Sew on buttons to correspond with buttonholes.

Designed by Ruth Maria Swepson
Phildar (UK) Ltd.

OPTIONS

This simple lace pattern could be used to make a lovely blanket for a baby, using a fingering or sport-weight machine-washable yarn. Cast on a multiple of 13 stitches for each pattern repeat, plus any edge stitches required at each side. Once completed, the blanket could be edged with knitted lace (see book, p. 70) or with purchased lace edging.

The same stitch pattern, knitted in cotton, could be used to make an attractive summer top. Make it sleeveless, with a slash neck; or, to show off a tan, make it to reach only to the underarms and join the front and back with narrow straps worked in garter stitch.

A supremely luxurious blend of angora, wool, and silk knits up into subtle random stripes in this classic cardigan embossed with discreet cables and bobbles.

SIZES

To fit 34[36:38:40]in bust loosely
Garment measures: 47[50:53:56]in at underarm
Length from shoulder: 24[25:26:27]in
Sleeve seam: 20½in
Note Instructions for larger sizes are given in brackets [].

MATERIALS

Noro Nadeshiko
18[18:20:20] 1¾oz/50g balls
Color shown: 5
Pair each of sizes 10 and 10½ knitting needles
8 buttons

GAUGE

11sts and 16 rows to 4in over st st worked on size 10½ needles

To save time, take time to check gauge.

ABBREVIATIONS

Bl – (bobble) K into front and back of next st twice, then K into front of same st once more, turn, (K5, turn, P5, turn) twice, using LH needle, lift 2nd, then 3rd, then 4th, then 5th st over first st and off needle.

For other abbreviations see book, p. 141.

BACK

Using smaller needles, cast on 66[70:74:78]sts. Work 8 rows K1, P1 rib.
Change to larger needles.
Beg with a K row, cont in st st until Back measures 14[15:16:17]in, ending with a P row.
Shape raglans:
Next row Bind off 3sts, K30[32:34:36]sts including st used in binding off, Bl, K to end.
Next row Bind off 3sts, P to end.
Dec one st at each end of next row and then every other row, *at the same time* working Bl above previous Bl on 3rd, then 4th row. (3 bobbles in all.)
P1 row. 52[56:60:64]sts.
Cont dec at each end of every other row as before, beg working cable panel as foll:
1st cable row K2 tog, K19[21:23:25], P2, K6, P2, K to last 2sts, K2 tog.
2nd row P20[22:24:26], K2, P6, K2, P to end.
3rd row K2 tog, K18[20:22:24], P2, C6B, P2, K to last 2sts, K2 tog.
4th row P19[21:23:25], K2, P6, K2, P to end.
5th row K2 tog, K17[19:21:23], P2, K6, P2, K to last 2sts, K2 tog.
6th row P18[20:22:24], K2, P6, K2, P to end.
7th row K2 tog, K16[18:20:22], P2, C6B, P2, K to last 2sts, K2 tog.
8th–12th rows Cont dec on every other row as before and keeping cable panel correct,

rep 6th row then 5th and 6th rows twice more.
Cont in cable patt as set by last 12 rows, dec on every other row until 24[26:26:28]sts rem, ending with a P row. Bind off.

POCKET LININGS (make 2)

Using larger needles, cast on 16sts. Beg with a K row, work 19 rows st st. Leave sts on a holder.

LEFT FRONT

Using smaller needles, cast on 32[34:36:38]sts. Work 8 rows K1, P1 rib.
Change to larger needles.
Beg with a K row, cont in st st until Front measures 6[6:7:7]in, ending with a P row.
Make pocket top:
Next row K11[12:13:14], using smaller needles (K1, P1) 8 times (16sts for pocket top), turn, leave rem 5[6:7:8]sts on larger needle, work 3 more rows in K1, P1 rib on 16 pocket top sts, bind off loosely in rib.
Using larger needles, K to end on rem 5[6:7:8]sts.
Insert Pocket Lining:
Next row P5[6:7:8], P across 16 Pocket Lining sts on holder, P to end.
Cont in st st on all sts until Front measures 12 rows less than Back to raglans, ending with a P row.
Make first bobble:
Next row K21[22:23:24], Bl, K10[11:12:13]. This row sets position for subsequent bobbles.
Work 2 rows, ending with a K row.
Shape V-neck:
Next row P2 tog, P to end.
K1 row, working Bl above first Bl as before.
Work 3 rows st st, ending with a P row.
Next row K21[22:23:24], Bl, K to last 2sts, K2 tog.
P1 row.
Beg cable panel:
Next row K16[17:18:19], P2, K6, P2, K4[5:6:7]. (This row sets position for cable panel.)
Cont working cable panel as for Back, P1 row.
Shape armhole:
Cont dec at neck edge on every 5th row from previous dec and keeping cable panel correct, bind off 3sts at beg of next row.
P1 row.
Keeping cable panel correct, and dec at neck edge as before, dec one st at armhole edge on next row and then every other row until 8[8:9:9]sts rem.
Cont working in st st only, without cable panel, dec at neck edge and armhole edge as before, until 2sts rem.
Next row Work 2 tog. Fasten off.

RIGHT FRONT

Work as for Left Front, reversing neck and armhole shaping and noting that "Make pocket top" will read as foll:
Next row K5[6:7:8], using smaller needles, (K1, P1) 8 times, leave rem 11[12:13:14]sts on larger needle.
Complete pocket top as for Left Front.
Complete as for Left Front, reversing position for bobbles and cable panel.

SLEEVES (make 2)

Using smaller needles, cast on 22[24:28:32]sts. Work 8 rows K1, P1 rib.
Change to larger needles.
Beg with a K row, cont in st st, inc one st at each end of first row and then every 4th row until there are 58[60:64:68]sts. Work 3 rows even, so ending with a P row.
Make first bobble:
Next row K29[30:32:34], Bl, K to end.
Work Bl above previous Bl in same way on 4th row. P1 row.
Shape raglans:
Bind off 3sts at beg of next 2 rows.
Dec one st at each end of next row, working Bl above previous Bl (3 bobbles in all).
Work 1 row.
Beg cable panel:
Next row K2 tog, K18[19:21:23], P2, K6, P2, K to last 2sts, K2 tog.
Cont in st st and cable panel as set, dec one st at each end of every other row until 16[16:16:18]sts rem, ending with a P row.
Bind off.

TO FINISH

Block each piece separately, but do not press.
Join raglan seams.
Button band Using smaller needles, cast on 4sts. Work in K1, P1 rib until band, when slightly stretched, fits up Left Front, along V-neck shaping to center back neck. Bind off in rib.
Buttonhole band Mark positions for 8 buttons on Right Front, first to come ½in from lower edge, last to come at beg of V-neck shaping, with 6 more evenly spaced between.
Using smaller needles, cast on 4sts and work in rib as for Button band, making buttonholes as markers are reached as foll:
Next row K1, P2 tog, yo, K1.
Bind off in rib.
Sew Button band to Left Front, easing to fit, ending at center back neck.
Sew Buttonhole band to Right Front in same way.
Join seam at center back neck.
Join side and sleeve seams.
Sew on buttons to correspond with buttonholes.
Press seams lightly if necessary.

Designed by Warm and Wonderful

Although the knitting is continuous, the pattern of squares gives this cardigan an attractive patchwork appearance.

SIZES

To fit 34–36[38–40]in bust
Garment measures: 37½[43½]in at underarm
Length from shoulder: 21[21½]in
Sleeve seam: 17[17½]in
Note Instructions for larger size are given in brackets [].

MATERIALS

Phildar Sagittaire 245
14[16] 1¾oz/50g balls
Color shown: Blanc
Pair each of sizes 1 and 3 knitting needles
8 buttons

GAUGE

28sts and 32 rows to 4in over st st worked on size 3 needles

To save time, take time to check gauge.

ABBREVIATIONS

M1 – lift strand running from base of st just worked to base of next st on to LH needle and work into back of it.
Inc 3 – (K1, P1, K1) all into next st.
MB – (Make bobble) (K1, P1, K1, P1, K1) all into next st, turn, K5, turn, P5, turn, K2tog, K1, K2tog, turn, sl 1, K2tog, psso.
For other abbreviations, see book, p. 141.

Note Instructions for each whole or half pattern square are given on back of card. Squares are worked in a given sequence, with first and every *uneven* row worked on RS and 2nd and every *even* row on WS.

CARDIGAN

Back
Using smaller needles cast on 102[120]sts. Work 27 rows K1, P1 rib.
Next row P7, *M1, P3, rep from * to last 8sts, M1, P8. 132[156]sts.
Change to larger needles and first set of squares:
1st patt row (RS) Work first row of square 1B[1A], 2A, 3A, 4A, 1A, 2B[2A].
2nd row Work 2nd row of square 2B[2A], 1A, 4A, 3A, 2A, 1B[1A]. Work 30 more rows.
Cont in patt as set. Work 30 more rows.
Beg 2nd set of squares:
1st row (RS) Work first row of square 4B[4A], 1A, 2A, 3A, 4A, 1B[1A].
2nd row Work 2nd row of square 1B[1A], 4A, 3A, 2A, 1A, 4B[4A].
Cont in patts as set. Work 30 more rows.
Beg 3rd set of squares:
1st row (RS) Work first row of square 3B[3A], 4A, 1A, 2A, 3A, 4B[4A].
2nd row Work 2nd row of square 4B[4A], 3A, 2A, 1A, 4A, 3B[3A].
Cont in patt as set. Work 28 more rows.

Shape armholes:
31st row Keeping patt correct, bind off 14[22]sts, work in patt to end.
32nd row Keeping patt correct, bind off 14[22]sts, work in patt to last 0[4]sts, K0[4]. 104[112]sts.
Beg 4th set of squares:
1st patt row (RS) K0[4], work first row of square 3A, 4A, 1A, 2A, K0[4].
2nd row K0[4], work 2nd row of square 2A, 1A, 4A, 3A, K0[4].
Cont in patt as set. Work 30 more rows.
Beg 5th set of squares:
1st row (RS) K0[4], work first row of square 2A, 3A, 4A, 1A, K0[4].
2nd row K0[4], work 2nd row of square 1A, 4A, 3A, 2A, K0[4].
Cont in patt as set. Work 30 more rows. K0[4] rows.
Shape shoulders:
Next row Bind off 26[30]sts, K to end.
Next row Bind off 26[30]sts, P to end.
Bind off rem 52sts.

LEFT FRONT

Using smaller needles, cast on 52[60]sts and work 27 rows K1, P1 rib.
Next row P6, *M1, P3, rep from * to last 7[3]sts, M1, P7[3]. 66[78]sts**.
Change to larger needles and first set of squares:

1st row (RS) Work first row of square 1B[1A], 2A, 3A.

2nd row Work 2nd row of square 3A, 2A, 1B[1A].

Cont in patt as set. Work 30 more rows.

Beg 2nd set of squares:

1st row (RS) Work first row of square 4B[4A], 1A, 2A.

2nd row Work 2nd row of square 2A, 1A, 4B[4A].

Cont in patt as set. Work 30 more rows.

Beg 3rd set of squares:

1st row (RS) Work first row of square 3B[3A], 4A, 1A.

2nd row Work 2nd row of square 1A, 4A, 3B[3A].

Cont in patt as set. Work 28 more rows.

Shape armhole:

31st row Keeping patt correct, bind off 14[22]sts, work in patt to end.

32nd row Work in patt to last 0[4]sts, K0[4]. 52[56]sts.

Beg 4th set of squares:

1st row (RS) K0[4], work first row of square 3A, 4A.

2nd row Work 2nd row of square 4A, 3A, K0[4].

Cont in patt as set. Work 30 more rows.

Beg 5th set of squares:

1st row K0[4], work first row of square 2A, 3A.

2nd row Work 2nd row of square 3A, 2A, K0[4].

Cont in patt as set until Front measures 5in from beg of armhole shaping, ending at front edge.

Shape neck:

Keeping patt correct, bind off 6[8]sts at beg of next row. Dec one st at neck edge on every row until 26[30]sts rem. Complete 32 rows of square patts. K0[4] rows.

Shape shoulder: Bind off rem 26[30]sts.

RIGHT FRONT

Work as for Left Front to **. **Change to larger needles and first set of squares:**

1st row (RS) Work first row of square 4A, 1A, 2B[2A].

2nd row Work 2nd row of square 2B[2A], 1A, 4A.

Cont in patt as set. Work 30 more rows.

Beg 2nd set of squares:

1st row (RS) Work first row of square 3A, 4A, 1B[1A].

2nd row Work 2nd row of square 1B[1A], 4A, 3A.

Cont in patt as set. Work 30 more rows.

Beg 3rd set of squares:

1st row (RS) Work first row of square 2A, 3A, 4B[4A].

2nd row Work 2nd row of square 4B[4A], 3A, 2A.

Cont in patt as set. Work 29 more rows.

Shape armhole:

32nd row Bind off 14[22]sts, work in patt to end. 52[56]sts.

Beg 4th set of squares:

1st row (RS) Work first row of square 1A, 2A, K0[4].

2nd row K0[4], work 2nd row of square 2A, 1A.

Carillon Patt

Square 1A (whole).

1st row K2, P2, K1 tbl, *P2, turn, cast on 4, turn, P2, K1 tbl, rep from * 3 times, P1.

2nd row K1, *P1, K2, P into front and back of each of 4 cast-on sts, K2, rep from * 3 times, P1, K2, P2.

3rd row K2, P2, K1 tbl, * P2, sl 1, K1, psso, K4, K2tog, P2, K1 tbl, rep from * 3 times, P1.

4th row K1, * P1, K2, P2tog, P2, P2tog tbl, K2, rep from * 3 times, P1, K2, P2.

5th row K2, P2, K1 tbl, *P2, sl 1, K1, psso, K2tog, P2, K1 tbl, rep from * 3 times, P1.

6th row K1, * P1, K1, P2tog, P2tog tbl, K1, rep from * 3 times, P1, K2, P2.

7th row K2, P2, K1 tbl, *P4, K1 tbl, rep from * 3 times, P1.

8th row K1, *P1, K4, rep from * 3 times, P1, K2, P2.

9th row P2, K1 tbl, P2, *turn, cast on 4sts, turn, P2, K1 tbl, P2, rep from * 3 times, K1.

10th row P1, *K2, P1, K2, P into front and back of each cast-on st, rep from * 3 times, K2, P1, K2.

11th row P2, K1 tbl, P2, * sl 1, K1, psso, K4, K2tog, P2, K1 tbl, P2, rep from * 3 times, K1.

12th row P1, *K2, P1, K2, P2tog, P2, P2tog tbl, rep from * 3 times, K2, P1, K2.

13th row P2, K1 tbl, P2, *sl 1, K1, psso, K2tog, P2, K1 tbl, P2, rep from * 3 times, K1.

14th row P1, K1, *K1, P1, K1, P2tog, P2tog tbl, rep from * 3 times, K1, P1, K2.

15th row P2, K1 tbl, *P4, K1 tbl, rep from * 3 times, P2, K1.

16th row P1, K2, *P1, K4, rep from * 3 times, P1, K2.

17th–32nd rows Rep first–16th rows.

Square 1B (half)

1st row P1, K1 tbl, rep from * as for square 1A twice, P2.

2nd row K2, rep from * as for square 1A twice, P1, K1.

3rd–8th rows Rep first–2nd rows 3 times, keeping square 1A correct.

9th row *P2, turn, cast on 4, turn, P2, K1 tbl, rep

from * once turn, cast on 4, turn, P2.

10th row *K2, P into front and back of each cast-on st, K2, P1, rep from * once, K2, P into front and back of each cast-on st, K2.

11th row *P2, sl 1, K1, psso, K4, K2tog, P2, K1 tbl, rep from * once, P2, sl 1, K1, psso, K4, K2tog, P2.

12th row K2, P2tog, P2, P2tog tbl, K2, *P1, K2, P2tog, P2, P2tog tbl, K2, rep from * once.

13th row *P2, sl 1, K1, psso, K2tog, P2, K1 tbl, rep from * once, P2, sl 1, K1, psso, K2tog, P2.

14th row K1, P2tog, P2tog tbl, K1, *P1, K1, P2tog, P2tog tbl, K1, rep from * once.

15th row *P4, K1 tbl, rep from * once, P4.

16th row K4, *P1, K4, rep from * once.

17th–32nd rows Rep first–16th rows.

Bramble Patt

Square 3A (whole)

1st row P26.

2nd and every other row As first.

3rd row P2, *K5, P1, rep from * 3 times.

5th row P2, *K2, MB, K2, P1, rep from * 3 times.

7th row As 3rd.

8th row As 2nd.

9th–32nd rows Rep first–8th rows 3 times.

Square 3B (half)

Work as for square 3A, but rep from * *once*, not 3 times, on 3rd, 5th and 7th patt rows.

Boxed Bobble Patt

Square 2A (whole)

1st and 3rd rows P26.

2nd row P1, *inc 3, P3tog, rep from * 5 times, P1.

4th row P1, *P3tog, inc 3, rep from * 5 times, P1.

5th–32nd rows Rep first–4th rows 7 times.

Square 2B (half)

Work as for square 2A, but rep from * *twice* instead of 5 times on every other row.

Seed Stitch Patt

Square 4A (whole)

1st row *K1, P1, rep from * to end.

2nd row As first

3rd row *P1, K1, rep from * to end.

4th row As 2nd.

5th–32nd rows Rep first–4th rows 7 times.

Square 4B (half) Work as for square 4A.

Cont in patt as set. Work 30 more rows.

Beg 5th set of squares:

1st row (RS) Work first row of square 4A, 1A, K0[4].

2nd row K0[4], work 2nd row of square 1A, 4A.

Cont in patt as set until Right Front matches Left Front to neck shaping, ending at front edge. Complete as for Left Front.

SLEEVES (make 2)

Using smaller needles, cast on 54[64]sts, and work 27 rows K1, P1 rib.

Next row P1, *M1, P1, rep from * to last st, P1. 106[126]sts.

Change to larger needles and square patt:

1st size only

1st row (RS) Work first row from square 1A, 2B, 3A, 2B, 1A.

2nd size only

1st row (RS) Work first row of square 4B over 10sts only, first row of 1A, 2B, 3A, 2B, 1A, work first row of 4B over 10sts only.

Both sizes

2nd–32nd rows Work each patt as set.

1st–32nd rows form Sleeve patt. Cont in patt until Sleeve measures 17[17½]in, ending with a WS row.

Shape cap:

Keeping patt correct, bind off 14[22]sts at beg of next 2 rows. 78[82]sts. Dec one st at each end of 3rd row, then every 4th row until 58[62]sts rem. Work one row. Bind off.

TO FINISH

Block each piece. Join shoulder seams.

Neckband With smaller needles and RS facing, pick up and K 30sts along right neck, 52sts along back neck and 30sts along left neck. 112sts.

Work 7 rows K1, P1 rib. Bind off in rib.

Button band Using smaller needles, cast on 12sts. Work in K1, P1 rib until band, slightly stretched, fits front edge. Bind off in rib.

Buttonhole band Mark positions for 8 buttons on Button band, one 6 rows from bottom, one ½in from top, with 6 spaced between.

Using smaller needles, cast on 12sts and work 5 rows K1, P1 rib.

6th row (make buttonholes) Rib 5, bind off 2, rib to end.

7th row Rib 5, cast on 2, rib to end.

Work as for Button band, making buttonholes as markers are reached. Bind off in rib. Set in Sleeves, easing any fullness at shoulder. Join side and sleeve seams.

Designed by Joan Chatterley's Knitwear

All you need to magic this glamorous wrap is a pair of large needles and some high-fashion yarn. Both the waist-tie and the button-up versions are knitted in easy stockinette stitch.

SIZES

To fit 32–34[36–38]in bust
Garment measures: 54[60]in
Length from shoulder: 18½[19¾]in
Note Instructions for larger size are given in brackets [].

MATERIALS

Pingouin 1920
7[8] 1¾oz/50g balls
Color shown: Azalée
Pair of size 10½ knitting needles
1 button for tie-wrap version
5 buttons for button-up version

GAUGE

13sts and 17 rows to 4in over st st worked on size 10½ needles

To save time, take time to check gauge.

ABBREVIATIONS

See book, p. 141.

Note Jacket is worked in one piece, beg at lower edge of Back.

MAIN PART (both versions)

Cast on 60[68]sts. Beg with a K row work in st st, shaping sides by inc one st at each end of every 4th row 5[7] times, then one st at each end of every other row 9[8] times in all. 88[98]sts.
Shape sleeves:
Cast on 2sts at beg of next 16[14] rows, then 6sts at beg of next 6[4] rows. 156[150]sts.
2nd size only Cast on 8sts at beg of next 2 rows. 156[166]sts.
Both sizes
Work even until work measures 17½[18¾]in, ending with a WS row.
Shape neck:
Next row K70[74]sts and leave these sts on a holder, bind off next 16[18]sts, K to end. Cont on rem 70[74]sts.
**Work 1 row.
Bind off 5[6]sts at neck edge on next row. Work 1 row. This completes back to shoulder line. Work 2 more rows.
Shape front neck:
Cast on 4[5]sts at beg of next row, then 4[5]sts at beg of every other row once and 5sts at beg of every other row once. 78[83]sts. Work even until piece measures 22½[24]in, ending with a RS row.
Shape sleeves:
Bind off 6[8]sts at beg of next row, 6sts at beg of every other row twice and 2sts at beg of every other row 8[7] times. 44[49]sts.
Shape sides:
Dec one st at beg of every other row 10[9]

times, then one st at beg of every 4th row 4[6] times in all. 30[34]sts.
Work 3 rows even so that Front measures same as Back, ending at side seam.
Button-up version only
Bind off rem sts.
Tie-wrap version only
Shape tie wrap:
Bind off 2sts at beg of next row and then every other row once, dec one st at beg of every other row once. Work 1 row. Rep these 6 rows 5 more times. 0[4]sts.
1st size only
Fasten off.
2nd size only
Bind off 2sts at beg of every other row twice. Fasten off.
Both versions – both sizes
With WS of work facing, rejoin yarn at neck edge sts on holder and work to end. Complete to match first side, working from ** to end, reversing sleeve shaping.

TO FINISH

Block but do not press.
Neck border With RS of work facing, pick up and K 18[19]sts evenly along left front neck, 36[38]sts along back neck and 18[19]sts along right front neck. 72[76]sts.
Bind off K-wise.
Tie-wrap version
Button band With RS of work facing, pick up and K 42[44]sts along slanting edge of Right Front, 60[66]sts along lower edge of Back and 42[44]sts along slanting edge of Left Front. 144[154]sts. Bind off K-wise.

Button-up version
Button band With RS of work facing, pick up and K 30[33]sts along slanting edge of Right Front, 60[66]sts along lower edge of Back and 30[33]sts along slanting edge of Left Front. 120[132]sts. Bind off K-wise.
Join side and sleeve seams.
Both versions
Button loop Using a strand of Pingouin 1920, make a double loop ¾in long, ½in below top neck edge at right front edge. Bind loop with buttonhole stitch. Sew button to Left Front to correspond with button loop.
Button-up version only
Button loops Make 4 more button loops on right front edge, the first to come ½in above lower edge, with 3 more evenly spaced up right front edge to top button loop. Sew on buttons to correspond with button loops.

Designed by Kate Jones

The fun begins the minute you slip on this flattering, bare-shoulders top, knitted in pure cotton. Wear it in the sun and under a summer moon, too.

SIZES

To fit 34[36:38]in bust
Garment measures: 34[36½:39]in at under-arm.
Length from top of Collar: 17[17:18]in (with collar turned over)
Note Instructions for larger sizes are given in brackets [].

MATERIALS

Scheepjeswol Mayflower Cotton 8
6 [7:7] 1¾oz/50g balls
Color shown: 530
Pair each of sizes 2 and 3 knitting needles
Size 2 circular needle

GAUGE

28sts and 40 rows to 4in over st st worked on size 3 needles

To save time, take time to check gauge.

ABBREVIATIONS

See book, p. 141.

BACK

Using smaller needles, cast on 120[128:136]sts. Work in K1, P1 rib for 4in.
Change to larger needles.
Beg with a K row, cont in st st until work measures 9[9:10½]in, ending with a P row.
Shape armholes:
Bind off 4sts at beg of next 2 rows and 2sts at beg of next 2 rows. Dec one st at each end of next 3 rows, then every 3rd row 6 times in all. 90[98:106]sts. Work even for 1¼in, ending with a P row. Leave rem sts on a holder.

FRONT

Work as for Back.

ARMHOLE BORDERS

Join side seams.
Using smaller needles and with RS facing, pick up and K 42sts along each armhole. Work in K1, P1 rib for ½in. Bind off in rib.

COLLAR

Using circular needle, cast on 45[48:51]sts, then with RS facing, pick up and K 3sts across left armhole border, K across 90[98:106] front sts on holder, pick up and K3sts across right front armhole border, cast on 45[48:51]sts, pick up and K 3sts across right back armhole border, K across 90[98:106] back sts on holder, pick up and K 3sts across left back armhole border. 282[304:326]sts.
Cont to work in rows.
Work in K1, P1 rib for 9in. Bind off loosely in rib.

TO FINISH

Block and press main pieces, foll instructions on yarn label, avoiding ribbing.
Join collar seam, reversing seam for 4in for turn-over.
Strap Using smaller needles, cast on 2sts. K90 rows. Bind off.
Sew strap in place, approx 5in away from inside collar side seam.
Press seams lightly if necessary.

Designed by Fiona McTague

Two cotton yarns – one smooth, one crunchy – add up to a cool summer number.

SIZES

To fit 30–32[34–36:38–40]in bust
Garment measures: 35½[39½:43¾]in at under-arm
Length from shoulder: 25[26:28½]in
Note Instructions for larger sizes are given in brackets [].

MATERIALS

Pingouin Coton Naturel 8 Fils (A)
3[4:4] 1¾oz/50g balls
Color shown: Blanc
Pingouin Coton Torsade (B)
3[4:4] 1¾oz/50g balls
Color shown: Celeste
Pair each of Sizes 3 and 7 knitting needles

GAUGE

19sts and 26 rows to 4in over st st worked on size 7 needles

To save time, take time to check gauge.

ABBREVIATIONS

M1 – lift strand running from base of st just worked to base of next st on to LH needle and work into back of it.

For other abbreviations see book, p. 141.

BACK

Using smaller needles and A, cast on 78[88:98]sts.
1st rib row *K1, P1, rep from * to end.
2nd row *K1, P1, rep from * to end.
Rep these 2 rows for 3in, ending with a first row.
Next row Rib 11[14:14], *M1, rib 11[12:14], rep from * to last 12[14:14]sts, M1, rib 12[14:14]. 84[94:104]sts.
Change to larger needles.
Using A and beg with a K row, work 8[8:10] rows st st, changing to B at end of last row.
Beg stripe patt:
Using B, work 16[17:18] rows st st, changing to A at end of last row. Using A, work 16[17:18] rows st st.**
These 32[34:36] rows form stripe patt.
Cont in patt, work 41[43:43] more rows. (Back measures approx 15½[16:16½]in.)
Shape armholes:
Bind off 2[3:3]sts at beg of next 2 rows, then dec one st at each end of every other row 9[9:10] times in all. Dec one st at each end of every 3rd row 7[7:8] times, then one st at each end of every 5th row 4[4:5] times in all, *at the same time* when 4th complete stripe patt rep has been completed, change to B and *shape neck* as foll:
Next row K to center 14[18:18]sts, bind off next 14[18:18]sts, K to end.
Complete each side separately:
Bind off 2 sts at neck edge on every other row 3[3:4] times in all. Work 1 row. (Back measures 25[26:28½]in.)

Bind off rem 7[9:9]sts.
With WS facing, rejoin yarn to rem sts and work to end. Complete to match first side.

FRONT

Work as for Back to **, ending with a WS row. (Front measures approx 9[9½:10]in.)
Divide for neck:
Next row Using B, K34[38:42]sts, turn and leave rem sts on a holder.
Keeping patt correct, dec one st at neck edge on every 16th[15th:14th] row 5[6:7] times in all, *at the same time*, when 80[84:88] rows have been worked in st st (Front measures approx 15½[16:16½]in) ending with a WS row, *shape armholes* as foll:
Bind off 2[3:3]sts at beg of next row, then dec one st at beg of every other row 9[9:10] times in all. Dec one st at beg of every 3rd row 7[7:8] times, then one st at beg of every 5th row until 7[9:9]sts rem.
Work even until Front matches Back to shoulder. Bind off rem sts. With RS of work facing, return to rem sts. Leave center 16[18:20]sts on a holder for center front neck. Rejoin yarn to rem 34[38:42]sts and complete to match first side.

TO FINISH

Block but do not press.
Join shoulder seams.
Armhole borders Using smaller needles and A, with RS of work facing, pick up and K 120[125:130]sts evenly around armhole. Bind off K-wise.
Collar Return to 16[18:20]sts on holder for center front neck. Using smaller needles and with RS of work facing, rejoin A.
Next row K 5[6:6], M1, K 5[6:7], M1, K 5[5:6], inc in last st. 19[21:23]sts.
Next row P1, *K1, P1, rep from * to end.
Next row K1, *P1, K1, rep from * to end.
Cont in rib as set until Collar, when slightly stretched, fits around neck edge.
Bind off in rib.
Sew Collar in place, stretching it slightly.
Sew end of right collar in place behind left collar.
Join side seams.

Designed by Kate Jones

A pretty cotton-linen blend is used for this airy summer top, featuring an unusual elliptical dropped-stitch motif.

SIZES

To fit 32–34[36–38]in bust
Garment measures: 37½[41½]in at underarm
Length from shoulder: 21¾[22¾]in
Note Instructions for larger size are given in brackets [].

MATERIALS

Scheepjeswol Linnen
5[6] 1¾oz/50g balls
Color shown: 250
Pair each of sizes 2 and 3 knitting needles

GAUGE

20sts and 44 rows to 4in over g st worked on size 3 needles

To save time, take time to check gauge.

ABBREVIATIONS

Ky2on – K next st, winding yarn twice over needle.
Ky3on – K next st winding yarn three times over needle.

For other abbreviations see book, p. 141.

BACK

Using smaller needles, cast on 109[119]sts and work in single rib as foll:
1st rib row (RS) K1, *P1, K1, rep from * to end.
2nd row P1, *K1, P1, rep from * to end.
Rep these 2 rows until Back measures 3½in, ending with a first row.
Next row K4[2], (K2 tog, K5[6]) 14 times, K2 tog, K5[3]. 94[104]sts.
Change to larger needles and patt:
K10 rows.
11th row (RS) K24[29], **, (Ky2on) 3 times, (Ky3on) 12 times, (Ky2on) 3 times, **, K52[57].
12th row K to end, dropping extra loops made on previous row off needle.
13th–20th rows K.
21st row K64[69], **, (Ky2on) 3 times, (Ky3on) 18 times, (Ky2on) 3 times, **, K6[11].
22nd row As 12th.
23rd–30th rows K.
31st row K6[11], rep from ** to ** of 21st row, K64[69].
32nd row As 12th.
33rd–40th rows K.
41st row K52[57], work from ** to ** of 11th row, K24[29].
42nd row As 12th.
43rd–50th rows K.
11th–50th rows form the patt.
Cont in patt until Back measures 12in, ending with a WS row.
Shape armholes:
Keeping patt correct, bind off 4sts at beg of next 2 rows. 86[96]sts.

Cont in patt until Back measures 9[10]in from beg of armhole shaping, ending with a WS row.
Next row K2[4], (inc in next st, K3) 21[23] times. 107[119]sts.
Beg with 2nd row, work 5 rows in rib as for waistband.
Bind off in rib.

FRONT

Work as for Back.

TO FINISH

Block the pieces, but do not press.
Join shoulder seams, leaving a space of approx 10½[11½]in at center for neck.
Armhole borders With RS facing and using smaller needles, pick up and K 137[149]sts evenly along straight edge of armhole.
Beg with a 2nd row, work in rib as for Back waistband for ¾in.
Bind off evenly in rib.
Work other border in same way. Sew borders in position to Front and Back at underarm.
Join side seams.

Designed by Julia Howe Knitwear

OPTIONS
Instead of seaming the front and back at the shoulder, you could fasten them with buttons and loops. Work in garter stitch up to the edge and bind off. Work crocheted slip stitch along both edges (see book, p. 140), working two- or three-chain button loops at the appropriate points on the front shoulder edges. Sew buttons to the corresponding points on the back edge.

The top could also be worked entirely in garter stitch, without the dropped-stitch motif.

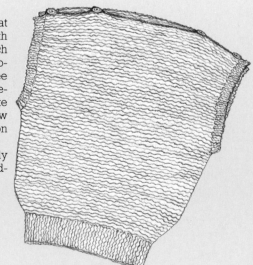

You're on holiday – if only in spirit – whenever you wear this delightful cotton sweater with its carefree assortment of bright colors arranged on a light cream, textured background.

SIZE

To fit 32–34in bust
Garment measures: 40in at underarm
Length from shoulder: 23½in
Sleeve seam: 15½in

MATERIALS

Scheepjeswol Cotton Miranda
6 1¾oz/50g balls in main color A (438 – cream)
Scheepjeswol Cotton Mayflower 8
1 1¾oz/50g ball in each of 7 colors: B (519 – dark blue), C (510 – red), D (526 – amber), E (565 – green), F (578 – gold), G (534 – pink) and H (511 – turquoise)
Pair each of sizes 5 and 7 knitting needles
Small quantity of fine cotton yarn matching color A for seams

GAUGE

20sts and 24 rows to 4in over st st worked on size 7 needles

To save time, take time to check gauge.

ABBREVIATIONS

M1 – lift strand running from base of st just worked to base of next st on to LH needle and work into back of it.
For other abbreviations see book, p. 141.

Note Use Cotton Mayflower 8 double throughout.
Strand colors not in use loosely across back of work (see book, p. 116).

FRONT

Using smaller needles and A, cast on 85sts.
1st rib row *K1, P1, rep from * to last st, K1.
2nd row *P1, K1, rep from * to last st, P1.
Rep these 2 rows for ¾in, ending with a 2nd row.
Change to larger needles.
Next row K10, *M1, K5, rep from * to end. 100sts.
P1 row.
Beg stripe and block patt:
Beg with a K row, cont working in st st throughout.
1st–8th rows Work (2 rows B, 2 rows A) twice.
9th row K1B, *3A, 2B, rep from *, ending last rep with K1B.
10th row P1B, *3A, 2B, rep from *, ending last rep with P1B.
11th–14th rows Rep 9th and 10th rows twice more. Break off B.
15th row Using A, K to end.
16th row Using A, P to end.
These 16 rows form patt. Rep patt rows 3 more times using C, then D, then E in place of B each time.

Shape armholes:
Using F, bind off 10sts at beg of next 2 rows. 80sts.
Work 2 rows A, 2 rows F and 2 rows A.
Next row K4A, *2F, 3A, rep from *, ending last rep with K4A.
Next row P4A, *2F, 3A, rep from *, ending last rep with P4A.
The last 2 rows establish the patt.
Cont in patt as set until 16 patt rows have been completed from beg of armholes. Rep patt rows twice more, using G, then H in place of F.**
Work 2 rows F, 2 rows A, 2 rows C, 2 rows A and 2 rows E.
***Shape shoulders:**
Using A, bind off 21sts at beg of next 2 rows. 38sts.
Work 3 rows in A. Bind off.

BACK

Work as for Front to **. Now work 2 rows D, 2 rows A, 2 rows G, 2 rows A and 2 rows B. Complete as for Front, working from *** to end.

SLEEVES (make 2)

Using A and smaller needles, cast on 40sts.
Work in K1, P1 rib for ¾in..
Change to larger needles.
Next row K2, *M1, K3, rep from *, ending last rep with K2. 53sts. P1 row.
Beg with a K row, cont in stripe and block patt as for Back, working in color sequence of C, D, E, F, G and H, *at the same time* inc one st at each end of every 5th row until there are 61sts, then at each end of every 4th row until there are 95sts.
Work 2 rows in A. Bind off.

TO FINISH

Block each piece separately and press lightly foll instructions on yarn label.
Join seams, using the finer cotton yarn.
Join shoulder seams.
Sew Sleeves in place matching center of Sleeve to shoulder seam and sewing final rows to bound-off sts at underarm, working as close to edge as possible. Fold last 3 rows worked in A to WS around neck edge and sew loosely in place.

Designed by Isabelle Higgins

> **OPTIONS**
> Using the same basic pattern and Cotton Miranda only, you could make a striped pullover. Work in random horizontal stripes of varying depth, changing colors as you like.

For the experienced knitter – a spectacular display of stitches worked in lustrous pure cotton in a delicious lemon sherbet color.

SIZES

To fit 34[36]in bust
Garment measures approx: 38[42]in at underarm
Length from shoulder: 21in
Sleeve seam: 17in
Note Instructions for larger size are given in brackets [].

MATERIALS

Anny Blatt Ecoss' Anny
17[20] 1¾oz/50g balls
Color shown: Paille
Pair each of sizes 5 and 7 knitting needles
Cable needle

GAUGE

20sts and 24 rows to 4in over st st worked on size 7 needles

To save time, take time to check gauge.

ABBREVIATIONS

M1 – lift strand running from base of st just worked to base of next st on to LH needle and P tb1.
Lt Tog – with RH needle behind LH needle skip one st, K next st tb1, with RH needle K both sts tb1.
Rt Tog – K2 tog leaving sts on LH needle, insert RH needle from front between 2 sts just knitted, K first st again.
Bl – (K1, P1, K1, P1, K1) into next st, turn, K5, turn, P5, turn, K2 tog, K1, K2 tog, turn, sl 1, K2 tog, psso.
For other abbreviations see book, p. 141.

Note A When working diagonal tassel panel the final 2sts, shown as *Lt Tog*, are moved one st to left to form diagonal line across Back and Front between tassel panel and cable panel. The same *Lt Tog* is later introduced on the RH side to form the diagonal line between st st panel and tassel panel.
Patts used for Sleeves are given out in full before Sleeve instructions and are referred to by name in the patt.

BACK

Using smaller needles, cast on 84[92]sts. Work 27 rows K2, P2 rib.
Next row P5[3], *M1, P5, rep from * to last 4sts, M1, P4. 100[110]sts.
Change to larger needles and tassel and cable patts:
1st patt row (RS) P5[10], (B1, P9) 4 times, B1, P7, (K4, P6) 4 times, K4, P3[8].
2nd row K3[8], (P4, K6) 4 times, P4, K7, P1, (K9, P1) 4 times, K5[10].
3rd row P5[10], (Lt Tog, P8) 4 times, *Lt Tog* (first 2sts of LH diagonal line), (P6, C4F) 5 times, P3[8].

4th row K3[8] (P4, K6) 5 times, P2, (K8, P2) 4 times, K5[10].
5th row P4[K1, Lt Tog, P6], (Rt Tog, Lt Tog, P6) 4 times, Rt Tog, *Lt Tog*, P5, (K4, P6) 4 times, K4, P3[8].
6th row K3[8], (P4, K6) 4 times, P4, K5, P4, (K6, P4) 4 times, K4[6], P3.
7th row P3[K2, Lt Tog, P4], (Rt Tog, K2, Lt Tog, P4) 4 times, Rt Tog, K2, *Lt Tog*, P4, (K4, P6) 4 times, K4, P3[8].
8th row K3[8], (P4, K6) 4 times, P4, K4, P6, (K4, P6) 4 times, K3[K4, P4].
9th row P2[K3, Lt Tog, P2], (Rt Tog, K4, Lt Tog, P2) 4 times, Rt Tog, K4, *Lt Tog*, P3, (K4, P6) 4 times, K4, P3[8].
10th row K3[8], (P4, K6) 4 times, P4, K3, (P8, K2) 5 times, P0[5].
11th row K1[K4, Lt Tog], Rt Tog, (K6, Lt Tog,

Rt Tog) 4 times, K6, *Lt Tog*, P2, (C4F, P6) 4 times, C4F, P3[8].

12th row K3[8], (P4, K6) 4 times, P4, K2, P51[56].

13th row K0[5], (Rt Tog, K8) 5 times, *Lt Tog*, P1, (K4, P6) 4 times, K4, P3[8].

14th row K3[8], (P4, K6) 4 times, P4, K1, P52[57].

First–14th rows set positions for tassel patt and cable patt.

Beg next patt rep:
15th row P5[10], (B1, P9) 4 times, B1, P5, *Lt Tog*, (K4, P6) 4 times, K4, P3[8].

16th row K3[8], (P4, K6) 4 times, P6, K5, (P1, K9) 4 times, P1, K5[10].

Cont in patt as set, working from 3rd patt row.

17th–32nd[24th] rows Cont in patt as set, working from 3rd patt row, moving *Lt Tog* one st to left on RS rows and P appropriate 2sts on WS rows to form diagonal line across Back, *at the same time* keeping cable patt correct and noting that C4F is worked on 19th and 27th rows.

1st size only
Note B Cont in patt as set, working beg and ends of rows as foll, so that the tassel panel is moved to the left and st st panel is introduced on the right:

33rd row Beg K1, P3 instead of P4.

34th row End K3, P1 instead of K4.

35th row Beg with *Lt Tog* instead of P3, noting that this *Lt Tog* now forms RH diagonal line across sweater, dividing tassel panel and st st panel.

36th row End with K1, P2 instead of K3, working C4F on cable panel.

37th row Beg K1, *Lt Tog*, K1, instead of P2, Rt Tog.

38th row End with P4, instead of P2, K2.

39th row Beg K2, *Lt Tog*, K5, instead of K1, Rt Tog, K6.

40th–42nd rows Keeping patt correct, cont moving *Lt Tog* one st to left on every RS row and P2 appropriate sts on WS rows, working new panel in st st on RH side.

43rd row Cont in patt, working C4F on cable panel.

44th–47th rows Cont in patt as set, moving *Lt Tog* one st to left as before and working beg or ends of rows as foll, to introduce a diagonal from left to right on RH side and beg working tile panel (see Sleeve instructions) on LH side.

48th row Beg P1, K2 instead of K3.

49th row End P1, *Rt Tog*, instead of P3.

50th row Beg P3 instead of K3.

51st row End K3, *Rt Tog*, K1, P1 instead of K4, P3, working C4F on cable panel.

52nd row Beg P7 instead of K3, P4.

53rd row End K1, *Rt Tog*, K3, P1 instead of K4, P3.

54th row Beg K5, P2 instead of K3, P4.

55th row P5, *Rt Tog*, P1, K4, P1, instead of P6, K4, P3.

56th row Beg P9, K4, instead of K3, P4, K6.

57th row End P3, *Rt Tog*, K2, P1, K4, P1, instead of P6, K4, P3.

58th row Beg P11, K2 instead of K3, P4, K6.

59th row End P1, *Rt Tog*, (K4, P1) twice, instead of P6, C4F, P3, working C4F on cable panel.

60th row Beg K11, P2, instead of K3, P4, K6.

61st–67th rows Keeping patt correct, cont moving *Rt Tog* one st to right on RS rows and P2 appropriate sts (also moving one st in same direction) on WS rows and working new diagonal panel on LH side in tile patt as set.

2nd size only
(See Note B, on first size.)
25th row Beg *Lt Tog*, K2 instead of K4.

27th row Beg K1, *Lt Tog*, K2, instead of K5 and working C4F on cable panel.

29th row Beg K2, *Lt Tog*, P6, instead of P10.

30th row End K6, P4, instead of K10.

31st row Beg K3, *Lt Tog*, P5, instead of P10.

32nd row End K5, P5, instead of K10.

33rd–42nd rows Keeping patt correct, move *Lt Tog*, one st to left on RS rows and P appropriate 2sts on WS rows, working new diagonal panel on RH side in st st, noting that C4F is worked on 35th row.

Cont in patt as set, beg working diagonal from left to right and introducing tile panel on LH side.

43rd row End P7, K1 instead of P8 and work C4F on cable panel.

44th row Beg P2, K6, instead of K8.

45th row End P5, *Rt Tog*, P1 instead of P8.

46th row Beg P4, K4 instead of K8.

47th row End P3, *Rt Tog*, K2, P1, instead of P8.

48th row Beg K4, P2, K2, instead of K8.

49th row End P1, *Rt Tog*, K4, P1, instead of P8.

50th row Beg P12 instead of K8, P4.

51st row End K3, *Rt Tog*, K1, P1, K4, P1, instead of C4F, P8, working C4F on cable panel.

52nd row Beg P12, instead of K8, P4.

53rd row End K1, *Rt Tog*, K3, P1, K4, P1 instead of K4, P8.

54th row Beg K10, P2, instead of K8, P4.

56th–67th rows Keeping patt correct cont moving *Rt Tog* one st to right on RS rows and P2sts on WS, also moving one st in same direction on WS rows, working panel on LH side in tile patt as set and working C4F on 59th row.

Both sizes
Cont working in diagonal patts, noting that on 99th–107th rows tassel panel is worked in rev st st.

108th row Work in patt.

109th row K37[42], *Lt Tog*, (P1, K4) 12[13] times, P1.

110th row P.

111th–116th rows Cont working appropriate diagonal panels in st st and tile patt, moving *Lt Tog* one st to left on RS rows and P2sts on WS rows as before. (Back measures approx 19½in.)
Work 10 rows K2, P2 rib. Bind off loosely in rib.

FRONT

Work as for Back.

SLEEVES (make 2)

(See note A.)
Tassel patt (over 31sts)

1st row (RS) P5, (B1, P9) twice, B1, P5.
2nd row K5, (P1, K9) twice, P1, K5.
3rd row P5, (Lt Tog, P8) twice, Lt Tog, P4.
4th row K4, (P2, K8) twice, P2, K5.
5th row P4, (Rt Tog, Lt Tog, P6) twice, Rt Tog, Lt Tog, P3.
6th row K3, (P4, K6) twice, P4, K4.
7th row P3, (Rt Tog, K2, Lt Tog, P4) twice, Rt Tog, K2, Lt Tog, P2.
8th row K2, (P6, K4) twice, P6, K3.
9th row P2, (Rt Tog, K4, Lt Tog, P2) twice, Rt Tog, K4, Lt Tog, P1.
10th row K1, (P8, K2) 3 times.
11th row P1, (Rt Tog, K6, Lt Tog) 3 times.
12th row P31.
13th row (Rt Tog, K8) 3 times, K1.
14th row P31.
These 14 rows form patt.

Cable patt (over 22sts)
1st row (RS) P4, K4, P6, K4, P4.
2nd row K4, P4, K6, P4, K4.
3rd row P4, C4F, P6, C4F, P4.
4th row As 2nd.
5th row As first.
6th–8th rows Rep 4th and 5th rows once, then 4th row once more.
These 8 rows form patt.

Tile patt (over 5sts)
1st row (RS) *P1, K4, rep from *.
2nd row P.
3rd row As first.
4th row As 2nd.
5th row As first.
6th row K.
These 6 rows form patt.

Using smaller needles, cast on 50sts.
1st row K2, *P2, K2, rep from * to end.
2nd row P2, *K2, P2, rep from * to end.
Rep these 2 rows 12 more times, then first row again.
Next row P2, *M1, P1, rep from * to last 2sts, P2. 96sts.

Change to larger needles and patt:
1st patt row (RS) K17, P5, *(B1, P9) twice, B1, P5, K1, P4, K4, P6, K4, P4, (P1, K4) 5 times.
2nd row (Work 2nd row tile patt) 5 times, 2nd row cable patt, P1, 2nd row tassel patt, P17. Position now set for 3 panels. Cont in patt as set, reading from individual patt instructions beg at 3rd patt row, inc one st at each end of every 8th row, taking extra sts into patt where possible, until there are 116sts.
Work even until Sleeve measures 17in, ending with a WS row.
Bind off loosely.

TO FINISH

Block each piece separately (apply steam if necessary, see book, p. 133).
Join shoulder seams at each side, leaving an opening approx 9½in long at center for neck opening and using a flat seam for ribbing.
Set in Sleeves, matching center of Sleeve to shoulder seam.
Join side and sleeve seams.
Press seams lightly if necessary.

Designed by Joan Chatterley's Knitwear

The subtle texture of seeded rib pattern enhances the lines of this simple pullover.

SIZES

To fit 38[40:42:44]in chest
Garment measures: 40[42½:45:47]in at underarm
Length from shoulder: 27[27½:28½:29]in
Sleeve seam: 18[18½:19:19½]in
Note Instructions for larger sizes are given in brackets [].

MATERIALS

Phildar Brisants
13[13:14:14] 1¾oz/50g balls
Color shown: Marengo
Pair each of sizes 2 and 5 knitting needles

GAUGE

28sts and 36 rows to 4in over ribbed patt worked on size 5 needles
For gauge sample cast on 33sts and rep patt rows for at least 4in.

To save time, take time to check gauge.

ABBREVIATIONS

See book, p. 141.

BACK

Using smaller needles, cast on 130[138: 146:154]sts and work in double rib as foll:
1st rib row K2, *P2, K2, rep from * to end.
2nd row K1, P1, *K2, P2, rep from * to last 4sts, K2, P1, K1.
Rep these 2 rows until Back measures 2½in, ending with a first row and inc one st in last st. 131[139:147:155]sts.
Next row Rib 1[5:4:3], *rib 6[6:6:7], inc in next st, rib 6[6:7:7], rep from * to last 0[4:3:2]sts, rib to end. 141[149:157:165]sts.
Change to larger needles and rib patt:
1st patt row K1, *K3, P1, rep from * to last 4sts, K4.
2nd row K1, *K1, P1, K2, rep from * to end.
These 2 rows form patt. Work in patt until Back measures 17[17½:18:18]in, ending with a WS row.
Shape armholes:
Bind off 6[8:8:8]sts at beg of next 2 rows and 3sts at beg of next 2 rows. 123[127:135: 143]sts. Dec one st at each end of next 4 rows, then one st at each end of every other row 4[4:5:6] times. 107[111:117:123]sts.
Work even until Back measures 27[27½:28½: 29]in, ending with a WS row.
Shape shoulders:
Bind off 7[7:8:8]sts at beg of next 4 rows and 7[8:9:10]sts at beg of next 2 rows.
Bind off rem 65[67:67:71]sts in rib.

FRONT

Work as for Back until armhole shaping has been completed. 107[111:117:123]sts.
Work even until Front measures 19[19½:20½: 21]in, ending with a WS row.
Divide for neck:
Next row Work 53[55:58:61]sts in patt, bind off one st, work in patt across rem 53[55:58: 61]sts.
Complete this side first.
Shape neck:
**Dec one st at neck edge *only* on every other row 32[33:33:35] times in all, keeping neck edge even once incs have been completed, *at the same time shaping shoulders* when work measures 27[27½:28½:29]in, ending at armhole edge, as foll:
Bind off 7[7:8:8]sts at beg of next row and then every other row once. Bind off rem 7[8:9:10]sts at beg of every other row once.**
With WS of work facing, rejoin yarn to rem sts at neck edge and work 2nd side to match first side, working from ** to **.

SLEEVES (make 2)

Using smaller needles, cast on 66[66: 70:70]sts and work in double rib as for Back until Sleeve measures 2½in, inc 3[7:3:7]sts evenly across last row. 69[73:73:77]sts.
Change to larger needles and patt:
Cont in patt as for Back, inc one st at each end of every 6th row until there are 111[115 :119:123]sts.
Work even until Sleeve measures 18[18½: 19:19½]in, ending with a WS row.
Shape sleeve cap:
Bind off 6[8:8:8]sts at beg of next 2 rows, then 3sts at beg of next 2 rows. 93[93:97: 101]sts. Dec one st at each end of next 4 rows, then one st at each end of every other row 25[25:27:29] times in all. 35sts.
Bind off 7sts at beg of next 5 rows.

COLLAR

Using smaller needles, cast on 210[218: 226:234]sts. Work in rib patt as for Back for 5½in.
Bind off loosely in rib.

TO FINISH

Block but do not press. Join shoulder seams.
Set in Sleeves.
Join side and sleeve seams.
Sew cast-on edge of Collar to neckline, overlapping Collar to the left and folding 1in at edge to outside.

Designed by Ruth Maria Swepson
Phildar (UK) Ltd.

OPTIONS
Use this attractive seeded rib pattern to make a matching scarf. First decide the width of the scarf: calculate the number of stitches to cast on by referring to the gauge given for the sweater. Work until the scarf is the desired length. A long fringe, looped into each end, would finish the scarf perfectly (see book, p. 32).

The diagonally-crossed ribs on this rugged crew-neck pullover give it an interesting lattice-work texture.

SIZES

To fit 38[40:42]in chest
Garment measures: 41½[43½:46½]in at under-arm
Length from shoulder: 27in
Sleeve seam: 19½in
Note Instructions for larger sizes are given in brackets [].

MATERIALS

Patons Beehive Shetland Chunky
16[17:18] 1¾oz/50g balls
Color shown: Wensleydale
Pair each of sizes 8 and 10 knitting needles

GAUGE

15sts and 20 rows to 4in over st st worked on size 10 needles

To save time, take time to check gauge.

ABBREVIATIONS

T2L – (Twist 2 left) With RH needle behind LH needle, skip first st, K 2nd st tbl, insert RH needle into backs of both sts and K2 tog tbl.
T2R – (Twist 2 right) K2tog, leaving sts on LH needle, then K first st again in normal way, then sl both sts off needle tog.
For other abbreviations see book, p. 141.

BACK

Using smaller needles, cast on 76[82:88]sts and work K1, P1 rib for 3in, inc 24sts evenly across last row. 100[106:112]sts.
Change to larger needles and patt:
1st patt row P.
2nd row (RS) * T2L, (T2R) twice, rep from * to last 4sts, T2L, T2R.
3rd and every other row P.
4th row K1, T2L, *T2R, (T2L) twice, rep from * to last st, K1.
6th row (T2L) twice, *K2, (T2L) twice, rep from * to end.
8th row K1, * (T2L) twice, T2R, rep from * to last 3sts, T2L, K1.
10th row T2R, *T2L, (T2R) twice, rep from * to last 2 sts, T2L.
12th row K3, * (T2R) twice, K2, rep from * to last st, K1.
These 12 rows form patt. Cont in patt until Back measures 27in, ending with a WS row.
Shape shoulders:
Keeping patt correct, bind off 11[12:13]sts at beg of next 6 rows.
Bind off rem 34sts.

FRONT

Work as for Back until Front measures 12 rows less than Back to shoulder shaping, ending with a WS row.
Shape neck:
Next row Work in patt across first 45[48:51]sts, turn and leave rem sts on a spare needle.
Cont on these sts for first side.
** Bind off 3sts at beg of next row and 2sts at beg of every other row 2 times. Dec one st at neck edge on every other row 5 times, *at the same time* when Front measures same as Back to shoulder ending at armhole edge, *shape shoulders* as for Back **. With RS of work facing, rejoin yarn to rem sts.
Next row Work in patt across first 10sts and sl on to a holder, work in patt to end.
Work 1 row in patt.
Complete to match first side, working from ** to **.

SLEEVES (make 2)

Using smaller needles, cast on 40[46:52]sts. Work in rib as for Back inc 18sts evenly across last row. 58[64:70]sts.
Change to larger needles and patt:
Work as for Back, inc one st at each end of every 4th row until there are 90[96:102]sts, working extra sts into patt.
Work even until Sleeve measures 19½in. Bind off.

TO FINISH

Block each piece separately, but do not press.
Neckband Join left shoulder seam. With RS facing and using smaller needles, pick up and K 34sts along back neck, 20sts down left side of neck, 10sts from holder at center front and 20sts up right side of neck. 84sts.
Work in K1, P1, rib for 1¼in. Bind off in rib.
Join right shoulder seam and neckband.
Measure 9[10:10½]in down from edge of shoulder seam, marking this point on both front and back.
Sew Sleeves in place between markers. Join side and sleeve seams.

Designed by Judy Dodson
Patons and Baldwins Ltd.

A wool yarn worked in a simple textured stitch makes a warm jacket for outdoor wear. Horn toggles complete the casual look.

SIZES

To fit 38[40:42:44:46]in chest
Garment measures: 43[45:47½:50:52½]in at underarm
Length from shoulder: 26½[26½:26½:28¼: 28¼]in
Sleeve seam: 20[20:20:21:21]in
Note Instructions for larger sizes are given in brackets [].

MATERIALS

Neveda Bistro
9[10:10:10:11] 1¾oz/50g balls in main color A (8238 – dark brown)
5[5:5:6:6] 1¾oz/50g balls in color B (8220 – medium brown)
5[5:5:6:6] 1¾oz/50g balls in color C (8209 – beige)
Pair each of sizes 6 and 7 knitting needles
5 horn toggles

GAUGE

20sts and 26 rows to 4in over patt worked on size 7 needles
For gauge sample cast on 23sts and rep 4 patt rows in 1 color for at least 4in.

To save time, take time to check gauge.

ABBREVIATIONS

See book, p. 141.

BACK

Using smaller needles and A, cast on 105[111:117:123:129]sts.
1st rib row *K1, P1, rep from * to last st, K1.
2nd row *P1, K1, rep from * to last st, P1.
Rep last 2 rows 7 more times, inc one st at each end of last row. 107[113:119:125:131]sts.
Change to larger needles.
K 2 rows.
Beg stripe patt:
1st patt row Using C, K2, *P1, K2, rep from * to end.
2nd row Using C, P2, *K1, P2, rep from * to end.
3rd row As first.
4th row Using C, K to end.
These 4 rows form patt. Cont in patt working in stripes of 4 rows B, 4 rows A and 4 rows C until 97[97:97:101:101] patt rows have been worked in all, placing a marker at each end of last row for underarm. Work 55[55:55:63:63] more rows in stripe patt. Bind off.

LEFT FRONT

Using smaller needles and A, cast on 48[51:54:57:60]sts.
1st rib row *K1, P1, rep from * to last 0[1:0:1:0]sts, K0[1:0:1:0].
2nd row P0[1:0:1:0], *K1, P1, rep from * to end.
Rep last 2 rows 7 more times, inc one st at each end of last row. 50[53:56:59:62]sts.
Change to larger needles.
K 2 rows.
Beg stripe patt:
Cont in stripe patt as for Back, working 16 rows.**
Divide for pocket:
Next row Work in patt across first 10sts, turn and cont on these sts only.
Work 31 more rows. Break off yarn and leave sts on a holder.
With RS of work facing, rejoin yarn to rem 40[43:46:49:52]sts and work 32 rows on these sts. Break off yarn.
Next row With RS of work facing, rejoin yarn to sts on holder, work in patt across these sts then across rem 40[43:46:49:52]sts. 50[53:56:59:62]sts.
Work 32[32:32:40:40] rows in stripe patt on all sts.
Shape neck:
***Dec one st at neck edge on next row and then every 5th row until 36[39:42:45:48]sts rem, placing a marker at side edge when Front matches Back to underarm.
Work even until Front matches Back to shoulder.
Change to smaller needles and A.
Work 10 rows K1, P1 rib as for waistband. Bind off in rib.

RIGHT FRONT

Work as for Left Front to **.
Divide for pocket:
Next row Work in patt across first 40[43:46:49:52]sts, turn and cont on these sts only.
Work 31 more rows on these sts. Break off yarn and leave sts on a holder.
Return to rem 10sts and work 32 rows in patt on these sts. Break off yarn.
With RS of work facing, rejoin yarn to sts on holder.
Next row Work in patt across 40[43:46:49:52]sts on holder, then across rem 10sts. 50[53:56:59:62]sts.
Work 31[31:31:39:39] more rows on all sts.
Shape neck:
Cont as for Left Front, working from *** to end.

SLEEVES (make 2)

Using smaller needles and A, cast on 51[51:51:57:57]sts. Work 16 rows K1, P1 rib as for Back, inc one st at each end of last row. 53[53:53:59:59]sts.
Change to larger needles.
K 2 rows.
Cont in stripe patt as for Back, inc one st at each end of 4th row and then every 5th row until there are 91[91:91:95:95]sts. Work even until 104[104:104:112:112] patt rows have been worked in all.
Change to smaller needles and A.
Work 10 rows K1, P1 rib as for Back. Bind off in rib.

TO FINISH

Block each piece, but do not press.
Button band and Collar Using larger needles and A, cast on 9sts and work 112[112:112:120:120] rows in g st.
Shape collar:
Cont in g st, inc one st at each end of next row and then every 8th row until there are 29sts. Work 90[90:90:100:100] more rows even in g st. Dec one st at each end of next row and then every 8th row until 9sts rem. Work 7 rows even.
Next row (make buttonholes) K3, bind off 3 sts, K to end.
Next row K to end, casting on 3sts over those bound off in previous row.
Work 22[22:22:24:24] rows even. Rep last 24[24:24:26:26] rows 3 more times, then 2 buttonhole rows once more (5 buttonholes). Work 6 rows even. Bind off.
Pocket borders Using smaller needles, A and with RS of work facing, pick up and K 27sts from top edge of pocket. Work 6 rows K1, P1, rib as for Back. Bind off in rib. Work 2nd Pocket border to match.
Pocket linings
Left pocket Using larger needles, A and with RS of work facing, pick up and K 25sts along inside edge of Left pocket, then cast on 11sts. 36sts.
**** Beg with a P row, work 31 rows st st. Bind off.
Right pocket Using larger needles, A and with RS of work facing, cast on 11sts then pick up and K 25sts along inside edge of pocket. 36sts. Work as for Left pocket from **** to end.
Sew Pocket borders neatly in place at each end. Sew Pocket linings to inside of Fronts. Join shoulder seams. Sew Sleeves in place between markers on Back and Front. Sew Button band and Collar in place. Join side and sleeve seams.
Sew toggles to Button band to correspond with buttonholes.

Designed by Alan Dart

> **OPTIONS**
> If you would prefer to make this cardigan without vertical pockets, the instructions can be altered quite simply. When working the fronts, omit "Divide for pocket" instructions, and continue to work across all the stitches. There will, of course, be no need to make the pocket linings.

An ingenious rib pattern worked in two colors creates a fascinating interplay of stripes on this striking pullover.

SIZES

To fit 38[40:42:44]in chest
Garment measures: 44¼[46½:48½:50½]in at underarm
Length from shoulder: 26¼[26½:26¾:27]in
Sleeve seam: 18½in
Note Instructions for larger sizes are given in brackets [].

MATERIALS

Neveda Bistro
9[9:10:10] 1¾oz/50g balls in main color A (8384 – blue)
6[6:7:7] 1¾oz/50g balls in color B (8290 – gray)
Pair of size 5 knitting needles
Pair of long size 7 double-pointed needles
3 buttons

GAUGE

15sts and 30 rows to 4in over rib patt worked on size 7 needles
For gauge sample cast on 17sts and rep 4 patt rows for at least 4in.

To save time, take time to check gauge.

ABBREVIATIONS

K1 below – K into st below next st on LH needle and sl both loops off tog.
P1 below – P into st below next st on LH needle and sl both loops off tog.
For other abbreviations see book, p. 141.

BACK

Using smaller needles and A, cast on 83[87:91:95]sts.
1st rib row (RS) K2, *P1, K1, rep from * to last st, K1.
2nd row *K1, P1, rep from * to last st, K1.
Rep these 2 rows for 3½in, ending with a WS row.
Change to double-pointed needles and patt:
1st patt row (RS) Using A, *P1, K1 below, rep from * to last st, P1. Do not turn.
2nd row (RS) Using B, P.
3rd row (WS) Using A, K1, *P1 below, K1, rep from * to end. Do not turn.
4th row (WS) Using B, K.
These 4 rows form patt. Cont in patt until Back measures approx 15in, ending with a first patt row.
Shape armholes:
Bind off 4sts at beg of next 2 rows. ** 75[79:83:87]sts. Work even in patt until Back measures 23in. Bind off.

FRONT

Work as for Back to **.
Divide for front neck:
Keeping patt correct, work 35[47:39:41]sts, turn and complete this side first. Cont in patt

until Front matches Back. Bind off.
With WS facing, rejoin yarn to rem sts, bind off next 5sts, work in patt to end. 35 [37:39:41]sts.
Complete to match first side.

LEFT SLEEVE AND HALF YOKE

Using smaller needles and A, cast on 41[43:45:47]sts. Work in K1, P1 rib for 3½in as for Back.
Change to double-pointed needles and patt:
Cont in rib patt as for Back, inc one st at each end of every 5th row until there are 87[89: 91:93]sts. Work even until Sleeve measures 18½in. Mark each end of last row with a contrasting thread.
Work even in patt for approx 1¼in, ending with a first patt row.
Shape Yoke:
Bind off 31sts at beg of next 2 rows. 25[27:29:31]sts.
Cont in patt on rem sts until Yoke measures approx 5½[6:6¼:6¾]in from bound-off sts, ending with a 2nd patt row.
Shape neck:
Bind off 4[5:6:7]sts at beg of next row.
Dec one st at neck edge only on next 5 rows, then on every other row 4 times. 12[13:14:15]sts.
Work even on rem sts until yoke measurement from bound-off sts at top of Sleeve equals half bound-off edge of Back.
Bind off rem sts.

RIGHT SLEEVE AND HALF YOKE

Work as for Left Sleeve and Half Yoke, reversing shaping by ending with a 4th patt row before "Shape neck".

TO FINISH

Block each piece separately, but do not press.
Join bound-off edges of shoulders to form center back neck.
Join bound-off edge of Back to straight edge of Back Yoke.
Join bound-off edges of Fronts to straight edges of Front Yoke.
Join rows from markers on Sleeves to bound-off sts at underarm of Front and Back. Join side and sleeve seams.
Neck border Using smaller needles, A and with RS facing, pick up and K 26[28:30:32]sts along right front neck, 30[32:34:36]sts along back neck and 26[28:30:32]sts along left front neck. 82[88:94:100]sts.
Work 7 rows K1, P1 rib. Bind off in rib.
Button band Using smaller needles, A and with RS facing, pick up and K 48sts up right front.
Work 7 rows K1, P1 rib. Bind off in rib.
Buttonhole band Work to match button border, making 4 buttonholes on 4th rib row as foll:
Next row Rib 4, (yo, K2 tog, rib 14) twice, yo, K2 tog, rib 10.
Sew on buttons to correspond with buttonholes.

Designed by Brenda Sparkes

This man's pullover in a slipstitch pattern is easier to make than its strong design suggests. The effect is of a triangular, neutral mesh over a rich, solid-color background.

SIZES

To fit 36–38[40–42]in chest
Garment measures: 42½[48½]in at underarm
Length from shoulder: 24½[26½]in
Sleeve seam: 18½[19½]in
Note Instructions for larger size are given in brackets [].

MATERIALS

Pingouin Confortable Sport
11[12] 1¾oz/50g balls in main color A (Cactus)
7[8] 1¾oz/50g balls in color B (Serbie)
Pair each of sizes 5 and 7 knitting needles
Size 5 circular or set of double-pointed needles

GAUGE

16sts and 28 rows to 4in over patt worked on size 7 needles
For gauge sample cast on 25sts and work 28 rows of patt.

To save time, take time to check gauge.

ABBREVIATIONS

M1 – lift strand running from base of st just worked to base of next st on to LH needle and work into back of it.
Sl 1P – Sl next st P-wise, with yarn at back of work on RS rows and at front of work on WS rows.
For other abbreviations see book, p. 141.

BACK

Using smaller needles and A, cast on 84[96]sts.
1st rib row *K1, P1, rep from * to end.
2nd row *K1, P1, rep from * to end.
Rep these 2 rows until work measures 3in, ending with a first rib row.
Change to larger needles.
P1 row, inc one st at end of row. 85[97]sts.
Beg patt:
1st patt row (RS) Using B, *K6, sl 1P, K5, rep from * to last st, K1.
2nd row Using B, *P6, sl 1P, P5, rep from * to last st, P1.
3rd row Using A, K.
4th row Using A, *K5, P3, K4, rep from * to last st, K1.
5th row Using B, *K5, sl 1P, K1, sl 1P, K4, rep from * to last st, K1.
6th row Using B, *P5, sl 1P, P1, sl 1P, P4, rep from * to last st, P1.
7th row Using A, K.
8th row Using A, *K4, P5, K3, rep from * to last st, K1.
9th row Using B, *K4, (sl 1P, K1) twice, sl 1P, K3, rep from * to last st, K1.
10th row Using B, *P4, (sl 1P, P1) twice, sl 1P, P3, rep from * to last st, P1.

11th row Using A, K.
12th row Using A, *K3, P7, K2, rep from * to last st, K1.
13th row Using B, *K3, (sl 1P, K1) 3 times, sl 1P, K2, rep from * to last st, K1.
14th row Using B, *P3, (sl 1P, P1) 3 times, sl 1P, P2, rep from * to last st, P1.
15th row Using A, K.
16th row Using A, *K2, P9, K1, rep from * to last st, K1.
17th row Using B, *K2, (sl 1P, K1) 4 times, sl 1P, K1, rep from * to last st, K1.
18th row Using B, *P2, (sl 1P, P1) 4 times, sl 1P, P1, rep from * to last st, P1.
19th row Using A, K.
20th row Using A, *K1, P11, rep from * to last st, K1.
21st row Using B, *K1, sl 1P, rep from * to last st, K1.
22nd row Using B, *P1, sl 1P, rep from * to last st, P1.
23rd row Using A, K.
24th row Using A, *P1, K11, rep from * to last st, P1.
25th row Using B, K12, *sl 1P, K11, rep from * to last st, K1.
26th row Using B, P12, *sl 1P, P11, rep from * to last st, P1.
27th row Using A, K.
28th row Using A, *P2, K9, P1, rep from * to last st, P1.
29th row Using B, *K1, sl 1P, K9, sl 1P, rep from * to last st, K1.
30th row Using B, *P1, sl 1P, P9, sl 1P, rep from * to last st, P1.
31st row Using A, K.
32nd row Using A, *P3, K7, P2, rep from * to last st, P1.
33rd row Using B, K2, *sl 1P, K7, (sl 1P, K1) twice, rep from * to last 11sts, sl 1P, K7, sl 1P, K2.
34th row Using B, P2, *sl 1P, P7, (sl 1P, P1) twice, rep from * to last 11sts, sl 1P, P7, sl 1P, P2.
35th row Using A, K.
36th row Using A, *P4, K5, P3, rep from * to last st, P1.
37th row Using B, *(K1, sl 1P) twice, K5, sl 1P, K1, sl 1P, rep from * to last st, K1.
38th row Using B, *(P1, sl 1P) twice, P5, sl 1P, P1, sl 1P, rep from * to last st, P1.
39th row Using A, K.
40th row Using A, *P5, K3, P4, rep from * to last st, P1.
41st row Using B, K2, *sl 1P, K1, sl 1P, K3, (sl 1P, K1) 3 times, rep from * to last 11sts, sl 1P, K1, sl 1P, K3, (sl 1P, K1) twice, K1.
42nd row Using B, P1, *(P1, sl 1P) twice, P3, sl 1P, (P1, sl 1P) twice, rep from * to last 11 sts, (P1, sl 1P) twice, P3, (sl 1P, P1) twice, P1.
43rd row Using A, K.
44th row Using A, *P6, K1, P5, rep from * to last st, P1.
45th row Using B, *K1, sl 1P, rep from * to last st, K1.
46th row Using B, *P1, sl 1P, rep from * to last st, P1.
47th row Using A, K.
48th row Using A, *K6, P1, K5, rep from * to last st, K1.
These 48 rows form patt. Cont in patt until work measures 14½[15¾]in. Place marker at

each end of next row for armholes. ** Cont in patt until 3 complete patt reps, then first 10[24] rows of 4th patt rep have been completed, and Back measures approx 24½[26½]in.
Shape shoulders:
Bind off 10[12]sts at beg of next 6 rows. Bind off rem 25sts loosely.

FRONT

Work as for Back to **. Cont in patt until 1[2] complete patt reps, then first 0[12] rows of 3rd patt rep have been completed and Front measures approx 16¼[17¾]in.
Shape neck:
Next row Work 42[48]sts in patt and place on a holder, bind off one st, work in patt to end. Complete this side first.
Work 1 row.
Next row K2 tog, work in patt to end.
Keeping patt correct, cont to dec one st at neck edge on every 5th row 11 times in all, noting that if the first st on needle at neck edge is to be slipped, it should be worked as a K or P st instead. 30[36]sts.
Work 1[3] rows.
Shape shoulder:
Bind off 10[12]sts at beg of next row and then every other row once. Work 1 row. Bind off rem 10[12]sts.
With WS of work facing, rejoin yarn to rem sts at neck edge, P2 tog, work in patt to end. Work to match first side.

SLEEVES (make 2)

Using smaller needles and A, cast on 42[46]sts and work in rib for 3in as for Back, ending with a first rib row.
Change to larger needles.
Next row P3[11], *M1, P6[12], rep from * to last 3[11]sts, M1, P3[11]. 49sts.
Cont in patt as for Back. Keeping patt correct, inc one st at each end of every 7th[6th] row, until there are 79[85]sts, taking extra sts into patt.
Work even in patt until Sleeve measures 18½[19½]in. Bind off loosely.

TO FINISH

Block, but do not press.
Join shoulder seams, matching patt.
Neck border Using circular or double-pointed needles, A and with RS of work facing, beg at right center front, pick up and K 93[103]sts evenly around neck edge.
1st row *K1, P1, rep from * to last st, K1.
2nd row *P1, K1, rep from * to last st, P1.
Rep these 2 rows until border measures 1¼in. Bind off loosely in rib.
Stitch edges of neck border in place, lapping the left side over the right side.
Sew Sleeves to Back and Front between markers.
Join side and sleeve seams.

Designed by Kate Jones

The pleasing texture of this basketweave stitch is equally successful in a slubbed cotton blend yarn and in a smooth yarn.

SIZES

To fit 38[40:42:44]in chest
Garment measures: 41[42½:45:46½]in at underarm
Length from shoulder: 24½[25:26¼:26½]in
Note Instructions for larger sizes are given in brackets [].

MATERIALS

Phildar Flammé Coton Viscose
11[11:12:12] 1¾oz/50g balls
Color shown: Perle
Pair each of sizes 2 and 3 knitting needles
6 buttons
or Phildar Brisants
7[8:8:9] 1¾oz/50g balls
Color shown: Beaujolais
Pair each of sizes 3 and 6 knitting needles
6 buttons

GAUGE

24sts and 30 rows to 4in over patt worked on size 3 needles
For gauge sample cast on 26sts and rep patt rows.

To save time, take time to check gauge.

ABBREVIATIONS

M1 – lift strand running from base of st just worked to base of next st on to LH needle and K tbl.
For other abbreviations see book, p. 141.

Note Instructions are the same, whether Flammé Coton Viscose or Brisants is used. Be sure to use the needles specified for the yarn (or those with which you can obtain the correct gauge).

BACK

Using smaller needles, cast on 105[111:117:123]sts.
1st rib row K1, *P1, K1, rep from * to end.
2nd row P1, *K1, P1, rep from * to end.
Rep these 2 rows until Back measures 3in, ending with a first row.
Next row Rib 5[7:3:5], *M1, rib 6[6:7:7], rep from * 15 more times, M1, rib to end. 122[128:134:140]sts.
Change to larger needles and patt:
1st patt row (RS) K.
2nd row P.
3rd and 5th rows K2, *P4, K2, rep from * to end.
4th and 6th rows P2, *K4, P2, rep from * to end.
7th and 8th rows As first and 2nd.
9th and 11th rows P3, *K2, P4, rep from * to last 5sts, K2, P3.
10th and 12th rows K3, *P2, K4, rep from * to last 5sts, P2, K3.
These 12 rows form patt. Cont in patt until Back measures 15[15:16:16]in, ending with a WS row.
Shape armholes:
Keeping patt correct, bind off 5sts at beg of next 2 rows. Dec one st at each end of next 5[7:9:11] rows. 102[104:106:108]sts.
Work 1 row.
Dec one st at each end of next row and then every other row 4 times in all. 94[96:98:100]sts.
Work even in patt until Back measures 9½[10:10¼:10½]in from beg of armhole shaping, ending with a WS row.
Shape shoulders:
Bind off 7sts at beg of next 8[8:6:6] rows and 0[0:6:6]sts at beg of next 0[0:2:2]rows.
Bind off rem 38[40:44:46]sts.

LEFT FRONT

** Using smaller needles, cast on 55[57:61:63]sts and work in rib as for Back for 3in.
Next row Rib 4, *M1, rib 8[8:9:9], rep from * 5 more times, M1, rib to end. 62[64:68:70]sts.
Change to larger needles and patt:

1st patt row (RS) K.
2nd row P.
3rd and 5th rows K2, *P4, K2, rep from * to last 0[2:0:2]sts, P0[2:0:2].
4th and 6th rows K0[2:0:2], *P2, K4, rep from * to last 2sts, P2.
7th and 8th rows As first and 2nd.
9th and 11th rows P3, *K2, P4, rep from * to last 5[1:5:1]sts, K2[1:2:1], P3[0:3:0].
10th and 12th rows P0[1:0:1], K3[4:3:4], *P2, K4, rep from * to last 5 sts, P2, K3.
These 12 rows form patt. Cont in patt until Left Front matches Back to underarm, ending with a WS row.
Shape armhole and front edge:
Next row Keeping patt correct, bind off 5sts, work in patt to last 2sts, K2 tog.
Work 1 row.
Dec one st at armhole edge on next 5[7:9:11] rows, then one st on every other row 4 times in all, *at the same time* dec one st at front edge on next and every other row 6[6:9:9] times in all, then one st on every 4th row 13 times in all. 28[28:27:27]sts.
Work even until Left Front matches Back to shoulder, ending with a WS row.
Shape shoulder:
Bind off 7sts at beg of next row and then every other row twice.
Work 1 row. Bind off rem 7[7:6:6]sts.

RIGHT FRONT

Work as for Left Front from ** to **.
1st patt row (RS) K.
2nd row P.
3rd and 5th rows P0[2:0:2], K2, *P4, K2, rep from * to end.
4th and 6th rows *P2, K4, rep from * to last 2[4:2:4]sts, P2, K0[2:0:2].
7th and 8th rows As first and 2nd.
9th and 11th rows K0[1:0:1], P3[4:3:4], *K2, P4, rep from * to last 5 sts, K2, P3.
10th and 12th rows K3, P2, *K4, P2, rep from * to last 3[5:3:5]sts, K3[4:3:4], P0[1:0:1].
These 12 rows form patt.
Complete Right Front to match Left Front, reversing shaping.

TO FINISH

Block the pieces, but do not press.
Join shoulder seams.
Button band Using smaller needles, cast on 9sts.
1st row (RS) K2, *P1, K1, rep from * to last st, K1.
2nd row P2, *K1, P1, rep from * to last st, P1.
Rep last 2 rows until band fits, stretched, up Right Front to center back neck (see book, p. 139).
Bind off in rib.
Buttonhole band Sew on Button band. Mark the positions for 6 buttons, the first to come 4 rows from lower edge, the last level with beg of front shaping, with 4 more evenly spaced between. Work Buttonhole band as for Button band, making buttonholes opposite markers as foll:
1st row (RS) Rib 4, bind off 2sts, rib to end.
2nd row Rib 3, cast on 2sts, rib to end.
Sew on Buttonhole band.
Armbands With RS of work facing and using smaller needles, pick up and K 113[117:123:127]sts evenly around the armhole edge.
Work in K1, P1 rib as for Back for 1in.
Bind off evenly in rib.
Join side seams and armbands.
Sew on buttons.

Designed by Julia Howe

Phildar (UK) Ltd.

The classic ribbed cardigan, interpreted here in a flecked, tweedy yarn, is a garment of great versatility.

SIZES

To fit 38[40:42:44]in chest
Garment measures: 43[45:47½:49¾]in at underarm
Length from shoulder: 26[26½:26¾:27]in
Sleeve seam: 19in
Note Instructions for larger sizes are given in brackets [].

MATERIALS

Scheepjeswol Nobel Tweed
18[19:20:21] 1¾oz/50g balls
Color shown: 5676
Pair each of sizes 6, 8 and 9 knitting needles
6 buttons

GAUGE

14sts and 32 rows to 4in over fisherman's rib worked on size 8 needles
For gauge sample cast on 17sts and rep 2 patt rows for at least 4in.

To save time, take time to check gauge.

ABBREVIATIONS

K1B – (K1 below) K into st below next st on LH needle and sl both loops off tog.
RH dec – (right-hand dec) sl 1 below (do not K it), sl 1, sl 1 below, replace last 2sts (3 loops) on LH needle, K2 tog, pass first sl st (2 loops) over.
LH dec – (left-hand dec) sl 1 below, sl 1, sl 1 below, replace last 3sts (5 loops) on left-hand needle and K3 tog.
For other abbreviations see book, p. 141.

BACK

Using smallest needles, cast on 75[79:83:87]sts.
1st rib row K1, *P1, K1, rep from * to end.
2nd row P1, *K1, P1, rep from * to end.
Rep these 2 rib rows for 3in, ending with a 2nd row.
Change to medium-sized needles and fisherman's rib:
1st patt row (RS) Sl 1, *P1, K1B, rep from * to last 2 sts, P1, K1.
2nd row Sl 1, *K1B, P1, rep from * to end.
These 2 rows form patt. Work even in patt until Back measures 16½in, ending with a WS row.
Place a marker at each end of last row. Cont in patt until Back measures 26[26½:26¾:27]in, ending with a WS row.
Bind off loosely, marking center 25[25:29:29]sts for back neck.

POCKET LININGS (make 2)

Using largest needles, cast on 19sts. Beg with a K row, work 5in in st st, ending with a P row and dec 2sts evenly in last row. 17sts. Leave sts on a holder.

LEFT FRONT

**Using smallest needles, cast on 37[39:41:43]sts. Work in rib as for Back for 3in.
Change to medium-sized needles and fisherman's rib:
Cont in patt as for Back until Front measures 8in, ending with a WS row.
Insert Pocket Lining:
Next row Work 10[11:12:13] sts in patt, sl next 17sts on to a length of yarn, work in patt across sts from first Pocket Lining, work in patt to end. 37[39:41:43]sts.
Cont in patt until Front matches Back to marker, ending with a WS patt row.**
Shape front:
Next row Work in patt to last 5sts, LH dec, work last 2sts in patt.
Work 11[11:11:9] rows even. Cont to work dec row as before on next row and then every 12th[12th:10th:12th] row 4[3:2:6] times in all.
1st, 2nd and 3rd sizes only
Rep dec row on next row and then every 14th[14th:12th] row 1[2:4] times in all.
All sizes
Work even on rem 25[27:27:29]sts until Front matches Back to shoulder, ending with a WS row.
Bind off loosely.

RIGHT FRONT

Work to match Left Front from ** to **.
Shape front:
Next row Work 2sts in patt, RH dec, work in patt to end.
Complete to match Left Front, reversing shaping and using RH dec in place of LH dec each time.

SLEEVES (make 2)

Using smallest needles, cast on 37[39:41:43]sts. Work in rib as for Back for 2in.
Change to medium-sized needles and fisherman's rib:
Cont in patt as for Back, inc one st, *one st in from edge*, at each end of every 7th row 7[11:11:16] times in all, then one st at each end of every 9th row 8[5:5:1] times in all, incorporating extra sts into patt. 67[71:73:77]sts.
Work even until Sleeve measures 19in.
Bind off loosely.

TO FINISH

Do not block or press.
Pocket tops Using smallest needles and with RS facing, K across sts from pocket top, inc 2sts evenly across 19sts.
1st row (WS) P2, *K1, P1, rep from * to last st, P1.
2nd row K2, *P1, K1, rep from * to last st, K1.
Rep last 2 rows twice more, then first row once. Bind off loosely in rib.
Sew pocket tops neatly to RS.
Sew Pocket Linings lightly to WS.
Join shoulder seams.
Button band Using smallest needles, cast on 9sts.
1st row (RS) K2, *P1, K1, rep from * to last st, K1.
2nd row P2, *K1, P1, rep from * to last st, P1.
Rep last 2 rows until band, slightly stretched, fits up Right Front to center back neck (see book, p. 139). Bind off.
Sew Button band in place.
Buttonhole band Mark positions for 6 buttons on Button band, the first to come 4 rows from cast-on edge, last to come level with beg of front shaping, with 4 more evenly spaced between.
Work as for Button band, making buttonholes as markers are reached as foll:
Next row (RS) Rib 4, bind off 2sts, rib to end.
Next row Rib to end, casting on 2sts over those bound off in previous row.
Sew Buttonhole band in place.
Join bands at center back neck.
Place center of bound-off edge of Sleeve to shoulder and sew in place between markers, easing to fit.
Join side and sleeve seams.
Sew on buttons.

Designed by Julia Howe

Scheepjeswol (UK) Ltd.

This echo-stripe, boatneck pullover for summer is refreshingly easy to make. Get the cool, clean look and feel by knitting it with pure slubbed cotton yarn, using simple stockinette stitch.

SIZES

To fit 36[38:40:42:44]in chest
Garment measures: 40[41:43:45:48]in at underarm
Length from shoulder: 23½[24½:25½:26:27]in
Sleeve seam: 17½[17½:17½:18:18]in
Note Instructions for larger sizes are given in brackets [].

MATERIALS

Patons Cotton Top
8[8:9:10:11] 1¾oz/50g balls in main color A (White)
1 1¾oz/50g ball in color B (Ultramarine)
Pair each of sizes 3 and 5 knitting needles

GAUGE

20sts and 26 rows to 4in over st st worked on size 5 needles

To save time, take time to check gauge.

ABBREVIATIONS

See book, p. 141.

BACK

Using smaller needles and A, cast on 92[96:102:108:114]sts.
1st rib row *K1, P1, rep from * to end.
2nd row As first.
Rep these 2 rows until work measures 3in.
Change to larger needles:
Next row K7[9:8:8:7], *inc one st in next st, K10[10:11:12:13], rep from * to last 8[10:10:9:9]sts, inc in next st, K to end. 100[104:110:116:122]sts.
Beg with a P row, work in st st until Back measures 5[5:5½:5½:6]in, ending with a P row and changing to B at end of row.
1st echo stripe:
Next row Using B, K50[52:55:58:61], changing to A on last st, using A, K to end.
Using A, work 9 rows st st, changing to B at end of last row.
Work 1 row in B, changing to A at end of row.
Using A, cont in st st until Back measures 12[12:12½:13:13½]in, ending with a P row.
2nd echo stripe:
Next row Using A, K50[52:55:58:61], changing to B on last st, using B, K to end, changing to A at end of row.
Using A, work 9 rows st st, changing to B at end of last row.
Work 1 row in B, changing to A at end of row.
Using A, cont in st st until Back measures 18½[19:19½:20½:21]in, ending with a P row.
Rep first echo stripe once more. Using A, cont in st st until Back measures 23½[24½:25½:26:27]in, ending with a P row.
Shape shoulders:
Bind off 5sts at beg of next 8[8:10:10:12] rows,

then 5[6:4:6:4]sts at beg of next 2 rows. 50[52:52:54:54]sts.
Next row P.
Beg with a P row, work 8 rows in st st. Bind off loosely P-wise.

FRONT

Work as for Back.

SLEEVES (make 2)

Using smaller needles and A, cast on 42[46:50:54:58]sts. Work in K1, P1 rib as for Back for 3in.
Change to larger needles.
Next row K3[5:4:4:6], *inc one st in next st, K6[6:7:8:8], rep from * to last 4[6:6:5:7]sts, inc in next st, K to end. 48[52:56:60:64]sts.
Beg with a P row, cont in st st inc one st at each end of every 4th row, *at the same time* when Sleeve measures 5[5:5½:5½:6]in, ending with a P row and changing to B at end of row, *work first echo stripe* as foll:
Next row Using B, K half number of sts on needle, including inc at each end, changing to A on last of these sts, K to end.
Using A, work 9 rows in st st, changing to B at end of last row.
Work 1 row in B, changing to A at end of row.
Working inc as before, and using A, cont in st st, *working 2nd echo stripe* when Sleeve measures 12[12:12½:13:13½]in, ending with a P row.
Next row Using A, K half number of sts on needle, including inc at each end, changing to B on last of these sts, using B, K to end, changing at A at end of row.
Using A, work 9 rows st st, changing to B at end of row.
Work 1 row in B, changing to A at end of row.
Using A, cont in st st, working inc as before, until there are 94[98:102:104:106]sts.
Work even until Sleeve measures 17½[17½:17½:18:18]in. Bind off.

TO FINISH

Block and press each piece lightly using a warm iron.
Fold Neckband to WS on P row at front and back neck edges forming a hem, and sew in place using slipstitch.
Join shoulder seams, matching neck edge hem neatly.
Mark underarm on Back and Front 9[9½:10:10¼:10½]in from shoulder seam. Sew Sleeves in place, matching center of Sleeve with shoulder seam.
Join side and sleeve seams. Press seams lightly if necessary.

Designed by Pip Hues

Traditional Fair Isle motifs, worked in a subtle mixture of colors, give this V-neck vest enduring appeal.

SIZES

To fit 36[38:40:42]in chest
Garment measures: 38[39½:41½:43½]in at underarm
Length from shoulder: 22½[23:23½:24]in
Note Instructions for larger sizes are given in brackets [].

MATERIALS

Anny Blatt No. 4
3[4:4:5] 1¾oz/50g balls in main color A (Saphir)
1[2:2:2] 1¾oz/50g balls in color B (Outremer)
2[2:2:3] 1¾oz/50g balls in color C (Havana)
1[2:2:2] 1¾oz/50g balls in color D (Ecru)
1[1:2:2] 1¾oz/50g balls in color E (Paille)
2[2:2:3] 1¾oz/50g balls in color F (Gris)
Pair each of sizes 3 and 6 knitting needles

GAUGE

26sts and 26 rows to 4in over Fair Isle patt worked on size 6 needles
For gauge sample, cast on 24sts and, working in st st, rep 8 patt sts and 22 patt rows shown on chart for at least 4in.

To save time, take time to check gauge.

ABBREVIATIONS

M1 – lift strand running from base of st just worked to base of next st and work into back of it.
For other abbreviations see book, p. 141.

Note When working patt from chart, read RS (K) rows from right to left and WS (P) rows from left to right, stranding and weaving colors not in use across back of work (see book, pp. 116–117).

BACK

Using smaller needles and A, cast on 111[115:121:129]sts.
1st rib row (RS) *K1, P1, rep from * to last st, K1.
2nd row *P1, K1, rep from * to last st, P1.
Rep these 2 rows for 3in, ending with a RS row.
Next row Rib 3[5:8:4], M1, (rib 8[7:7:8], M1) 13[15:15:15] times, rib to end. 125[131:137:145]sts.
Change to larger needles.
Joining in colors as required, cont working in patt from chart (see Note), rep 8 patt sts 15[16:17:18] times across row and working first 2[1:0:0]sts and last 3[2:1:1]sts on K rows and first 3[2:1:1]sts and last 2[1:0:0]sts on P rows as shown on chart, until Back measures 14½in, ending with a P row**.
Shape armholes:
Bind off 3sts at beg of next 2 rows. Dec one st

at each end of every row until 107[113:119:127]sts rem, then at each end of every other row until 95[101:107:113]sts rem.
Work even until Back measures 22½[23:23½:24]in, ending with a P row.
Shape shoulders:
Bind off 11sts at beg of next 4 rows and 5[7:9:11]sts at beg of foll 2 rows. 41[43:45:47]sts.
Leave rem sts on a holder.

FRONT

Work as for Back to **.
Shape armholes and neck:
Next row Bind off 3sts, work 57[60:63:67]sts in patt, including st used in binding off, K2 tog, turn and leave rem sts on a holder. Complete this side first. Work 1 row.
***Dec one st at neck edge on next and every other row, *at the same time* dec one st at armhole edge on every row until 49[52:55:59]sts rem. Dec one st at each end of every other row until 37[40:43:45]sts rem. Keeping armhole edge even, cont dec at neck edge only on next and every other row until 33[40:43:45]sts rem, then on every 3rd row until 27[29:31:33]sts rem.
Work a few rows even until Front matches Back to shoulder, ending with a P row.
Shape shoulder:
Bind off 11sts at beg of next row and then every other row once. 5[7:9:11]sts.
Work 1 row. Bind off rem sts.
With RS facing, sl center st on to a safety pin, rejoin yarn to rem sts, K2 top and work in patt to end.
Next row Bind off 3sts, work in patt to end.
Complete to match first side, from *** to end, reversing shaping.

TO FINISH

Block and press each piece separately, foll instructions on yarn label and omitting ribbing. Join right shoulder seam.
Neckband Using smaller needles, A and with RS facing, pick up and K 58[60:62:64]sts down left side of neck, K center st from pin, marking it with a contrasting thread; pick up and K 58[60:62:64]sts up right side of neck, K 41[43:45:47]sts from back neck holder, dec 3sts evenly. 155[161:167:173]sts.
1st rib row *P1, K1, rep from * to within 2sts of center st, P2 tog, P1, P2 tog tbl, **K1, P1, rep from ** to end.
2nd row K1, *P1, K1, rep from * to within 2sts of marked st, K2 tog tbl, K1, K2 tog, **K1, P1, rep from ** to last st, K1.
Rep these 2 rows until neckband measures 1¼in.
Bind off in rib, still dec at each side of center st.
Join left shoulder seam.
Join neckband seam.
Armhole borders Using smaller needles, A and with RS facing, pick up and K 100[104:108:112]sts all around armhole edge. Work 1¼in rib as for neckband. Bind off in rib.
Join side seams and armhole borders.
Press seams if necessary.

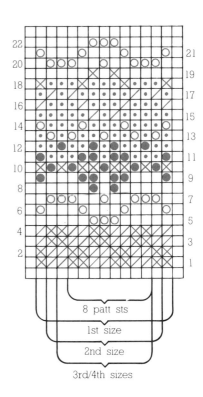

8 patt sts
1st size
2nd size
3rd/4th sizes

KEY

☐ = A (blue)   ⊙ = D (white)
⊠ = B (navy)   ● = E (yellow)
⊘ = C (gold)   · = F (gray)

Designed by Anne Matheson

This traditional Aran pullover suits old and young, male and female alike. Its rich, contrasting textures include trinity stitch, Irish moss stitch, claw stitch, and a generous OXOX cable.

SIZES

To fit 28[30:32:34:36:38:40]in chest/bust
Garment measures: 30[31½:34:35½:38:40:42½]in at underarm
Length from shoulder: 19[20½:22:23½:25:25½:26]in
Sleeve seam: 14½[15½:16½:17½:18:18½:19]in
Note Instructions for larger sizes are given in brackets [].

MATERIALS

Pingouin Sport Laine
15[16:18:19:21:22:24] 1¾oz/50g balls
Color shown: Ecru
Pair each of sizes 5 and 7 knitting needles
Cable needle

GAUGE

21sts and 27 rows to 4in over Irish moss st worked on size 7 needles
For gauge sample cast on 24sts and work as foll:
1st row (K1, P1) 12 times.
2nd and 3rd rows (P1, K1) 12 times.
4th row As first.
Rep these 4 rows for at least 4in.

To save time, take time to check gauge.

ABBREVIATIONS

Pfb – P into front and back of next st.
Kfb – K into front and back of next st.
Inc 2 – (K1, P1, K1) into front of next st.
CP7 – sl next 2sts on to cable needle and hold at back of work, K1, K2 from cable needle, K next st, sl next st on to cable needle and hold at front of work, K2, K1 from cable needle.
C5B – sl next 3sts on to cable needle and hold at back of work, K2, K3 from cable needle.
C5F – sl next 2sts on to cable needle, hold at front of work, K3, K2 from cable needle.
For other abbreviations see book, p. 141.

BACK

Using smaller needles, cast on 85[89:97:99:107:111:117]sts.
1st rib row (RS) P1, *K1, P1, rep from * to end.
2nd row K1, *P1, K1, rep from * to end.
Rep these 2 rows until work measures 2½[2½:2½:3:3:3½:3½]in, ending with a first row.
Next row Rib 13[15:17:17:19:21:23], *P7, Kfb, (P1, Pfb) 3 times, P1, Kfb, P7*, (K1, P1, inc 2, P1, K1, P1) 2[2:2:3:3:3:4] times, rib 0[0:4:0:4:4:0], Kfb, rep from * to * once more, rib 13[15:17:17:19:21:23]. 100[104:112:116:124:128:136]sts. (This inc row sets position for each patt.)
Change to larger needles and patt:
1st patt row (RS) (K1, P1) 6[7:8:8:9:10:11] times (for Irish moss st), P1, *K7 (for claw patt), P2, K10 (for cable patt), P2, K7 (for claw patt)*, P18[18:22:26:30:30:34] (for trinity st panel), rep from * to * once more, P1, (P1, K1) 6[7:8:8:9:10:11] times (for 2nd Irish moss st panel).
2nd row (P1, K1) 6[7:8:8:9:10:11] times, K1, *P7, K2, P10, K2, P7*, K1, (inc 2, P3 tog) 4[4:5:6:7:7:8] times, K1, rep from * to * once more, K1, (K1, P1) 0[7:8:8:9:10:11] times.
3rd row (P1, K1) 6[7:8:8:9:10:11] times, P1, *CP7, P2, K10, P2, CP7 *, P18[18:22:26:30:30:34], rep from * to * once more, P1, (K1, P1) 6[7:8:8:9:10:11] times.
4th row (K1, P1) 6[7:8:8:9:10:11] times, K1, *P7, K2, P10, K2, P7 *, K1, (P 3 tog, inc 2) 4[4:5:6:7:7:8] times, K1, rep from * to * once more, K1, (P1, K1) 6[7:8:8:9:10:11] times.
These 4 rows form patt for Irish moss st over 12[14:16:16:18:20:22]sts at each side, the claw patts and for trinity st patt over center

18[18:22:26:30:30:34]sts, and are rep throughout.
5th row Work 12[14:16:16:18:20:22]sts in Irish moss st, P1, *K7, P2, C5B, C5F, P2, K7 *, P18[18:22:26:30:30:34], rep from * to * once more, P1, work 12[14:16:16:18:20:22]sts in Irish moss st.
6th–9th rows As 2nd–5th.
10th–12th rows As 2nd–4th.
13th–18th rows Rep first–4th rows once, then first and 2nd rows once more.
19th row Work 12[14:16:16:18:20:22]sts in Irish moss st, P1, *CP7, P2, C5F, C5B, P2, CP7 *, P18[18:22:26:30:30:34], rep from * to * once more, P1, work 12[14:16:16:18:20:22]sts in Irish moss st.
20th row As 4th.
21st row As first.
22nd row As 2nd.
23rd row As 19th.
24th row As 4th.
These 24 rows form patt for cable panel. Cont in patt as set until work measures 12¼[13½:14½:15¾:16½:17:17]in, ending with a WS row.
Shape armholes:
Bind off 6[6:7:7:8:8:10]sts at beg of next 2 rows. 88[92:98:102:108:112:116]sts. Work even until work measures 19[20½:22:23½:25:25½:26]in, ending with a WS row.
Shape shoulders and neck:
Bind off 8[8:9:9:8:8:8]sts at beg of next 2[2:2:2:4:4:4] rows.
Next row Bind off 8[8:9:9:8:8:8]sts, work in patt across next 18[19:20:22:17:18:19]sts and leave these 19[20:21:23:18:19:20]sts on holder (includes st used in binding off) for right back, bind off next 18[20:20:20:24:26:28]sts tightly, work in patt to end.
Cont on rem 27[28:30:32:26:27:28]sts for left back.
Bind off 8[8:9:9:8:8:8]sts at beg of next row and 10[10:11:12:12:12:12]sts at neck edge at beg of next row. 9[10:10:11:6:7:8]sts.
Bind off rem sts.
With WS facing, rejoin yarn to rem sts at neck edge for right back.
Bind off 10[10:11:12:12:12:12]sts, work in patt to end. 9[10:10:11:6:7:8]sts.
Bind off rem sts.

FRONT

Work as for Back until there are 12[12:12:14:14:14:16] rows less than Back to shoulder, ending with a WS row.
Shape neck and shoulders:
Next row Work 37[38:40:42:43:44:45]sts in patt and leave these sts on a holder for left front, bind off next 14[16:18:18:22:24:26]sts tightly, work in patt to end.
Cont on rem 37[38:40:42:43:44:45]sts for right front.
Work 1 row.
**Bind off 4sts at beg of next row, 2sts at same edge on every other row 3[3:3:3:3:3:2] times and one st on every other row 2[2:2:3:3:3:5] times. 25[26:28:29:30:31:32]sts.
Keeping neck edge even, bind off 8[8:9:9:8:8:8]sts at beg of next row and then every other row 1[1:1:1:2:2:2] times. 9[10:10:11:6:7:8]sts.

Work 1 row. Bind off rem sts.
With WS facing, rejoin yarn to rem sts at neck edge for left front. Complete to match right front, working from ** to end.

SLEEVES (make 2)

Using smaller needles, cast on 41[41:45:47:51:55:57]sts. Work in K1, P1 rib for 2½[2½:2½:3:3:3½:3½]in as for Back, ending with a first row.
Next row (WS) P0[0:0:0:0:2:2], Kfb, (P1, Pfb) 3 times, P1, Kfb, (P1, Pfb) twice, P1, (K1, P1, inc 2, P1, K1, P1) 2[2:2:3:3:3:4] times, rib 0[0:4:0:4:4:0], Kfb, (P1, Pfb) twice, P1, Kfb, (P1, Pfb) 3 times, P1, Kfb. P0[0:0:0:0:2:2]. 60[60:64:68:72:76:80]sts.
Change to larger needles and patt:
1st patt row (RS) K0[0:0:0:0:2:2], P2, K10 (for cable panel), P2, K7 (for claw patt), P18[18:22:26:30:30:34] (for trinity st), K7 (for claw patt), P2, K10 (for cable panel), P2, K0[0:0:0:0:2:2].
This row establishes the position of each patt.
Cont in patt as set, working center trinity st patt as for Back and keeping cables and claw patts correct.
Work 5 rows.
Inc one st at each end of next row and then every 8th row 3[2:1:3:2:2:1] times in all, then every 6th row 7[10:12:10:12:12:14] times in all noting that first 7[7:7:7:7:5:5] extra sts at each side form claw patt as soon as possible, next st forms P1 and rem sts are worked in Irish moss st. 82[86:92:96:102:106:112]sts.
Work even until Sleeve measures 14½[15½:16½:17½:18:18½:19]in; place a marker at each end of last row.
Work 8[8:10:10:12:12:14] rows even.
Shape cap:
Bind off 3[5:6:6:7:9:10]sts at beg of next 2 rows, 8sts at beg of next 2 rows, 12sts at beg of next 2 rows and 8sts at beg of next 2 rows. 20[20:24:28:32:32:36]sts.
Bind off rem sts tightly.

TO FINISH

Block each piece separately, but do not press.
Join right shoulder seam, matching patts.
Neckband With RS facing and using smaller needles, pick up and K 50[52:54:58:62:66:70]sts around front neck edge and 41[43:45:47:51:53:55]sts across back neck. 91[95:99:105:113:119:125]sts.
Beg with a 2nd row, work 5 rows K1, P1 rib as for Back. Bind off loosely in rib.
Join left shoulder seam and ends of neckband.
Sew bound-off edges of Sleeves to sides of armholes, matching rows above markers on Sleeves to bound-off sts of armhole.
Join side and sleeve seams.
Press seams lightly if necessary.

Designed by Philippa Wolledge
Pingouin

Asymmetrical styling and warm, wearable colors make a handsome pullover with a youthful accent.

SIZES

To fit 36[38:40:42]in chest
Garment measures: 40[42:44½:46½]in at underarm
Length from shoulder: 21½[22½:23½:24½]in
Sleeve seam: 23½[24½:25¼:26]in
Note Instructions for larger sizes are given in brackets [].

MATERIALS

Jaeger Luxury Spun Double Knitting
7[7:7:8] 1¾oz/50g balls in main color A (Barley)
5 1¾oz/50g balls in color B (Mink)
1 1¾oz/50g ball in color C (Jet)
(Alternative yarn: Patons Clansman Double Knitting)
Pair each of sizes 3 and 6 knitting needles
Set of 4 size 3 double-pointed needles

GAUGE

22sts and 28 rows to 4in over st st worked on size 6 needles

To save time, take time to check gauge.

ABBREVIATIONS

See book, p. 141.

Note When working patt from chart, use separate balls of yarn for each color, joining in as necessary (see book, p. 115). Do not carry colors across back, but break them off and rejoin every 6 rows. Leave long ends at each join to be darned in for at least 1in once knitting has been completed.

BACK

Using smaller pair of needles and A, cast on 96[100:108:112]sts.
1st rib row K1, *K2, P2, rep from * to last 3sts, K3.
2nd row K1, *P2, K2, rep from * to last 3sts, P2, K1.
Rep these 2 rows 9 more times, inc 14[16:14:16]sts evenly across last row. 110[116:122:128]sts.
Change to larger needles and patt:
Beg working st st, foll chart, reading RS rows from right to left and WS rows from left to right. **Work in colors as marked for Back on chart as foll:
1st patt row (RS) K33[35:37:39] B, K22sts from chart, K55[59:63:67] A.
2nd row K1 A, P54[58:62:66] A, P22sts from chart, P32[34:36:38] B, K1 B.
***3rd–36th rows** Cont working 22sts from chart in patt as set, keeping colors correct on each side of 22 chart patt sts, until 36 chart patt rows have been completed.
These 36 rows form patt. Rep 36 patt rows once more, then first 8[12:16:20] rows once more, thus ending with a P row.

Shape armholes:
Keeping 22 chart patt sts correct, bind off 12sts at beg of next 2 rows. *** 86[92:98:104]sts. Work even in patt for 62[64:66:68] more rows, ending with a 36th[6th:12th:18th] chart patt row.

Shape shoulders:
Keeping 22 chart patt sts correct, bind off 8[8:9:10]sts at beg of next 4 rows and 7[9:9:9]sts at beg of next 2 rows, thus ending with a 6th[12th:18th:24th] chart patt row. Sl rem 40[42:44:46]sts on to a holder.

FRONT

Work as for Back to **. Work in colors as marked for Front on chart as foll:

1st patt row K55[59:63:67] A, K22sts from chart, K33[35:37:39] B.

2nd row K1 B, P32[34:36:38], P22sts from chart, P54[58:62:66] A, K1 A.

Cont in patt as set, foll chart as before, and keeping colors correct on each side of 22 chart patt sts. Work as for Back from *** to ***. 86[92:98:104]sts.

Work even in patt for 50[52:54:56] more rows, ending with a 24th[30th:36th:6th] chart patt row, thus ending with a P row.

Shape neck:

Next row Using A, K30[32:34:36]sts, turn and leave rem sts on a holder.

Next row Using A, bind off 3 sts, P to last st, K1.

Cont in A, dec one st at neck edge on next 3 rows.

Work 1 row even.

Dec one st at neck edge on next row. 23[25:27:29]sts. Work 5 rows even, ending with a P row.

Shape shoulder:

Bind off 8[8:9:10]sts at beg of next row and then every other row once.

Work 1 row. Bind off rem 7[9:9:9]sts.

With RS of work facing, sl next 26[28:30:32]sts on to a holder for center neck. Rejoin B to rem sts and K to end.

Next row K1, P to end.

Complete to match first side, reversing shaping and making dec at neck edge by working sl 1, K1, psso on K rows and P2 tog tbl on P rows.

LEFT SLEEVE

Using smaller pair of needles and A, cast on 48[48:52:52]sts. Work 40 rows in rib as for Back, ending with a 2nd row.

Change to larger needles.**

Beg with a K row, cont in st st, inc one st at each end of next row and then every 4th row until there are 98[102:104:108]sts.

Work even until Sleeve measures 20½[21: 21½:22]in, ending with a P row. Mark each end of next row with a contrasting thread and work 14 more rows st st. Bind off.

RIGHT SLEEVE

Work as for Left Sleeve to ****. Change to B and complete to match Left Sleeve, working from **** to end.

TO FINISH

Block and press pieces foll instructions on yarn label.

Neckband Join shoulder seams. With RS of work facing, using set of double-pointed needles and A, pick up and K 40[42:44: 46]sts along back neck, 13sts down left front neck, 26[28:30:32]sts from center front sts on holder, and 13sts up right front neck. 92[96:100:104]sts. Arrange sts evenly on 3 needles.

Next round *K2, P2, rep from * to end. Rep last round 19 more times. Bind off in rib using larger needle.

Join top edges of Sleeves to armhole edge, joining rows above marker threads to bound-off sts of armhole shaping.

Join side and sleeve seams.

Fold Neckband in half to WS and slipstitch in place, ensuring an easy fit over head.

Press seams lightly if necessary.

Designed by Betty Barnden

Triffic

FRONT
☐ = col. B
⊡ = col. A
⊠ = col. C

BACK
☐ = col. A
⊡ = col. B
⊠ = col. C

← 22 sts →

34

This versatile, soft pullover, knitted in a mohair blend and textured with zigzags and bobbles, is sized to fit teenagers and adults too.

SIZES

To fit 30–32[34–36:38–40]in bust
Garment measures: 35½[40½:45½]in at under-arm
Length from shoulder: 22[22½:23]in
Sleeve seam: 18in
Note Instructions for larger sizes are given in brackets [].

MATERIALS

Pingouin Orage
8[9:10] 1¾oz/50g balls
Color shown: Azur
Pair each of sizes 5 and 8 knitting needles

GAUGE

16sts and 25 rows to 4in over patt worked on size 8 needles
For gauge sample cast on 21sts and work rows 1–30 of patt instructions.

To save time, take time to check gauge.

ABBREVIATIONS

MB – make bobble as foll: K1, P1, K1, P1, K1, all into same st. Turn, P5. Turn, K5. Turn P5. Turn, sl 2nd, 3rd, 4th and 5th sts on LH needle over first st on LH needle, pull tightly and sl rem st on to RH needle.

For other abbreviations see book, p. 141.

BACK

**Using smaller needles, cast on 70[80:90]sts. Work in K1, P1, rib for 3in, inc one st at end of last row. 71[81:91]sts.
Change to larger needles and patt:
1st patt row (RS) *K5, P1, K4, rep from * to last st, K1.
2nd row *P4, K1, P1, K1, P3, rep from * to last st, P1.
3rd row *K3, (P1, K1) twice, P1, K2, rep from * to last st, K1.
4th row *P2, (K1, P1) 3 times, K1, P1, rep from * to last st, P1.
5th row *(K1, P1) twice, K3, P1, K1, P1, rep from * to last st, K1.
6th row *K1, P1, K1, P5, K1, P1, rep from * to last st, K1.
7th row *K1, P1, K7, P1, rep from * to last st, K1.
8th row *K1, P3, K3, P3, rep from * to last st, K1.
9th row *K3, P5, K2, rep from * to last st, K1.
10th row *P2, K7, P1, rep from * to last st, P1.
11th row *K1, P9, rep from * to last st, K1.
12th row *P1, K4, MB, K4, rep from * to last st, P1.
13th row As 11th.
14th row As 10th.
15th row As 9th.
16th row As 8th.

17th row As 7th.
18th row As 6th.
19th row As 5th.
20th row As 4th.
21st row As 3rd.
22nd row As 2nd.
23rd row As first.
24th, 26th and 28th rows P.
25th, 27th and 29th rows K.
30th row P.
These 30 rows form patt. **
Cont in patt until Back measures 22[22½:23]in, ending with a WS row.
Shape shoulders:
Bind off 24[28:32]sts at beg of next 2 rows.
Leave rem 23[25:27]sts on a holder.

FRONT

Work as for Back from ** to **. Cont in patt until Front measures 19¼[19½:20]in, ending with a WS row.
Shape neck:
Next row Keeping patt correct, work 29[33:37]sts in patt, K2 tog, turn and leave rem sts on a holder.
Dec one st at neck edge on every row until 24[28:32]sts rem.
Work even until Front matches Back to shoulder shaping, ending with a WS row.
Shape shoulder:
Bind off rem sts.
With RS of work facing, sl center 9[11:13]sts on to a holder, rejoin yarn to rem sts, K2 tog, work in patt to end.
Complete to match first side, reversing shaping.

SLEEVES (make 2)

Using smaller needles, cast on 40sts and work in K1, P1 rib for 2½in, inc one st at end of last row. 41sts.
Change to larger needles and patt:
Beg with a 20th patt row, work as for Back, *at the same time shaping sides* by inc one st at each end of every 7th row once and then every 4th row until there are 61sts.
Work even until Sleeve measures 18in, ending with a 30th patt row. Bind off.

TO FINISH

Block the pieces, but do not press.
Join right shoulder seam.
Neckband With RS of work facing, using smaller needles and beg at left shoulder, pick up and K 15sts down left side of neck, K9[11:13]sts from holder at front neck, inc 2sts evenly, pick up and K 15sts up right side of neck and K23[25:27]sts from holder at back neck, inc 4sts evenly. 68[72:76]sts.
Work in K1, P1 rib for 3in.
Bind off loosely in rib.
Join left shoulder and neckband seams. Fold Neckband in half to WS and slipstitch loosely in place.
Measure 7½in from each shoulder on Front and Back and mark with a contrasting thread. Sew in Sleeves between markers.
Join side and sleeve seams.
Press seams lightly if necessary.

Designed by Janet Biggs

Pingouin

OPTIONS

Using the same stitch pattern, you could easily make an attractive pillow cover. Make sure that the number of stitches cast on is divisible by 10 plus 1 extra stitch.
A more delicate texture could be achieved using a sport yarn. The bobbles can be worked in afterward (see p. 120) using small amounts of bright-colored yarn. Use a neutral color for the background and arrange the bobble colors to form a rainbow sequence.

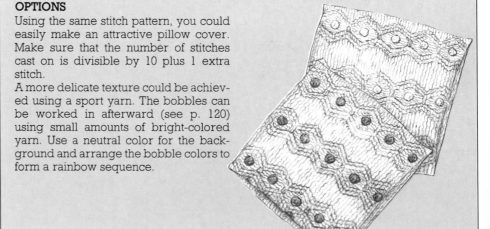

An exceptionally stylish sweater suitable for both boys and girls features a placket neck and square buttons which echo the checked motif of the upper part of the garment.

SIZES

To fit 28[30:32]in chest
Garment measures: 29½[32:33½]in at underarm
Length from shoulder: 16½[18½:20]in
Sleeve seam: 12[13½:15]in
Note Instructions for larger sizes are given in brackets [].

MATERIALS

Patons Beehive Double Knitting
5[5:6] 1¾oz/50g balls
Color shown: 6009
Pair each of sizes 3 and 6 knitting needles
3 square buttons

GAUGE

22sts and 30 rows to 4in over g st rib worked on size 6 needles
For gauge sample cast on 30sts and rep g st rib patt rows for at least 4in, working patt rep only from * on 2nd row, thus omitting edge sts.

To save time, take time to check gauge.

ABBREVIATIONS

See book, p. 141.

BACK

Using smaller needles, cast on 81[87:91]sts.
1st rib row *K1, P1, rep from * to last st, K1.
2nd row *P1, K1, rep from * to last st, P1.
Rep these 2 rows 7 more times, inc one st at each end of last row. 83[89:93]sts.
Change to larger needles and g st rib:
1st patt row (RS) K.
2nd row P4[2:4], *K5, P5, rep from * to last 9[7:9]sts, K5, P4[2:4].
These 2 rows form g st rib patt. Work 52[64:76] more rows in g st rib patt.
Beg rib and g st check patt:
1st patt row (K1, P1) twice [once:twice],* K5, P1, (K1, P1) twice, rep from * to last 9[7:9]sts, K5, (P1, K1) twice[once:twice].
2nd row (P1, K1) twice[once:twice], P5, *K1, (P1, K1) twice, P5, rep from * to last 4[2:4]sts, (K1, P1) twice[once:twice].
3rd–6th rows Rep first and 2nd rows twice more.
7th row K.
8th row P4[2:4], *K5, P5, rep from * to last 9[7:9]sts, K5, P4[2:4].
9th–12th rows Rep 7th and 8th rows twice. These 12 rows form rib and g st check patt.**
Shape armholes:
Keeping rib and g st check patt correct, bind off 6sts at beg of next 2 rows. 71[77:81]sts. Dec one st at beg of every row until 63[67:69]sts rem.
Work 39 rows even. Bind off sts.

FRONT

Work as for Back to **.
Shape armhole and divide for front opening:
Next row Bind off 6sts, patt 32[35:37] (including st left on needle after bind-off), turn and leave rem sts on a holder.
Complete this side first.
*** Work 1 row.
Keeping front edge even and patt correct, dec one st at beg of next row and then every other row until 28[30:31]sts rem. Work even in patt for 24 rows, ending at front edge.
Shape neck:
Next row Bind off 4sts, patt to end. Work 1 row.
Next row Bind off 2sts, work in patt to end.
Rep last 2 rows 4 more times. 14[16:17]sts.
***
Work 4 rows even. Bind off rem sts.
With RS of work facing, rejoin yarn to rem sts, bind off 7sts, work in patt to end. 38[41:43]sts.
Shape armhole:
Next row Bind off 6sts, work in patt to end. Work as for first side from *** to ***. Work even for 3 rows. Bind off rem sts.

SLEEVES (make 2)

Using smaller needles, cast on 41[47:51]sts and work 16 rows K1, P1 rib as for Back, inc one st at each end of last row. 43[49:53]sts.
Change to larger needles and g st rib patt:
Cont in patt as for Back, inc one st at each end of 5th row and then every 6th[7th:8th] row until there are 63[69:73]sts. Work even until 62[74:84] patt rows have been worked in all.
Change to rib and g st check patt:
Cont in patt as for Back. Work 12 rows.
Shape top:
Bind off 6sts at beg of next 2 rows. 51[57:61]sts.
1st and 2nd sizes only
Dec one st at beg of next 2 rows. 49[55]sts. Work 2 rows.
1st size only
Rep last 4 rows twice more. 45sts.
All sizes
Dec one st at beg of every row until 25sts rem. Bind off rem sts.

TO FINISH

Block each piece, but do not press.
Button band Using smaller needles and with RS of work facing, pick up and K 24[26:28]sts from right side of front opening for a boy or left side for a girl. Work 11 rows K1, P1 rib. Bind off in rib.
Buttonhole band Using smaller needles and with RS of work facing, pick up and K 24[26:28]sts along left side of front opening for a boy or right side for a girl. Work 3 rows K1, P1 rib.
Next row (make buttonholes) Rib 4, (bind off 2sts, rib 5[6:7] including st left on needle after bind-off) twice, bind off 2sts, rib to end.
Next row Work in rib, casting on 2sts over those bound off in previous row.
Work 6 rows K1, P1 rib. Bind off in rib.
Collar Using larger needles, cast on 3sts. Cont working in g st, inc one st at each end of 5th row and then every 4th row until there are 21sts. Work even for 72 rows. Dec one st at each end of next row and then every 4th row until 3sts rem.
Work 4 rows even. Bind off rem sts.
Join shoulder seams.
Sew front bands neatly in place to base of front opening, with Buttonhole band on top.
Sew Collar in place.
Set in Sleeves.
Join side and sleeve seams.
Sew on buttons to correspond with buttonholes.

Designed by Alan Dart

Fashion plus! Mathematical symbols, numbers, and exclamation marks in crisp navy on a cream background add up to a winning formula – a neat, round-neck cotton pullover for the young.

SIZES

To fit 26[28:32:34]in chest/bust.
Garment measures: 34[36½:39½:42]in at underarm
Length from shoulder: 20[21½:22½:23½]in
Sleeve seam: 17[18:19½:19½]in
Note Instructions for larger sizes are given in brackets [].

MATERIALS

Neveda Double Cotton
10[10:12:12] 1¾oz/50g balls in main color A (3004 – cream)
2[2:2:2] 1¾oz/50g balls in color B (3021 – navy)
Pair each of sizes 3 and 6 knitting needles

GAUGE

18sts and 26 rows to 4in over st st worked on size 6 needles

To save time, take time to check gauge.

ABBREVIATIONS

See book, p. 141.

Note Scatter numbers over body and sleeves at random, using individual charts for each number and reading RS (K) rows from right to left and WS (P) rows from left to right. Work as many or as few numbers as desired. Use the intarsia method (see book, p. 115) to work the numbers. For best results plan the placement of the numbers on a graph paper drawing (see book, p. 40).

When working a ÷ or ! from chart, work the bobble on a RS row as foll: K to position of bobble, K into front and back of next st twice, then into front again, (turn, P5, turn, K5) twice, using LH needle lift 2nd, 3rd, 4th and 5th sts over first st and off needle.

BACK

Using smaller needles and A, cast on 78[84:90:96]sts. Work 10 rows K1, P1 rib.
Change to larger needles.
Beg with a K row, cont in st st, working numbers in B at random from individual charts, until Back measures 19[20:21½:22]in, ending with a P row and making sure that last number has been completed.
Shape neck and shoulders:
Next row K27[30:33:36], turn and complete this side first.
Dec one st at neck edge on next 7 rows, ending at armhole edge.
Next row Bind off 6[7:8:9]sts, K to last 2sts, K2 tog.
P1 row.
Keeping neck edge even, bind off

6[7:8:9]sts at beg of next row and then 7[8:9:10]sts at beg of every other row once. Fasten off.
With RS facing, sl next 24sts on to a holder for center neck, K to end.
P1 row.
Complete to match first side, reversing shaping.

FRONT

Work as for Back.

SLEEVES (make 2)

Using smaller needles and A, cast on 40[40:42:42]sts. Work 10 rows K1, P1 rib.
Change to larger needles.
Beg with a K row cont in st st, inc one st at each end of next row and then every 5th row until there are 80[82:84:86]sts.
Work even until Sleeve measures 17[18:19½:19½]in, ending with a P row.
Bind off loosely.

TO FINISH

Block and press each piece on WS, foll instructions on yarn label.
Join right shoulder seam.
Neckband With RS facing, using smaller needles and A, pick up and K 92sts around neck edge, including working across 24sts at center back and center front. Work 6 rows K1, P1 rib in A, 1 row in B.
Bind off loosely in rib using B.
Join left shoulder seam.
Fold Sleeves in half and sew in place, matching center of Sleeves to shoulder seams.
Join side and sleeve seams.
Press seams lightly if necessary.

Designed by Warm and Wonderful

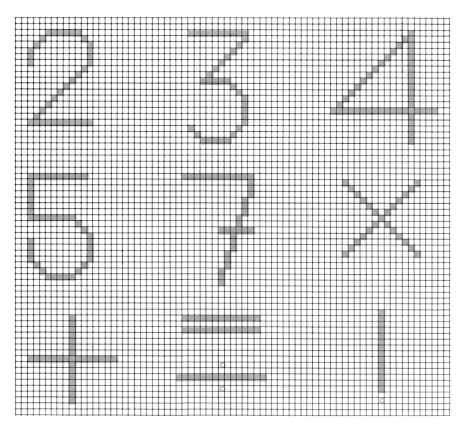

○ = bobble—5sts and 4 rows

Bright-colored diamonds add sparkle to this shawl-collared sweater dress.

SIZES

To fit 24[26:30]in chest
Garment measures: 26[29:32]in at underarm
Length from shoulder: 24½[26½:28]in
Sleeve seam: 12[12:12½]in
Note Instructions for larger sizes are given in brackets [].

MATERIALS

Patons Clansman Superwash Double Knitting
7[8:9] 1¾oz/50g balls in main color A (2448 medium blue)
1 1¾oz/50g ball in each of 4 colors: B (7286 – light blue), C (2498 – red), D (11 – navy) and E (7789 – yellow)
Pair each of sizes 3 and 6 knitting needles
1 toggle (optional)

GAUGE

23sts and 32 rows to 4in over diamond patt worked on size 6 needles
For gauge sample cast on 24sts and work patt rep of 6sts from diamond patt chart 4 times in all on each row. Work at least 4in.

To save time, take time to check gauge.

ABBREVIATIONS

See book, p. 141.

Note When working pattern from chart, carry yarn not in use across back of work using stranding method (see book, p. 116).

DRESS

Sleeve and Bodice (worked in one piece)
Right Sleeve Using smaller needles and A, cast on 43[45:49]sts.
1st rib row *K1, P1, rep from * to last st, K1.
2nd row *P1, K1, rep from * to last st, P1.
Rep these 2 rows for 2in, ending with a 2nd row, inc 4sts evenly across last row. 47[49:53]sts.
Change to larger needles.
Beg working embossed diamond patt from Chart, beg with a 7th patt row, reading RS rows from right to left and WS rows from left to right, at the same time inc one st at each end of 5th[9th:9th] row once and then every 4th row until there are 71[77:89]sts and 50[64:78] rows in all have been worked in diamond patt.
Beg working color patt in st st from chart, reading RS rows from right to left and WS rows from left to right as before, at the same time inc on every 4th row from previous dec until there are 83[87:95]sts. Work even until 32nd patt row has been completed. **
Work even, using A, and resume embossed diamond patt as already established, beg with a 13th patt row.
1st and 2nd sizes only Work 9 rows.

3rd size only
Work 1 row.
All sizes
***Shape back neck:
Keeping embossed diamond patt correct, work 42[44:48]sts, turn and leave rem 41[43:47]sts on a holder.
Dec one st at neck edge on 3rd and 7th row. 40[42:46]sts.
Work even until back neck measures 3½in. Bind off.
Left Sleeve
Work as for Right Sleeve to **.
Work even, using A, and resume embossed diamond patt as already established, beg with a 13th patt row.
1st and 2nd sizes only
Work 10 rows.
3rd size only
Work 2 rows.
All sizes
Complete as for Left Sleeve, working from *** to end.

SKIRT (worked in one piece)

Using smaller needles and A, cast on 151[169:187]sts. Work in K1, P1 rib as for Sleeve for 2½in.
Change to larger needles and patt:
Beg at 7th patt row, working embossed diamond patt from chart as foll:
7th row (RS) P3[0:3], *K1, P5, rep from * to last 4[1:4]sts, K1, P3[0:3].
8th row K3[0:3], P1, *K5, P1, rep from * to last 3sts, K3[0:3].
Cont in embossed diamond patt as set working 9th–14th rows of chart once. Now rep first–14th rows of embossed diamond patt until Skirt measures 18[19:20]in, or length required, ending with a WS row.
Bind off loosely.

TO FINISH

Block and press pieces lightly under a damp cloth foll instructions on yarn label.
Join bodice pieces at center back.
Collar Using smaller needles, A and with RS of work facing, K41[43:47]sts from right front holder, pick up and K 31 sts along back neck, K41[43:47]sts from left front holder. 113[117:125]sts. Work in K1, P1 rib as for Sleeve for 6in. Bind off in rib.
Wrap Right Collar over Left Collar and pin in place.
Join skirt seam.
Join Skirt to Bodice, matching center back seams and making sure that both pieces of Collar are securely sewn in.
Make a button loop at lower edge of Collar and sew on toggle to correspond if desired.

Designed by Ruth Herring

COLOR PATTERN

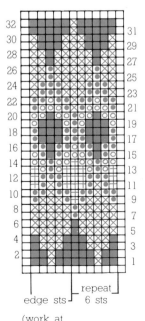

(work at end of K rows, beg of P rows)
edge sts — repeat 6 sts

EMBOSSED DIAMOND PATTERN

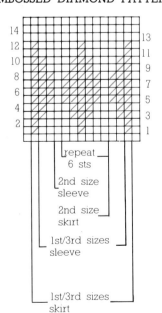

repeat 6 sts
2nd size sleeve
2nd size skirt
1st/3rd sizes sleeve
1st/3rd sizes skirt

KEY

☐ = K on RS, P on WS
☑ = P on RS, K on WS
■ = main col A (medium blue)
⊠ = col B (light blue)
⊡ = col C (red)
⊙ = col D (navy)
⊞ = col E (yellow)

This attractive child's cardigan combines stylish raglan sleeves with a traditional Fair Isle pattern. Worked in charming, carousel colors, it is equally suited to boys and girls.

SIZES

To fit 26[28:30]in chest
Garment measures: 29½[31½:33½]in at under-arm
Length from shoulder: 17[18½:20½]in
Sleeve seam: 12½[14:15½]in
Note Instructions for larger sizes are given in brackets [].

MATERIALS

Scheepjeswol Luzern
3[4:5] 1¾oz/50g balls in main color A (6438 – medium blue)
1[1:2] 1¾oz/50g balls in each of 3 contrasting colors: B (6412–white), C (6487–yellow) and D (6442 – gold)
2 1¾oz/50g balls in contrasting color E (6444 – red)
1 1¾oz/50g ball in contrasting color F (6474 – pale blue)
Pair each of size 6 and 8 knitting needles
7 buttons

GAUGE

20sts and 20 rows to 4in over st st worked on size 8 needles

To save time, take time to check gauge.

ABBREVIATIONS

M1 – lift strand running from base of st just worked to base of next st on to LH needle and work into back of it.

For other abbreviations see book, p. 141.

Note Work Fair Isle patt from chart, reading RS (odd-numbered) rows from right to left and WS (even-numbered) rows from left to right. Each patt rep is worked over 16sts with extra sts for different sizes shown at side of chart. Carry yarn not in use across back of work, using the stranding and weaving methods (see book, pp. 116–117).

BACK

Using smaller needles and A, cast on 61[65:69]sts.
1st rib row (RS) *K1, P1, rep from * to last st, K1.
2nd row *P1, K1, rep from * to last st, P1.
Rep last 2 rows for 2½in, ending with a RS row.
Next row Rib 4[5:2], M1, *rib 6[5:5], M1, rep from * 8[10:12] more times, rib to end. 71[77:83]sts.
Change to larger needles, Fair Isle patt:
Beg with a K row, cont working in st st in patt from chart, rep 16 patt sts 4[4:5] times in all across row and working first 3[6:1]sts and last 4[7:2]sts on K rows and first 4[7:2]sts and last 3[6:1]sts on P rows as indicated. Cont in patt until Back measures 10½[11½:13]in, ending with a P row.
Shape raglans:
Bind off 3sts at beg of next 2 rows. Dec one st at each end of every other row until 45[51:57]sts rem, then at each end of every row until 21[23:25]sts rem.
Leave rem sts on a holder.

LEFT FRONT

Using smaller needles and A, cast on 29[31:33]sts and work in K1, P1 rib for 2½in as for Back, ending with a RS row.
Next row Rib 4[2:2], M1, *rib 3[4:4], M1, rep from * 6 more times, rib to end. 37[39:41]sts.
Change to larger needles, Fair Isle patt:
Beg with a K row, cont in st st working from chart, rep 16sts twice across row and working first 3[6:1]sts and last 2[1:8]sts on K rows and first 2[1:8]sts and last 3[6:1]sts on P rows as indicated, until Front matches Back to raglan shaping, ending with a P row.
Shape raglan:
Bind off 3sts at beg of next row.
Work 1 row.
Dec one st at beg of every other row until 24[26:26]sts rem, then at same edge on every row until 22 sts rem, ending with a P row.
Shape neck:
Next row Work 2 tog, work 15sts in patt, turn and leave rem 5sts on a holder.
Cont dec one st at raglan edge as before, *at the same time* dec one st at neck edge on every row until 6sts rem.
Cont dec at raglan edge *only* until 2sts rem.
Work 2 tog. Fasten off.

RIGHT FRONT

Work as for Left Front, reversing shaping and noting that chart will be read by working first 1[0:7]sts and last 4[7:2]sts on K rows and first 4[7:2]sts and last 1[0:7]sts on P rows as indicated.

SLEEVES (make 2)

Using smaller needles and A, cast on 31sts and work in K1, P1 rib for 2½in as for Back, ending with a RS row.
Next row Rib 2, M1, *rib 4, M1, rep from * 6 more times, rib to end. 39sts.

Change to larger needles, Fair Isle patt:
Beg with a K row, cont working in patt from chart, beg with a 13th[11th:11th] row, rep 16 patt sts twice across row and working first 3sts and last 4sts on K rows and first 4sts and last 3sts on P rows as indicated, *at the same time* inc one st at each end of 3rd row once and then every 7th[6th:6th] row until there are 51[55:59]sts.
Work even until Sleeve measures approx 12½[14:15½]in, ending on same patt row as Back at beg of raglan shaping.
Shape raglans:
Bind off 3sts at beg of next 2 rows. Dec one st at each end of every other row until 23[25:29]sts rem, then at each end of every row until 3[5:5]sts rem. Leave rem sts on a holder.

TO FINISH

Block and press foll instructions on yarn label, omitting ribbing.
Join raglan seams.
Join side and sleeve seams.
Neckband Using smaller needles, A and with RS facing, beg at Right Front and K5sts from holder, pick up and K 9sts up right side of neck, K3[5:5]sts along right side of neck, K3[5:5]sts along Right Sleeve, K21[23:25]sts along Back dec 4sts evenly, K3[5:5]sts along Left Sleeve, pick up and K 9sts down left side of neck and 5sts from holder. 51[57:59]sts.
Work in K1, P1 rib as for Back for 1¼in, beg with a 2nd (WS) row.
Bind off evenly in rib.
Button band Using smaller needles and A, cast on 9sts.
1st rib row (RS) K2, *P1, K1, rep from * twice more, K1.
2nd row K1, *P1, K1, rep from * 3 more times.
Rep these 2 rows until Button band, when slightly stretched, fits up Right Front (for a boy, Left Front for a girl) to top of neckband.
Bind off evenly in rib.
Sew Button band in place.
Buttonhole band Mark positions for 7 buttons on Button band, the first to come ¾in above lower edge, last to come in center of neckband, with 5 more evenly spaced between.
Work as for Button band, making buttonholes as markers are reached as foll:
1st buttonhole row (RS) Rib 3, bind off 3sts, rib to end.
2nd row Rib to end, casting on 3sts over those bound off in previous row.
Sew Buttonhole band in place.
Sew on buttons to correspond with buttonholes.
Press seams.

Designed by Anne Matheson

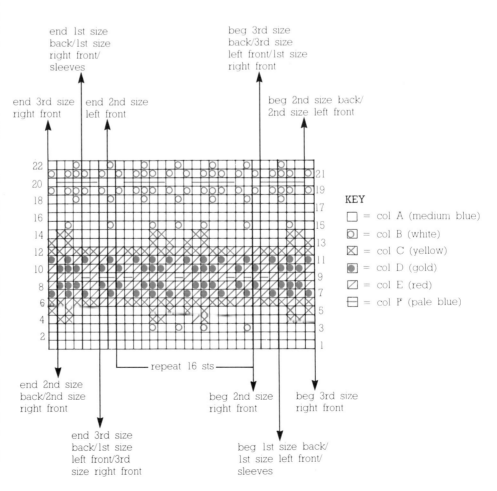

end 1st size
back/1st size
right front/
sleeves

beg 3rd size
back/3rd size
left front/1st size
right front

end 3rd size
right front

end 2nd size
left front

beg 2nd size back/
2nd size left front

KEY

☐ = col A (medium blue)
⊙ = col B (white)
⊠ = col C (yellow)
⊙ = col D (gold)
⧄ = col E (red)
⊟ = col F (pale blue)

repeat 16 sts

end 2nd size
back/2nd size
right front

beg 2nd size
right front

beg 3rd size
right front

end 3rd size
back/1st size
left front/3rd
size right front

beg 1st size back/
1st size left front/
sleeves

Nautical motifs, worked in Swiss darning, enliven this jacket, with its sailor collar and sturdy zipper.

SIZES

To fit 26[28:30:32]in chest
Garment measures: 31[33:35:37½]in at underarm
Length from shoulder: 15½[17:18:19½]in
Sleeve seam: 8½[9:10:10½]in
Note Instructions for larger sizes are given in brackets [].

MATERIALS

Pingouin Pingostar
4[5:5:5] 1¾oz/50g balls in main color A (Cerise)
2 1¾oz/50g balls in color B (Ecru)
1 1¾oz/50g ball in each of 3 colors: C (Noir), D (Persan) and E (Bleu franc)
Pair each of size 6 and 7 knitting needles
Tapestry needle for Swiss darning
12[12:14:14]in heavy-weight plastic zipper

GAUGE

17sts and 23 rows to 4in over st st worked on size 7 needles

To save time, take time to check gauge.

ABBREVIATIONS

See book, p. 141.
Note When working motifs from charts, work the areas shown in solid colors. The areas marked as symbols indicate the position for the Swiss darning.

Use a combination of stranding and intarsia methods (see book, pp. 115–116) to work the knitted motifs.

BACK

Using smaller needles and C, cast on 66[70:74:80]sts. Cont in K1, P1 rib, working 1 row C, 9 rows B and 2 rows C.
Change to larger needles.
Beg with a K row, cont in st st throughout.

Beg with a K row, cont in st st throughout. Using A, work 20[24:28:36] rows.
Work fish motif:
Cont working in st st and foll chart, reading RS (uneven) rows from right to left and WS (even) rows from left to right, beg at 5th chart row placed as foll:
Next row K26[28:30:33]A, 1E, 4A, 4E, join in 2nd ball of A, K31[33:35:38]A.
Cont in patt as set, working from 6th row of chart until 30th chart row has been completed. Break off contrasting colors.
Using A only, cont in st st until Back measures 14½[16:17:18½]in, ending with a P row.
Shape neck:
Next row K24[25:26:29], turn and complete this side first.
Bind off 2sts at beg of next row. Dec one st at neck edge on next row. 21[22:23:26]sts.
P1 row. Bind off.
With RS facing, rejoin yarn to rem sts. Bind off next 18[20:22:22]sts, K to end.
Dec one st at end of next row. Bind off 2sts at beg of next row.
P1 row. 21[22:23:26]sts. Bind off.

LEFT FRONT

Using smaller needles and C, cast on 32[34:36:40]sts. Work 12 rows rib as for Back, inc one st at center of last row on *first, 2nd and 3rd sizes only.* 33[35:37:40]sts. **

Change to larger needles.
Using A and beg with a K row, work 16[20:24:32] rows st st.

Work "B" motif:
Cont working in st st and foll chart reading RS and WS rows as for fish motif, placed as foll:

1st chart row K11[12:12:15]A, 14C, join in 2nd ball of A, K8[9:11:11]A.

2nd row P8[9:11:11]A, 15C, 10[11:11:14]A.

3rd row K0[10:10:13]A, 2C, 12D, join in 2nd ball of C, K2C, 8[9:11:11]A.

Cont working "B" motif from 4th row of chart as set, until motif has been completed. Break off contrasting colors.

Using A only, cont in st st until Left Front measures 12[12½:14:15]in, ending with a P row.

Shape neck:
Dec one st at neck edge on every row until 21[22:23:26]sts rem. Work even until Front matches Back to shoulder. Bind off.

RIGHT FRONT

Work as for Left Front to **.

Change to larger needles.
Using A and beg with a K row, work 18[22:26:34] rows st st.

Work boat motif:
Cont working in st st and from chart, reading RS and WS rows as for fish motif, beg at 15th boat motif row placed as foll:

Next row K14A, 2D, 17[19:21:24]A.

Next row P6[8:10:13]A, 1D, 8A, 5D, 2A, 2D, join in 2nd ball of A, P9A.

Cont working motif in patt as set, working from 17th row of chart until Right Front measures same as Left Front to neck shaping, ending with a P row.

Shape neck:
Keeping motif patt correct, dec one st at neck edge only on every row until 21[22:23:26]sts rem.

Work even until Right Front matches Left Front to shoulder. Bind off.

SLEEVES (make 2)

Using smaller needles and C, cast on 34[38:42:46]sts. Work 12 rows rib as for Back, inc 3sts evenly across last row. 37[41:45:49]sts.

Change to larger needles.
Using A and beg with a K row, cont in st st inc one st at each end of 5th row once and then every 6th[8th:8th:8th] row until there are 47[51:55:59]sts.

Work even until Sleeve measures 8½[9:10: 10½]in. Bind off.

COLLAR

Right side
Using smaller needles and C, cast on 33[35:35:37]sts.

Next row (RS) Using C, K1, *P1, K1, rep from * to end.

Break off C. Join in B.

Cont working in rib as set with B, dec one st at end of next row and at same (neck) edge until 19[21:19:21]sts rem.

Work 10[12:10:10] rows even.

Next row Cast on 2sts, rib to end. 21[23:21:23]sts ***.

Work 1 row.

Break off yarn and leave sts on a holder.

Left side
Work as for right side to *** reversing shaping.

Next row Rib to end, then cast on 18[20:22:22]sts for back neck, with RS facing

work across right side sts on holder. 60[66:64:68]sts.

Work even on these sts until work measures 3½[4:4½:4½]in from back neck. Break off B. Join in C. Work 2 more rows in rib. Bind off in rib.

TO FINISH

Block and press lightly foll instructions on yarn label, omitting ribbing.

Work Swiss darning (see book, p. 37) as shown on charts for each individual motif.

Join shoulder seams.

Pin Collar to neck edge with RS facing WS of neck. Sew in place, using backstitch.

Fold Sleeves in half and sew in place matching center of Sleeve to shoulder seam.

Join side seams.

Sew in zipper.

Press seams lightly if necessary.

Designed by Ruth Herring

KEY Knitted areas
- ■ = main col A (red)
- ☐ = col B (white)
- ■ = col C (black)
- ▨ = col D (turquoise)
- ☐ = col E (blue)

Swiss darning
- ⊡ = col B (white)
- ⊠ = col C (black)
- ⊙ = col D (turquoise)
- ⊞ = col E (blue)

OPTIONS
You could easily substitute a different initial – perhaps the child's own first initial – for the "B" used here. Make it approximately the same size and shape as the "B" and transfer the letter on to graph paper. (See book, p. 42.)

Any of these motifs could be used on a different garment, such as a pullover or overalls.

FISH MOTIF
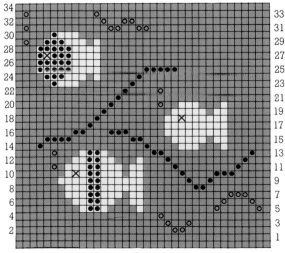

B MOTIF
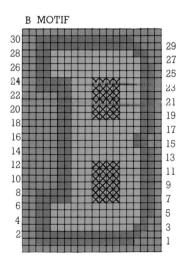

BOAT MOTIF
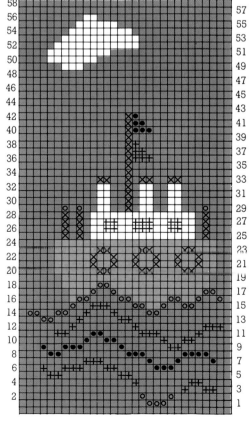

This girl's yoked bathrobe, designed to flatter, is knitted in a simple seed stitch which enhances the yarn's mother-of-pearl tones. The garter stitch edging, tie closures and the heart-shaped pocket provide attractive finishing touches.

SIZES

To fit 22[24:26]in chest (3[5:7] years)
Garment measures: 26[27½:29]in at underarm
Length from shoulder: 25½[28½:30½]in
Sleeve seam: 9¾[11½:12¼]in
Note Instructions for larger sizes are given in brackets [].

MATERIALS

Scheepjeswol Voluma Colori (A)
6[7:8] 1¾oz/50g balls
Color shown: 5394
Scheepjeswol Voluma (B)
1 1¾oz/50g ball
Color shown: 4323
Pair each of sizes 5 and 6 knitting needles

GAUGE

20sts and 32 rows to 4in over seed st worked on size 6 needles
For gauge sample cast on 23sts and work patt row for at least 4in.

To save time, take time to check gauge.

ABBREVIATIONS

See book, p. 141.

BACK

Using smaller needles and B, cast on 121[125:129]sts. K 3 rows.
Change to larger needles and A.
K 1 row.
Beg seed st patt:
1st patt row (WS) P1, *K1, P1, rep from * to end.
2nd row P1, *K1, P1, rep from * to end.
The 2nd row forms patt. Cont in patt until Back measures 19[21½:23]in, ending with a WS row.
Shape yoke:
Next row (K2 tog) 23[21:19] times, (K1, K2 tog) 9[13:17] times, (K2 tog) 24[22:20] times. 65[69:73]sts.
Work 2in more in seed st, ending with a WS row.
Shape armholes:
Keeping patt correct, bind off 4sts at beg of next 2 rows. Dec one st at each end of next 3 rows. 51[55:59]sts.
Work 1 row.
Dec one st at each end of next row and then every other row twice. 45[49:53]sts.
Work even until armholes measure 4½[5:5½]in, ending with a WS row.
Shape shoulders:
Bind off 4sts at beg of next 6[4:2] rows and 0[5:5]sts at beg of next 0[2:4] rows. 21[23:25]sts. Leave rem sts on a holder.

LEFT FRONT

Using smaller needles and B, cast on 61[63:65]sts. K 3 rows.
Change to larger needles and A.
K 1 row.
Cont in seed st patt as for Back until Front matches Back to yoke, ending with a WS row.
Shape yoke:
Next row (K2 tog) 11[11:9] times, (K1, K2 tog) 5[7:9] times, (K2 tog) 12[10:10] times. 33[35:37]sts.
Work even in patt until Front matches Back to underarm, ending with a WS row.
Shape armhole:
Keeping patt correct, bind off 4sts at beg of next row.
Work 1 row.
Dec one st at armhole edge on next 3 rows.
Work 1 row.
Dec one st at armhole edge on next row and then every other row twice. 23[25:27]sts.
Work even in patt until Front measures 2[2:2½]in less than Back to shoulder shaping, ending with a RS row.
Shape neck:
Bind off 4[5:5]sts at beg of next row. Dec one st at neck edge on next 5 rows, then on every other row 2[2:3] times. 12[13:14]sts. Work even until Front matches Back to shoulder, ending with a WS row.
Shape shoulder:
Bind off 4sts at beg of next row and then every other row 1[1:0] time. 4[5:10]sts.
Work 1 row.
Bind off 4[5:5]sts at beg of next row and then every other row 0[0:1] time.

RIGHT FRONT

Work to match Left Front, reversing shaping.

SLEEVES (make 2)

Using smaller needles and B, cast on 35[39:41]sts. K 3 rows.
Change to larger needles and A.
K 1 row.
Cont in seed st patt as for Back, inc one st at each end of every 10th[9th:9th] row until there are 47[55:59]sts and working extra sts into patt. Work even until Sleeve measures 9¾[11½:12¼]in, ending with a WS row.
Shape sleeve cap:
Bind off 4sts at beg of next 2 rows. 39[47:51]sts.
1st size only
Dec one st at each end of next row and then every 4th row 3 times in all. 33sts.
Work 1 row.
All sizes
Dec one st at each end of next row and then every other row until 19[19:23]sts rem, dec one st at each end of every row until 13sts rem. Bind off.

TO FINISH

Block the pieces, if necessary, but do not press.
Join shoulder seams.
Neck border Using smaller needles, B and with RS of work facing, pick up and K 59[61:67]sts evenly around neck. K 3 rows. Bind off.
Right front border Using smaller needles, B and with RS of work facing, pick up and K 120[134:142]sts from right hem to top of neck border. K 3 rows. Bind off.
Left front border Work as for Right front border, from top of neck border to left hem.
Ties (make 4) Using smaller needles and B, cast on 39sts. K 4 rows. Bind off.
Pocket Using smaller needles and B, cast on 5sts, K 1 row. Cont in g st, inc one st at each end of next 4 rows. 13sts.
Work 1 row.
Inc one st at each end of next row and then every other row until there are 29sts. K 10 rows.
Next row K14, sl 1, K1, psso, K to end.
Next row K2 tog, K10, K2 tog, turn and cont on these sts for first side. K 1 row.
Dec one st at each end of next row and then every other row until 4sts rem. Bind off.
With RS of work facing, rejoin yarn to rem sts and complete to match first side. Sew Pocket in place.
Set in Sleeves.
Join side and sleeve seams.
Sew two Ties at neck edge and two 6in below neck edge.

Designed by Julia Howe

Scheepjeswol (UK) Ltd.

Knitted smocking and a demure collar give this dress real charm.

SIZES

To fit 20[22:24]in chest
Garment measures: 23[24:25]in at underarm
Length from shoulder: 17[17¾:18½]in
Sleeve seam: 8½[9½:11]in
Note Instructions for larger sizes are given in brackets [].

MATERIALS

Pingouin Pingofine
4[4:5] 1¾oz/50g balls in main color A (Vieux rose)
1 1¾oz/50g ball in color B (Ecru)
Pair each of sizes 1 and 3 knitting needles
Cable needle
3 small buttons

GAUGE

26sts and 36 rows to 4in over st st worked on size 3 needles

To save time, take time to check gauge.

ABBREVIATIONS

M1 – lift strand running from base of st just worked to base of next st on to LH needle and K tbl.
SM5 – (smock 5) Sl 5sts just worked on to cable needle, wind B from left to right around sts on cable needle twice, leave B on WS of work, sl sts from cable needle back on to RH needle.
For other abbreviations see book, p. 141.

BACK

Using smaller needles and A, cast on 111[117:123]sts using the double cast-on method (see book, p. 101)
1st row (RS) K to end, working into front loop only of each cast-on loop.
2nd row P.
3rd row K.
4th row P.
5th row (make eyelets) K1, *yo, K2 tog, rep from * to end.
6th row P.
7th row K.
8th row P.
9th row (make hem) * With point of RH needle, pick up first loop from cast-on edge, sl on to LH needle and K this loop tog with first st, rep from * to end.
10th row P.
Change to larger needles:
Beg with a K row, cont in st st until Back measures 12½[13:13½]in, ending with a K row.
Shape armholes:
Bind off 4sts at beg of next 2 rows. 103[109:115]sts.
Shape yoke:
Next row P to end, inc 4[2:0]sts evenly across row. 107[111:115]sts.

Beg smock patt:
1st patt row (RS) P3, *K1, P3, rep from * to end.
2nd row K3, *P1, K3, rep from * to end.
3rd row P3, *K1, P3, K1, SM5, P3, rep from * to end.
4th row As 2nd.
5th row As first.
6th row K3, P1, K3[K3:K3, P1, K3], *P1, K3, P1, SM5, K3, rep from * to last 4sts, P1, K3.
These 6 rows form patt. Work even in patt until armhole measures 1¼[2:2½]in, ending with a WS row.
Divide for opening:
Next row Work 51[53:55]sts in patt, turn and leave rem sts on a holder.
Keeping patt correct, work even on these sts until armhole measures 4½[4¾:5]in. Bind off.
With RS of work facing, rejoin yarn to rem sts, bind off next 5sts for center back neck, work in patt to end.
Complete to match first side.

FRONT

Work as for Back, omitting back opening, until armholes measure 14[14:18] rows less than Back, ending with a WS row.
Shape neck:
Next row Work 47[48:49]sts in patt, turn and leave rem sts on a holder.
Dec one st at neck edge on next 8 rows, then one st on every other row 2[2:4] times in all. 37[38:37]sts. Work 1 row. Bind off.
With RS of work facing, rejoin yarn to rem sts, bind off center 13[15:17]sts loosely, work in patt to end. Complete to match first side.

SLEEVES (make 2)

Using smaller needles and B, cast on 31[35:37]sts.
1st rib row (RS) K1, *P1, K1, rep from * to end.
2nd row P1, *K1, P1, rep from * to end.
Rep these 2 rows until Sleeve measures 1½in, ending with a first row.
Next row Rib 4, (M1, rib 6[7:7]) 4 times, M1, rib 3[3:5]. 36[40:42]sts.
Change to larger needles and A.
Beg with a K row, cont in st st, *shaping sides* by inc one st at each end of every 5th row 8[7:4] times in all, then one st at each end of every 7th row 2[4:8] times in all. 56[62:66]sts.
Work even until Sleeve measures 9[10:11½]in. Bind off.

TO FINISH

Block and press pieces separately, avoiding smocking and ribbing.
Buttonhole band With RS of work facing, using smaller needles and A, pick up and K 23sts along right back opening.
1st row P1, *K1, P1, rep from * to end.
2nd row (buttonholes) K1, P1, (yo, P2 tog, rib 6) twice, yo, P2 tog, K1, P1, K1.
Work 2 more rows in rib. Bind off in rib.
Button band Work to match Buttonhole band along left back opening, omitting buttonholes.

Join shoulder seams.
Left collar
Using smaller needles and B, cast on 41[45:49]sts.
1st row (RS) K2, *P1, K1, rep from * to last st, K1.
2nd row P2, *K1, P1, rep from * to last st, P1.
Rep these 2 rows until collar measures 2in.
Bind off in rib.
Sew Left collar in position from center back neck to center front.
Work Right collar as for Left collar. Sew in place from center front neck to center back.
Sew Sleeves in place, matching center of Sleeve to shoulder seam and joining Sleeves to Front and Back at underarm.
Join side and sleeve seams.
Sew on buttons.

Designed by Julia Howe Knitwear

OPTIONS

If you prefer, this pretty dress could be made with a simple round neck, either by working a narrow single crochet border around the neck edge (see book, p. 140), or by picking up stitches and working a few rounds of K1, P1 rib in the contrasting yarn. Use the same size needles as specified for the collar.

Dress your baby for warmth and comfort in this neat, fresh outfit. The two-tone style uses an attractive combination of solid color and stripes.

SIZES

To fit 0–6[6–12] months
Top
Garment measures: 20½[22½]in at underarm
Length from shoulder: 8½[10]in
Sleeve seam: 5[6]in
Pants
Inside leg seam: 8½[9½]in
Note Instructions for larger size are given in brackets [].

MATERIALS

Anny Blatt Baby Blatt
4[5] 1¾oz/50g balls in main color A (Eau)
1 1¾oz/50g ball in color B (Blanc)
Pair each of sizes 1 and 2 knitting needles
4 small buttons for Top
4 small snaps for underflap
Waist length of elastic for Pants

GAUGE

26sts and 56 rows to 4in over g st worked on size 2 needles

To save time, take time to check gauge.

ABBREVIATIONS

M1 – lift strand running from base of st just worked to base of next st on to LH needle and work into back of it.
For other abbreviations see book, p. 141.
Note When working in patt, twist colors tog on WS to avoid forming holes (see book, p. 115), carrying B loosely up back of work.

TOP

Back

Using smaller needles and A, cast on 67[73]sts.

1st rib row (RS) K1, *P1, K1, rep from * to end.

2nd row P1, *K1, P1, rep from * to end.

Rep these 2 rows for ¾in, ending with a 2nd row, inc one st at end of last row. 68[74]sts.

Change to larger needles and patt:

1st patt row (RS) K51[57]A, K17B.

2nd row K17B, K51[57]A.

3rd row Using A, K to end.

4th row As 3rd.

These 4 rows form patt. Cont in patt until Back measures 4½[5]in, ending with a WS row.

Shape sleeves:

Cast on 28[34]sts at beg of next 2 rows. 124[142]sts.

Work even until narrow (cuff) edge measures 4[4½]in.

Shape shoulders:

Bind off 52[59]sts at beg of next 2 rows. 20[24]sts. Leave rem sts on a holder.

Left Front

Using smaller needles and A, cast on 47[53]sts. Work in K1, P1 rib for ¾in as for Back, ending with a 2nd row.

Change to larger needles and patt:

1st row (RS) Using B, K to end.

2nd row As first.

3rd row Using A, K to end.

4th row As 3rd.

These 4 rows form patt. Cont in patt until Front matches Back to sleeve, ending with a WS row.

Shape sleeve:

Next row Cast on 28[34]sts, K to end. 75[87]sts.

Work even until narrow (cuff) edge of sleeve measures 3[3½]in, ending with a WS row.

Shape neck:

Next row K59[68], turn and leave rem sts on a holder.

Dec one st at neck edge on next 4 rows, then one st at same edge on every other row 3[5] times in all. 52[59]sts.

Work even until Front matches Back to shoulder, ending with a WS row. Bind off.

With RS of work facing, rejoin yarn to rem sts, bind off next 6sts loosely, K to end.

Dec one st at neck edge on next 4 rows, then one st at same edge on every other row 3[5] times. 3[4]sts.

Work even until 2nd side of neck matches first side, ending with a RS row. Bind off.

Right Front

Using A throughout, work to match Left Front, reversing shaping.

To finish

Join shoulder seams.

Neckband With RS facing, using smaller needles and A, pick up and K 37[45]sts evenly around front neck, K across 20[24]sts on holder for back neck inc one st, pick up and K 33[41]sts evenly around front neck. 91[111]sts. Work in K1, P1 rib for ¾in as for

Back. Bind off in rib.

Buttonhole band Mark positions for 4 buttonholes on Right Front, the first to come at top of neck, last to come ½in above lower edge, with 2 more evenly spaced between.

Using smaller needles and A, cast on 9sts.

1st rib row (RS) K2, *P1, K1, rep from * to last st, K1.

2nd row P2, *K1, P1, rep from * to last st, P1.

Rep last 2 rows until band, when slightly stretched, fits up Right Front to neck, then bind off in rib, *at the same time* making buttonholes as markers are reached as foll:

Next row (RS) Rib 3, yo, K2 tog, rib to end.

Sew buttonhole band in place.

Cuffs With RS facing, using smaller needles and A, pick up and K61[61]sts evenly across narrow edge of sleeve. Work in K1, P1 rib for ¾in as for Back. Bind off in rib.

Join side and sleeve seams.

Sew on buttons to correspond with buttonholes. Sew on snaps to fasten Left Front edge to Right Front.

PANTS

Back – right leg

Using smaller needles and A, cast on 25[29]sts. Work in K1, P1 rib for ¾in as for Top Back, ending with a first row.

Next row Rib 3, *M1, rib 4[6], rep from * 4[3] more times, M1, rib 2. 31[34]sts.**

Change to larger needles.

Beg with a RS row and using A throughout, cont in g st until Right Leg measures 8½[9½]in, ending with a WS row. Leave sts on a holder.

Back – left leg

Work as for right leg to **.

Change to larger needles and patt:

1st patt row (RS) K14[17]A, K17B.

2nd row K17B, K14[17]A.

3rd row Using A, K to end.

4th row As 3rd.

These 4 rows form patt. Cont in patt until left leg matches right leg, ending with a WS row. Cut off yarn.

Join legs:

***Next row** With RS facing, K across 31[34]sts on holder for right leg, cast on 6sts, K across 6 cast-on sts, K across left leg sts in patt as set. 68[74]sts.

Work even in patt until legs measure 16[18]in, ending with a WS row.

Shape back:

Next row K64[67], turn.

Next row Sl 1, K59[62], turn.

Next row Sl 1, K55[58], turn.

Next row Sl 1, K51[54], turn.

Cont in this way, working 4sts less on every row until you have worked the row "Sl 1, K27[30], turn."

Next row Sl 1, K to last 2sts, K2 tog. 67[73]sts. Work 1 row.

Change to smaller needles.

Work in K1, P1 rib for 1½in as for Top. Bind off in rib.

Front – right leg

Using A throughout, work as for Back left leg.

Front – left leg

Work as for Back right leg to **.

Change to larger needles and patt:

1st patt row (RS) K17B, K14[17]A.

2nd row K14[17]A, K17B.

3rd row Using A, K to end.

4th row As 3rd.

Complete as for Back right leg.

Join legs:

Keeping patt correct, join legs as for Back, working from ***, then work even until Front measures 1½in less than Back, thus omitting Back shaping.

Change to smaller needles.

Work in K1, P1 rib for 1½in. Bind off in rib.

To finish

Join side and leg seams.

Fold waistband in half to WS and slipstitch in place, leaving an opening for elastic. Thread elastic through waistband and fasten securely. Close opening.

Designed by Julia Howe Knitwear

OPTIONS

You can work many variations on this design by changing the stitch pattern or colors. You could, for example, make the top entirely in stripes, using three or more colors, and use one of the colors for the pants. Or you could make the outfit in one color, perhaps using a different stitch pattern, such as seed stitch, or even basketweave (pp. 59 and 60, respectively). Be sure to make a gauge sample of whatever stitch pattern you choose and adjust the number of cast-on stitches where necessary.

Pearl cotton yarn gives crisp definition to the little Dutch boys and girls on this three-piece outfit for a toddler.

SIZES

To fit 18[20:22:24]in chest
Sweater
Chest measures: 20½[21½:24½:25½]in
Length from shoulder: 10¾[11:11½:14]in
Sleeve seam:
Beret (2 sizes)
Lower edge: 14¼[17¾]in
Center to edge: 6¾[7]in
Shorts
Waist to crotch: 7½[8½:9:9]in
Leg seam: 2¾[2¾:3¼:3½]in
Note Instructions for larger sizes are given in brackets [].

MATERIALS

Patons' Cotton Perlé
6[6:6:8] 1¾oz/50g balls in main color A (Ultramarine)
2[2:2:2] 1¾oz/50g balls in color B (White)
Pair each of sizes 3 and 6 knitting needles
3 sets of double-pointed needles: sizes 3, 6 and 7; size B crochet hook; 3 bead buttons; shirring elastic.

GAUGE

22sts and 29 rows to 4in over st st worked on size 6 needles
26sts and 26 rows to 10cm over two-color patt worked on size 6 needles
To save time, take time to check gauge.

ABBREVIATIONS

M1 – lift strand running from base of st just worked to base of next st on to LH needle and work into back of it.
For other abbreviations see book, p. 141.
Note When working patt from chart, strand yarn not in use across WS. Read odd rows (K) right to left; even rows (P) left to right.

SWEATER

Back
**Using smaller pair of needles and A, cast on 49[55:59:65]sts.
1st rib row (RS) K1, *P1, K1, rep from * to end.
2nd row P1, *K1, P1, rep from * to end.
Rep these 2 rows until work measures 1¼in, ending with a first row.
Next row Rib 8[6:7:7], M1, (rib 2[3:2:3], M1) 16[14:21:17] times, rib to end. 66[70:79:83]sts.
Change to larger needles.
Joining in and breaking off B as required, *place chart 1 as foll, at the same time* working first 0[0:11:11]sts at beg of K rows and last 0[0:11:11]sts at end of P rows as indicated.
1st patt row (RS) Using A, K0[2:1:3] (chart 1 as first row) 3 times, K0[2:1:3].
2nd row Using A, P0[2:1:3] (chart 1 as 2nd row) 3 times, P0[2:1:3].**

Cont in patt, working appropriate rows of chart 1 until Back measures approx 10¾[10¾:10¾:13½]in, ending with a 32nd [32nd:32nd:16th] patt row.
Using *A only,* work as foll:
2nd, 3rd and 4th sizes Beg with a K row, work 2[4:2]rows st st.
All sizes Cont in st st *shaping shoulders* by binding off 11[11:13:14]sts at beg of next 2 rows, then 11[11:13:13]sts at beg of foll 2 rows. Leave rem 23[26:27:29]sts on a holder.

Front
Work as for Back from ** to **, beg chart 1 with a first[first:17th:17th] patt row.
Cont in patt, working from chart until Front measures approx 9½[9½:9¾:12¼]in, ending with a 24th[24th:10th:24th] patt row.
Cont in patt, *divide for neck* as foll:
Next row Work 26[27:31:32]sts in patt, leave rem sts on a holder; turn.
Cont on these 26[27:31:32]sts for first side, dec one st at neck edge on next 4[5:5:5] rows. 22[22:26:27]sts.
Work 3[2:0:2] rows in patt, ending with a

32nd[32nd:16th:32nd] patt row.
Using *A only,* work as foll:
2nd, 3rd and 4th sizes Beg with a K row, work 2[4:2] rows st st.
All sizes Cont in st st, shape shoulder by binding off 11[11:13:14]sts at beg of next row.
Work 1 row. Bind off rem 11[11:13:13]sts.
With RS facing, slip center 15[16:17:19]sts on a spare needle, rejoin appropriate color to rem sts, patt to end. Work to match first side, reversing shapings.

Sleeves

Using smaller needles and A, cast on 27[29:33:33]sts and work in rib as for Back for 1¼in, ending with a first row.

1st, 3rd and 4th sizes Rib 7[8:8], M1, rib 13[16:16], M1, rib to end. 29[35:35]sts.
2nd size Rib 14, M1, rib 15. 30sts.
Change to larger needles.

Beg with a K row, work in st st, shaping sides by inc one st at each end of first[3rd:6th: 11th] row and then every 4th[4th:5th:5th] row until there are 53[58:59:61]sts.
Work even until Sleeve measures 8¼[9¾: 10¾:12¼]in, ending with a P row. Bind off.

To finish

Block the pieces; press if necessary.
Join right shoulder seam.
Neck Border With RS facing, using A and smaller needles, pick up and K8[10:10:10]sts down left side of neck, K15[16:17:19]sts from front neck holder, pick up and K8[10:10: 10]sts up right side of neck, then K 23[26:27: 29]sts from Back, dec one st at center. 53[61:63:69]sts. Beg with a 2nd row, work in rib as on Back for 2in, ending with a 2nd row. Bind off loosely in rib, using larger needle. Fold neck border in half to WS and sew loosely in position. Join left shoulder to beg of 2nd shaping.
Shoulder opening Using crochet hook and A, work 2 rows sc all around opening, including neck border, working 3 button loops on front edge of 2nd row, first at beg of neck border and rem 2 along opening. *To make a button loop*: ch 2, skip 1 sc.
Place center of sleeve tops to shoulder seams and sew in position. Join side and sleeve seams. Sew on buttons.

BERET

Using set of four smallest needles and A, cast on 82[98]sts. Divide evenly on 3 needles and mark first st of round.
1st round * K1, P1, rep from * to end. Rep this round once.
Next round Rib 20[24], M1, rib 41[49], M1, rib 21[25]. 84[100]sts.
Change to set of four medium-size needles.
Work in st st (every round K) for 3 rounds.
Change to set of four largest needles.
Joining in and breaking off B as required, work in patt from chart B, rep 4 patt sts, 21[25] times across.
Change to set of four medium-size needles.
Using *A only* work in st st for 2 rounds.
Next round K10[5], M1, (K21[10]M1) 3[9] times, K11[5]. 88[110]sts.
Work 3[4] rounds.
Next round K11[5], M1, (K22[11], M1) 3[9] times, K11[6]. 92[120]sts.
Work 3[4] rounds.
Next round K7[6], M1, (K11[12], M1) 7[9] times, K8[6]. 100[130]sts.
Work 2 rounds.
Next round K7[5], K2 tog, (K10[11], K2 tog) 7[9] times, K7[6]. 92[120]sts.
Work 0[1] round.
Change to set of four largest needles.
Joining in and breaking off B as required, work in patt from chart 2, rep 4 patt sts 23[30]

times across.
Change to set of four medium-size needles.
Using *A only* work in st st for 1 round.
Next round K10[5], K2 tog, (K21[10], K2 tog) 3[9] times, K11[5]. 88[110]sts.
Change to set of four largest needles.
Joining in and breaking off B as required, work in patt from chart 3, rep 22 patt sts 4[5] times across and dec where indicated. 8[10]sts. Break yarn, draw through rem sts and pull up tightly. Fasten off.

To finish

Cut out circle of cardboard slightly larger than Beret at widest point, place inside Beret and *gently* steam *above* Beret until it lies flat. Using A and B tog, make a small pompon (see book, p. 31) and sew to Beret.

SHORTS

Left leg

Using smaller needles and A, cast on 47[51:55:61]sts.
1st rib row (RS) K1, * P1, K1, rep from * to end.
2nd row P1, * K1, P1, rep from * to end.
Rep these 2 rows until work measures ¾[¾:1¼:1¼]in, ending with a 2nd row and inc one st at end of last row. 48[52:56:62]sts.
Change to larger needles.
Beg with a K row, work in st st until leg measures 2¾[2¾:3¼:3½]in, ending with a P row. Leave sts on a holder.

Right leg

Work as for left leg.
Divide for Front and Back With RS facing and using larger needles, sl first 24[26:28:31]sts from left leg on a spare needle, rejoin A to rem sts, K24[26:28:31], cast on 4[4:6:6]sts, K24[26:28:31]sts from right leg, leave rem 24[26:28:31]sts on a spare needle; turn. 52[56:62:68]sts.
Beg with a P row, work in st st on these 52[56:62:68]sts for Front until work measures 6¼[7:7¾:7¾]in from crotch, ending with a K row.
Next row P8[9:10:11], P2 tog, (P15[16:18:20], P2 tog) twice, P8[9:10:11], 49[53:59:65]sts.
Change to smaller needles.
Beg with a first row, work in rib as for left leg for 1¼in, ending with a 2nd row. Bind off evenly in rib.
Complete Back With RS facing and using larger needles, rejoin A to 24[26:28:31]sts from right leg, K these sts, cast on 4[4:6:6]sts, then K across 24[26:28:31]sts from left leg. 52[56:62:68]sts.
Work as for Front.

To finish

Block the pieces; press if necessary.
Join side and inside leg seams.
Thread 3 rounds of shirring elastic through the waistband. Fasten off.

Designed by Cornelia Gracey

Patons and Baldwins Ltd.

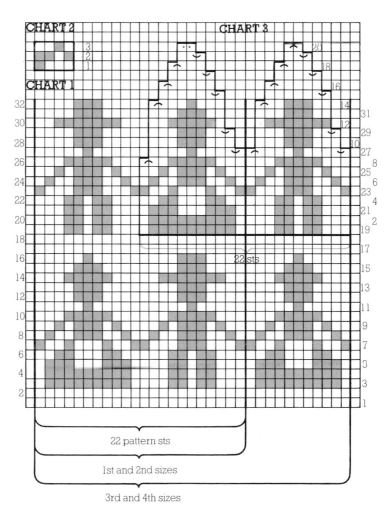

CHART 2 CHART 3
CHART 1

22 sts

22 pattern sts
1st and 2nd sizes
3rd and 4th sizes

Delicate bluebell lace pattern makes an exquisite christening gown with matching bonnet and bootees. The skirt is lined for a graceful shape and extra warmth.

SIZE

To fit: Up to 3 months
Garment measures: 19in around chest
Length from shoulder: 29in
Sleeve seam: 7in

MATERIALS

Phildar Luxe 3-ply
Dress
4 1¾oz/50g balls
Bonnet
1 1¾oz/50g ball
Bootees
1 1¾oz/50g ball
Pair of size 2 knitting needles
¾yd of 48in-wide voile
3yd narrow lace
3yd narrow ribbon
1yd wide ribbon
5 small buttons

GAUGE

26sts and 40 rows to 4in over skirt patt worked on size 2 needles
For gauge sample cast on 34sts and rep 8 skirt patt rows for at least 4in.

To save time, take time to check gauge.

ABBREVIATIONS

M1P – make 1 P-wise by lifting strand running from base of st just worked to base of next st on to LH needle and P tbl.
P2sso – pass 2 sl sts over.
For other abbreviations see book, p. 141.

GOWN

Main part
Cast on 274sts.
**1st row (RS) K.
2nd row P.
3rd row (Make picot hem) K2, * yo; K2 tog, rep from * to end.**
Beg with a P row, work 3 rows st st.
Beg skirt patt:
1st patt row K1, *yo, sl2 tog, K1, p2sso, yo, K5, rep from * to last st, K1.
2nd and every other row P.
3rd row As first.
5th row K1, *K3, yo, sl 1, K1, psso, K1, K2 tog, yo, rep from * to last st, K1.
7th row K1, * yo, sl2 tog, K1, p2sso, yo, K1, rep from * to last st, K1.
8th row P.
These 8 rows form skirt patt. Cont in patt until Skirt measures approx 23½in from picot hem, ending with a 7th patt row.
Shape bodice:
Next row *P2 tog, rep from * to end. 137sts.
Make ribbon slots:
Next row K1, *yo, K2tog, rep from * to end.
Next row P.

Beg bodice patt:
1st row (RS) K14, (yo, sl2 tog, K1, p2sso, yo, K5, yo, sl2 tog, K1, p2sso, yo – called "panel 1"), K19, rep panel 1, K27, rep panel 1, K19, rep panel 1, K14.
2nd and every other row P.
3rd row P1, (K3, P1) 3 times, K1, rep panel 1, K1, P1, (K3, P1) 4 times, K1, rep panel 1, K1, P1, (K3, P1) 6 times, K1, rep panel 1, K1, P1, (K3, P1) 4 times, K1, rep panel 1, K1, P1, (K3, P1) 3 times.
5th row K14, (K3, yo, sl 1, K1, psso, K1, K2 tog, yo, K3 – called "panel 2"), K19, rep panel 2, K27, rep panel 2, K19, rep panel 2, K14.
7th row K2, (P1, K3) 3 times, (yo, sl2 tog, K1, p2sso, yo, K1, yo, sl2 tog, K1, p2sso, yo, K1, yo, sl2 tog, K1, p2sso, yo – called "panel 3"), K3, (P1, K3) 4 times, rep panel 3, K3, (P1, K3) 6 times, rep panel 3, K3, (P1, K3) 4 times, rep

panel 3, (K3, P1) 3 times, K2.

8th row P.

These 8 rows form bodice patt. Cont in patt until bodice measures 1½in, ending with a RS row.

Divide for armholes:

Next row P31 and leave these sts on a holder for Right Back, bind off 7sts, P61 (including st left on needle after bind off) and leave these sts on a holder for Front, bind off 7sts, P to end.

Left back

Cont in patt as set on rem 31sts until armhole measures 4in, ending with a RS row.

Shape shoulder:

Bind off 9sts at beg of next row and then every other row once. Leave rem 13sts on a holder.

Right back

With RS facing, rejoin yarn to 31sts for Right Back and complete to match Left Back, reversing shaping.

Front

With RS facing, rejoin yarn to 61sts on holder for Front. Cont in patt on these sts until Front measures 8 rows less than Right Back to shoulder shaping, ending with a WS row.

Divide for neck:

Next row Work 23sts in patt, K2 tog, turn and leave rem sts on a holder.

Cont in patt on these 24sts, dec one st at neck edge on next 6 rows. 18sts.

Work 1 row.

Shape shoulder:

Bind off 9sts at beg of next row.

Work 1 row.

Bind off rem 9sts.

With RS facing, sl center 11sts on a holder, K2 tog, patt to end. Complete to match first side, reversing shaping by working 1 more row before "Shape shoulder".

Sleeves (make 2)

Cast on 40sts and work as for Main part of gown from ** to **. Beg with a P row, work 2 rows st st.

Make ribbon slots:

Next row P2, *yo, P2 tog, rep from * to last 2sts, P2.

Next row K.

Next row P1, *M1P, P2, M1P, P1, rep from * to end. 66sts.

Cont in patt as for Main part skirt, until Sleeve measures approx 7½in from picot hem, ending with a 7th patt row. Bind off.

To finish

Block but do not press.

Join shoulder seams.

Neck border With RS facing, K13sts from left back holder, pick up and K 10sts down left side, K11sts from center holder, pick up and K 10sts up right side and 13sts from right back holder. 57sts.

Next row P.

Next row (Make picot) K1, *yo, K2 tog, rep from * to end.

Beg with a P row, work 2 rows st st. Bind off.

Join sleeve seams to within ⅝in of top.

Set in Sleeves, gathering to fit and joining free edges of sleeve seams to bound-off sts at underarm.

Join center back seam, leaving an 8in opening.

Fold picot hems to WS at neck, wrist and lower edge and slipstitch in place.

Back border With RS facing, beg at top of neck border and pick up and K 59sts down right back to base of opening then 59sts up left back to top of neck border. 118sts. Bind off loosely.

Make 5 button loops, evenly spaced, on Right Back between top of Skirt and top of neck border. (To make button loop, sew 3 even strands of thread on to edge of fabric; cover threads with closely worked button-hole stitch.)

Sew buttons to left back to correspond with button loops.

Cut 20in of lace, finish ends, then gather and sew to lower edge of neck border.

Underskirt

Sew lace across 48in width of voile. Trim underskirt to same length as gown skirt. Join back seam, leaving 2in opening at top. Gather to fit waist, fasten gathering thread securely and sew in place to WS.

Ribbon trim Cut two 16in lengths of narrow ribbon and thread through wrists, starting and ending ¾in from seam on back of Sleeve. Thread 60in of ribbon through waist, beg and ending at center front.

BONNET

Cast on 101sts.

1st row (RS) K.

2nd row P.

3rd row (Make picot hem) K1, * yo, K2 tog, rep from * to end.

Beg with a P row, work 3 rows st st.

Beg patt:

1st patt row (RS) K1, yo, sl2 tog, K1, p2sso, yo, *K5, yo, sl2 tog, K1, p2sso, yo, rep from * to last st, K1.

2nd and every other row P.

3rd row As first.

5th row K4, * yo, sl 1, K1, psso, K1, K2 tog, yo, K3, rep from * to last st, K1.

7th row K1, * yo, sl2 tog, K1, P2sso, yo, K1, rep from * to end.

8th row P.

These 8 rows form patt. Cont in patt until Bonnet measures approx 4½in from picot hem, ending with a 7th patt row.

Shape back:

Next row Bind off 35sts, P31, bind off rem 35sts.

With RS facing, rejoin yarn to rem 31sts.

1st patt row K.

2nd row P.

3rd row K3, *P1, K3, rep from * to end.

4th row P

5th and 6th rows As first and 2nd.

7th row K1, P1, *K3, P1, rep from * to last st, K1.

8th row P.

These 8 rows form patt. Cont in patt dec one st at each end of next row and then every 8th row until 21sts rem.

Work a few rows even, until center section fits along bound-off sts of back, ending with a P row.

Cut yarn and leave sts on a holder.

To finish

Fold picot hem to WS and slipstitch in place. Join back seams.

Neck border With RS facing, pick up and K 21sts along side, work (K6, K2 tog) twice, K5 across sts on holder, pick up and K 21sts along 2nd side. 61sts.

Complete as for neck border of gown.

Gather lace and sew around face edge.

Cut wide ribbon in half and sew in place on each side.

BOOTEES

Cast on 31sts.

1st row (RS) (K1, yo) twice, K11, yo, K1, yo, K3, yo, K1, yo, K11, (yo, K1) twice.

2nd and every other row P.

3rd row K2, yo, K1, yo, K13, yo, K1, yo, K5, yo, K1, yo, K13, yo, K1, yo, K2.

5th row K3, yo, K1, yo, K15, yo, K1, yo, K7, yo, K1, yo, K15, yo, K1, yo, K3.

7th row K4, yo, K1, yo, K17, yo, K1, yo, K9, yo, K1, yo, K17, yo, K1, yo, K4.

8th row P. 63sts.

Now cont working in panel patt as for gown bodice.

1st row K26, rep panel 3 as in 7th bodice patt row, K26.

2nd and every other row P.

3rd row K1, (K3, P1) 6 times, K1, rep panel 1 as in first bodice patt row, K1, (P1, K3) 6 times, K1.

5th row K26, rep panel 1, K26.

7th row K2, (P1, K3) 6 times, rep panel 2 as in 5th bodice patt row, (K3, P1) 6 times, K2.

8th row P.

These 8 rows form patt.

Shape top of foot:

Next row Work 38sts in patt, turn.

Next row P13, sl 1 P-wise, turn.

Next row K2 tog, work 11sts in patt, K2 tog tbl, turn.

Next row P13, sl 1 P-wise, turn.

Rep the last 2 rows, 9 more times.

Next row K2 tog, work 11sts in patt, K2 tog tbl, work in patt to end. 41sts.

Next row P2 tog, P37, P2 tog. 39sts.

Next row K2, *yo, sl2 tog, K1, P2sso, yo, K1, rep from * to last st, K1.

Next row P.

Next row K1, *K5, yo, sl2 tog, K1, P2sso, yo, rep from * to last 6sts, K6.

Work 15 more rows in patt as set.

Make picot:

Beg with a P row work 2 rows st st.

Next row K1, *yo, K2 tog, rep from * to end.

Beg with a P row work 2 rows st st. Bind off.

To finish

Fold picot hem at top to WS and slipstitch in place.

Join seam at back and along sole.

Thread 16in narrow ribbon through patt at each ankle.

Designed by Barbara Clarkson

Phildar (UK) Ltd.

Delicate lace, worked in fine cotton yarn, covers two plump square pillows and a matching bolster. All are backed with contrasting cotton satin and have concealed zippers, which allow easy removal for cleaning.

SIZE

Pillow cover
To fit 14in square pillow
Bolster cover
To fit 18in (7in diameter) bolster

MATERIALS

Phildar Perlé No. 5
Pillow cover
2 1¾oz/50g balls for each pillow cover
Color shown: Sorbet
16in of 48in-wide cotton satin in a contrasting color for each pillow
Bolster cover
3 1¾oz/50g balls
20in of 48in-wide cotton satin in a contrasting color
Pair of size 2 knitting needles
5 size 2 double-pointed knitting needles
14in square pillow
18in-long bolster (7in diameter)
12in lightweight zipper for each pillow cover and for bolster cover

GAUGE

30sts and 38 rows to 4in over Patt 1 worked on size 2 needles
For gauge sample cast on 32sts and rep Patt 1 for at least 4in.

To save time, take time to check gauge.

ABBREVIATIONS

B1 – (bobble 1) (K into front and back of next st) twice, turn, P4, turn, K4, turn, P4, turn, (K2 tog) twice, pass first st over 2nd st.
For other abbreviations see book, p. 141.

SQUARE MEDALLION

Using 5 double-pointed needles, cast on 124sts and distribute evenly on 4 needles.
1st round K.
2nd round *Sl 1, K1, psso, K27, K2 tog, rep from * to end. 116sts.
3rd round *Sl 1, K1, psso, K1, (yo, K2 tog) 12 times, K2 tog, rep from * to end. 108sts.
4th round K.
5th round *Sl 1, K1, psso, K1, yo, K2 tog, K18, yo, (K2 tog) twice, rep from * to end. 100sts.
6th round *Sl 1, K1, psso, K21, K2 tog, rep from * to end. 92sts.
7th round *Sl 1, K1, psso, K1, yo, K2 tog, K14, yo, (K2 tog) twice, rep from * to end. 84sts.
8th round K.
9th round *Sl 1, K1, psso, K1, yo, K2 tog, K5, B1, K6, yo, (K2 tog) twice, rep from * to end. 76sts.
10th round *Sl 1, K1, psso, K15, K2 tog, rep from * to end. 68sts.
11th round *Sl 1, K1, psso, K1, yo, K2 tog, K2,

B1, K1, B1, K3, yo, (K2 tog) twice, rep from * to end. 60sts.
12th round K.
13th round *Sl 1, K1, psso, K1, yo, K2 tog, K2, B1, K3, yo, (K2 tog) twice, rep from * to end. 52sts.
14th round *Sl 1, K1, psso, K9, K2 tog, rep from * to end. 44sts.
15th round *Sl 1, K1, psso, K1, yo, K2 tog, K2, yo, (K2 tog) twice, rep from * to end. 36sts.
16th round K.
17th round *Sl 1, K1, psso, K1, yo, K2 tog, yo, (K2 tog) twice, rep from * to end. 28sts.
18th round *Sl 1, K1, psso, K3, K2 tog, rep from * to end. 20sts.
19th round *Sl 1, K1, psso, yo, K3 tog, rep from * to end. 12sts.
20th round *Sl 1, K2 tog, psso, rep from * to end. 4sts.
Break off yarn. Thread through rem sts and fasten off.

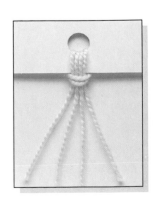

ROUND MEDALLION

Using 4 double-pointed needles, cast on 6sts and distribute evenly on 3 needles.
1st round *Yo, K1, rep from * to end. 12sts.
2nd, 4th, 6th, 8th and 10th rounds K.
3rd round *Yo, K2, rep from * to end. 18sts.
5th round *Yo, K3, rep from * to end. 24sts.
7th round *Yo, K4, rep from * to end. 30sts.
9th round *Yo, K5, rep from * to end. 36sts.
11th round *Yo, K6, rep from * to end. 42sts.
12th round *K1, yo, sl 1, K1, psso, K4, rep from * to end.
13th round *Yo, K7, rep from * to end. 48sts.
14th round *K1, yo, K2tog, yfwd, sl 1, K1, psso, K3, rep from * to end.
15th round *Yo, K8, rep from * to end. 54sts.
16th round *K1, (yo, K2tog) twice, yo, sl 1, K1, psso, K2, rep from * to end.
17th round *Yo, K9, rep from * to end. 60sts.
18th round *K1, (yo, K2tog) 3 times, yo, sl 1, K1, psso, K1, rep from * to end.
19th round *Yo, K10, rep from * to end. 66sts.
20th round *K1, (yo, K2tog) 4 times, yo, sl 1, K1, psso, rep from * to end.
21st round *Yo, K11, rep from * to end. 72sts.
22nd and 24th rounds P.
23rd and 25th rounds K.
Bind off loosely.

PATTERN 1

1st patt row (RS) *K2, yo, sl 1, K1, psso, rep from * to end.
2nd row *P2, yo, P2tog, rep from * to end.
These 2 rows form patt.

PATTERN 2

1st patt row (RS) *K3, yo, sl 1, K1, psso, K2, K2tog, yo, K1, yo, sl 1, K1, psso, rep from * to end.
2nd and every other row P.
3rd row *(K1, K2tog, yo, K1, yo, sl 1, K1, psso) twice, rep from * to end.
5th row *K2tog, yo, K3, yo, sl 1, K1, psso, K2tog, yo, K1, yo, sl 1, K1, psso, rep from * to end.
6th row P.
These 6 rows form patt.

PILLOW COVER

Make 1 Square Medallion.
Border
Using pair of needles and with RS facing, pick up and K 30sts from 1 side of square, then cast on 42sts. 72sts.
^^Work 3 rows g st.
Cont working in either Patt 1 or Patt 2.
Work 48 rows in patt.
Bind off.**
***With RS facing and working clockwise around square, pick up and K 30sts up next side of square and 42sts from side of previously-worked patt strip. 72sts.
Work from ** to ** once more.
Cont to pick up and cast on sts, then work in patt on rem 2 sides of square, working from *** to end.

TO FINISH

Block and press knitting foll instructions on yarn label.
Join seam.
Cut two 15in squares from fabric for each pillow (see cutting layout).
Baste knitted square to RS of 1 fabric square.
Place RS of fabric squares tog and sew tog on one edge 1½in from each end, taking ⅝in seam allowance.
Insert zipper into opening.
Open zipper and, with RS of squares tog, baste then sew around rem 3 sides, taking ⅝in seam allowance.
Neaten raw edges by overcasting.
Turn cover RS out and remove basting.

BOLSTER COVER

Main tube
Using pair of needles, cast on 168sts.
Work 36 rows in Patt 1.
Work 2 rows g st.
Next row Cast on 5sts, K to end.
Next row Cast on 5sts, K to end. 178sts.
Beg Patt 2:
1st patt row K5, work in patt to last 5sts, K5.
2nd row P5, work in patt to last 5sts, P5.
Keeping 5sts at each end in st st, cont in patt until 36 rows of Patt 2 have been worked.
Work 4 rows g st.
Keeping 5sts at each end in st st as before, work 36 rows in Patt 1.
Work 4 rows g st.
Keeping 5sts at each side in st st as before, work 36 rows in Patt 2.
Work 2 rows g st.
Next row Bind off 5sts, K to end.
Rep last row once more. 168sts.
Work 36 rows in Patt 1.
Bind off.
Bolster ends
Make 2 Round Medallions.

TO FINISH

Block and press pieces foll instructions on yarn label.
With RS tog, join side seams to form a tube, leaving st st section open.
Gather each end of tube on to edge of Round Medallions.
Turn knitted tube RS out.
Cut 1 rectangle 19in wide × 23½in long from fabric (see cutting layout).
Cut 2 circles, 8in in diameter, from fabric.
Placing RS tog fold fabric rectangle in half so that the two 19in sides are tog.
Taking ⅝in seam allowance throughout, sew down 3½in at each end of 19in side, leaving 12in opening at center.
Press seam open.
Placing RS tog, sew circle to each end of tube.
Turn tube RS out and place inside knitted cover.
Baste st st seam allowance to matching fabric seam allowances.
Insert zipper into opening.
Remove basting.

Designed by Alan Dart

> ### OPTIONS
> Both the square medallion and the round medallion are attractive patterns which could be used individually to make pretty placemats, worked in white or cream cotton.

CUTTING LAYOUT, TWO PILLOWS AND BOLSTER

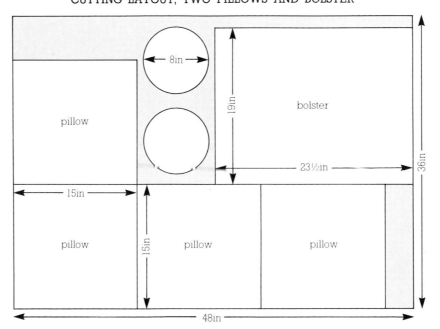

ACKNOWLEDGMENTS
We would like to thank the following people who assisted in the preparation of THE KNIT KIT: **Jo Cole, Julie Dumbrell, Kathy Maben, Winifred Muir, Shelley Turner, Pat Hunter.**

Photographic Credits
Key *b* bottom *t* top *l* left *r* right
1/5 **Roger Phillips**; 8/13, 14/15 **Roger Phillips**, inset **Jackie Hurst**; 16 **Roger Phillips**; 17 **Jackie Hurst**; 18/22 **Roger Phillips**; 24, 28/29 **Charlie Stebbings**; 30/33 **Roger Phillips**; 34/37 **Peter Smith**; 38/39 **Roger Phillips**; 43 **Peter Smith**; 44/45 **Charlie Stebbings**; 46/51, 51/53, 55/57 **Roger Phillips**; 58/75 **Peter Smith**; 77, 80, 84, 88 **Charlie Stebbings**; 92*t* **David Grey**, *bl* **Steve Campbell**, *br* **David Grey**; 96*t* **David Grey**, *b* **Steve Campbell**; 98/99 **Roger Phillips**; 102, 104/105, 107/109, 112/114, 116, 119, 121, 127, 132, 139 **Peter Smith**

Artwork Credits
Key *c* chart *b* bottom *t* top
10, 12, 15 **Hayward & Martin**; 17, 23, 25/27, 30/32 **Stan North**; 34/37 **Carole Johnson**; 39 **Stan North**; 40/41 *t* **Hayward & Martin**, *b* **Stan North**; 42 **Stan North**; 45/46 **Terry Evans**; 47 **Stan North**; 48/49 **Terry Evans**; 50 **Hayward & Martin**; 51/53 **Terry Evans**; 54 **Hayward & Martin**; 55, 57 **Terry Evans**; 68/69 **Hayward & Martin**; 77 **Terry Evans**; 78/79 **Stan North**; 80 **Terry Evans**; 81 **Stan North**; 82/83 **Hayward & Martin**; 84 **Terry Evans**; 85 **Stan North**; 87 **Hayward & Martin**; 88 **Terry Evans**; 89 **Stan North**; 90 **Hayward & Martin**; 93/95, 97 **Carole Johnson**; 100/104, 106/140 **Coral Mula**, 115/117*c*, 127*c* **Hayward & Martin**

Suppliers' Credits
10/14 Baskets: **David Mellor** Wool: **Ries Wools, Laines Couture** 18/19 Needles: **Pingouin Kensington**, 60 Kenway Road, London S.W.5. Beads supplied by **Bead Warehouse** Buttons supplied by **The Button Box**

USEFUL ADDRESSES
The following companies can supply information regarding the nearest retailer and/or mail order suppliers of the yarns used in the knitting patterns.

Anny Blatt
Laines Anny Blatt
24770 Crestview Court
Farmington Hills
Michigan 48018

Argyll
Estelle Designs & Sales Ltd
1135 Queen St East
Toronto
Ontario MIN 2R3
Canada

Jaeger, Patons
Susan Bates Inc
212 Middlesex Avenue
Route 9A
Chester
Connecticut 06412

Neveda
Neveda Yarn Company
230 Fifth Ave
New York
New York 10001

Noro
Knitting Fever
180 Babylon Turnpike
Roosevelt
New York 11575

Phildar
Phildar Inc
6438 Dawson Blvd
Norcross
Georgia 30093

Pingouin
Pingouin Corporation
PO Box 100
Highway 45
Jamestown
South Carolina 29453

Plassard
Joseph Galler, Inc
27 West 20th Street
New York
New York 10011

Rowan
Westminster Trading
Corporation
5 Northern Boulevard
Amherst
New Hampshire 03031

Scheepjeswol
Scheepjeswol USA Inc
115 Lafayette Ave
North White Plains
New York 10603

Tiber
Merino Wool Co, Inc
230 Fifth Ave
New York
New York 10001

PATTERNS
Suppliers' Credits

1 Hat: Dickins & Jones
Earrings: Accessorize
Bracelet: Detail
Skirt: Dickins & Jones

2 Hat: The Hat Shop
Earrings: Dickins & Jones
Bracelet: Merola
Shirt: Simpson
Pants: Dickins & Jones

3 Earrings: Detail
Bracelet: Pilot
Top: Simpson
Pants: Review

4 Scarf: Dickins & Jones
Shirt: Marella
Sweater: Benetton
Pants: Empire Stores

5 Earrings: Dickins & Jones
Pearl & rhinestone necklaces: Chanel
Pearl necklace: Accessorize
Gold chain: Dickins & Jones
Silk top: Chanel

6 Earrings: Detail
Jeans: Benetton
Boots: Hobbs

7 Jewelry: Michaela Frey
Skirt: Dickins & Jones

8 Earrings: Pilot

9 Scarves: Benetton
Jewelry: Detail
Pants: Flip

10 Glasses: Clive Kay
Jeans: Benetton

11 Earrings: Dickins & Jones
Pants: Aquascutum

12 Earrings: Detail
Pants: Benetton

13 Earrings: Detail
Bracelets: Dickins & Jones
Watch: Paul Smith
Skirt: Flip

14 Earrings: Michaela Frey
Bracelet: Pilot
Skirt: Simpson

15 Earrings: Dickins & Jones
Brooch: Merola
Blouse: Empire Stores
Skirt: Dickins & Jones

16 Earrings: Detail
Bracelet: Michaela Frey
Top: Simpson
Pants: Aquascutum

17 Earrings: Dickins & Jones
Skirt: Pamela Furs & Things, stand Y8, Antiquarius

18 Earrings: Dickins & Jones
Bandeau: Persiflage, stand Y8, Antiquarius
Pants: Dickins & Jones

19 Jewelry: Pilot
Pants: Monsoon

20 Earrings: Dickins & Jones
White bracelet: Dickins & Jones
Blue bracelet: Accessorize
Skirt: Dickins & Jones

21 Earrings: Pellini
Skirt: Penny Black

22 Earrings: Detail
Pants: Penny Black

23 Earrings: Michaela Frey
Bracelet: Accessorize
Pants: Dickins & Jones

25 Shirt: S. Fisher
Pants: Paul Smith

26 Shirt: S. Fisher
Pants: S. Fisher

28 Shirt: S. Fisher

29 Cotton vest
Shirt: Dickins & Jones
Pants: Grey Flannel
Wool vest
Glasses: Clive Kay
Bow tie: Paul Smith
Shirt: New Man

30 Shirt: Blazer
Pants: Sprint

31 Pants: Paul Smith

32 Shirt: Stand Z8, Antiquarius
Pants: Blazer

33 Man's Aran
Scarf: Aquascutum
Shirt: Aquascutum
Pants: Simpson
Girl's Aran
Shirt: 012
Pants: 012

34 Pants: Paul Smith

35 Shirt: 012
Pants: La Cicogna

36 Glasses: Clement Clarke
Pants: 012

37 Pants: La Cicogna

39 Shirt: 012
Belt: Joannas Tent
Jeans: Bambino

40 T shirt: 012
Pants: Dickins & Jones

43 Bootees: La Cicogna

44 Bootees: La Cicogna

ACKNOWLEDGEMENTS
We would like to thank the following people who assisted in the preparation of the patterns
Key *c* chart *b* bottom *t* top

Photographic Credits
1/32 **David Grey**; 33*t* **David Grey**; 33*b* **Steve Campbell**; 34/45 **Steve Campbell**; 46 **Christine Hanscombe**. Inset wool samples by **Jackie Hurst**

Artwork Credits
2, 3, 8, 9, 32, 34, 37/47, 48*c* **Hayward & Martin**; 11, 15, 18, 21, 35 **Carole Johnson**